PYTHON
PRESS

Peter Cowman
The Sheltermaker's Manual
Volume 2

Peter Cowman is an architect, eco-builder, writer and teacher delivering Courses & Workshops internationally on the subject of Living Architecture. He was born and educated in Dublin, Ireland, graduating from the School of Architecture, University College Dublin in 1976. Apart from his work as an architect, at various points of his nomadic life Peter has worked as a salesman, an art gallery director, a handyman and as a full-time parent. He began teaching people how to design their own homes in 1989, a task which he still pursues as director of the Living Architecture Centre. Never having had a mortgage himself, Peter has a special interest in the creation of affordable, low-impact, mortgage-free buildings and has developed a unique timber framing system for cost-conscious self-builders. Originator of the 'Sheltermaker' and 'Living Architecture' concepts Peter's work has been widely publicised in both print as well as broadcast media, worldwide.

The Sheltermaker's Manual

Volume 2

Peter Cowman

PYTHON PRESS

For sheltermakers everywhere ...

Special thanks to: Siãn Cowman, Johnny Gogan, Gerard Greene, John Long, Mary Dineen-Long, Brendan Lyons, Alanna Moore, Sharon Ray, Bairbre Madden-Reddy, Jim O'Donnell, Leo Regan, Deirdre Stephens, Leitrim Co. Enterprise Board, Sligo-Leitrim VEC, Tommy Waters

PYTHON
PRESS

© Peter Cowman 2013

First published as part of 'The Handbook of House Design & Construction Volume 2' ISBN 0 9519365 1 4

Printed on acid free paper by Lightning Source
Lightning Source Inc., an Ingram Content Group Inc. company, is committed to manufacturing books in a manner that both respects the environment and helps preserve the world's natural resources.

ISBN 978-0-9757782-7-2

Published by:
Python Press
P.O. Box 929
Castlemaine
Victoria 3450
Australia

EMail:
pythonpress@gmail.com

Web:
pythonpress.com

Design & Illustration
Peter Cowman

Cover: EconoSpaceMaking
Photo by Peter Cowman

Contents

Planning & Building Regs180

Site Analysis 197

Layout 212

Costing 280

Planning & Working Drawings 316

Appendices 317

Introduction to Volume 2 of The Sheltermaker's Manual (2013)

Volume 1 of *The Sheltermaker's Manual* deals primarily with the formulation of a clear and all-encompassing *Brief*, the learning of measurement, drawing and modelmaking techniques, the familiarisation with basic structural principles, the importance of setting a clear direction in respect of environmental considerations, and, the formulation of a practical approach to building location and orientation and, the composition of a suitable building fabric. *Volume 2* builds on that foundation.

Continuing the established methodology of tackling each relevant topic in turn, *Volume 2* allows the sheltermaker to steadily approach the goal of creating a plan! This contrasts to the usual design methodology of creating a plan first - which, as we are all aware of, can cause insurmountable problems in respect of designing as well as living.

Volume 2 begins with the examination and selection of materials and products that might possibly be used in the construction process. A decision on a suitable construction methodology follows that. Building services - plumbing, drainage and electrical - are then examined, along with issues of planning and building regulation. Next, the topic of location and site analysis are dealt with leaving the way open for a plan to be formulated. This approach is based on common sense and has proven itself, in practice, to produce first rate results. Sheltermakers are well advised to closely adhere to this course of action.

As will have been discovered from work carried out in respect of *Volume 1,* there are many hidden aspects to the process of sheltermaking. I think of these as the 'invisible architecture'. Unseen yet powerful in the effect they exert, one will ignore such aspects of the design process at one's peril.

What is invisible architecture and what activates it? Well, to answer the second question first - the sheltermaking process itself activates it! The articulation of one's dreams; the making of drawings and models; the careful examination of existing buildings; the articulation of one's bottom line in respect of harmonisation with the natural world; the realisation that the sun is at the heart of all sheltermaking ambitions; etc. etc. All of these engagements activate, awaken and embolden our natural sheltermaking instincts! This awakening inevitably challenges much of one's conditioning and oftentimes, one's sense of security. Because these effects are invisible - but nonetheless keenly felt - it can be hard to discern exactly what is going on. This is normal and hints at the nature of invisible architecture itself. We might think of this as an aspect of the Universe, which, as was described in the *Introduction* to *Volume 1*, is composed of space-time.

The inside and outside of buildings not only comprise space-time but the inside and outside of people too! This is the source of our dreams and the reason why buildings, particularly our homes, play such an important part in us living our lives fully. So, we might think of invisible architecture not only in terms of physical buildings but also in terms of our dream world and the lives we have to live. This allows us to appreciate the vitality of creating shelters that reflect who we are inside. In effect what happens is that sheltermakers make their inner world visible and habitable by conscious engagement with their inner selves. Invisible architecture therefore is who we are!

This is the great secret of architecture evidenced in the *Sacred Geometry*, *Feng Shui* and *Vastu Shastra* traditions. While such secrets continue to inform eastern traditions, in the west, the prevalence of rational thinking has assured the suppression of such intangibles in the methodologies of the architectural profession and of other building designers.

When awareness of the power of 'living one's architecture' is appreciated we are presented with a dynamic tool for change. Change is characteristic of life and a vital component of the sustainable agenda, which at it's heart, is all about sustaining life.

The current official interpretation of sustainability however is quite the opposite - it's all about non-change and sustaining the *status quo*! As can be clearly seen this threatens people and planet alike! The reason why such an absurd agenda can prevail is largely because we have lost touch with who we are and our purpose in life. Material considerations rank highest and science disputes the existence of anything immaterial. We are invited to inhabit a soulless world in which love, compassion, joy, intuition and their invisible companions are consigned to the wastebasket.

Sheltermaking offers an unrivalled opportunity to those seeking to escape such a deadening world in the search for a fuller and more meaningful life. This is not to suggest that it is simply a matter of ordering such a life online or of engaging someone to create it on one's behalf. Rather, this approach suggests a complete revision of how one lives one's life, obtains one's food, disposes of ones waste, sets one's values, relates to their fellow humans, moves from place to place and so on. Interestingly, this is not all that difficult to achieve. It is the reactions to such alternative living that pose the biggest threats to the realisation of such dreams. If such reactions are not taken into account or underestimated, the sheltermaker will find him or herself threatened by the full force of what has become an outmoded way of life.

While the focus of *The Sheltermaker's Manual* is on the design and construction of buildings suited to a new way of life the invisible aspects of such engagement are vital to appreciate. The simplest way to think of this is to give careful consideration to how one spends one's time. Because space and time are inseparable and because space and time are the essence of the invisible parts of ourselves and of buildings, consideration of how we spend our time tells us much about how we currently live and about how we might spend our time in a new world of our dreaming.

Inevitably, time needs to be given over to such consideration! Further, we need to connect with others in our search for meaningful answers. Using living architecture as a foundation for such discussion will prove to be most enlightening! To do this successfully we first have to inform ourselves of, and become conversant with, the abstract and invisible aspects of our lives - who we are, where we are going and how we plan to get there! Sharing such insights with others inevitably leads to the possibility of shared sheltermaking activity. With our sheltermaker genes activated in this way we suddenly find ourselves in a new world full of possibility, love, hope and excitement. In this way we change our lives, our relationships and our way of sheltering ourselves, shaping our world according to our dreams.

Peter Cowman
February 2013

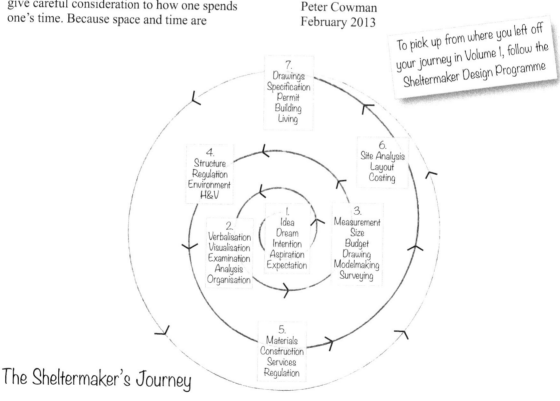

To pick up from where you left off your journey in Volume I, follow the Sheltermaker Design Programme

The Sheltermaker's Journey

The process of investigating and selecting materials with which to realise your design ambitions now begins. The selection of these will be based on your previous decisions about the *Structural, Environmental* and *H&V* aspects of your design. The pending exercise can be imagined as the selection of ingredients with which to make a meal.

If you wish to have a frame structure, to create a healthy internal environment, to use sustainable materials or to have high levels of insulation, you will have to use timber extensively in your building.

Timber is the most critical and important building material that exists. Because it is a natural material, timber manages to stimulate a wide range feelings and responses which, if not properly assessed, can critically imbalance a project. A full understanding of the nature and performance of timber, or wood, as it is commonly referred to, is therefore essential to the success of any design.

Begin by reading the *Timberfile* as far as *'Wood Conversion'* on page 10. The critical information contained in these pages is as follows:

- When trees are felled and the timber in them is made ready for building, it is called wood.
- There are two basic types of wood - softwood and hardwood.
- All wood contains a certain percentage of moisture.
- The Moisture Content of wood, when in use, determines how safe it will be from decay.
- Decay in wood is a consequence of its actual food content - desirable to fungi and insects.

It is that latter issue - decay - that is responsible for the bulk of adverse reactions to the use of wood for building purposes. This is a deep-seated fear and should not be underestimated. While you yourself might be fully aware of the emotional issues concerning the use of wood for building, others involved in the design/construction process may not be so informed. For example, lenders, insurers, friends and relatives may well have a different attitude to the use of wood and may well insist on imposing their views to you. Generally, the evocation of fear is the method used to dissuade people from the widespread use of wood for building purposes. Because it's aimed at our emotional selves - as opposed to our rational selves - the invocation of fear can be devastating to the natural evolution of a building design.

Next: SDP29 - Wood - The Facts, page 11

Timberfile

It is virtually impossible to build a house without using timber. Because of this, it is vital to develop an understanding of the nature of this unique substance. In comparison to other building materials, timber evokes a very strong response in people. Attitudes range from adulation to fear.

Timber always has been used in the creation of human shelter as well as for the production of tools, implements, vessels, paper and other essential items. As well as this, it has always been an important fuel.

Wood

Timber is the name given to wood that has been cut and dried. Wood is the major component of trees that are the largest plants that grow on the earth.

The growth process of trees is fuelled by the light and heat of the sun. Nutrition and water are provided by the earth. The natural balance of this growth process is an inherent part of the smell, feel and appearance of wood. This contributes to the materials' usefulness and appeal as a building material.

The growth of trees is fuelled by the sun and by the earth. The natural balance of this process is an inherent part of the smell, feel and appearance of wood, making it a very useful and versatile building material.

Tree Classification

Botanically, trees are identified by reference to Class. Common Classes are Pine, Fir, Oak and Larch. Within these Classes, trees are further identified by Species.

Class of Tree	Species of Tree Within its Class
Spruce	European Silver
Larch	Japanese European

It is common to identify trees by type rather than by using the exact botanical classification system. Two basic types of trees exist - Conifer and Broadleaf.

Two basic types of trees exist - Conifer and Broadleaf

Conifer trees have needles and cones. The wood they produce is called softwood. Broadleaf trees have broad leaves. The wood they produce is called hardwood.

The terms *softwood* and *hardwood* refer to the physical structures of these woods. It does not necessarily mean that all *softwoods* are soft and all *hardwoods* are hard.

Conifer trees have needles and cones. The wood they produce is called softwood.

Common Softwoods
Produced by Conifer Trees

Larch
Red Deal
Yellow Pine
Baltic Redwood
Whitewood
White Deal
Western Red Cedar
Douglas Fir

Common Hardwoods
Produced by Broadleaf Trees

Oak
Mahogany
Beech
Ash
Birch
Teak
Maple
Sycamore

Broadleaf trees have broad leaves. The wood they produce is called hardwood.

Wood Growth

In spring, when a trees' annual growth cycle begins, water and nutrients are drawn up through the root system and delivered to the leaves or needles of the tree. Once there, this raw sap is combined with sunlight and carbon dioxide to produce food sap. This food sap is then distributed to the tree in a layer of tissue immediately beneath the bark. Some of the food is used to produce new cells and some is put aside for winter.

Conifer trees generally keep their needles in winter .... except for Larch

In one growing season the new wood that is produced by the tree appears as an individual ring within the trunk. A growth ring consists of 2 bands of new wood - a light coloured band of wood produced in the spring and a darker band of wood produced in the summer. These 2 bands are referred to as *earlywood* and *latewood* respectively. Slow growing trees have narrow growth rings while trees of rapid growth have wider ring patterns.

Broadleaf trees generally shed their leaves in winter ... except for Eucalyptus

The cells making up the earlywood are large in comparison to those making up the latewood to accommodate the large amount of raw sap that the tree needs in the spring. This accounts for its lighter colour.

Apart from producing new wood during the growing season, trees also set aside food for winter. While all cells contain a certain amount of food, special food storage cells also exist called parenchyma. These radiate out from the centre of the trunk and the lines they follow are called *medullary rays*.

In spring, water and nutrients are drawn up through the root systems of trees to fuel the growth cycle.

In one season of growth the new wood that is produced forms an individual ring within the tree trunk.

Sapwood & Heartwood

The wood within the tree trunk that channels raw sap upwards to the needles or leaves is called the sapwood. This consists of the outermost portion of the trunk.

Wood within the trunk that has ceased to function as a conductor for raw sap is known as heartwood. Heartwood acts primarily to support the weight of the tree.

Each year a ring of sapwood is converted into a ring of heartwood. Often heartwood can be distinguished by its darker colour.

The wood within a tree trunk that channels raw sap is known as sapwood. Wood that has ceased to do this is called heartwood.

The Components of Wood

Wood is mainly composed of the elements carbon, oxygen and hydrogen. These are extracted from the water and air that the tree absorbs. Wood can also contain resin, tannin, oil, calcium, gum, silica, syrup and so on.

Carbon, oxygen and hydrogen are present in wood in the form of cellulose, hemi-cellulose, lignin and water. Cellulose and hemi-cellulose are the substances that make the wood strong. Lignin is the substance that binds the wood cells together. Water is the vehicle for food transportation and it also gives elasticity to the wood.

Wood is made up of:
Carbon, Oxygen & Hydrogen

Plus
Resin, Tannin, Oil, Gum, Silica & Syrup

In the form of:
Cellulose & Hemi-cellulose for strength
Lignin for binding
&
Water for elasticity

Cellulose accounts for about half the dry weight of wood and hemi-cellulose about one quarter. These substances are the main components of paper as well as being used in the production of alcohol for motor spirit, in the making of insulation, synthetic textiles, films, lacquers and even explosives.

Dry weight refers to the weight of wood when the water content has been completely removed. This is a convenient artificial state used for measurement - when all the water is removed from wood it becomes brittle and breaks apart. The amount of water present in wood varies. Freshly felled wood can contain more that its own weight in water, while in fully seasoned timber the water content accounts for about one fifth of its weight.

Lignin accounts for about one fifth of the dry weight of wood. Because lignin softens at high temperatures wood can be bent into a desired shape when it is steamed.

The resins, oils and other substances sometimes present in wood account for only a small proportion of its dry weight. These substances give various woods their characteristic colour, scent and resistance to decay and are present in the heartwood. They are often referred to as *extractives*. When these are removed from the wood they yield such substances as rosin, oil of turpentine and tannin. The presence of these extractives is what gives heartwood its darker colour.

While both softwoods and hardwoods are basically composed of cellulose, hemi-cellulose, lignin and water, the type of cells making up these two wood types differ from each other. The difference between various softwoods and hardwoods is accounted for by this difference in cellular structure.

Softwood

Softwood is the type of wood produced by all conifer trees. Softwood cells are called tracheids. They are about 3mm long, hollow and have minute holes in their walls, called pits. These pits allow for the passage of sap between adjoining tracheids. Tracheids run in lines upwards from the roots and outwards along the branches. It is these lines that give the wood its grain.

Tracheids formed in the early part of the growing season have thin walls to allowing large amounts of sap to flow through them. These form the lighter portion of the annual growth rings called the earlywood. Tracheids

All wood contains water because without it the wood will disintegrate.

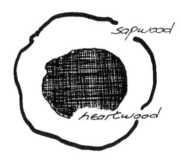

Resin, oil, tannin and so on, are contained in the heartwood. This gives heartwood its darker colour and its ability to resist decay. These substances also give the various woods their characteristic colour, scent and odour.

All wood is made up of cellulose, hemi-cellulose and lignin. However, it is the way in which these substances are used in the formation of wood cells that differentiates softwoods from hardwoods.

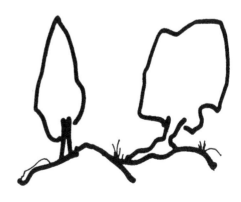

formed in the later part of the growing season have thick walls to give support to the tree during the winter. These form the darker portion of the annual growth rings, the latewood.

Food storage cells, called *parenchima*, are also formed in the growing season. These are confined to the medullary rays that radiate out from the centre of the trunk. In some trees, resin ducts are also formed in the latewood. Resin is waste matter secreted by the tree.

Trees are a remarkable source of renewable sheltermaking material

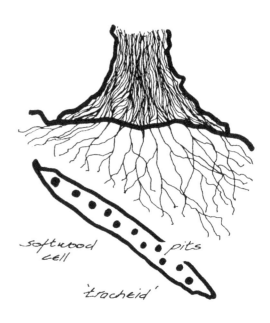

Softwood cells are called tracheids. These run in lines upwards from the roots giving the wood its grain.

Hardwood

Hardwood is the type of wood produced by all broadleaf trees. The cells making hardwood are called pores and fibres.

Pores are hollow, open-ended cells with holes in their walls called pits. Pits allow for the passage of sap between adjoining cells. Pores vary in size according to tree type. In oak, for example, they are quite large while in beech they are comparatively small. It is the presence of pores in the end grain of a piece of wood that distinguishes softwoods from hardwoods.

In all hardwoods, fibres surround the pores and make up the bulk of the wood. Their function is to give the tree strength. Pores and fibres normally run in lines upwards from the roots and outwards along the branches. It is the lines of these cells that gives the wood its grain. Food storage cells, called parenchima, form the medullary rays radiating out from the centre of the tree trunk.

Woods that have a concentration of large pores within the earlywood and smaller pores within the latewood are called ring porous - oak, elm and ash for example. Woods with a fairly even distribution of pores within the earlywood and latewood are known as diffuse porous - mahogany, beech and birch for example.

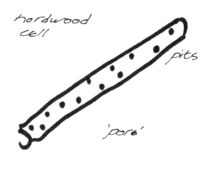

Hardwood cells are called pores and fibres. Pores are open-ended tubular cells. These are surrounded by fibre cells. It is the presence of pores in the end grain of a piece of wood that identifies it as a hardwood.

Green Wood

To obtain wood for building purposes trees have to be felled. A felled tree contains sap and the wood is referred to as being green. To use the wood for building the sap should be removed. To make this process as easy as possible trees are usually felled during the dormant period of the growth cycle when they contain the least amount of sap.

The amount of sap that green wood contains is referred to as it's Moisture Content. This is a measure of the weight of sap that the green wood contains in relationship to the weight of the wood when it has been completely dried. This measure is expressed as a percentage. Green wood can have a moisture content more than 100%, meaning that the weight of sap present weighs more than the wood substance itself.

There are many reasons why wood has to be dried to be used for building. The most important reason is that green wood, particularly sapwood, is rich in food and, as such, is the target of fungi and insects who wish to eat it. This food is stored in the medullary rays and within the cell walls. If it is devoured the strength of the wood is reduced.

In order for fungi and insects to eat the food, the wood generally has to have a Moisture Content of 25 to 30%. Wood is at its most vulnerable when it is freshly cut. To render green wood safe from attack it's Moisture Content (MC) has to be reduced below the 25% level. While it might seem sensible to completely remove the moisture from wood to keep it safe, this would result in the wood becoming brittle and falling apart.

Apart from the initial need to remove the sap from green wood, wood at all stages of its life must be maintained at a reasonable Moisture Content. Even after the sap has been removed the hollow wood cells maintain their ability to absorb water. If the amount of this absorption raises the moisture content above 25% the wood again becomes vulnerable to attack. Maintaining a reasonable Moisture Content is the fundamental principle of using wood for building.

While certain woods have an inbuilt ability to resist attack from fungi and insects, it is the heartwood of these species that is resistant. This is mainly due to the extractives present in these woods. The sapwood of all species, due to its food content, is always vulnerable.

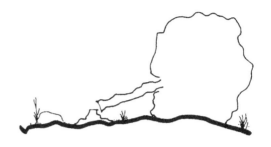

A felled tree contains sap and the wood is referred to as being green. Green wood can have a Moisture Content in excess of 100%. This means that the sap content of the wood outweighs the actual wood content itself.

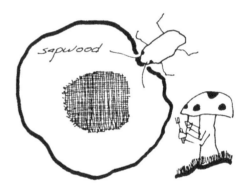

Green wood, particularly green sapwood, has a high food content. This makes it the target of fungi and insects that wish to eat it.

To protect wood from being devoured by fungi and insects requires that the Moisture Content be reduced to a safe level: 25 - 30%

Maintaining a reasonable Moisture Content is the fundamental principle of using wood for building.

Weather conditions are in themselves not enough to raise the Moisture Content of wood constructions to a dangerous level.

It should be borne in mind that the ability of wood to absorb and to release water is a distinct advantage in the creation of a living, breathing building. While it might be feared that the Moisture Content of your timber building would exceed the critical 25% level, this would only happen if the timber were exposed to a constant source of moisture from a leaking gutter, by soaking it up from the ground or some other defect. Damp weather and rain are not in themselves enough to raise Moisture Content to a critical level. It is in this area that a proper understanding of the nature of wood is essential to using the material freely and with confidence. Even if naturally resistant heartwood is to be used this does not obviate the need for proper construction and detailing practice.

To counteract the vulnerability of sapwood to fungal and insect attack it is normal practice to poison the food supply within the wood. Great care has to be taken with this as the introduction of toxic substances into the wood render it dangerous to all forms of life.

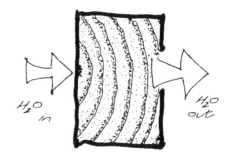

The ability of wood to absorb and release moisture is a distinct advantage in the creation of healthy living environments.

The poisoning of wood to render it safe from fungal and insect attack is dangerous to all life forms.

Wood Conversion

To properly remove the sap from freshly felled trees, the trunks are first delimbed and then cut into smaller pieces. The delimbed trunk is known as a log and the cutting of this is called conversion. When wood has been converted it becomes known as timber. The sawn pieces themselves are known as sections.

Conversion usually takes place in a sawmill. This process is carried out to expose as much of the wood surface as possible ensuring that it dries evenly. If a log is left in one piece the outer part of it dries while the inner portion remains wet. There are various ways of sawing up logs to yield usable sections of timber.

A timber section where the angle of the broad face to the growth rings is less than 45° is called flat sawn. Where the angle is greater than 45° it is called quarter sawn. Flat sawn sections are more liable to shrink across the grain when dried or to distort or split in comparison to quarter sawn sections. It is a more economical conversion method, however. Quarter sawn sections are usually confined to uses such as boat building or for flooring that will be subject to hard wear. Also, quarter sawing is sometimes used to best display the attractive ray pattern in some decorative hardwoods such as oak.

a log

When a tree has been felled and delimbed it is called a log.

The process of sawing a log into smaller pieces is called conversion. Converted wood is called timber.

The pieces of timber themselves are called sections.

To make it ready for building purposes timber, in the form of trees, is felled, cut and dried, resulting in the availability of seasoned sections of wood in a range of sizes. Generally, for building purposes, softwoods are used.

Even after seasoning (drying), wood continues to absorb and release moisture as it seeks to come into balance with its surroundings. This is a distinct advantage of the use of wood for building purposes.

Wood has a great appeal to our senses, and as such, it is an ideal building material.

The facts of this are to be found in pages 10 -15. You should carefully read these pages and consciously deal with any adverse reactions that you have to the information.

Next: SDP30 - Wood - Technical Facts & Figures, page 16

Wood from a local sawmill can be an economical option for the cost-conscious sheltermaker

Seasoning Timber

The process of drying converted timber is known as seasoning. This can either be carried out naturally by allowing air to circulate through the converted sections or the timber can be placed in a kiln where the moisture content is reduced artificially.

Properly seasoned timber will always be less prone to attack by fungi and insects, will have better stability and strength, will be lighter in weight, less corrosive to metal fastenings and will be more pleasant to handle. It will also accept surface finishes more easily.

In some cases, sections of green timber are used for building. The advantages of this lie in the fact that the timber is less prone to split and is easier to cut. Also, when green timber is nailed the nails rust in making them less likely to pull out. Green timber, when used in this way, must then be allowed to dry naturally and care must be taken to ensure that the consequent shrinkage does not cause distortion or undue stresses in the structure.

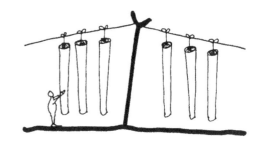

The process of reducing the Moisture Content of timber is called seasoning.

The seasoning of timber can be carried out naturally or artificially ... by air or by kiln drying.

Air Drying

Air drying utilises the ability of air to carry moisture away from the converted timber. This process is very similar to the way in which air carries away moisture from our skin by evaporation. To facilitate this process the timber is placed in a drying shed, a structure that is open at the sides and has a roof over it. The timber is stacked so that each piece is exposed on all sides.

The length of the air drying process depends on the prevailing conditions in the drying shed and can range from several months to as long as a year. Most rapid drying takes place in the late spring and early summer. When the drying process is complete the bulk of the moisture within the timber will be gone - evaporated away. The actual Moisture Content will then normally be about 20%.

Timber will always strike a balance with its surroundings either picking up or shedding moisture as necessary. This balance that the timber achieves with its surroundings is known as equilibrium. Generally speaking, timber should be allowed some time to adjust to its environment before it is finally fixed in position to allow it to establish a proper equilibrium with its surroundings.

Air drying involves exposing the timber sections to the air within a drying shed. This will reduce the Moisture Content to about 21%

The air drying of timber takes from six months to one year.

Kiln Drying

An alternative to air drying timber is to dry it in a kiln under controlled conditions. Kiln dried timber can be dried down to quite small Moisture Contents, as low as 8%. Even after kiln drying however, timber will pick up moisture from its surroundings and find its own equilibrium.

Kilns vary in size and type but the conditions under which they operate are basically all the same. The timber is stacked within the kiln so that as much of its surface area as possible is exposed. The air within the kiln is then heated up and is circulated around the timber removing moisture by evaporation, in much the same way as air drying does. Because the process is much more rapid than air drying, the humidity and temperature of the circulating air need to be very carefully controlled. If this is not done there is a danger that the outer layers of timber will dry too quickly, trapping moisture within the timber and causing splits and unacceptable internal stresses. This condition is called case hardening.

The time required for kiln drying varies from several days to twelve weeks, according to quality, species and the initial and desired Moisture Content of the timber. A good quality timber can be safely dried more rapidly than poor quality and the size of the timber sections is also a factor. Some white timbers can lose their light colour in the kiln drying process and with others their strength and suitability for joinery work can be impaired. Kiln dried timbers can also display a dead quality in comparison to those that have been air dried.

The main advantage of kiln drying is the speed at which the drying can be realised in comparison to natural methods, though it is more expensive. It also has an advantage in that the risk of attack by fungi and insects is minimised because the Moisture Content is reduced so rapidly after felling.

When introduced into a new environment, kiln dried timber will inevitably absorb airborne moisture and swell as it finds its equilibrium.

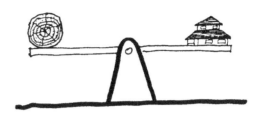

Timber will always strike a balance with its surroundings - either picking up or shedding moisture. This is called: finding its equilibrium.

Kiln drying can reduce the Moisture Content of timber to as low as 8%.

Even kiln dried timber with a low Moisture Content will pick up moisture from its surroundings and find its equilibrium.

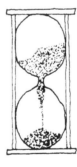

Kiln drying offers the most rapid seasoning process available.

Timber Movement

Timber moves all the time. It swells and shrinks as it absorbs and releases water vapour. Timber will always adjust to the atmosphere that it is in, establishing a balance or equilibrium with its surroundings. Swelling and shrinkage in timber is called movement.

Initial shrinkage commences when green timber is dried below its fibre saturation point. This is the point at which all the moisture has been removed from the cell cavities. This usually occurs at between 28-30% moisture content. At this point the remaining moisture is stored in the cell walls. When some of this is removed the cells themselves shrink in size and it is the accumulated reduction in size of all the cells together that cause shrinkage.

The extent of shrinkage depends on the species of the timber as well as on the way it has been converted - flat or quarter sawn. In flat sawn sections this movement - called tangential shrinkage - will be about twice that of the equivalent size quarter sawn section - called radial shrinkage. Tangential shrinkage can be estimated at 1% for every 3% change in Moisture Content below 30%. Radial shrinkage is about half this. Shrinkage due to a fall in initial moisture content is always greater than the shrinkage that occurs as timber finds its equilibrium. Generally, those timbers used in building construction do not exhibit measurable shrinkage along the grain.

Once timber has been seasoned its moisture content will never return to the levels it had in its green state unless it is immersed in water. Even then, many timbers will not absorb such great quantities of water to return them to a Moisture Content of 100% or more. Where airborne moisture - water vapour - is the only moisture that timber in use is liable to absorb, its Moisture Content will always remain relatively low.

Because Moisture Content is an important factor in preserving timber from attack by fungi and insects, controlling the amount of water that timber is likely to absorb in use is critical. Once timber is situated so that it is not in contact with a constant source of water, particularly its end grain, the timber will remain dry enough to be free of decay. Rain and damp conditions are not in themselves capable of wetting carefully detailed and constructed timber to the point where decay is likely to occur.

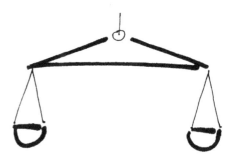

Timber in service is all the time either absorbing or releasing moisture as it keeps its equilibrium.

The movement caused by this means that the timber is either swelling or shrinking.

Timber shrinks when all the moisture held in its cell cavities has been removed. This occurs at between 28-30% Moisture Content. This causes the timber to shrink, principally across the grain. This means that the depth and width of the timber section is reduced in size while the length of the section is not affected.

In the case of timber swelling - this causes the depth and width of the timber section to increase in size.

Maintaining a reasonable Moisture Content is a critical element in the keeping of timber safe from fungal and insect attack in a natural manner.

The reality of timber movement is an important factor in the selection of appropriate surface finishes for the material. Finishes such as oil paint that have no elasticity will crack when the timber swells. When subsequent drying takes place the escaping moisture will then cause the paint to peel. A worse scenario is where the moisture cannot escape and by remaining in the timber causes the Moisture Content to rise to a dangerous level thereby setting up ideal conditions for decay. This can also occur where improperly seasoned timber is sealed with a surface coating trapping moisture within the material.

Dealing with the realities of timber movement, moisture content, fibre saturation and so on can seem a daunting task. The material seems to have a mind of its own and will simply not stay still! That movement should ever be seen as a problem in timber is a peculiarity of how we view the material.

The feel, smell, look and sound of the timber are the factors that must guide the creative process. It is this sensual contact with timber that will allow one to enjoy and exploit its potential to create natural, safe, healthy and sensually alive spaces. If one insists on applying pure logic to the design and building process then the materials that are selected will reflect this bias and, for all practical purposes, will be dead materials - those that will not move, change or be unpredictable in any way. Of course, the spaces that will be created from these materials will inevitably reflect this dead quality.

In truth, the ability of timber to adjust to the relative humidity of its surroundings is a great bonus to those wishing to create a healthy internal environment. Because timber is hygroscopic - it can absorb and release airborne moisture - it will act as a regulator of the internal relative humidity when used in the fabric of the building. Furthermore, its use will allow for a breathable construction to be created if this is a design aim. More than any other building material, timber requires a response from our senses to properly evaluate its widespread advantages in creating proper living environments.

The Characteristics of Timber

Apart from its strength and versatility as a building material, timber displays certain characteristics that might best be described as its sensuous qualities. These qualities vary from species to species and distinguish one timber from another especially with their appeal to our senses - how the timber smells, how it feels and how it looks.

Timber is forever moving slightly as it absorbs and releases moisture. Any surface finish that is applied to timber should recognise this fact.

Timber is a living material and must be appreciated through the senses.

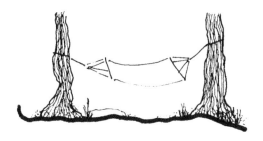

Timber is an ideal material with which to create natural living environments.

30 Sheltermaker Design Programme
Wood - Technical Facts & Figures

The information contained in pages 15 onwards set out many technical facts and figures about wood. At this juncture, much of this information is not critical to the progress of your project, however reading through all of it is a good idea.

Tucked away within these technical facts and figures is more information on the emotional aspects of using wood for building purposes. Particularly, *'Timber & Fire'* and *'Timber Decay'* on pages 30 -32 need to be studied, followed by a close reading of *'Timberfear'* on page 43.

The normal method of dealing with the issue of decay in wood is to 'preserve' it. Wood preservation usually involves the use of toxic chemicals which act by killing any life forms which threaten to devour the food contained within the wood. Chemical preservatives are threatening to all forms of life - not just insects and fungi. A natural preservative, such as borax, combined with careful detailing are the only safe alternatives to chemical preservation. *'Wood Preservation'* is dealt with in pages 46-53.

Print the *Construction Worksheet* and outline the use you will make of wood in your project. Create a new file entitled *Construction* in which to store this and other information. This can include information collected on wood and wood-based products.

Next: SDP31 - Choosing Other Materials & Products, page 70

Timber is the ideal framing material

These qualities are normally referred to as *texture, grain, figure, scent, colour* and even *taste*. Apart from giving sensuous appeal to the timber, some of these qualities also affect the performance of the timber when it is used for building. For example, grain has an important bearing on the strength of the timber while scent and taste affect the ability of the timber to resist decay. Some of these qualities also assist in distinguishing one timber from another.

Texture

Texture refers to the size of the cells making up the timber and is perceived a visual as well as a tactile quality. Fine texture means that the timber is composed of small cells and coarse texture means the timber is made up of large cells. Most softwoods are fine textured, while oak, a hardwood, is described as being coarse textured due to its relatively large cell size. It is the cell size that gives timber its looks, in other words whether it appears to be fine or coarse textured. As well as this the cell size affects how the timber reacts to being smoothed or planed. If it is fine textured it will plane very smooth, if it is coarse textured it will have a coarser finish.

Apart from cell size, texture also refers to the colour contrast apparent between the earlywood and the latewood. Within a timber where there is little colour contrast between earlywood and latewood the timber is said to have an even texture. Where there is a distinct contrast apparent, the timber is said to have an uneven texture. Diffuse porous hardwoods such as beech, and softwoods with growth rings having slight contrasting spring and summer woods, such as white pine, are known as even textured timbers. Ring porous hardwoods such as elm and softwoods having strongly contrasting zones of spring and summer wood, such as Douglas Fir, are said to be of uneven texture.

Grain

Grain describes the line or direction of the fibres and cells within the timber as they appear on the surface of the section. Also it is perceived as an alternation of colour between zones of spring and summer wood in the growth rings. There are several kinds of grain - straight grain, irregular grain, spiral grain, interlocking grain and diagonal grain.

Straight grain is where the cells are parallel to the long side of the section. It is relatively strong and easy to work. Irregular grain is where the fibres are inclined

The sensuous qualities of timber are normally referred to as texture, grain, figure, scent, colour and even taste!

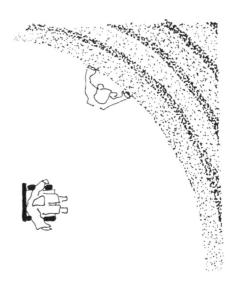

Texture means how a piece of timber looks and feels ... and how the earlywood and latewood contrast with each other.

17

and wavy producing alternating darker and lighter waves like stripes on the surface. This is relatively weak timber and it can be difficult to work but can be highly decorative on account of the irregularly curved surface pattern. The irregularity is often due to the presence of knots.

Spiral grained timber is where the cells are arranged spiral. This reduces the timbers strength and makes it difficult to work. Interlocking grain is where the cells in successive growth rings are inclined in opposite directions. This timber may be subject to excessive twisting when being seasoned and is not easy to work but its strength is not seriously affected.

Diagonal grain occurs where straight grained timber has been badly converted. This reduces its strength.

End grain refers to the arrangement of exposed fibres on the cross cut surface of the timber. Here the circular pattern of the growth rings will usually be visible.

Grain means the line and direction that the wood cells follow.
Straight grain is where the wood cells run straight and parallel.
Straight grained timber is strong and easy to work.

Colour

Timbers display a large variation in colour from white, to brown, to yellow, red, green, pink and even black. The majority of timber that one will use for general carpentry work however, will inevitably be softwoods falling into the brown/white/yellow/pinkish red categories. Where there are variations in shading or where the colour of the timbers you are using is very light and without much body, a stain, seal or paint will enhance their appearance. This type of finish will help to unify variations in natural timber colour and will also help to relieve the monotony you can sometimes get if you are using a lot of wood for surfaces. Such surfaces, if not finished in this way, can have a very busy appearance which takes from the overall quality of the material.

Care should be taken that any paints or stains used internally do not lead to pollution of the internal environment of your home or seal up the timber so that it cannot breathe. Timbers with a good natural colour can be used in particular situations - for beams, columns or for features such as an internal threshold.

Timber exposed externally can be stained, sealed or painted. It should be remembered not to seal these so that they cannot breathe. External timber that is left without any surface finish will eventually lose its natural colour due to the effects of ultra violet light, weathering to a silver grey colour.

End grain means the arrangement of exposed cells or fibres on the end of a piece of timber where the growth ring pattern is usually visible.

Pale softwoods should normally be painted. Only natural and safe materials should be used to do this.

Figure

Figure refers to the ornamental markings seen on the cut surface of timber, formed by the cell structure of the wood. Figure is influenced by the arrangement of different cell tissues particularly the pattern made by the medullary rays in hardwoods. The grain and colour of the wood and the variations between early and late wood also influence figure.

Straight grained, flat sawn timber has only a plain figure whereas quarter sawn hardwood can have beautiful figure, showing beautiful markings particularly when it is has an irregular grain and the rays are exposed. Oak, for example, that is quarter sawn to disclose relatively large sections of the broad medullary rays on the cut surface.

Timber must always be allowed to breathe ... naturally.

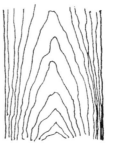 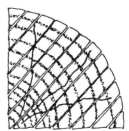

Figure as a discernable sensuous quality of timber, applies mainly to hardwoods such as oak.

Good figure is best exploited by quarter sawing the timber.

Taste

All timbers have their own characteristic taste. This natural taste varies according to the extractives with they contain - resin, oils tannin and so on. Generally natural taste is not likely to be an influence on the selection of timber, though in particular situations, such as in work tops on which food will be prepared, it is important. In this regard sycamore is the timber of choice.

Taste however is of considerable importance in assessing the safety of timber in regard to your health. You should be able to chew on a piece of wood that is to be used in the construction of your home without worrying that it might make you sick. Timber that has been impregnated by certain preservatives will be toxic in order to kill fungi or insects that might attempt to devour it. Needless to say such substances are a danger to all forms of life. This taste test is a very good indicator of whether or not the timber in your home will pose a danger to your health.

The taste of a particular timber is important where it might come directly in contact with food. Sycamore is the best timber to use in such cases.

Scent

In terms of scent, all woods have an agreeable smell. The particular scent that a timber displays depends on the resins and oils present in the timber, especially in the heartwood. This natural quality of wood can be utilised to create a wonderful scented internal environment stimulating all your sense organs. Stains, sealants and paints, where used, should be made from natural ingredients enhancing the original scent of the timber and creating a natural, living environment.

Defects In Timber

Apart from variations in grain due to growth or conversion factors, timber can be subject to other variations in quality. These are usually referred to as defects and can reduce the strength of the timber, make it difficult to convert, spoil its appearance and present difficulties in working and finishing.

Knots, bark pockets, shakes, deadwood, resin pockets, checks, ribbing, splits, cupping, bowing, warp and wany edges are all conditions that come under the heading of defects in timber.

Knots are the most frequent defects likely to be encountered in converted timber. They are caused by branches being enclosed by sound wood within the growing tree. They affect the strength of the timber by causing deviation in the grain and they may fall out, leaving a hole in the section.

Shakes appear as a separation in the cellular structure of the timber. They usually occur between or through the growth rings. Resin pockets are cavities within the timber containing resin. All the above are the result of natural causes.

Checks are separations of the cellular structure along the grain forming a crack in the timber that does not extend through the section from one side to the other. Checks usually occur across or through the growth rings and can occur anywhere along the section. They are caused by unequal drying.

Ribbing is a more or less regular corrugation of the surface of the timber caused by differential shrinkage of early and late wood.

Splits are separations in the cellular structure of the timber along the grain. They extend through the section from one side to the other usually at the ends of the section.

Cupping is curvature from edge to edge across the section of the timber making it deviate from a flat plane.

Bowing is curvature in a piece along its length making it deviate from a flat plane.

Warp or twist is distortion in the section causing all faces to deviate from a flat plane. All the above defects are due mainly to seasoning problems.

The Taste Test - can you safely chew on a piece of timber that is to be used in your home?

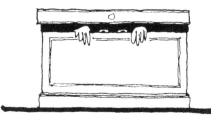

The smell of timber is one of its most sensuous qualities. Remember the smell of your grandmother's cedar chest?

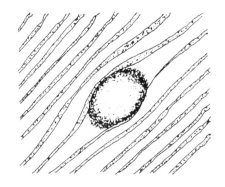

Knots

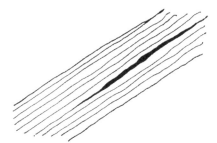

Shakes

Defects in timber can reduce its strength, make it difficult to convert, spoil its appearance and present difficulties in working and finishing.

Waney edges are remains of the original rounded surface of log remaining on the timber section. This defect is a problem in the conversion process.

All of these conditions are readily apparent by visual inspection. Apart from the presence of a reasonable number of sound knots, timber displaying any of the above characteristics cannot be regarded as being of first quality and so should be available at a reduced price to the buyer.

Cupping

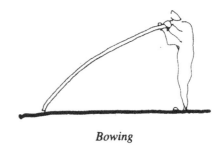

Bowing

Warp & Twist is a combination of Cupping & Bowing

Identifying Timber

Apart from the more commonly recognised timbers such as mahogany, teak, pine and oak, the task of identifying particular timbers is a difficult one. For those handling timber from day-to-day, indicators such as smell, feel, grain and workability - not to talk of labelling! - make the task seem easy.

In general, the distinction between softwood and hardwood is the one most easily made. Softwoods are generally paler in colour, lighter in weight and their end grain has a consistent structure possibly displaying a distinct growth ring pattern. Hardwoods, on the other hand, are usually darker in colour, seem denser, and their end grain displays the pores characteristic of this type of wood. The use of a magnifying glass to examine end grain will always be of help in distinguishing between soft and hardwoods.

Even with a microscope it is often impossible to distinguish between softwoods, for example the anatomical structure of Sitka and European Spruce are indistinguishable. A pronounced contrast between earlywood and latewood is a feature of both Larch and of Douglas Fir. Spruces display little contrast between earlywood and latewood.

If you wish to become accomplished at the ready identification of timber you need to visit a sawmill or timber yard, poke around, ask questions and pick someone's brain. If you are lucky you can get some off-cuts and these can be identified and marked. In any exercise designed to improve your identification skills,

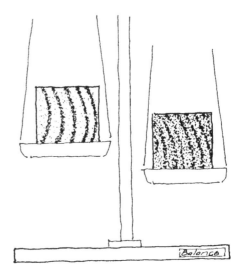

Softwood generally is paler, lighter in weight and has a distinct growth ring pattern ...

Hardwood is usually darker in colour, heavier in weight, denser and displays open pores on its end grain.

it is important not only to look but to handle the material and to smell it. Also, while you are doing this, enquire as to the cost of the various timbers available and keep a good record of this information - it will probably be the decisive factor at the end of the day as to which timbers you select for use. Also, a visit to a forest is also a good idea in order to identify the standing trees. When one realises the ability of the material in terms of creating shelter, even the lowly Sitka plantations become places of wonder.

When one appreciates the abilities of timber in constructing clean, dry and healthy buildings, even the lowly Sitka plantations become places of wonder.

Timber Sizes

Converted timber is normally available in a range of standard sizes and lengths. A British Standard also exists covering this topic - BS 4471. Basic sawn section sizes for softwood are as follows, measured in millimetres at 20% moisture content:

Section sizes will vary according to location ... always try to use what is available locally from renewable sources

	75	100	125	150	175	200	225	250	300
16 X	75	100	125	150					
19 X	75	100	125	150					
22 X	75	100	125	150					
25 X	75	100	125	150	175	200	225	250	300
32 X	75	100	125	150	175	200	225	250	300
36 X	75	100	125	150					
38 X	75	100	125	150	175	200	225		
44 X	75	100	125	150	175	200	225	250	300
47 X	75	100	125	150	175	200	225	250	300
50 X	75	100	125	150	175	200	225	250	300
63 X		100	125	150	175	200	225		
75 X		100	125	150	175	200	225	250	300
100 X		100		150		200		250	300
150 X				150		200			300
200 X						200			
250 X								250	
300 X									300

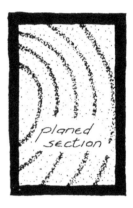

Standard timber section sizes are reduced by 4-5mm in depth and in width when they are planed smooth.

PAO means 'planed all over' i.e. the timber section is planed smooth.

Standard hardwood section sizes are more variable than standard softwood section sizes and lengths.

When planed, these section sizes will be reduced by 4-5mm in overall size. Basic lengths of softwood range from 1800mm rising in 300mm increments to 7200mm. Generally, lengths over 4800mm carry a surcharge.

Hardwoods are normally available in standard thicknesses of boards - 19; 25; 32; 38; 50; 63; 75 & 100mm, available in variable widths. It is probable that your use of hardwood will be minimal because of the costs involved or your attitude towards what is happening to the rain forest. However, odd lots of locally grown hardwood do become available at times and it is possible to obtain random sections which you can put to specific use in your home. Due to the proliferation of Dutch Elm disease for example, quantities of elm are frequently available from small local sawmills.

It is worth watching out for locally available lots of hardwood at small sawmills ...for example, elm.

Timber Grading & Strength

For its weight, timber is an extremely strong building material particularly its ability to sustain tensile loading along the grain. Being a natural material, timber is subject to variation in quality and this has to be taken into account in assessing the ability of what is available to the builder to sustain the loads it will be subject to in use - generally for floor, roof and wall construction.

To bring some uniformity to the question of assessing the strengths of various timbers in carrying loads Stress Grading rules have been developed. These allow both for the visual grading as well as for the machine grading of different species.

Visual Stress Grading is based on the assessment of the appearance of the timber by considering the size and position of characteristics such as knots which will affect the ability of the timber to carry the loads it is likely to be subjected to in use.

Machine Stress Grading measures the actual stiffness of the timber by passing it through a machine. Generally, machine stress grading is carried out on softwood which is the most commonly used timber in house construction. Hardwoods are generally graded visually.

Various national standards exist for stress grading softwoods, for example, American Lumber Standards (ALS), British Standard 4978: 1973 and the Irish SR 11: 1988. The provisions of SR 11 are broadly in compliance with BS 4978. Timber which has been stress graded in accordance with one of these standards carries a stamp to this effect.

SR 11 is devoted to grading both native Irish as well as imported structural timber for use in house building. It requires that the moisture content of all structural timber shall not exceed 22% at the time of fixing. Visual as well as mechanical grading is covered by the standard. Timbers graded mechanically carry the designation 'M'. There are three grades:

General Structural - GS & MGS
Special Structural - SS & MSS
Machine Grade - M75

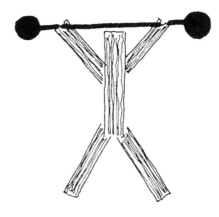

Timber Stress Grading involves the assessment of how strong particular sections of softwood are.

Stress Grading is carried out either visually or by machine.

National Standards exist for Stress Graded softwoods. Such timber carries a stamp to this effect.

TIMBER SPAN TABLES — FOR DOMESTIC CONSTRUCTION

INTRODUCTION

This information sheet is based on SR11 — 1988: 'STRUCTURAL TIMBER FOR DOMESTIC CONSTRUCTION' and shows maximum Span Tables for Floor Joists, Ceiling Joists, Roof Rafters and Purlins as used in domestic construction.

The section of timber required for a particular application is selected by reference to Span Tables.

How Long?   How wide?   How Deep?

To take into account the different strength abilities of the timber species covered by SR 11 three Strength Classes are designated:

Strength Class - SC A
Strength Class - SC B
Strength Class - SC C

In practice timber sections of appropriate size and strength for particular uses are selected by reference to Span Tables and the Strength Class Table. The Strength Class Table covers softwood species, grades and strengths. The Span Tables cover floor joists, ceiling joists, roof rafters and roof purlins.

The tables can be used in several ways. One method is to select a species and strength class of timber using the Strength Class Table then, by reference to the appropriate Span Table, finding out the size of section that is required to safely cover the span.

For example: You wish to use Sitka Spruce - SC A to make a floor that spans a distance of 4 meters. What size section will be required to do this?

Refer to the Floor Joist Span Table and you will see that under SC A you have a choice of spacing the joists at 300, 400 or 600mm centres.

Follow down the 300 column until you come the figure 4.04, then read off on your left the section size - 35x200mm. This is the size of timber you will have to use to make your floor and each joist will have to be 300mm from the next.

If the joists are spaced at 400mm centres a 44x225 section will be needed. At 600mm centres, a 63x225mm section will have to be used.

You will also see as you follow this exercise that for the 35x200 and the 44x225mm sections 'bridging is required at 1350mm'. Bridging involves inserting support pieces between the joists to counteract their tendency to lean sideways.

Following the same exercise for Sitka Spruce- SC B, you will see that 44x175mm joists @ 300mm centres, 44x200mm joists @ 400mm centres, or 44x225mm joists @ 600mm centres will have to be used to make your floor.

TGBI
Grade **SS** Strength Class **SCB**
BS 4978/SR11
Reg. No. 100/738

TGBI
Grade **SS** Strength Class **SCC**
BS 4978/SR11
Reg. No. 100/738

TGBI
Grade **M75** Strength Class **SCC**
BS 4978/SR11
Reg. No. 100/738

Deciding which size section to use will be a matter of the cost of the various size sections and their availability. If the joists are to be left exposed this will also be a factor in your decision. The cost of sawn timber is calculated per cubic meter. In the above example, based on the volume of wood involved, the 44x225 joists in either SC A or SC B would offer the best value.

This will illustrate the importance of beginning to collect information on the availability of timber locally and its cost. If this data is available to you when you reach the detailed design stage an economical structure can be planned. If timber sizes are calculated on the basis of the Tables alone you may be in for some shocks when you begin to order materials!

FLOOR JOISTS

Size of Joist (mm)	STRENGTH CLASS								
	SC A			SC B			SC C		
	Spacing of Joists								
	300	400	600	300	400	600	300	400	600
	permissible span of joists in metres								
35 × 100	2.02	1.81	1.48	2.12	1.92	1.67	2.21	2.00	1.74
35 × 115	2.33	2.07	1.69	2.43	2.21	1.92	2.54	2.30	2.00
35 × 125	2.54	2.24	1.83	2.65	2.40	2.09	2.76	2.50	2.18
35 × 150	3.04	2.66	2.17	3.18	2.88	2.51	3.31	3.01	2.62
35 × 175	3.54	3.08	2.51	3.71	3.37	2.93	3.87	3.51	3.05
35 × 200†	4.04	3.50	2.85	4.25	3.85	3.34	4.42	4.01	3.49
35 × 225†	4.51	3.91	3.19	4.78	4.33	3.73	4.98	4.51	3.93
44 × 100	2.19	1.98	1.66	2.29	2.08	1.81	2.39	2.16	1.89
44 × 115	2.52	2.28	1.89	2.63	2.39	2.07	2.74	2.48	2.16
44 × 125	2.74	2.48	2.05	2.87	2.59	2.25	2.98	2.71	2.35
44 × 150	3.28	2.98	2.43	3.44	3.12	2.72	3.58	3.25	2.83
44 × 175	3.84	3.45	2.82	4.02	3.65	3.16	4.18	3.79	3.30
44 × 200	4.38	3.92	3.20	4.59	4.16	3.62	4.78	4.33	3.77
44 × 225†	4.94	4.38	3.57	5.17	4.69	4.08	5.38	4.88	4.24
63 × 150	3.71	3.37	2.91	3.89	3.52	3.07	4.04	3.64	3.20
63 × 175	4.33	3.93	3.37	4.54	4.12	3.58	4.72	4.28	3.73
63 × 225	5.58	5.06	4.28	5.83	5.29	4.61	6.07	5.51	4.80
75 × 150	3.94	3.58	3.11	4.12	3.74	3.26	4.29	3.89	3.40
75 × 175	4.60	4.17	3.63	4.81	4.37	3.80	5.01	4.54	3.96
75 × 225	5.91	5.37	4.67	6.19	5.61	4.89	6.44	5.84	5.09

25

TIMBER SPAN TABLES —
FOR DOMESTIC CONSTRUCTION

INTRODUCTION

This information sheet is based on SR11 — 1988: 'STRUCTURAL TIMBER FOR DOMESTIC CONSTRUCTION' and shows maximum Span Tables for Floor Joists, Ceiling Joists, Roof Rafters and Purlins as used in domestic construction. The Tables shown are for three Strength Classes of softwood timber: SC A / SC B / SC C and cover most common timber sizes used in Ireland. All spans are given **on plan** (including roof rafters) and refer to the clear span between the points of support.

The timber sizes shown are the minimum permissible sizes for timber at a moisture content of 22%.

TIMBER

These Tables can be used for both Irish and Imported softwood timber graded to BS.4978:1988. Timbers appropriate to a particular Strength Class are selected on a species/grade combination as shown below:

SOFTWOOD SPECIES	STRENGTH CLASSES		
	SC A	SC B	SC C
Irish Timber:			
Sitka Spruce	GS	SS	M75
Norway Spruce	GS	SS	M75
Douglas Fir	GS		SS
Larch		GS	SS
Imported Timber:			
Whitewood*1		GS	SS
Redwood*1		GS	SS
Fir-Larch*2		GS	SS
Spruce-Pine-Fir*2		GS	SS
Hem-Fir*2		GS	SS

*1 — European
*2 — Canadian

MOISTURE CONTENT

It is a requirement of SR11 that the Moisture Content of all structural timber, including preservative treated timber, shall not exceed 22% at the time of fixing.

END CONDITION

The bearing condition assumed is a simple support at the ends of the members. No allowance has been made for notching or drilling, which reduces the strength of a member.

MINIMUM BRIDGING

Members marked† in the tables require bridging at intervals of 1350mm.

LOADING AND DESIGN ASSUMPTIONS

The loads are suitable for domestic houses up to 3 stories.

The following loading and design assumptions are taken:

Floor Joists	:	
UDL**	:	0.30 KN/M² Dead Load
		1.50 KN/M² Live Load
Factors	:	1.1 Load Sharing
		1.0 Load Duration
Ceiling Joists	:	
UDL**	:	0.25 KN/M² Dead Load
		0.25 KN/M² Live Load
Factors	:	1.0 Load Sharing
		1.0 Load Duration
Point Load	:	0.9 KN*1
UDL**	:	0.25 KN/M² Dead Load
Factors	:	1.0 Load Sharing
		1.25 Load Duration
Roof Rafters	:	
UDL**	:	0.68 KN/M² Dead Load*2
UDL**	:	0.75 KN/M² Live Load
Factors	:	1.1 Load Sharing
		1.25 Load Duration
Point Load	:	0.9 KN/M*1
UDL**	:	0.68 KN/M² Dead Load*2
Factors	:	1.1 Load Sharing
		1.5 Load Duration
Purlins	:	
Maximum loading from above cases		
Factors	:	1.0 Load Sharing

**UDL   Uniformly distributed load.
*1   Point load placed so as to produce maximum stress or deflection in a member.
*2   Concrete tiles measured on slope.

DEFLECTION

Limited to 0.003 times the span except in the case of the roof rafters where the limit is 0.004 times the rafter span.

RAFTER SPANS

The Rafter Spans shown in the tables are measured **on plan** and are **clear spans** from wall-plate to purlin or purlin to ridge. The following formula may be used to convert spans on plan to spans on slope:

Span on Slope = Span on Plan x K

Correspondingly:

(Span on Plan = Span on Slope ÷ K)

Roof Pitch (Degrees)	20°	25°	30°	35°	40°
K valves	1.06	1.12	1.18	1.24	1.30

Intermediate roof pitch K values, may be interpolated.

FLOOR JOISTS

Size of Joist (mm)	STRENGTH CLASS								
	SC A			SC B			SC C		
	Spacing of Joists								
	300	400	600	300	400	600	300	400	600
	permissible span of joists in metres								
35 × 100	2.02	1.81	1.48	2.12	1.92	1.67	2.21	2.00	1.74
35 × 115	2.33	2.07	1.69	2.43	2.21	1.92	2.54	2.30	2.00
35 × 125	2.54	2.24	1.83	2.65	2.40	2.09	2.76	2.50	2.18
35 × 150	3.04	2.66	2.17	3.18	2.88	2.51	3.31	3.01	2.62
35 × 175	3.54	3.08	2.51	3.71	3.37	2.93	3.87	3.51	3.05
35 × 200†	4.04	3.50	2.85	4.25	3.85	3.34	4.42	4.01	3.49
35 × 225†	4.51	3.91	3.19	4.78	4.33	3.73	4.98	4.51	3.93
44 × 100	2.19	1.98	1.66	2.29	2.08	1.81	2.39	2.16	1.89
44 × 115	2.52	2.28	1.89	2.63	2.39	2.07	2.74	2.48	2.16
44 × 125	2.74	2.48	2.05	2.87	2.59	2.25	2.98	2.71	2.35
44 × 150	3.28	2.98	2.43	3.44	3.12	2.72	3.58	3.25	2.83
44 × 175	3.84	3.45	2.82	4.02	3.65	3.16	4.18	3.79	3.30
44 × 200	4.38	3.92	3.20	4.59	4.16	3.62	4.78	4.33	3.77
44 × 225†	4.94	4.38	3.57	5.17	4.69	4.08	5.38	4.88	4.24
63 × 150	3.71	3.37	2.91	3.89	3.52	3.07	4.04	3.64	3.20
63 × 175	4.33	3.93	3.37	4.54	4.12	3.58	4.72	4.28	3.73
63 × 225	5.58	5.06	4.28	5.83	5.29	4.61	6.07	5.51	4.80
75 × 150	3.94	3.58	3.11	4.12	3.74	3.26	4.29	3.89	3.40
75 × 175	4.60	4.17	3.63	4.81	4.37	3.80	5.01	4.54	3.96
75 × 225	5.91	5.37	4.67	6.19	5.61	4.89	6.44	5.84	5.09

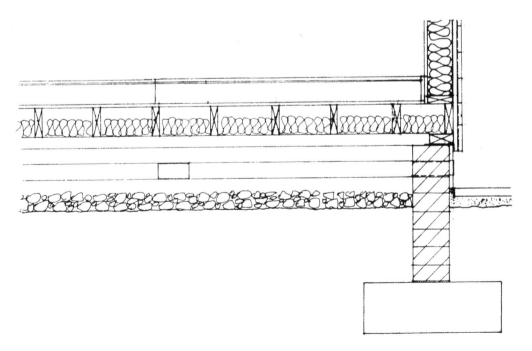

CEILING JOISTS

Size of Joist (mm)	STRENGTH CLASS								
	SC A			SC B			SC C		
	Spacing of Joists								
	300	400	600	300	400	600	300	400	600
	permissible span of ceiling joists in metres								
35 × 100	1.42	1.39	1.35	1.84	1.81	1.76	1.94	1.92	1.86
35 × 115	1.82	1.78	1.71	2.24	2.21	2.14	2.37	2.33	2.26
35 × 125	2.10	2.05	1.96	2.53	2.48	2.40	2.67	2.62	2.53
35 × 150	2.88	2.79	2.64	3.26	3.19	3.07	3.45	3.37	3.24
35 × 175	3.74	3.60	3.37	4.05	3.94	3.76	4.28	4.16	3.97
35 × 200†	4.57	4.44	4.13	4.86	4.72	4.48	5.13	4.98	4.72
44 × 100	1.76	1.72	1.66	2.06	2.01	1.96	2.16	2.14	2.07
44 × 115	2.24	2.19	2.09	2.50	2.46	2.38	2.64	2.59	2.51
44 × 125	2.59	2.52	2.40	2.81	2.76	2.67	2.98	2.92	2.81
44 × 150	3.42	3.34	3.20	3.63	3.55	3.40	3.84	3.75	3.58
44 × 175	4.23	4.12	-3.93	4.50	4.37	4.17	4.75	4.62	4.39
44 × 200	5.07	4.93	4.68	5.39	5.23	4.95	5.69	5.51	5.20

†Bridging required at 1350mm

Roof Angle 20 degrees or more

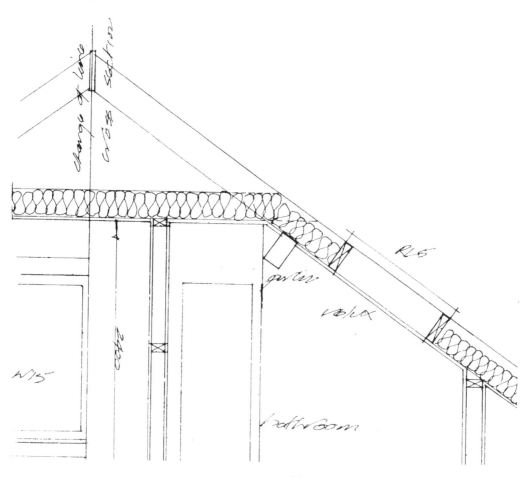

28

ROOF RAFTERS

Roof Angle 20 — 40 degrees   With purlin support at mid-span

Size of Rafter (mm)	SC A			SC B			SC C		
	300	400	600	300	400	600	300	400	600
	permissible span of rafters in metres								
35 × 100	2.35	2.03	1.65	2.70	2.35	1.90	2.92	2.53	2.08
35 × 115	2.65	2.30	1.88	3.05	2.65	2.15	3.30	2.85	2.33
35 × 125	2.85	2.47	2.03	3.28	2.85	2.33	3.53	3.08	2.50
35 × 150	3.33	2.90	2.38	3.80	3.30	2.72	4.10	3.58	2.92
35 × 175	3.78	3.30	2.70	4.30	3.75	3.08	4.63	4.05	3.33
44 × 100	2.67	2.30	1.88	3.08	2.67	2.17	3.33	2.90	2.35
44 × 115	3.03	2.63	2.13	3.47	3.03	2.47	3.78	3.28	2.67
44 × 125	3.25	2.83	2.30	3.75	3.25	2.65	4.05	3.50	2.88
44 × 150	3.80	3.30	2.70	4.38	3.80	3.10	4.72	4.10	3.35
44 × 175	4.35	3.78	3.10	4.95	4.32	3.55	5.35	4.65	3.83
44 × 200	4.85	4.22	3.47	5.53	4.82	3.97	5.97	5.20	4.28

*Span of roof rafter is measured on plan

ROOF PURLINS

Strength Class	Purlin Size (mm)	Span of Roof Rafter in metres								
		1.25	1.50	1.75	2.00	2.25	2.50	2.75	3.00	3.25
		permissible purlin span in metres								
SC A	75 × 225	3.16	3.12	2.82	2.63	2.56	2.40	2.35	2.21	2.17
	75 × 175	2.63	2.42	2.24	2.17	2.02	1.87	1.73	1.59	1.56
	75 × 150	2.26	2.17	1.90	1.84	1.59	1.55	1.42	1.39	1.36
	63 × 225	3.03	2.80	2.61	2.43	2.37	2.21	2.16	2.02	1.89
	63 × 175	2.43	2.23	2.05	1.89	1.84	1.60	1.56	1.53	1.40
	63 × 150	2.17	1.89	1.72	1.57	1.53	1.39	1.36	1.33	1.30
SC B	75 × 225	3.22	3.26	3.14	3.04	2.86	2.79	2.63	2.58	2.43
	75 × 175	2.64	2.61	2.41	2.34	2.27	2.12	2.07	2.03	1.89
	75 × 150	2.34	2.23	2.05	1.98	1.93	1.78	1.74	1.60	1.57
	63 × 225	3.07	3.12	2.91	2.82	2.65	2.58	2.43	2.38	2.24
	63 × 175	2.62	2.40	2.31	2.14	2.08	2.03	1.89	1.85	1.72
	63 × 150	2.24	2.04	1.96	1.90	1.75	1.61	1.57	1.54	1.41
SC C	75 × 225	3.38	3.41	3.37	3.16	3.07	2.90	2.83	2.78	2.63
	75 × 175	2.86	2.72	2.62	2.53	2.36	2.30	2.25	2.11	2.07
	75 × 150	2.55	2.43	2.24	2.17	2.01	1.95	1.91	1.87	1.74
	63 × 225	3.31	3.26	3.13	3.03	2.85	2.78	2.62	2.57	2.42
	63 × 175	2.73	2.61	2.51	2.33	2.27	2.11	2.06	2.02	1.89
	63 × 150	2.44	2.23	2.04	1.98	1.92	1.87	1.73	1.60	1.57

Timber & Fire

A frequent argument against the use of timber for house construction is its alleged vulnerability to fire. In truth, the majority of the world's houses are timber based. Even in such places as California, where brush fires are common, timber continues to be the material of choice when it comes to making houses.

One reason why the thought of a timber house strikes fear in people is because they imagine their property being destroyed by fire. Or they imagine themselves and their families being put at unnecessary risk. It is important to separate the fear of property loss from the fear of the loss of life or injury. Timber houses are at no greater risk from being consumed by fire than solid ones. As far as personal injury is concerned, the furnishings in a home constitute a greater danger to the occupants in the event of accidental fire than anything else. Even in conventional bricks and mortar construction, floors, doors, stairs and roof are of timber construction. Indeed if they were made of anything else one would think it strange!

Our fear of house fires seems to be a genetic inheritance, a carry-over from times when a timber dwelling was likely to be ignited by invaders. The castle, on the other hand, was built solid, strong and tall and was safe from the stray torches of enemies. In this day and age, such fears are not sustainable in reality. It makes no sense to deny oneself the pleasure of being housed using a natural sensuous material because of an outdated fear, just as it makes no sense to build a modern castle that is cold and damp in order to be safe from invaders.

As far as the facts of timber and fire are concerned - timber is a very difficult material to ignite. Anyone who has tried to set a log on fire can verify this - you hold a flame to the face of the log and other than charring the surface and producing some smoke, nothing happens! This experiment can also be tried with a piece of 44x100mm timber, a fairly typical size section used in house construction. Wood is in fact one of the most fire resistant structural materials available. In the unlikely event of a fire in a timber house, a properly designed timber frame will remain standing in a fire of several hours duration.

It is interesting however to understand how wood burns. At temperatures below 150°C all that happens is that some of the moisture within the wood is released. Between 150°C and 250°C inert gases such as carbon dioxide are released. When the temperature exceeds 250°C an appreciable release of flammable gases occurs resulting from the decomposition of hemicellulose. At this point

Timber is the most commonly used material for housebuilding ....worldwide!

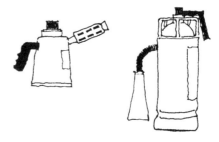

Timber houses are at no greater risk from fire than bricks and mortar ones.

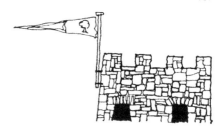

A fear of house fires is a genetic inheritance that has little relevance to the world as we now live in it.

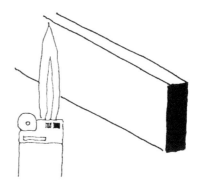

Timber, in the section sizes used for housebuilding, is a very difficult thing to ignite, requiring a temperature in excess of 250°C.

ignition may occur. This is followed by breakdown of the cellulose at temperatures above 320°C. Although complete combustion can be achieved at temperatures between 300 and 400°C, higher temperatures are required for the release of gases rather than liquids. The gases liberated include hydrogen, carbon monoxide and methane. It is the ignition of these gases which cause flames to appear on the surface of the wood. Even so, the emission of such gases may not be sufficient to allow sustained burning to take place.

What all this means is that wood is difficult to ignite and has to be subjected to high temperatures to really get it to burn. Because wood is a poor conductor of heat, little of the heat produced by the combustion of the flammable gases reaches the inner layer of the wood and this remain at a temperature below that required for combustion. This means that even though a timber column or beam might be on fire it is only the surface that will be burning, the charring effect of the fire will in fact protect the inside of the timber.

For optimum fire resistance, a piece of structural timber should have as small a surface area as possible. The corollary of this is that small sections of wood with a large surface area will burn very easily. This is readily verifiable of course - when trying to light a fire we use sticks which have a large surface area in relation to their volume.

In the attitude of Fire Authorities, timber, in the thicknesses used in building, is considered to be not easily ignitable.

Because timbers char at predictable rates their resistance to fire can be estimated allowing timber structures to be designed to withstand fire. For commonly used softwoods with a density above 420kg/m3, the rate of charring is assessed at 20mm in _ hour for each exposed side and at 25mm for less dense species. Timber can also be treated with flame retardants.

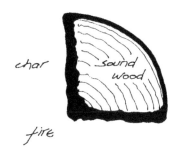

When timber does burn it chars on the surface and thereby protects itself.

The easiest way to get wood to burn is to use sections with a large surface area relative to their volume ... like the sticks one would use for kindling.

One of the oldest houses in the world is wooden, Japanese ... and was built ...1000 years ago!

Timber Decay

Apart from the fear of fire, the use of timber for housebuilding purposes also generates a fear of decay. Decay in timber is usually called rot.

"Will my house last?" is a question often asked. The answer is that there is no good reason why it should not last. The oldest surviving house in the world is a wooden Japanese structure that is 1000 years old.

Despite the wealth of answers to assuage this fear of decay, people oftentimes retain nagging doubts about the question of lasting. Oftentimes these fears are accompanied by horror stories or the worry that a timber house will involve a lot of maintenance. Further, there is often a concern about what other people will think of you if you live in a wooden house. Despite this, when asked, even people with deep reservations about timber houses will always wish to use wood for stairs, floors and certainly for the roof of their new home. Now, the roof of most houses is the flimsiest part of the construction. Despite thick masonry walls and concrete floors, the roof will be made of rafters, felt and slates. If anyone were to propose replacing such a roof with a 'lasting' material such as concrete they would be met with strong resistance!

What this means is that we are conditioned to think of houses in a particular way. Walls are solid, roofs are made of wood. Ground floors are made of concrete. We accept this conditioning without question or imagine that there has to be a good reason why things are the way they are. The reason why houses are the way they are usually has little to do with the comfort, health or safety of the owners and occupants!

"What about the climate?" is another frequent question, "Is it not too damp?"

The answer to this is: "What about your timber roof, are you not worried about your roof in this climate?"

The curious thing about this sequence of doubt, question and argument is that it has no end. When each question is answered, there is always another, no matter how skillful or truthful the reply, the examples or the logic might be. "That's all very well, but ..."

The truth is there is no point in trying to convince anyone to build a timber house rather than a bricks and mortar one. All one can do is present the facts and allow people choose.

How long should a house last?

How long should a human body last?

How long should a car last?

How long should a refrigerator last?

It is Property Values we are told that never die!

```
WOOD    RULES

NO  EXCESS  MOISTURE
NO  GROUND  CONTACT
NO  RUNNING
NO  SHAKES
NO  CHECKS
NO  BOWING
NO  NAKED  FLAMES


          BY  ORDER
```

To set up the conditions whereby timber in construction will decay, requires ... extreme carelessness.

To overcome a fear of timber the realities of the material have to be appreciated. The material has to be handled, looked at, listened to. Further, one has to seek out situations in which timber can be said to have failed and one has then to understand why that decay happened in the first place and what could have been done to prevent it. The design of a timber building must acknowledge the realities of the material, must accept its living nature, its sensuous qualities, and its response to being lovingly and sensitively handled at all stages of the building process. In other words the material becomes an integrated part of your design aims, the vehicle to help you physically create a home and to endow its spaces qualities of healthiness, sensuousness and perfume.

In terms of facts - timber does decay under certain conditions because it is devoured by fungi or insects who feed on the food stored within the wood. This erosion reduces the strength of the timber. Some timbers are more resistant to decay than others. The moisture content of the wood is a critical factor in the decay process. Timber most at risk needs to have a moisture content of between 30-40%. Like all natural processes, the decay process is a slow one. Timber, to be at risk, must remain wet for a considerable period. Timber that has been wetted and that can then dry out will remain free of decay. To set up the conditions whereby timber will decay or rot requires carelessness.

Durability

Durability is a technical term used to classify timbers according to their natural ability to resist decay. The tests used in this classification are based on 50x50mm sections of heartwood being placed directly into the ground. The usefulness of this test is limited as far as the building designer is concerned for several reasons. Firstly, timber should never be placed directly into the ground or be placed in a situation where it is exposed to a constant source of moisture. Secondly, as will inevitably be the case, cost will be a dominant factor in your design programme. This will mean that your choice of timber will largely be based on cost. This means that timber containing sapwood will have to be used. The sapwood of all timber is susceptible to decay due to the large food content within this part of the wood. This limits the usefulness of classifying heartwoods according to their natural durability. This information, however, is a reasonable guide to the nature of various timbers and is included for this reason.

The sapwood of all timber is susceptible to decay due to its stored food content.

The heartwood of some timbers can resist decay due to the presence of oils, tannin and other natural substances.

When used with care and sensitivity timber can last indefinitely.

Classification of timber according to the natural durability of heartwood.

Tests are carried out by placing a 50x50mm section of heartwood *directly into the ground*.
There are 5 degrees of classification:

Perishable: *less than 5 years*
Alder, ash, beech, birch, holly, hornbeam, horse chestnut, lime, London plane, poplar, sycamore, willow.

Non-durable: *5-10 years*
Elm, Norway Maple, pines, Red Oak, spruces, silver firs, western hemlock.

Moderately durable: *10-15 years*
Cherry, Douglas fir, larches, Lawson cypress, Turkey oak, walnut.

Durable: *15-25 years*
Sweet chestnut, oak, robinia, western red cedar, yew.

Very Durable: *more than 25 years*
Leyland cypress.

Timber does not deteriorate due to age alone and under favourable conditions it can last indefinitely. Different species vary considerably in their ability to resist attack and often there is substantial variability within a species and even within an individual tree. The darker woods are often held to be more durable than the lighter ones. This is true if the dark colour is due to the presence of natural resins or tannins that have a preservative effect making the wood more resistant to fungal attack. In some timbers, resistance to attack relates to the structure of the wood. Hardwoods are not necessarily more durable than softwoods. All sapwood is prone to decay because this is the part of the living tree that is used for food storage purposes. Fungal and insect attack relates directly to this fact.

Timber permanently and completely immersed in fresh water will not decay as there is insufficient oxygen available for decay fungi to carry out the process of breakdown. Soft rot however can occur but its rate of progress is so slow than timber over 75x75mm in size is hardly affected. Salt water can act as a timber preservative and a heavy salt deposit on the surface of wood is a protection against fungal decay. The greatest hazard to timber immersed in sea water is from marine borers.

Timber permanently immersed in fresh water will not decay.

Salt water can act as a timber preservative.

A heavy salt deposit on the surface of timber will give protection against fungal decay.

Weathering

Timber of all species, when exposed outdoors in its natural state, is subject to weather changes that alters its surface and colour. Also, warping can occur, loss of surface fibres, surface roughening and checking. Once the weathering process has been completed no further change in appearance occurs.

The fully weathered appearance of external timber depends on the degree of exposure to the sun and rain. Only the outer layer of the timber is affected. With continuous exposure, the surface of all woods turns grey due to the effects of ultra violet light. Further weathering characteristics are loss of surface fibres. This process - defilibration - is slow however, leading to a loss of 6mm of timber in 100 years! Biological attack by moulds, fungi and moss will occur where timber cladding is not allowed to dry out properly after wetting.

The intermittent wetting and drying of exposed timber can cause checks and cracks develop in the surface and can cause warping. Moderate to low density woods are less at risk and it is better to use boards that are fixed vertically rather than horizontally. For best results, the width of cladding boards should not exceed eight times their thickness. All cladding should be protected by adequate roof overhangs.

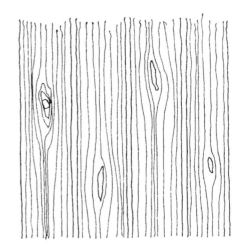

Vertical timber cladding is preferable to horizontal cladding.

Also, remember to provide generous roof overhangs ....

and ...

timber left unfinished externally will weather to a pleasant silver-grey colour.

Fungal Attack

Fungi are plants of the mushroom tribe and are the principal cause of decay in timber used in far northern and southern latitudes. This decay or rot results in the loss of strength and weight within the timber and oftentimes a change of texture and colour. Some species, by virtue of their extractives, are resistant to fungal attack. Typically only the inner, or heartwood zone contains these extractives.

The spores of fungi are widespread and timber can be infested with spores being blown onto it. These spores, or seeds, germinate on the surface of the timber pushing out hype into the wood. These are tiny thread-like tubes that pierce the cells of the timber branching out into a mat or mycelium. The hyphae secrete enzymes which break down the wood providing food for the fungus. The spores often grow into bracket-like fruit bodies which in turn produce many millions of spores.

Fungi are the main cause of decay in timber used in far northern latitudes.

35

Growing trees are also susceptible to attack by wood destroying fungi - some of which can persist after felling and conversion. These can continue to cause decay until the wood is properly seasoned. It is believed that all timber, no matter how sound it may appear, is infected in some degree with fungus. This can lie dormant in the wood until the establishment of the right conditions for it to become active.

The early stage of decay is characterised by bleached or discoloured streaks or patches in the wood, the general texture remaining more or less unchanged - this effect is also known as doaty, dosy, dozy and foxy! Ultimately they can reduce the strength of the timber significantly by digesting wood tissue. Wood is subject to fungal attack at any stage in its existence, given certain conditions.

Food: This is provided by the wood.
Oxygen: Provided by the air present.
Moisture: Provided by the moisture water present in the timber. A moisture content of 25-30% is dangerous. A moisture content of 30-40% is hazardous.
Temperature: The timber needs to be between 20-32°C. The greatest risk occurs above 27°C. Most fungi will not grow if the temperature exceeds 40°C or is at freezing point.

The absence of any one of the four conditions required for fungal attack on timber will prevent fungal decay from taking place. In normal circumstances it is difficult to control air and temperature conditions. It is therefore usual that the moisture and food conditions are controlled. This is done by ensuring a low moisture content and/or by ensuring that the food content of the wood will not be consumed. This is oftentimes achieved by treating the wood with toxic substances. The water vapour in humid air alone will not provide sufficient moisture to support decay.

Wood Destroying Fungi :
Moulds & Stains
White & Brown Rot
Soft Rot

Moulds & Stains: Moulds and Stains are caused by microscopic fungi which feed on substances within the cell cavity or attached to the cell walls of sapwood causing staining. The distinction between moulding and staining is largely made on the basis of depth. Deep-seated stains are referred to as sap or blue stain. Superficial discolouration of timber is called mould. Both moulds and stains can grow very rapidly.

Fungi like to feed on the food stored within the sapwood of timber. Even standing trees can be subject to fungal attack.

In seasoned timber 4 Conditions have to be satisfied to allow fungal attack to be successful:
1. Food must be present in the timber.
2. Air must be present.
3. There must be sufficient moisture in the timber. (MC 25-30%)
4. The temperature must be right. (+27°C)

The best protection against fungal attack is to maintain the timber at a reasonable Moisture Content.

In practical terms these fungi do not cause loss of strength in the timber they attack but can they reduce the value of timber or spoil its appearance. The sapwood of green softwood is most at risk. Sap stain or mould attack that has been retarded by seasoning can revive if the moisture content of the timber increases. A moisture content above 25% is required for active sap-stain development. Mould growth can continue down to about 20% however. To prevent moulding and staining, felled logs should be converted as soon as possible.

White & Brown Rot: The two main forms of decay in timber leading to loss of strength and eventual collapse, are distinguished by the colour of the decayed timber - white or brown, indicating attack by white or brown rot. With white rot, both the lignin and the cellulose are usually consumed in the attack, causing the wood to loose colour and to appear whiter than normal. With brown rot, the cellulose only is removed and the wood takes on a browner colour, tending to crack across the grain and to collapse. These fungi differ from mould and stain fungi in that they obtain their nutrition by digesting the structural components of the wood tissue.

Timber rots are sometimes referred to in terms of wet and dry rot. This can cause some confusion as it lends to the belief that some rots do not require moisture to attack the timber. This is not true - all rots require a high level of moisture to carry out their destruction. Dry Rot is no different. However if dry rot becomes established and the source of the moisture is withdrawn, the fungus can produce its own water and continue to survive. This can often be the case where a leaky gutter or a damp wall has wetted timber allowing the fungus to establish itself. When the source of the moisture is withdrawn, by repairs being carried out for example, the fungus can continue living.

White and brown rots have exotic Latin names. Here are some common ones:
Coniophora Cerabella
Called Cellar rot, this is the commonest fungus causing timber decay in buildings. Its presence is usually associated with water leaks, etc. Such an outbreak will not spread to other, drier, parts of the building. Sheet/plate like fruit bodies may vary from olive green to yellow to brown with a cream white margin. Thin brown-black strands sometimes occur on the surface of the decayed wood. Produces darkened shrinkage cracks running mainly along the grain, though often the surface skin of the wood remains sound. Spores are produced in small pimples. Wood becomes dark brown, sometimes with yellow streaks.

All Rots require that the timber they attack have a very high Moisture Content to carry out their destruction.

Dry Rot is no exception.

With White Rot the lignin and cellulose in the timber is consumed.

With Brown Rot, the cellulose in the timber is consumed.

Timber will oftentimes provoke a fearful response in the wary ... this is a reflection of our own mortality

Fibroparia vaillantii / Poria vaillantii:

Mycelium makes white or cream coloured skin on surface of wood. Forms thin strands up to 3mm in diameter that are flexible when dry. The fruit bodies are soft white plates with pores 2 to 13mm long. Requires high moisture content to become established and is associated with water leaks, etc. from which it will not spread to other parts of the building. Wood becomes brown and splits into cubes when dry.

Paxillus panuoides:

Mycelium on surface are hairy or woolly and dull yellow, sometimes with violet tinges. Strands are dull yellow in colour. Fruit bodies are fleshy and fan or shell shaped with gills underneath. Requires high moisture content to cause decay. Wood is initially yellow turning later to dark brown or reddish brown.

Amyloporia Xantha / Poria xantha:

Generally no mycelium appear on wood surface though some may be seen in cracks. Strands are thin, white and often chalky in appearance. Fruit bodies form yellow pore layer with small tubes up to 3mm long. Commonly associated with decay in greenhouses. Causes brown cubical rot.

Lentinus lepideus:

Mycelium sometimes appear on surface and are white with brown or purple tinges. These are usually present in shrinkage cracks. No strands are formed. Fruit bodies are brown, mushroom type with a tough woody consistency and gills on undersurface. Cylindrical forms often found with branching growths. Commonly associated with decay of timber that has been inadequately treated with creosote, especially in ground contact. Causes a brown cubical rot, often with a characteristic aromatic odour.

Love that wood!
EconoSpace under construction

Corolius versicolor /Polystictus versicolor:

Causes initial white flecking with the wood being very much bleached eventually. No shrinkage cracks and original volume of wood is retained. Occasionally white mycelium sheets formed on surface. No strands formed. Fruit brackets are up to 80mm across, grey and brown on top. Its hairy surface may be zoned concentrically with a creamy pore surface underneath. Commonest cause of white rot in hardwoods, especially in ground contact.

Merulius Lacrymans / Also Serpula Lacrymans:

This is the well known Dry Rot. These fungi have the ability to produce their own moisture once they have become established. The subsequent drying out of the timber will not destroy these organisms. Mycellum develop into thick greyish cords that may be over 6mm in diameter. When dry they become brittle. May spread away from timber through brickwork and plaster. The strands throw off hyphae whenever they meet timber and carry the water supply for digestion of the timber, which becomes friable, powdery and dull brown in colour, accompanied by a distinctive mushroom-like smell.

Fleshy fruit bodies form either a flat plate or a bracket. The spores are rust coloured. They can be carried by wind, animals or insects and throw out minute hollow white silky threads (hyphae). Produces charred /corrugated effect. Occurs in damp places. Wood becomes brown and splits into cubes.

Soft Rot: Soft rot is caused by fungi related to the moulds rather than those responsible for the brown and white rots. These can grow within the walls of wood tissue and usually manifest themselves by an initial softening of the surface layers of the wood. Digests cellulose cells. Most likely to be troublesome in situations too wet to permit brown or white rots - fence posts in water-logged soils, in boats and other wet environments. Marine fungi are of the soft rot type.

Reading about fungal attack is no fun! This is because what is being witnessed is death and destruction, a subtle reminder to us of the nature of the natural decay process itself, practical recycling in action. That fungi might be a low form of life and are doing their best to survive is no comfort. Being intelligent beings however, we can easily outsmart the fungi and deny them the use of our timber for food and shelter. Simply keeping our wood dry will always do the trick.

Timber decay is ...
Natural Recycling in action.

To retard this process
.... keep timber dry!

A timber frame is a skeleton which is fleshed with walls, floor and roof

Insects

Apart from fungi, the other hazards to timber that can cause decay are insects. These fall into two categories - insects which attack the wood of living trees and fresh felled roundwood, and those which attack converted timber. In northern latitudes, insect attack on standing or freshly felled trees is not significant. Wood wasp larvae can sometimes cause slight damage by boring into trees. Forest longhorn beetles lay their eggs in round timber that is already subject to fungal decay. Bark beetles can attack felled trees from which bark has not been removed. These insects do not attack seasoned timber.

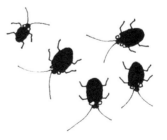

Apart from fungi, certain insects can
attack timber causing it to decay.

Insects that attack seasoned timber rarely do so until the timber is 7-8 years old. These cause damage by laying eggs allowing larvae to bore into the wood. Some woods are more prone to attack than others, sapwood more than heartwood. Some insects will not attack wood unless it has been already infected with a fungus. The most common attacks come from:

Ernobis mollis:

These beetles are 3-6mm long, red or chestnut brown, covered in silky hairs. Eggs are laid in the bark of softwoods. The larvae are covered in fine golden hairs and are up to 6mm long when fully grown. They have a life cycle of 1 year. Their borings are confined to the bark and outermost zones of sapwood. Brown and white grit containing spherical pellets emerges from their 2.5mm diameter exit holes. Attack is confined to wood with wany edges with bark still remaining on them and will die out if bark is removed.

Wood Wasps - Siricidae:

Pests of sickly standing trees or freshly felled softwood logs. The eggs are laid through the bark and into the wood. The larvae that hatch from them tunnel into both the sapwood and heartwood, eventually emerging through circular holes.

Ambrosia beetles - families Scolytidae & Platipodidae:

These are small beetles called pin hole borers or ambrosia beetles, mainly confined to temperate or tropical regions. There are over 1000 species and they attack both softwoods and hardwoods usually freshly felled wood, though they are occasionally found in standing trees. The eggs are laid under the bark and develop into larvae that bore holes of up to 2mm in diameter. The surface of these become covered in fungal growth which is the primary food for the larvae. A high moisture is needed to allow an attack. Infestation dies out when timber is dried.

Furniture Beetle / Woodworm (Anobium Punctatum):

This is the commonest insect to attack wood in northern latitudes. Unlike most other wood-boring insects, which attack in the wake of fungal decay, woodworm is able to invade the sapwood and heartwood of sound, dry wood. This beetle is about 3-5mm long and dark brown in colour. It alights on timber between May and August, laying small white eggs in minute cracks and crevices on the surface of the wood, particularly unprotected end grain and old exit holes. The eggs develop into larvae/worms that are comma-shaped and about 4-5mm long. These penetrate into the wood by knawing 2mm bore holes. The worms grow to about 8mm long and continuously bore through the wood for one to three years

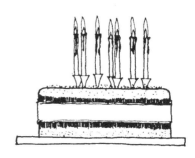

Timber needs to be 7-8 years old before insects might attack it to raid its stored food content.

The insects that cause woodworm attack between May and August, laying their eggs on the surface of the timber.

The insect eggs grow into worms which then bore through the wood.

When these worms emerge from the timber they leave a tell-tale exit hole ....

40

They finish near the surface of the wood, emerging in June or July, pupate and from this a beetle develops to repeat the cycle.

Woodworm attack can be identified only after the worms emerge, leaving their tell-tale holes. Gritty dust emerges from these when the timber is struck. Small pellets will also emerge. Woodworm attacks softwoods and hardwoods, preferring old timber. Both furniture and structural timber can be attacked. Plywood made from birch or alder and bonded with animal glues are particularly susceptible.

Powder Post Beetle - (Lyctus):

There are several varieties of this beetle that are classified under the name, lyctidae. They are the most serious pests of wood and wood-based products, particularly plywood. Attacking only hardwoods, susceptibility depends on two main factors - the pores of the timber must be large enough in diameter to allow for egg to be laid and the timber must have a high starch content because this is what the worms feed on. Softwoods not attacked.

The beetles are usually about 3-5mm long and red, brown or black in colour. They have short antennae. The larvae are small, with one brown oval spot on each side of the 8th segment. They are up to 6mm long when fully grown, emerging chiefly between June and August leaving an exit hole 1.5mm in diameter. They have a life cycle of 1 year. A fine flour-like dust is produced from the holes. The sapwoods of oak, ash, hickory and elm are particularly at risk, especially during the seasoning process. Neither softwoods nor diffuse porous hardwoods are at risk, because the beetles requires pores of up to 1mm in diameter in which to lay their eggs.

Sheltermaking is a communal activity

Bostrychidae (Also referred to as Powder Post Beetles):

These beetles are from 6-25mm long with short antennae. The eggs are laid in specially bored tunnels by the adult beetle. The larvae are over 6mm long. These make tunnels filled with a flour-like dust. Sapwood of partially or recently dried timber can be attacked, mainly tropical timber, especially hardwoods.

Powder post beetles of the family Anobiidae infest hardwoods and softwoods. A beetle of this family known as the 'old house borer' causes damage to seasoned pine floors and joists.

Death Watch Beetle (Xestobium Rufovillosum):

This beetle is a less widespread pest than furniture beetle or powder post beetle. It causes extensive damage in ancient structural hardwoods and is usually confined to old buildings. Attack usually follows in the wake of decay, particularly that caused by roof leakages - once larvae are established in pockets of rotten wood, they are able to spread to adjacent sound timber. Most UK infestations have been in oak, but other hardwoods and softwoods may be attacked.

The beetles are 6-8mm long, chocolate brown, mottled with patches of short yellowish hairs on thorax and wing cases. These attack timber between March and June laying eggs in cracks and crevices of decayed wood and also in old exit holes. The larvae are up to 8mm long and hairy in appearance. They can live for up to a decade in the infected wood making 3mm diameter bore holes. The bore holes are filled with grit that will contain small bun-shaped pellets. Circular exit holes are made, about 3mm in diameter. Attack is almost entirely confined to hardwoods especially oak but the wood must be partially decayed by a fungus before an attack can take place.

The beetle makes a ticking sound during the mating period - May or June - by tapping its head on the side of the hole. It will not attack dry timber that is free from rot.

Polish grain store

House Longhorn Beetle - Hylotrupes bajulus (Cerambycidae):

Also known as the Camberly beetle. These beetles are 10-20mm long, grey, black or brown in colour. Eggs are laid between July and September. These are 2mm long and spindle shaped laid in splits and cracks on softwood sapwood. The larvae are greyish white and their segmented bodies taper towards the tail. They can reach 30mm long when fully grown. Their borings are large and packed with dust containing cylindrical pellets. The exit holes are 6-9mm diameter.

The sapwood of softwoods attacked, chiefly roof timbers. Life cycle may vary from 3-11 years. At present it is confined to parts of Surrey, Berkshire and Hampshire, though it is a common destructive pest in Continental Europe and in tropical and temperate regions.

Termites:

Termites are essentially a problem of tropical and sub-tropical regions but are also found in some temperate countries - France, Korea and Germany. Their distribution is limited by low temperatures and/or altitude.

There are two main types that attack timber in service - dry-wood termites and subterranean termites. There are 1800 species known and of these 10% have been recorded as doing damage to buildings. 53 species are serious pests. Of these 10 are dry-wood types.

Drywood termites live entirely inside the timber on which they are feeding, often hollowing large timbers but leaving a thin shell for protection. Attack may be well advanced before being recognised. Termites need very little moisture to survive.

Subterranean termites live in nests in mounds or cavities in the ground. They posess a different form of colony organisation from the dry-wood termites. The nest may be up to hundreds of meters from the attack but movement is always within protective tunnels or runways constructed by the foraging workers from earth and chewed wood. They can get into a building through wood that is in contact with the ground, through crevices in the foundations and through clay tunnels that they build over the surface of masonry etc. They require moisture to survive.

A common protection against subterranean termite invasion is the insertion of a sheet of copper into the bottom of walls. This projects 100mm and is angled at 45deg to prevent their passage.

Very few woods have a natural resistant to termite attack. Close grained heartwood of California redwood has some resistance. Very resinous heartwood of southern pine is practically immune from attack.

Component of traditional Latvian log house

Timberfear

Timberfear is a fear of using timber as a building material. This is a frequent phenomenon affecting many people. It is important to understand the nature of this fear in order to evaluate the limitations and restrictions that it can impose on you as a house designer.

While it is accepted that many people choose to create their homes from concrete and other solid materials, where this choice is made on the basis of avoiding the wholehearted use of timber, it could be said that *timberfear* is a controlling factor in the design process.

Timberfear is best characterised in this way - a reluctance to make and live in a timber home based on an irrational fear of the material.

Timberfear is an irrational fear of using timber as a building material.

It is a deep unconscious recognition of our own mortality.

Perhaps the best example of the irrational nature of *timberfear* is in the general attitude to roof construction. The accepted norm is that roofs are made of timber. Now, a wall made from timber is merely a roof standing upright. A refusal to accept a timber wall while advocating a timber roof typifies *timberfear*.

Timberfear can easily make the difference between creating a warm, sensuous, healthy home and creating a cold, hard and possibly damp one. On another level, it can deny you the possibility of creating a low-cost, self-build home, free of huge mortgage liabilities.

Fear of decay is the cornerstone of *timberfear*, impelling people towards the use of concrete, plastic and metal, materials which are supposedly immune to decay. On a deep level, *timberfear* is a recognition of our own mortality, the fact that the very substance of our bodies will decay at some point in the future and be no more. We unconsciously express this by making houses that will 'last' indefinitely, outliving us and remaining as a permanent testimony of our existence. The pyramids of Egypt are the ultimate expression of this, massive stone constructions that are in fact the permanent homes of their dead occupants.

Another argument cited against timber is the resale value of timber houses. While there is no particular evidence to support this fear, it is nonetheless an often cited argument. In truth a beautiful home, no matter how made, will always command a good market. Apart from this, the preoccupation with future value cannot be ignored - why is it that the future value of our homes is so critical? We all know that a car will continue to lose value from the moment it leaves the showroom. The notion of a car that will last our lifetimes and our children's lifetime is a crazy one. Yet we demand this kind of return from our homes.

In times when people created their homes out of income and from the resources they had available to them, the notion of future value was never considered as an important design consideration. This modern preoccupation is in fact a product of the way we pay for our houses - by borrowing large sums of money and paying for them over long periods of time. This forges an almost unbreakable link between continuous secure employment and the home. Further, it fosters the notion of future value as being of critical importance because the borrowed monies grow magically into quite enormous amounts. Naturally, the future value of the home has to compare with these inflated figures otherwise the borrower would feel cheated.

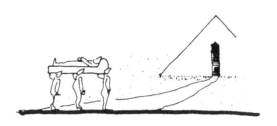

The Pyramids of Egypt are the ultimate in permanent, long-lasting homes.

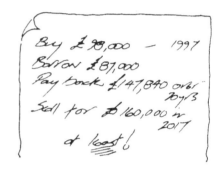

Buy £98,000 – 1997
Borrow £87,000
Pay back £147,840 over 70yrs
Sell for £160,000 in 2017
at least!

When building out of income, future value never seems to be of particular importance ..... in contrast to mortgaging ... where future value is all important.

The link between Work and Home Ownership, as it presently exists, is a reflection of Industrialised Society and Patriarchy ....
This creates very male oriented houses, lacking in sensitivity ... the opposite of what a home really is all about.

44

This link between employment and home has other critical aspects. If one's job disappears, the ownership of the home, and consequently survival, comes immediately under threat. This flaw in the system has only been too well revealed by recent world economic events. If one imagines building out of income, or on the basis of small borrowings, it is possible to circumvent these anomalies and to remain free of the crushing burden that the mortgage system brings to bear on peoples lives. It further allows the preoccupation with future value to be lessened.

The link between work and home is very much an aspect of industrial society and also of patriarchy. That is, the way our homes are created and paid for is very much a male invention. This unfortunately is very much in contrast to how homes are lived in and used. It is generally women and children who spend the most time there while the man goes out to work. This forces women and children to exist within what are very much male inspired surroundings - surroundings created on the basis of a mental rather than a sensual approach to design. To describe this as a form of enslavement is perhaps too strong a statement but nonetheless, it is a notion that many would agree with. Even men are described as being 'wage slaves', toiling to make their mortgage repayments. That such considerations should be aspects of *timberfear* might seem surprising. Yet, on reflection, it is the very essence of *timberfear* - the desire for an endless unchanging present.

If our homes cannot liberate us, allowing for relaxed and contented lives to be lived within them and allowing for freedom of choice as to how one spends one's time, then something is very much wrong.

If the home cannot accommodate some work activities or entertain the possibility of a home based business being operated from it, then the design is flawed and will only reinforce the notion that the only way to own a home is to have a secure job.

It might be said that there is only one justification for *timberfear* and that is the danger that timber preservatives can pose to the health of the home occupants.

Homes should be liberating, relaxing, contenting and fulfiling places .... otherwise, something is wrong!

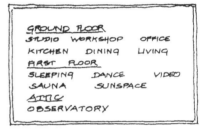

GROUND FLOOR
STUDIO   WORKSHOP   OFFICE
KITCHEN   DINING   LIVING
FIRST FLOOR
SLEEPING DANCE   VIDEO
SAUNA   SUNSPACE
ATTIC
OBSERVATORY

Every home should be able to fully accommodate within itself any work and/or leisure activity that you might wish to undertake.

Traditional Latvian log house, Co. Mayo, Ireland

Timber Preservation

One of the characteristics of timber constantly being alluded to by many people is the materials' supposed vulnerability to decay. While it can be seen that proper design and construction practices diminish this risk, the more common approach to this topic is the preservation of timber.

Preservation is based on the theory that if the food supply in timber, on which fungi and insects feed, is protected, then these organisms will not be able to attack the timber for the purpose of obtaining food and shelter. This protection generally takes the form of poisoning the timber. Such a drastic measure can pose a serious danger to the occupants of a home as the toxins used are harmful to all forms of life, not merely to fungi and insects.

Timber has always been treated - 'preserved' - by employing natural methods such as charring to ensure it's lasting quality. However, the modern approach to preservation is a theoretical and sometimes dangerous one. Oftentimes, the way preserved timbers are used assumes that they have been rendered immune from decay and that they can then be employed in much the same way as steel, concrete or plastic, supposed decay-proof materials. This is of course not the case and preserved timbers have been known to fail because they were carelessly used. Preservation treatment is never a substitute for good design.

Because all commercial preservatives are applied in liquid form, the way in which the timber can be made to absorb them is critical to their effectiveness. When some softwoods have been seasoned, the pits in the cell walls close up, making it very difficult for the preservative to penetrate deeply into the timber. Because hardwoods are made up of open-ended pores, their treatment with liquid preservatives is much easier.

Effective preservation treatment depends upon several factors:

1. *The preservative used.*
2. *The method of its application.*
3. *The amount of preservative absorbed.*
4. *The depth of penetration.*
5. *The hazards to which the timber is exposed in service.*
6. *The species of the timber.*

*Timber is normally preserved by rendering it toxic to fungi and insects. Extreme care needs to be taken with this approach ... because conventional preservatives threaten all life forms. There is **no** substitute for good detailing and design when using timber in construction.*

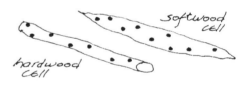

When softwood is seasoned, the pits within the cell walls close up, making it difficult to impregnate the timber with liquid preservatives .... hardwoods, on the other hand, because they contain open-ended cells, can be treated more easily and effectively by impregnation treatments.

Ideally, an effective preservative should be repellent to fungi and insects, safe for persons handling the timber, odourless, non-irritant, permanent, able to penetrate the timber deeply, cheap, readily available, non-corrosive to metal fastenings, non-flammable and it should allow the timber to receive a finishing coat.

Four hazard categories are normally used to assess the need for preservation treatment:

A - Preservation Unnecessary:
Situations of negligible risk.
Situations where the use of preservatives have unacceptable consequences.
Situations where cost is important.

B - Preservation Optional:
Situations of low decay risk.
Situations where remedial action/repairs are simple.

C - Preservation Desirable:
Situations of unacceptable decay risk.
Situations where remedial action/repairs are impossible.

D - Preservation Essential:
Timber exposed to a continually hazardous environment which cannot be protected by design.

Preservation Treatments

There are various methods of applying timber preservatives.

Brushing/Spraying:

This type of treatment is the easiest to achieve but the level of protection is quite limited as the penetration of preservative into the timber is normally shallow. Unplaned timber, however, will absorb more than planed sections. Organic solvent type preservatives are commonly applied this way, as are borate solutions and creosote.

The preservative should be liberally applied so that as much as possible is absorbed, particularly into end grain, joints and cracks. A second application several days after the first may also be needed - or as soon as the first coat is surface dry to allow the preservative liquid to keep moving into the timber. For lasting protection on exposed timber, the application must be

《 No such substance exists!

Air is the best preservative of all.

Good ventilation will always maintain timber at an agreeably low Moisture Content, protecting it against decay.

Timber should never be installed so that it is directly touching the earth ... or any other constant source of moisture.

All preserved timber should be handled with extreme care ... or not at all.

47

repeated at regular intervals. This is best done in the summer when the wood is dry and more absorbent.

Organic solvent type solutions can be applied satisfactorily at normal temperatures. Creosote can be heated to obtain better penetration and a cleaner treatment.

Deluging:
In this process timber is fed through a tunnel on a conveyor system as a preservative is sprayed or flooded over it. Mostly used for tar oils, though water based and organic solvent type treatments can also be used. The timber is in contact with the preservative for only a few seconds and the treatment equates with a short 10 second dip in a tank or a liberal brush/spray application. This process is often used for the rapid and uniform treatment of freshly felled and freshly sawn timber to prevent sapstain and mould growth.

Dipping/Soaking/Immersion:
This involves timber being submerged in a tank of preservative for a period of time. This can range from a few seconds or minutes to several hours or days - referred to as dipping, soaking and steeping. Effective against insect attack, less successful against fungi.

The degree of treatment will depend on the preservative used, the species of timber, and the length of the treatment. In pine sapwood, for example, penetration is much deeper than in less permeable woods such as spruce or hemlock, where it may be only a millimetre or two, even with long periods of immersion. In pine sapwood the degree of treatment achieved in three minutes is double that achieved after 10 seconds. To double this again requires over 30 minutes of soaking. A 3 minute immersion is suitable for the protection of redwood external joinery that is to be painted in service. A 1 hour immersion is acceptable for pine cladding. Internal structural timbers can also be treated in this way.

Organic solvent type preservatives are normally used for this treatment, though long periods of soaking - over 1 hour - are rare. However, long steeping periods are sometimes used with creosote.

Diffusion:
Diffusion is a treatment for freshly felled wood that utilises the fact that moisture can move freely within the green timber. The process involves immersing freshly felled green wood or the converted timber in a solution of sodium borate for up to two months. When it is removed it is close-stacked under an impervious sheet for several weeks. During this time the soluble active ingredient

Timber preservation is a mental solution to a natural problem ..

The natural solution to the problem of timber decay is to apply sense to the matter ....

Sense says that timber is beautiful, natural, renewable, smells and looks good, feels good, tastes okay, sounds great, is warm, cosy and strong ... and that, like all earthly life, it will have an end ....

But, in the meantime, with caring, sensitivity and love, it will provide shelter and warmth and comfort for a long as your life needs it.

Sensitive sheltermaking allows us to overcome the fears which demand the use of timber preservatives

48

diffuses through the sap and the timber is deeply penetrated by the preservative. The timber is then dried. Thorough impregnation can be achieved even in timbers difficult to treat by any other method giving good protection against fungi and insects.

Timber treated with boron is suitable for general building work where protection is required against decay or insects, however it should be painted in exposed places to prevent the boron being leached from the surface by rain.

Hot and Cold/Open Tank:

This process is normally used with creosote. The seasoned timber is immersed in tank or drum of hot creosote for several hours. This causes the air in the cell cavities to expand and escape from the tank. The tank is then allowed to cool overnight and the contracting air pulls creosote into the timber. Practically the whole of the absorption occurs during the cooling period which may last many hours. The next day the tank is reheated and the expanding air expels the excess creosote.

Well-seasoned sawn timber of small dimension should be soaked for 2/3 hours and then cooled for 4/5 hours. Larger timbers require longer time.

Double Vacuum Pressure Treatment:

Also known as Vac-Vac. This process has been around for the past 20 years and is widely used. It is carried out by placing the timber in a treatment chamber and drawing a partial vacuum on this. The vacuum is maintained for a short period before flooding the chamber with an Organic Solvent Preservative such as pentachlorphenol. The vacuum is then released and the timber is allowed to remain in the solution for an hour under atmospheric pressure or possibly under forced pressure. After the chamber is emptied of preservative, a second vacuum is drawn, designed to recover some of the solution and produce a dry surface.

Treated timber is ready for gluing in a couple of days but permeable timber may take longer. Timber can be primed and painted. Originally developed for the treatment of redwood external joinery required to be painted in service, the treatment is now widely used for the treatment of timber in building and construction work.

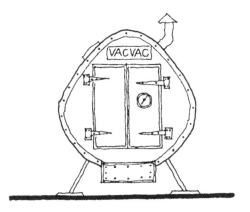

Double Vacuum Pressure Treatment, or Vac Vac as it is called, is the commonest form of preservation used. Watch out for greenish coloured timber!

Air dried, unpreserved timber sheltered and housed the species before any of these preservative chemicals were even thought about.

Timber Preservatives

Timber preservatives are often referred to as 'biocides', meaning they act both as fungicides as well as insecticides. All commercial products are compromises, some working more effectively on insect attack than on fungal attack and vice versa.

Oil based preservatives:

Widely used for 150 years and formerly a by-product from the production of town gas. Now produced from natural gas or crude oil and as a by-product of the manufacture of smokeless fuels and coke. These preservatives are a mixture of many organic compounds that are readily toxic to organisms. Some fungi however are resistant.

Characteristics: Relatively insoluble in water and resistant to being dissolved away, making them particularly suitable for external work. They also provide a degree of water repellency that helps control dimensional movement. They have an unpleasant characteristic odour and can stain adjacent materials. Non-corrosive to metals but they attack plastics. Treated timber presents no special fire hazard after several months of drying but it cannot be painted over. Treated timber is unsuitable for internal use.

Products: Coal tar creosote
Coal tar oil

Application: By pressure treatment, immersion or brushing.

Unleachable metallic salts:

These preservatives are organic solvent based which means they contain volatile compounds that evaporate after application. These can be harmful. Only use in well ventilated conditions. These vapours are also flammable and care should be taken when handling them. A fire risk is also attached to freshly treated timber. Evaporation can continue after the initial 'drying' period.

Characteristics: Mostly resistant to leaching but experience some loss due to evaporation. Suitable for interior/exterior use. Not generally corrosive to metals. Non-staining. Treated timber is clean in appearance and can be painted and glued. Treatment does not cause swelling and can be safely applied to machined wood. Water repellent additives can be included to retard moisture change in service.

Sheltermaking is about setting yourself free - not supporting toxic industries

Products: Copper naphthenate
Zinc Naphthenate
Pentachlorophenol (PCP)
Synthetic creosote
Tributyltin Oxide
Chlorinated naphtalene
Tributyl tin oxide (TBTO)

Copper and zinc napthenates applied in organic solvent solutions are effective preservatives due to their metallic content. Primarily fungicidal in nature, their effectiveness against insect attack is high after application but is lost after some time. Pentachlorophenol (PCP) is primarily a fungicide with only limited activity against insect attack. Combined PCP-zinc napthenate formulations are also sometimes used. Tributyl tin oxide (TBTO) is one of range of trialkid tin compounds claimed to be effective preservatives. Proprietary formulations often contain a contact insecticide such as gamma-Hexachlorocyclohexane (HCH), gamma-BHC, lindane or dieldrin.

Application: By pressure treatment, immersion, deluging, brush or spray.

Water soluble preservatives - inorganic salts dissolved in water:

Waterborne preservatives suffer the disadvantage that the zone of wood penetrated by the preservative solution swells and has to be redried before use. There are two types of this preservative - in one type the preservative chemicals remain soluble in water and can be leached from the timber if exposed to rain. In the second type, the mixtures of inorganic salts in the water solution react with the timber over a period of several days after application and form precipitates which are virtually insoluble in water and permanently incorporated into the wood.

Simple low-impact shelters do not have to cost the earth

Characteristics: Timber treated with water borne preservatives salts should be left for a period of 14 days before metalwork is introduced. If this is not possible fasteners of non-ferrous metal except aluminium should be used. Solutions containing copper sometimes give softwoods a greenish tinge. Treated timber can be painted and glued. Non-staining and non-flammable. Timber must be redried after treatment. Most effective against insects, particularly longhorn beetle and termites.

Products: Copper-chrome-arsenic (CCA)
Copper/chrome (CC)
Flouro/chrome/arsenate dinitrophenol
Copper-chromium-boron (CCB)
Zinc chloride
Sodium fluoride;
Magnesium silicoflouride
Mercuric chloride
Copper sulphate
Alkyl ammonium compounds (AAC)
PCP in water borne carrier
Sodium Pentachlorophenoxide (NaPCP)

Sensitive sheltermaking has the potential to reveal the mysteries of life ... no toxins allowed!

CCAs are the most common types of waterborne preservatives though their use is becoming restricted. CCA and CC undergo chemical changes within the wood and become resistant to leaching. They are suitable for interior and exterior use. Copper is toxic to fungi, and arsenic is toxic to insects as well as certain brown rot fungi that are tolerant to copper. Copper-chromium-boron (CCB) has a slower rate of fixation than CCA.

Alkyl ammonium compounds (AAC), are effective against fungi and insects but not against Lyctids. Pentachlorophenol (PCP) in a water solution has been found to be effective in the USA. Sodium Pentachlorophenoxide (NaPCP) is a sodium salt of PCP. It is used extensively as the standard chemical for prevention of sap stain, often in conjunction with borate solutions. Borates posess both fungicidal and insecticidal properties. They are used alone as well as in multi salt formulations.

Application: By pressure treatment.

Borax Solutions:
Borax is a natural mineral from obtained from salt lakes.

Products: Boric Salt
Boric Acid

Borax is a natural, safe and easily obtainable timber preservative.

Characteristics: Boric Acid is a mild, mineral acid derived from borax and sulphuric acid - sodium octoborate. It is an effective, non-volatile medium for wood preservation and is no more toxic than cooking salt. Applied as a strong solution, it has good fungicidal, insecticidal and fire retardant properties. It is colourless, odourless and non-poisonous to mammals, though it leaches out of wood exposed to rain. It is often fortified with a mouldicide such as sodium pentachlorophenoxide.

Application: By diffusion treatment and brushing.

Beechwood pitch:

Beechwood pitch is an extract of beech wood. The preservative itself contains pitch, alcohol, pinewood terpene alcohol, lecitin, pinewood resin, linseed oil and liquid ammonia. Generally, for deep penetration, it is necessary for timber to be dried to its likely service level before being treated.

Timber Based Products

Aside from its use as a sawn material for straightforward building applications, timber is also used for the production of sheet materials such as plywood, medium density fibreboard (MDF), insulating board, hardboard and other building boards. Paper, of course, is the most familiar wood based material. Laminated timber, woodwool slabs and cellulose fibre insulation also are widely used for building purposes.

Building Boards

The use of wood to create building boards has many advantages. It offers an economical use of timber and of forest and sawmill residues, produces materials with less variability than sawn timber, offers greater widths of boards, standard sizes and products that are less prone to movement. On the negative side, some board materials contain binders and/or glues such as formaldehyde that pose a potential health hazard. In addition, the manufacturing process can oftentimes destroy some of the natural appeal of the wood itself. Chipboard would be a good example of this. Overall however, timber board materials offer the designer a wide range of products allowing for a variety of end uses, from flooring to walling to general sheeting and structural applications.

The range of board materials available is quite extensive - plywood, blockboard, laminboard, chipboard, fibreboard, hardboard and medium density fibreboard. Generally these are all produced in a standard 8'x 4' sheet size. (2440x1220mm)

Plywood:

Plywood sheets consist of a number of layers of wood veneer glued together. Wood veneers are thin layers of wood produced from whole logs that are pared lengthways by machine. The thickness and number of the layers vary according to the type of plywood being

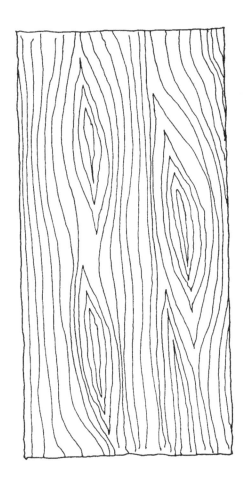

Many building boards are produced in 8 foot X 4 foot sheets ... which is ...
1220 X 2440mm
1200 X 2400mm sheets are also available.

53

produced. The alternate layers of veneer are laid with the grain at right angles to each other. This gives the plywood good strength and dimensional stability. A product such as phenol-formaldehyde resin is used to bond the veneers which usually number three or more. Sheets vary in thickness from several millimetres to several inches.

A variety of woods are used in the production of plywood - birch, Douglas Fir, pine and larch for example. Plywood is also available with a surface veneer of a quality hardwood timber such as oak or mahogany, giving the sheets a high level of finish.

Edge of plywood sheet.

Various grades of plywood are produced from shuttering to marine to decorative 'ply'. WBP plywood is guaranteed 'water and boil proof' allowing it to be safely used under sever conditions of exposure. 'Exterior' grade is suitable for use out of doors. Generally grade depends on the quality of the veneers used, particularly those of the exposed faces, as well as on the adhesive. British Standard 6566 governs the 'WBP' quality of most plywoods used for construction, while BS 5268 Part 2 governs structural qualities. These Standards recognise that the quality and grading of plywood is controlled in their country of origin and these products are so marked:

USA: APA PS 1-83
Canada: CSA 0151 (for Softwood ply)
        CSA 0121 (for Douglas Fir ply)
Sweden: SBN 1775:5

The bulk of softwood ply comes from North America, Scandinavia and Russia, while hardwood ply come from Brazil and Malaysia.

Beware of all manufactured board products!

The uses to which plywood can be put in house construction are many and varied. For structural use, plywood is an excellent sheathing material for timber framed walls and roofs. It also makes excellent flooring and panelling and can be used to construct strong beams and columns. It uses for furniture and cabinet making are also numerous. In fact, plywood is indispensable in the making of any home. Lower quality plywood, such as 'shuttering plywood' offer excellent value for the low-cost designer/builder.

Blockboard and Laminboard:
Blockboard is made up of strips of wood less than 30mm wide, laid side by side and glued together to form a thin slab. These are then veneered on both faces. The veneer is laid at right angles to the grain of the core and is normally of good finished quality. With laminboard, the core consists of strips of veneer on edge glued together with a

Traditional wattle+daub, or, lathe+plaster are ideal substitutes for timber board materials

good quality veneer on both faces. Used mainly for built-in work, both these sheet materials are of somewhat heavier quality than straightforward plywood. Useful for desktops, seats, doors and other similar applications.

Chipboard:
First developed in Germany during the last war, chipboard is composed of resin coated wood chips which are then pressed into sheets, from 3-50mm thick. Used for flooring and as the basic material of many fitted kitchens, chipboards are produced in 4 grades - Standard/Flooring/Moisture Resistant and Moisture Resistant Flooring. Moisture Resistant Flooring will not however withstand prolonged wetting. BS 5669:1979 is the governing standard.

Chipboard is available with a plain finish or with wood and paper veneers. Boards with melamine and plastic laminates are also made. Difficult to screw into and liable to disintegrate, chipboard is the least appealing of the board materials. It is also considered that the formaldehyde content of the resins used in its manufacture can pose a health hazard.

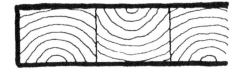

Beware of all manufactured board products!

Fibreboards:
The term 'fibreboard' applies to all board materials made up from wood fibres bonded together. These include hardboard and medium density fibreboards. The governing standard is BS 1142. However, the term is more frequently used to describe low-density boards or insulating boards of less than 240 kg/m3. These range in thickness from 10-25mm. Brittle and soft, but with excellent heat and sound insulation properties, these boards are useful as linings in floors and behind wall panelling.

Standard Hardboard:
Boards with a density of not less than 800 kg/m3, are described as standard hardboard. They range in thickness from 2-6.4mm. Useful for sheeting, for use in built-in units, for lightweight partitions, bulkheads and for furniture. Melamine covered boards are also available.

Tempered Hardboard:
These are boards with densities exceeding 960kg/m3, and containing moisture resistant oils. These have superior strength properties and good moisture resistance. Thicknesses range from 3.2-12.7mm. Used for structural purposes, for built-in units, for sheeting and even for external use.

Edge of blockboard sheet.

Traditional woven hazel wall and ceiling panels with clay plaster ... ideal materials for the cost-conscious self-builder

Medium Density Fibreboard (MDF):

This is an excellent material with many applications particularly for built-in work. Suitable for desktops, seating, tables and so on, MDF has an excellent smooth finish and can be machined to produce a decorative finish. Exterior grade boards are also produced. Governed by BS 6100, boards range from 6-50mm in thickness. Boards for use externally are also made and MDF doors are produced for internal as well as external applications.

Oriented Strand Board (OSB):

OSB is made by coating thin strands/flakes of wood - mainly Scots pine - with phenolic resin and wax. Alternate layers are laid at right angles to each other to yield strength properties comparable to plywood. A big brother of chipboard, OSB is used for wall sheathing, roofing and flooring. Available from 9-18mm thick. Difficult to finish pleasantly.

Woodwool Slabs:

These consist of strands of timber, shredded from short roundwood billets. These are mixed with wet cement to form slabs 50-60mm thick, sometimes with metal edgings to give them tensile strength. Mainly used for roofing, woodwool slabs have quite good insulating properties. Occasionally used for walling also.

Laminated Timber:

Small sections of timber are oftentimes glued together to form larger sections. This type of timber product is known as laminated timber. Often used to make up large beams, lamination is also used for making window frames. The technique allows for problems of twisting and warping to be counteracted by carefully laying sections of timber together so that they pull against each other. It also allows for large beams and columns to be made economically from small sections. Curved sections can also be produced.

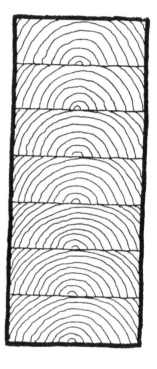

Section of laminated beam.

Cork:

Cork is produced from the bark of the cork oak tree. This is treated to produce small granules that are then bonded together to form boards or sheets. An excellent insulating material, cork is also used for flooring.

External Finishes for Timber

When exposed externally, timber, depending on its type, will weather. Due to the action of rain and sun, the exposed surfaces will become bleached and grey. Greying is caused by the loss of natural colouring materials due to the effects of sunlight. Where such an appearance is acceptable the timber can be left unfinished. This is often the case where cedar shingles are used and a pleasant silvery-grey colour results. It is important however, wherever natural weathering is used as a finishing treatment, that all exposed wood is well ventilated to prevent mould growths. It is also important that the fixing method of untreated external cladding can allow for replacement should this become necessary.

There are four basic types of external finishes for timber - preservatives, paints, varnishes and exterior wood stains.

Preservatives:

Preservative treated timber is often used in exposed situations. Depending on the type of substance used, paint, varnish or wood stains are often applied as a finish to such timber.

Where creosote or tar oil preservatives have been used it is not possible to apply another finish over these. An occasional brush treatment on such timber will renew its colour. Care needs to be taken however in choosing such treatment for your home. These preservatives have a very strong odour.

Timber treated with water-borne or organic solvent type preservatives can all be finished with paint, varnish or stain or they can be left unfinished to weather naturally. In the case of boron brush-treated timber it is essential to seal this against the rain that will wash away the preservative salts. If a 'natural' preservative is desired beechwood pitch would provide a better treatment externally.

Paints:

Paints are opaque coatings applied in several coats over wood. They change its appearance, mask its texture and allow for a variety of colours to be used. Their use is both practical as well as decorative, allowing for a particular appearance to be obtained and of course, this can be altered at the whim of the homeowner. On the downside, paint has to be renewed occasionally.

Natural finishes such as linseed oil will be found to be the most economical and user-friendly

A wide variety of natural paints can be made easily and economically from simple ingredients such as flour, water, clay, skimmed milk, lime, bicarbonate of soda ...

It is critical to the success of external work that the correct paint is used. This means using a paint that is permeable - water repellent and breathable. This will prevent water itself from penetrating the timber while allowing it to absorb and release water vapour as is required by its nature. If a sealing paint is used this breathing function will be halted resulting in peeling, cracking, blistering and possibly, in decay. Breathable paints are often erroneously called *micro porous paint*.

In selecting exterior paints for woodwork it is also important to choose products from reputable manufacturers and to apply these according to their recommendations. Water and solvent based products are available and of these, the water based variety will be found to be the most pleasant and safest to work with. When carefully and properly applied external paintwork should last for at least five years before renewal becomes desirable. Both conventional 'chemical' as well as 'natural' paints are available.

Timber clad EconoSpace with linseed oil painted exterior

Varnish:

Varnishes are essentially paints without colour pigmentation. These allow the natural grain of the wood to remain visible. There are basically two types of varnish - conventional and permeable.

Conventional varnishes are similar to conventional sealing paints though they often include a ultra-violet radiation filter to stop the wood from losing its colour. They are also solvent based. Permeable varieties can either be solvent or water based and allow the timber to breathe naturally. Conventional as well as natural products are available.

Varnish is a more exacting finish, requiring that the timber itself is consistent in quality and colour to produce a quality effect. The renewal period is also shorted than for paints at approximately three years.

Exterior wood stains:

Wood stains can be seen as an alternative to paints or varnish in that they allow for a variety of colours to be used while the natural grain of the wood remains visible. They are also permeable, allowing the timber to breathe while repelling water itself. The range of colours available is restricted however. Both solvent and water based varieties are manufactured and most wood stains contain a preservative to inhibit mould and fungal growth.

Sand-lime plaster+whitewash on hemp-lime walling

The maintenance period with wood stains will vary with exposure, though a 3-5 year cycle would be normal. It is however, the ease of renewal that gives these products their greatest appeal. Far less exacting to apply than either paint or varnish the time required to re-stain exterior timber would be far less that for either of the alternatives. Conventional and natural products are available.

Interior Finishes for Timber

Internal timber, because it is shielded from the effects of wind and rain, requires far less protection to that exposed externally. In many cases no finish is necessary at all. This is particularly true of timber used structurally, though a preservative treatment might be used in these situations. Care needs to be taken here however that substances likely to pose a health risk to the occupants are not employed. Boron type treatments should be considered for this. In terms of finishes themselves, the health risks involved in the use of many conventional products should be carefully evaluated. It is all too easy to create an otherwise healthy internal environment and then to disrupt this with hazardous vapours. The wide range of natural products now available should be given close consideration when choosing internal finishes for wood as well as for finishes generally.

Interior finishes should pose no threat to the buildings' occupants

Paints:

The advantages of using paint is that it allows for colour to be used creatively. A secondary advantage is that otherwise uninspiring-looking wood can be disguised and enhanced. All too often wood, especially wood panelling in walls and ceilings, creates too busy an effect for comfort. A further advantage of paint is that colour schemes can be changed at will, radically altering the feeling within a particular space or spaces. Colour schemes also allow for changes in furniture, fabrics, carpeting and lighting to be harmonised.

As with external paints, internal paints should be chosen for their quality and the recommendations of manufacturers should be carefully followed. Water based products are best and those products produced naturally are best of all. A variety of paint effects can also be produced though these require more skill than straightforward paint application that can be carried out by almost anyone.

Protecting children from toxic finishes is particularly important

Products are available for almost all internal surfaces, including floors. Paints with a vinyl/plastic content seal surfaces and these then cannot breathe.

Varnishes:

Varnishes are best applied to quality features allowing the natural appearance of the wood to be revealed. Again, care needs to be taken not to create too busy an effect by exposing too much timber. Natural products should be considered not only in terms of price but also in terms of smell, appearance and lasting effects.

Stains:

Features such as ceiling beams can often be stained to good effect. Floors of whitewood or plywood can also be given a solid colour to enhance their appearance. Similarly, plywood or blockboard when used to create built-in units, can be stained to create a particular colour effect. The colour range of stains is however quite limited. The colours chosen for use also have long term implications in contrast to paints whose colours can be altered far more easily.

Care needs to be taken in selecting stains to ensure that their vapours do not upset the balance of the internal environment. Products carrying any type of warning on the container should be very carefully used. Natural products should be chosen wherever possible.

Sealers:

Seals are thinned varnishes or lacquers and they are used to prevent absorption of surface coatings such as waxes into timber, particularly timber floors.

Wax:

Waxes are transparent surface coatings that are laid over stains or sealers. Wax provides protection without forming a thick coating on the surface. Suitable for floors, furniture and built-in units. Natural waxes such as carnauba and beeswax are readily available. Waxed floors however require more frequent attention than do varnished ones.

Paraffin wax of the type used for home canning is particularly suitable for wood kitchen utensils, cutting boards and other wood kitchen surfaces.

Oil:

Commonly called 'Danish oils', these surface treatments penetrate the wood and form no noticeable film on the surface. Two or more coats are normally applied, followed sometimes by a wax topcoat. Tung oil, linseed oil and resin oils are readily available. Vegetable oils are non-drying and are suitable for finishing and maintaining wood kitchen utensils. It should be borne in mind that any finish used for eating utensils is safe and non-toxic.

Natural finishes will be found to be the most pleasant for interior use

Common Softwoods

Common Name: Sitka Spruce / Silver Spruce

Botanical Name: *Picea Sitchensis*

Characteristics: This timber has good working qualities, displays little moisture movement and is noted for its natural lustre. Sometimes referred to as 'white deal', the timber finishes very well. The timber can vary in colour from pale white to pinkish white to greyish brown. It has a coarse texture Compared to the 'redder' woods, it is less resinous and has less conspicuous growth rings. When dry, the sapwood and heartwood are indistinguishable.

Knots are normally small - less than 25mm in diameter, hard and widely spaced. The distance between whorls of knots often exceeds 1m. Dead knots are less troublesome than in other species. These usually remain tight because the bark casing is thin. Shrinkage of knots is small also.

Sitka and European spruces are often machine graded for structural work such as in trussed rafters and timber frames. Selected timbers of both species can be used for joinery, though the European variety is preferable due to a lower incidence of spiral grain. This tendency in Sitka spruce can cause twisting in sawn wood for structural use. Usually regarded as a low strength timber, when graded to the GS grade of BS 4978 qualifies for lowest strength class of BS 5268 - meaning that it has lower strength properties than most other imported and home grown softwoods. Under the SR 11 grading system it is considered to be equivalent in strength to Douglas fir. Because of its low density spruce has good strength/weight ratio. Canadian Sitka was the preferred material in days of wooden aircraft manufacture because of this. Howard Hughes constructed the largest aircraft ever built out of spruce and named it the 'Spruce Goose'.

The heartwood of Sitka spruce is impermeable to wood preservatives and the sapwood can be penetrated only in its green condition. The converted wood dries quickly and well however.

Uses: Sawn timber; paper pulp; fibreboard; chipboard; MDF; plywood; furniture; musical instruments; boat frames; oars; masts.

Common Name: Norway/European Spruce

Botanical Name: *Pices abies*

Characteristics: Similar to Sitka Spruce but it usually has a broader band of sapwood and is less prone to twist. Shrinkage on conversion is also marginally lower.

Uses: San timber; paper pulp; chipboard; MDF; laminated beams; furniture; flooring.

Common Name: Scots pine

Botanical Name: *Pinus sylvestris*

Characteristics: Known as *red deal*, the timber has a fine texture and good working qualities, with medium moisture movement. The colour varies considerably with the creamy white sapwood being quite distinct from the pale orange/brown heartwood. Growth rings are prominent.

The timber works well with machine and hand tools though it tends to split around nails in dry timber. It absorbs preservatives well. The sapwood is susceptible to attack by blue stain fungi, especially during humid late summer and autumn months. It offers no significant problems in drying though in some situations the dried wood exhibits appreciable movement in changing humidity conditions causing unsightly gaps to appear in joints and increasing the risk of decay. It is a stronger timber than the spruces.

Uses: Sawn timber; external cladding; furniture; plywood; flooring; poles.

Common Name: Corsican Pine

Botanical Name: *Pinus nigra*

Characteristics: Similar to Scots Pine though it is more difficult to season. The drying timber will actually absorb water in the late autumn and winter months. It displays largely spaced whorls of knots and a much larger proportion of sapwood than other conifers. Good penetration and retention of preservatives can be achieved. It is less prone to movement after drying than Scots pine. The sawn wood similar to Scots pine but it usually has wider growth rings and a coarser texture. It works and finishes well.

Uses: Sawn timber; piers; jetties; poles; wood-wool slabs.

Common Name: Lodgepole Pine

Botanical Name: *Pinus contorta*

Characteristics: A pale yellowish wood with a medium texture. It displays good working qualities, has a small moisture movement and glues well. It resembles Scots pine and is sometimes used as a substitute for red deal though it has a somewhat lower strength. Even quite wide ringed timber gives a near-perfect machined finish. It shrinks less than Scots and is more stable in changing humidities making it better for joinery and furniture uses.

Uses: Sheeting; joinery; flooring; furniture; paper pulp; pallets.

Common Name: Larch

Botanical Names: *Larix decidua*
Larix Kaempferi
Larix eurolepis

Characteristics: A very strong timber though it is apt to split when nailed. Excellent for use out-of-doors. Resinous and knotty. The highest grade of sawn larch was traditionally used for boat skins and also sometimes used for vat making.

The wood is reddish brown with a fine texture. It displays good working qualities though the moisture movement can be quite large. It has conspicuous growth rings, dries rapidly but has a tendency to warp. Once dry, it is staple in use. It is one of the hardest and toughest softwoods and is significantly stronger than Scots pine. It had excellent natural durability characteristics and is resistant to preservation treatment.

Uses: External cladding; posts; rails; boats; poles; trellis work.

Common Name: Douglas Fir

Botanical Name: *Pseudotsuga menziesii*

Characteristics: Also called *Oregon Pine*. This is an excellent timber with a high strength/weight ratio and a fine to medium texture. The timber has off-white sapwood contrasting with salmon pink heartwood. It ages to a pleasant mellow brown. It displays conspicuous growth rings, is straight grained and

63

resinous. Its strength properties are marginally better than Scots Pine and it has a better natural resistance to decay. It dries quickly and well though it is difficult to treat it with preservatives under pressure. The timber works and finishes well though large knots can be encountered and it may split on nailing. It has a small moisture movement. Stainless steel fittings should be used due to the extractives present in the wood.

Uses: Heavy structural work; railway sleepers; chemical vats; tanks; flooring; decking; external cladding; plywood; poles; furniture; laminated timber; garden furniture.

Common Name: Lawson Cypress

Botanical Name: Chamaecyparis lawsoniana

Characteristics: Often called *cedarwood*. This is an almost featureless timber, even-textured, creamish white with a persistent spicy scent. It displays no difference between early and latewoods. It has moderate strength properties and is moth repellent allowing it to be used for wardrobe linings, cedar chests, etc. Leyland Cypress (*Cupressocyparis leylandii*) is a related species displaying generally the same characteristics though it is more durable.

'Cedar' embraces a number of dissimilar and botanically unrelated species which have in common a yellowish to red/brown colour and a fragrant or spicy odour. These include Western Red Cedar (*Thuja plicat*), true cedars (*Cedrus atlantica/libani* and *deodora*), Japanese Cedar (*Cryptomeria japonica*), Port Orford Cedar (*Chamaecyparis lawsoniana*) and pencil cedars (*Juniperis* species). These red/brown timbers have excellent natural durability, though strength is around 10% lower than spruce. Because of its low density this wood has an excellent strength/weight ratio however. In damp conditions it can be corrosive to steel and galvanised or stainless steel fastenings should be used.

Uses: Furniture; external cladding.

Common Name: Fir

Botanical Name: Abies species

Characteristics: Firs, particularly the European silver fir (*Abies alba*), Grand Fir (*Abies grandis*) and Noble Fir (*abies procera*) produce off white to pale brown wood superficially resembling spruce with comparable strength properties but giving a better, less woolly finish. They are also more amenable to treatment with preservatives. They have good nailing properties and selected wood is suitable for furniture and built-in units.

Common Name: Western Hemlock

Botanical Name: *Tsuga heterophylla*

Characteristics: Hemlock has an almost featureless pale brown colour with no marked difference between heartwood and sapwood. Its strength properties fall between Scots pine and spruce. It glues very well.

Common Name: Yew

Botanical Name: *Taxus baccata*

Characteristics: This is the strongest, hardest, heaviest and one of the most durable softwoods. A narrow band of white sapwood is readily distinguished from the much darker heartwood and it has pronounced growth rings. The earlywood is cinnamon brown with plain chocolate bands of latewood. This was the traditional material for the longbow. Excellent for turning and for decorative work.

Common Name: Giant Redwood

Botanical Name: *Sequoia semperviren*

Characteristics: A soft, low density timber that is highly durable. The ruddy brown heartwood contrasts with a creamy white sapwood. It has relatively low strength properties but is an excellent cladding.

Common Hardwoods

Common Name: Alder

Botanical Name: *Alnus* genus

Characteristics: A dull brown-pink, light, even textured, low strength, easily workable timber. Traditionally used for clogs, hat blocks and artificial limbs. Takes preservatives easily.

Common Name: Ash

Botanical Name: *Fraxinus excelsior*

Characteristics: This is one of the most valuable native hardwood species. The timber has good strength and is easily worked giving a smooth finish. It has good resistance to impact loading making it the preferred species for tool and implement handles, for vehicle construction, oars, racquets, hurley sticks and furniture/turnery use. The colour varies from off-white to yellowish white. It is somewhat coarse in appearance due to large pores and has obvious annual rings.

Common Name: Beech

Botanical Name: *Fagus sylvatica*

Characteristics: This is an even textured, coffee coloured timber. Kiln dried timber has a pinkish tinge. It displays no pronounced difference between sapwood and heartwood. It works, nails and screws well. Traditionally used for many types of tools such as jack planes, mallets and file handles, for furniture, chair backs and legs as well as for school furniture. It is also used for steam bent work and to make plywood and toys. It is good for use in floors and is permeable to wood preservatives.

Common Name: Birch

Botanical Names: *Betula pubescens*
Betula pendula

Characteristics: This is one of the strongest native woods. Off-white to pale pinkish brown, the wood is almost featureless, displaying no difference between sapwood and heartwood. It shows no rays and the annual rings are very faint. It works and stains well.

Its uses are similar to beech - furniture, toys, tool handles, flooring, clothes pegs and plywood. It takes preservatives well.

Common Name: Cherry

Botanical Name: Prunus species

Characteristics: This is an even textured wood with pale sapwood distinct from medium brown heartwood. It is quite strong - stronger than oak. It is used for furniture, panelling and cabinet making. It is resistant to preservative treatment and is good for turning and veneer.

Common Name: Sweet Chestnut

Botanical Name: Castanea sativa

Characteristics: The light brown heartwood of this timber resembles oak. The sapwood is a much paler creamy brown. It is easy to work, durable, stable, attractive and moderately strong. It is good for furniture production and internal joinery and ideal for outdoor work, especially glazing bars and mullions. It tends to split on nailing and so needs pre-boring. It is also used for hop poles, bean rods, walking sticks and umbrella handles. In contrast, Horse Chestnut (*Aesculus* spp.) has moderately low strength properties, is non durable and is only suited to such uses as shelving.

Common Name: Elm

Botanical Name: Ulmus species

Characteristics: The yellowish white sapwood of this timber contrasts with the golden or reddish brown heartwood. Its strength properties are moderately low - equivalent to spruce. It is often regarded as the most handsome of the native hardwoods. Used for coffin boards, garden furniture and chair seats, it requires kiln drying to prevent warping in service. It also has applications in civil engineering - for sea defenses and port installations. It makes good weather boarding and is permeable to preservation.

Wych Elm (*Ulmus glabra*) resembles other species of Elm superficially but has better strength properties, generally superior to Oak. It has a lustrous green colour and, apart for the uses to which the other Elm is put, it is used in boat building and to make wheels.

Common Name: Hornbeam

Botanical Name: Carpinus betulus

Characteristics: This is a white timber displaying no difference between sapwood and heartwood. It is strong, hard and heavy and was traditionally used for machinery parts and industrial floors as it has good abrasion resistance.

Common Name: Lime

Botanical Name: Tilia species

Characteristics: An even textured pale brown timber of moderate strength. Used for wood carving, beehives, kitchen implements and brushware.

Common Name: Oak

Botanical Names: Quercus robor
Quercus petraea

Characteristics: This is a familiar timber of good natural durability. It is handsome, resists abrasion and, apart from being hard, it is not particularly strong. The off-white sapwood is paler than the light brown heartwood. When quarter sawn it displays an attractive ray pattern. Used for coffin boards, shop fittings, furniture, joinery, veneer, frames, boats, ladder rungs, turnery and barrel making. Also it is much used for flooring. Red oaks and Turkey oaks are less durable but take preservatives well.

Common Name: Poplar

Botanical Name: Populus species

Characteristics: This is a lightweight, low strength timber. It is off-white usually with no difference displayed between the sapwood and heartwood. The absence of taints makes it very suitable for use with food. It is also used in the making of matches, though it is difficult to ignite. Employed in situations where fire hazards exist and also for food containers/boxes. Also used for furniture, joinery, pallets and packing cases.

Common Name: Sycamore

Botanical Name: *Acer pseudoplatanus*

Characteristics: This is a very useful wood with moderately good strength properties. It is hard, has good stability, an off-white colour and it works easily, though with a tendency to split. An absence of taints makes it suitable for use with food, kitchen and dairy implements, draining boards and chopping blocks. It is abrasion resistant and can be washed repeatedly. It is also used for furniture, joinery, toys as well as for violin making and textile woodware, especially bobbins.

Summary

It is virtually impossible to build a house without using timber.

Maintaining a reasonable Moisture Content is the fundamental principle of using wood for building.

The ability of wood to absorb and release moisture is a distinct advantage in the creation of healthy living environments.

Timber is a living material and must be appreciated through the senses.

Timber houses are at no greater risk from fire than bricks and mortar ones.

When used with care and sensitivity timber can last indefinitely.

The practice of poising timber to preserve it is dangerous to all forms of life.

Air is the best timber preservative of all.

A simple and economical timber frame which can be finished with a variety of natural materials

Cedar boarding makes an effective and durable exterior cladding

31 Sheltermaker Design Programme
Choosing Other Materials & Products

Apart from understanding the properties and special qualities of wood, it is necessary to evaluate and select other *Materials & Products* to use in the creation of your building design.

Begin by reading pages 71-79. This will provide the necessary overview, the most critical aspects of which are:

- The manufacturing process of *Materials & Products* from the 'raw' to the 'finished' state.
- The 'true' cost of *Materials & Products* in monetary and environmental terms.
- The impact of *Materials & Products* on living systems.
- How selected *Materials & Products* might be recycled.

Pages 79-87 deal with *'Raw Materials'* while pages 87-102 cover *'Products'*. A reading of this information will allow you to begin collecting brochures and samples. Of equal importance will be the collection of information on cost and availability. Store all information in the *Construction* File.

One may find it easier, at this stage, to eliminate the use of certain *Materials & Products,* as opposed to making final selections. For example, one might rule out the use of PVC windows and doors, synthetic paints and concrete blocks. In any event, the 'final' selection of *Materials & Products* will only take place after consideration of *Construction*, conditions attached to borrowings, detailed site analysis, planning considerations, the availability of skills locally and so on.

At this stage what is important is to recognise the deeper aspects of selecting *Materials & Products* and to assess the feel of these. Outline the *Materials & Products* which most appeal to you on the *Construction Worksheet.*

Next: SDP32 - Choosing A Construction System, page 105

Salvaged double glazing units in purpose made frames in EconoSpace

Materials & Products

Small buildings are best made from materials that are freely available locally. It is a good idea therefore, to go to a local builders supplier at an early stage in the project to see what they stock and to become familiar with building materials and products in their unbuilt state. Many of the items you will see will look awfully crude and raw and some you will not even know what they are! None of this matters particularly. You are just looking and feeling and sensing what these things are like. Does something feel good? Does it look good? Does it smell good? These are the responses that you must entertain in order to narrow down the field of materials and products that you are willing to surround yourself with in your home. Sensing materials in this way will allow you to organise a file entitled *Materials & Products* which will comprise catalogues, notes and even samples along with the relevant prices of these things. It should be borne in mind when assembling price information, that building costs are made up of two elements - material costs and labour costs.

The range of materials used today has changed very little from that used for building purposes throughout history - wood, stone, clay, sand, metal, cloth. Of course the modern products made from these materials would be quite sophisticated in comparison to their former counterparts. Plastic would be a significant modern addition to this range.

With the exception of wood and cloth, all these materials are derived from the earth itself, including plastic. While all materials are of natural origins they cannot all be considered to be natural materials as the process of their manufacture into products may alter them in such a way that their original natural qualities are radically altered.

What materials are available locally ?

Do these materials ....

Look good ?

Smell good ?

Feel good ?

Sound good ?

Taste good ?

Many building materials originate in the earth ....
Clay, Stone, Lime, Oil, Sand, Metal

But beware of what might happen to these in a factory!

71

The use of man made chemicals in modern manufacturing processes can oftentimes introduce dangerous substances into otherwise benign materials as well as producing quantities of waste that cannot easily participate in the earth's natural recycling process. Manmade chemicals can be particularly dangerous in this respect as they generally do not recycle naturally and so cause an imbalance in the environment. This type of imbalance can be extremely hazardous to life. Because of this, all the materials and products that one chooses to use in a building project should be scrutinised from their raw material state to their finished state in order to make a reasoned assessment of their likely effect on one's health as well as their effect on the wider world.

A house is an enclosure that excludes the outdoor climate while creating an indoor one. The materials and products from which this enclosure is made - the building fabric - will effectively surround the inhabitants, isolating them from the outside world. What this means is that the indoor climate, or environment, must be carefully made to ensure that the occupants will be safe inside it - that they have sufficient air to breath, that their bodies are kept at a pleasant temperature, that the effects of benign natural radiation can reach them, that they are not subjected to dangerous substances and so on. In short, what you want to achieve is an internal environment that is pleasant, safe and natural. The creation of this type of environment in large part depends on the materials you choose to make your building with and how these are put together.

The outlines for the type of internal environment you wish to create within your building will be described in your *Brief*, particularly in the *Abstract Analysis* for each space and your stated requirements in regards to *Heating & Ventilation*. *Internal Environment* includes everything from the quality of space, to the quality of light, to the quality of air within the building. Because we perceive these qualities through our senses it is vital that the materials and products chosen to emulate these qualities are selected by using our senses also. It is all too easy to select items on the basis of cost or by succumbing to sophisticated advertising or pressure. In other words it is easy to allow our heads to make the decisions while ignoring what the heart has to say in the matter.

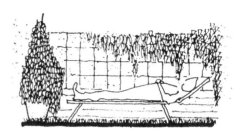

Choose building materials and products that will be good for your health!

Making a healthy and safe internal environment depends on the materials and products you select to make your building with.

Use your senses to guide you.

Good ventilation is essential in creating a healthy home.

The earth has always provided people with the raw materials with which to create their homes.

Modern Building Materials

The majority of modern building materials are mostly derived from the same source as their historical counterparts - the earth itself. Many new materials and products have been developed from these basic raw materials using technology. Oil is a good example of this. Building components that are wholly or partially made from oil by-products are very common. They include PVC windows and doors, damproof courses, paints and preservatives.

When evaluating the use and worth of any building material or product it is important to be aware of the general process that has been used to convert the raw material into a usable form. This process, in the case of stone for example, would be the quarrying, shaping, transporting and laying of the material. In the case of wood, the process required to make the wood ready for use is to fell the tree, to transport it, to cut it, to dry it, to distribute it and to fix it. It might also be subjected to chemical preservative treatment.

An awareness of the processes involved in making raw materials usable will reveal what that raw material has been subjected to, what chemicals have been used and how much energy has been needed to do it all. This information will give some idea of how the original character of the material is likely to have changed and what the consequences of the process have been in terms of waste and emissions. It will also give you an idea what might be in the material that might be harmful to you or to the environment, both when it is in use or when it is no longer needed. The ability of a material or product, when it has been discarded, to be recycled is also very important. Can it be reused or if it is to become waste, can it be recycled without causing harm to the wider environment?

The building materials you surround yourself with should feel good, look good, smell good and maybe even taste good! The walls, floors and roof of your building - the building fabric - will all impact your senses constantly while you are within them, so it is important to carefully consider what these elements are made from and how they have been produced. If the materials in your home are benign materials, your senses will signal your defence mechanisms to relax. This will make you feel good, ensure your good health and generally make a most appealing internal environment!

Raw Material -
to Product -
to Use
Analysis:

Extraction ...
Transportation ...
Treatment ...
Packaging ...
Storage ...
Transportation ...
Display ...
Advertising ...
Sale ...
Transportation ...
Use ...

Reuse?

Are the materials and products I want to use, safe and friendly in every respect?

Energy, Materials & Products

Energy is one of the most pertinent topics of our age, particularly its cost. This cost is perceived both in monetary as well as in environmental terms. In relation to the design and construction of a home, energy has a major bearing on how your building is heated and on the selection of materials from which to make the building fabric. As with the wider question of global energy usage, the cost both in monetary as well as in environmental terms will be of concern to the designer.

Quite an amount of the energy involved in the making of building materials and products is used to convert the raw material into a usable state. When an energy source such as oil is used to do this the monetary cost of the energy itself is high and the environmental cost in terms of the emissions and waste is also high. These are costs that consumers, whether they buy these products or not, must pay for.

Earthly matter might best be described as being a mixture of substance and energy. Substance is the part of something that we can touch and feel and energy is the invisible glue that holds it all together. This energy content that matter contains was either 'locked-in' when the earth was formed or it was beamed down from the sun, captured and stored. The energy within uranium for example, derives from the formation of the earth, while the energy within oil, wood and gas is derived from the sun.

All substance is made from a standard kit of parts called atoms. Atoms are tiny particles that are held together by energy. What makes one substance different from another is the number and arrangement of these atoms and the amount of energy needed to hold them together. Chalk and cheese, for example, are both made from the same kind of atoms. What makes chalk different from cheese is the number of atoms it contains, the way they are arranged and the amount of energy needed to hold the atoms together. Because all matter is made from identical atoms, in theory chalk can be changed into cheese by rearranging its atoms. This is true. To carry out this process however, energy has to be used to break up the chalk atoms and yet more energy is needed to glue them back in the correct order to make the cheese. It is this factor, the energy required, that makes the conversion of chalk into cheese impractical and, of course, costly. In terms of building materials it is also the energy factor that has a major bearing on the practicality and cost of converting the raw materials into usable products.

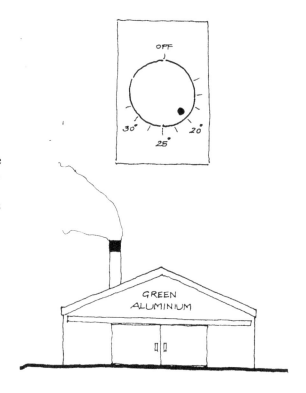

The heating of a home and the conversion of the raw materials with which to make it, can demand a large amount of energy.

This level of energy usage can have a negative impact on the environment ...

So, be careful and use materials that have not demanded a lot of energy to produce ... timber, for example.

To make chalk into cheese requires a lot of energy!

*To make ...
ore into metal
... oil into plastic
... stone into cement
... requires a lot of energy also!*

High energy usage produces a lot of waste, which leads to pollution.

While energy might be thought of as an abstract, insubstantial thing, when it has to be extracted from a substance such as oil in order to use it to convert chalk into cheese, or stone into cement, or ore into metal, the process of extracting that energy produces waste - carbon dioxide, sulphur etc. - products which have difficulty recycling themselves and therefore end up causing pollution. It is all too easy to think of 'cost' as meaning the price of something in pounds or dollars. What cost really means is, how much of a mess is this going to make and is it worth it for what we are going to get out of it?

Now, when you see a bag of cement in the builders suppliers, don't just ask what it costs, think what has gone into making it. Or better still, drive out to the factory and see what the process is like. The point I am making is that you should not isolate yourself from the processes that have gone into making the building materials you select to build your house from. Do not think of them purely in terms of their monetary cost, but think of how sensitive the process has been, because, like it or not, the process has become part of the material. If you do go out to the cement factory, try and stop by a sawmill on your way home. Go stand in the drying shed and feel the difference in how cement and wood are produced and the effect this has on them.

In energy terms alone, the amount of energy needed to produce a tonne (1000 kilos) of sawn timber would also produce:

500 kilos of bricks
330 kilos of cement
250 kilos of chipboard
50 kilos of glass
38 kilos of steel
30 kilos of polyethylene
31 kilos of PVC
30 kilos of lead
25 kilos of zinc
20 kilos of copper
4 kilos of aluminium

The Nature of Building Materials

All building materials and products carry with them qualities derived from their origins and from the process used to prepare them. Stone, for example, displays qualities of solidity, longevity and permanence in its raw state. These are the natural qualities of stone, its Identikit. These qualities have traditionally been exploited to impart to stone buildings qualities of strength, longevity and

Using salvaged materials is a low-energy option ... but beware - only gather what is in good condition and carefully consider the work involved in rendering the materials useful

Ask yourself ...
How much energy has gone into producing the materials and products I am going to build with ?

Has this energy usage produced polluting waste ...

And ...

Can the material or product that I am buying be usefully and safely recycled ?

beauty. Cement, on the other hand, although it is derived from stone, is processed so as to obliterate these natural qualities. When cement is used to make concrete, the absence of natural appeal results in a rather cold, dead material. Although concrete might be regarded as having both strength as well as longevity its lack of beauty cannot be ignored.

Wood has natural qualities of strength, aroma, beauty, flexibility and warmth that can readily be utilised to contribute to the making of beautiful spaces. The process of preparing wood for use can vary from simple cutting and air-drying to sophisticated kiln-drying and pressure impregnation treatments with preserving chemicals. All these processes have their own effect on wood and alter its natural qualities accordingly. This means that not only is it important to make a careful selection of materials when creating a home, but of equal importance is the investigation of the process to which the material has been subjected to make it usable.

We perceive the natural qualities of materials through our senses, particularly by touch, smell and sight. This type of perception allows us to feel the nature of these materials and allows us to select appealing materials, particularly for the inside of buildings where their effect will most impact our senses and therefore our sense of well-being. It is of particular importance to design with aroma in mind, choosing materials that appeal to our sense of smell, our strongest sense.

Workpersonship

Just as it is important to be aware of the natural qualities inherent in building materials, it is equally important for the person using these materials to appreciate these qualities in order that they can be properly exploited during construction.

The level of appreciation that it is possible to have for any material is related to how much of the original natural qualities remain after manufacture. While it is not always true that the manufacturing process inevitably takes from these natural qualities, it is true that the nature of any machine process that a material might be subjected to invests that material with a machine quality. As a general principle, it can be considered that the qualities of all building materials and products relate directly to the amount of care and sensitivity that have been applied to them in taking them from their raw state to a finished state.

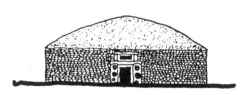

The Identikit of Stone
Solidity
Longevity
Permanence

The Dead Materials Society

Most Famous Alumnus
Concrete

But ..
Wood has it all ... strength, aroma, beauty, flexibility, warmth, recyclability ...

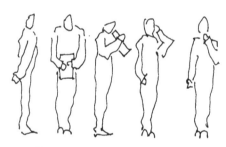

Use your senses when choosing building materials ... look, feel, smell, hear and even taste them!

The natural qualities of all building materials must be appreciated and exploited when building with them.

Concrete, for example, starts its life in the earth where the portland stone from which it largely derives was originally formed. It is extracted from the ground mechanically, transported to a factory mechanically, subjected to heat and chemical treatment, then bagged mechanically and finally transported to the end user. This dry cement powder is then mixed with sand, gravel and water and placed in a mould. When sufficient water has evaporated from this mix, the mould is removed and the resulting concrete is revealed. The process does not evoke a caring response in either the building operatives or the eventual occupants of the building!

If no care at all is applied to the preparation of a material or to how it is used, no care will be evident in the finished product. Care is a purely human quality that can be added to a building by sensitively assembling the components from which it is to be made. It is in this regard that the quality of workmanship in any building project is so important. If a building worker can work with materials that have been produced sensitively and can invest the building work with care, the end user - the building occupants - will benefit from this care because it will clearly evidence itself in the finished product.

Stonemasons, carpenters and joiners all share a tradition of fine workmanship, a deep knowledge of their materials and an ability to produce work of the highest standard. This tradition is closely allied to the practice of creating space - architecture - and persons properly trained in these trades will be an invaluable addition to any building project. The very word 'architect' is itself derived from the Greek words for 'chief carpenter'. Modern methods of training persons in the building trades have changed much from the old system of Apprentice, Journeyman and Master. Coupled with modern methods of producing materials and of design, these changes have done much to diminish the quality of modern buildings.

It is of critical importance that a careful selection of materials and products is made for any building project and that the building operatives involved in their assembly are given every opportunity to exercise care and become involved in the creative aspects of their work. If this is done, the commitment to achieving a particular standard of care will benefit the eventual occupants considerably. Such encouragement cannot be given by employing persons on the basis of the number of concrete blocks they can lay per hour! Neither can it be had by noting in a Specification that 'all work shall be carried out with sensitivity and care.' Rather, this is a quality that can only be achieved by direct communication on a human level, by praising good work and by encouragement.

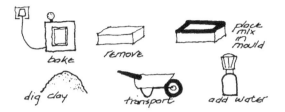

dig clay   *transport*   *bake*   *remove*   *place mix in mould*   *add water*

**Raw Material
To Finished Product
Chain**

How much care and sensitivity has been invested in this process ?

How sensitive is the material or product to you ... and to the environment ...now and in the future ?

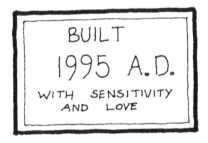

BUILT
1995 A.D.
WITH SENSITIVITY
AND LOVE

Care & Sensitivity are essential parts of any building project.

Sensitive materials and careful work lead to sensitive and cared for buildings.

Care is a purely human quality.

Select materials and products carefully.

Encourage good work and initiative.

Avoid the lump!

77

Standards

Standards exist for many of the materials and products used in modern buildings. These Standards are normally set by National Authorities who evaluate these materials and products to assess their suitability for the uses for which they are intended. When materials and products are being chosen it is wise to consider items which conform to a relevant Standard.

Typical of such Standards are the Irish Standards indicated by the initials I.S. followed by a number. For example, I.S. 1:1963 is the number of the Irish Standard for Cement. This Standard is produced in written form by the relevant testing Authority. Cement which meets the criteria set out in the Standard document may then carry the Standard Mark. This mark is simply a repetition of the initials I.S. and the Standard number - I.S. 1:1963.

Another common Standard is the British Standard indicated by the letters B.S. and the relevant number. For example B.S. 1230 is the British Standard for gypsum plasterboard.

Agrement Certificates are another form of International Standard. Like Irish and British Standards, Agrement Certificates carry a number which indicates that the material or product that they refer to has been tested and passed by an independent evaluator.

Healthy Houses

A major consideration in the selection of building materials and products must be whether or not these materials are likely to be harmful to the building occupants. Materials that have been subjected to chemical processes in their manufacture oftentimes release gas and particles that can be harmful. Chipboard is a good example of this. Under certain conditions of moisture and heat, chipboard releases formaldchyde gas which can be harmful if inhaled.

Materials which are potentially hazardous to one's health should be avoided in any building project. Exposure to such materials will activate the body's immune system to fight the effects of the noxious substances to which the body is being exposed. The level of activity associated with these defence exercises can be quite minor, but any constant exposure to unsafe materials will keep the immune systems always on the alert. Consequently, the body will be unable to properly relax and renew its defenses. This will manifest itself as stress.

Where possible, select materials and products that conform to a recognised Standard.

Avoid dangerous substances and building materials ... because they activate your immune system and leave it in the on position ... this leads to stress and a weakening of your ability to fend off other, possibly more serious, attacks. Be particularly careful about paints, stains, preservatives and varnishes.

Stress can stem from physical causes such as fumes and bacteria or from non physical causes such as man made electromagnetic radiation. Bedroom areas particularly need to be protected from all possible sources of stress as it in sleep that the immune system has the best chance of renewing itself. The long term effects of constant exposure to harmful substances and radiation is a severe weakening of the immune system. Such weakness can render the body unable to adequately ward off a major attack on the body such as an illness, and this, of course, can have very serious consequences for one's health.

Generally speaking, if the process by which a material has been produced from the raw material to its finished state, is, at all times in that process, respectful to life, then the material will be safe to use. It is a good idea to begin assembling samples of materials and products at an early stage of the design process. This way you can become familiar with these substances and their likely effects on you and on your family. This is particularly true of finishes such as paints and stains - if you cannot bear the smell of an open paint tin in the room, look for an alternative product! Our immune systems are activated by our senses. We must learn to trust this information and not to rely solely on our mental faculties when making decisions in regard to materials and products.

It is important to remember that the furnishings of your home should also be subjected to the same scrutiny as the materials and products from which it is to be made. Carpets, curtains, bedding materials and appliances should all be carefully selected.

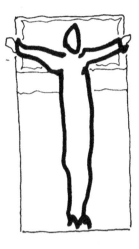

Your home should be a place where you can relax physically and mentally and, ideally, be under no stress whatsoever!

Your immune system is activated by your senses ... so listen to what your senses tell you and let your Mind take a back seat for a change!

Raw Materials

Clay is one of the most sensuous, low-cost, useful, beautiful and easily-worked materials that one could use

Earth:

Buildings always have a strong connection to the earth. Inevitably they stand on it and usually many of the materials from which a building is made are earth materials - stone, clay, metal and so on.

The earth is a vast recycling system and all earth materials have in their nature the inclination to return to the earth. Erosion due to the action of wind, rain and ground moisture all contribute to the gradual breaking down of earth materials, a process of recycling them back into the earth from which they came. Our bodies are partially composed of earth materials and will eventually return to the earth in one form or another. Our connection with the earth is undeniable even if we all resist the idea of dying and returning to it as recyclable waste.

The Earth is the source of all building materials ... and it is to the Earth that many of these are always striving to return.

It is important to realise the nature of earth materials when they are being used for building, especially their tendency to recycle. This tendency however can easily be retarded by conscious design. This is usually done by protecting them from being wet. Water is an essential part of the natural decay process and air also plays an important role in this.

Earth materials can be used to provide a built environment with a very strong sense of the earth. This is especially true when earth, in the form of mud and clay, is exploited as a building material. Abundant, local and easily worked, earth is always readily available. Their tendency to decay however is very strong unless they are kept extremely dry. They can be used to make floors, walls, and even roofs. Like stone, earth has no ability to withstand tensile loading but it works very well in compression. Usually straw, animal hair or similar binders are used to give earth some strength under tensile loading.

In early building forms, branches bound together with mud - wattle and daub - was in widespread use. Mud was also used to produce mortar for binding stones together. Adobe bricks are made by drying shaped sections of wet clay in the sun. Roof tiles can be made in the same way. When wet clay is fired in a kiln a very durable substance emerges. Baked clay has many uses in modern buildings. Pipes, bricks, tiles, sinks, toilets, crockery and various other items are made from this. Dry earth also has a good ability to store heat.

Stone:
Stone is a naturally occurring building material that exists in the earth either in small lumps or in large blocks. Where these lumps of stone are relatively small they can be used to make foundations, walls, floors, beams and even roofs. Where stone occurs in huge blocks - rock - it has to be cut into smaller pieces before it can be used. Granite, limestone, quartz, marble and sandstone are all types of stone that can be used for building.

Small stones which occur either on the surface of the ground or immediately under it, can be used directly to build with without cutting or even using any bonding material. More commonly a bonding material is used and this can be anything from mud to mortar. It all has the same effect - it bonds all the stones together so that they don't move. When stone has been used in this way to build a house it is usually covered over afterwards with some sort of plaster for the sake of appearance and to lend it a degree of weathertightness.

The Earth is the original Recycler.

Earth is an abundantly useful material ... allowing for the making of ... floors, walls, bricks, tiles, pipes, pots, plates .... and ... it is an excellent heat storage medium.

Stone is used traditionally for foundations, walls, floors, roofs, cills, lintols ...

It can be dry built or bound with mud... or mortar.

Where large blocks of stone are cut for building they are usually shaped into rectangular blocks to facilitate transportation and to make them easy to lay one on top of the other. When this is being done careful regard has to be paid to the natural bed of the stone to ensure its best performance.

The compressive strength of stone and its poor ability in tension means that it has to be used in a load bearing fashion when building with it. The early stone structures that still survive on the planet employ either corbelling or the post and beam system. Later developments introduced the arch and the flying buttress. The flying buttress is a building device whereby the horizontal loads of a stone structure can be safely transferred to the ground.

Of its nature stone is hard, cold, durable and usually heavy. Sometimes it is waterproof but this is not always the case. Formed in the earth in ancient fiery upheavals, stone usually carries with it qualities of lasting which can be utilised in building design. Ancient stone constructions exist all over the earth testifying to this quality.

The craft of stonemasonry is a very ancient one and its practitioners have played a vital role in the history and development of architecture. Apart from its main use as a structural material, stone has always been carved and decorated to enhance its natural qualities.

Building with stone is time consuming and requires a considerable degree of skill. Buildings stones, especially granite should be tested for radon emission before they are incorporated into a structure. Apart from its use to make walls, stone can be used to make chimneys, steps, worktops, floors and can also be used as a means of storing heat. Stone in the form of slate is a good roofing material. Dry built stone can be used for making boundary walls. Stones sensitively laid in gravel can make a simple sculpture garden as employed in Japanese garden design. Gravel - small rounded stones - used on its own, is ideal for paths as well as for courtyard areas. When used in this way the gravel should be edged by a series of upright stones to contain it.

One of the main drawbacks of using stone can be the high cost of quarrying, transportation and the slow construction time involved in using it. More than any other material the stone you use should be local, preferably out of the very ground that you are building on.

Often stone is used for filling prior to the laying of a concrete floor slab, under a driveway or for levelling a site. All types of rock fill are unstable unless they have

The Natural Qualities of Stone
Hard
Cold
Permanent
Heavy
Indestructible

been well compacted. Extreme care should be taken when fill is being built over. In general, ways can usually be found that avoid using fill and these options should be exercised wherever possible.

Sand:

Sand is a granular material made up of small particles of silica rock. Building sand is quarried from the earth wherever it occurs. For building purposes it has many uses - for making mortar, concrete and external plaster. It is also used as a covering for rock fill prior to the laying of concrete ground floor slabs. Sea sand should not be used in the making of concrete as it contains salt.

Sand is a useful medium for filtering water. It can also be used as a bed for the making of paths. Sand can provide a pleasant decorative garden as used in the Japanese way - raked to produce a pleasant decorative effect.

Silica is used as the basis of photoelectric cells allowing electricity to be made from light. The other great use of sand is in glassmaking, allowing light to be brought inside of buildings while excluding the weather. Coloured glass can also be used to transform dull grey light into something more cheerful and pleasant. Glass is also very useful for trapping solar radiation. Sand is an excellent heat storage medium.

Gypsum:

Gypsum is another earth material with a long history of use in building. In its raw form gypsum is calcium sulphate rock and it is mined underground. It is a mineral evolved from salt deposits laid down by the evaporation of water from the earth's surface at some time in the distant past.

Gypsum is mined in large blocks, crushed and then pulverised into a fine powder. It is then heated and its natural water content is evaporated off. This leaves what is called Plaster of Paris behind. After this, certain chemicals are added to assist in the workability of the plaster when water is added to it in a working situation. These are known as retardants.

Plaster of Paris is used for internal decorative plasterwork and for moulded objects. The addition of a moulded plaster cornice to a ceiling will do a lot to take the bare look off a wall and ceiling junction. Plaster roses and other decorative plaster motifs can also be applied to ceilings to good effect. These types of plaster decoration are available premade and are very easy to install and affix.

Beware of building on stone fill.

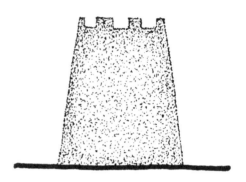

Sand is useful for ... making mortar, concrete and external rendering ... for filtering water ... for paths and Japanese Gardens ... for making glass and photovoltaic cells ... for storing heat and reflecting solar radiation ... and ...
for playing with.

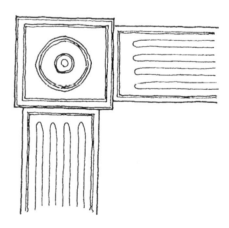

Gypsum is a natural mineral deposit useful for making plaster and plasterboards ... and for producing decorative cornices and mouldings.

Gypsum plaster is also used to cover internal wall surfaces by wet application. Plasterboard is gypsum plaster that has been mixed and set in the factory to a regular thickness then faced with paper. It is used internally to face walls and ceilings. All types of gypsum products have a good ability to absorb and release water vapour. This is of benefit where a natural internal environment is being created. Plasterboard is also fireproof.

Companies producing gypsum plaster issue information on their products and the standards to which they are made. These will include information on the ingredients of the finished products, how they should be used, sizes etc. A builders providers will give you prices on these also.

All earth products can carry with them traces of radon gas, gypsum included. The source of the gypsum should be checked to see if you can find out if it is radon infected or not. You would have to try and do this through the manufacturer. Plaster that has had formaldehyde added to it at any stage should be avoided.

Cement:
Cement is probably the earth material that is most extensively used in modern building. Consisting mainly of powdered Portland Stone and other earth derived additives, cement is factory produced as a fine dry powder. This is delivered in 50kg paper sacks.

Cement is used as the main ingredient in many building components and finishes. Depending on what is being made and constructed, cement is mixed with other ingredients including water to produce a wet plastic substance that hardens when placed in position.

The most extensive use of cement is in the making of concrete. Concrete is a mixture of cement, sand and crushed stone. These are mixed together in careful proportions depending on the use to which the concrete is being put. Because it is applied in a wet plastic form, concrete requires that some type of mould or formwork is used to hold it in place until it has hardened.

Like its natural counterpart, stone, concrete works extremely well under compressive loads, in other words, when it is being pushed in on itself. Under tensile loads - when it is being pulled apart - it has no strength whatsoever. To rectify this shortcoming steel is introduced into the concrete in the form of steel bars. Steel works extremely well in tension. This combination of concrete and steel is known as reinforced concrete. Reinforced concrete works extremely well in tension and in compression.

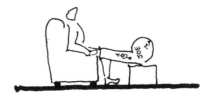

Plaster of Paris has many uses, both practical as well as decorative.

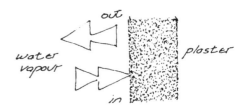

Plaster is hygroscopic, meaning that it can absorb and release water vapour and help to regulate internal humidity.

Plaster and plasterboards are also useful for fireproofing.

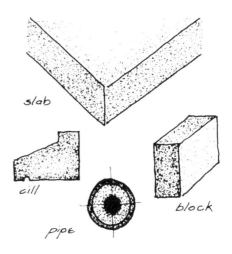

Cement is used in the making of ... concrete slabs, blocks, pipes, window cills, lintols, hearths and floors.

Concrete is a naturally cold material and it conducts heat very well. If it is heated on one side, for example, it will continually conduct heat away to its colder side. Oftentimes, insulation is placed under reinforced concrete ground floor slabs to minimise this heat loss to the cold ground below.

Concrete blocks are made from cement, sand, gravel and water. They are normally factory made and are used to build walls. They are made either solid or hollow and are produced in a range of standard sizes. Regular in shape, predictable in size and flat for ease of laying, the concrete block is in fact, a manmade stone. One concrete block is the same as another so no thought or feeling is required on the part of the blocklayer to select the appropriate one for the particular piece of work that is being done. This makes blocklaying a very mechanical process and the resulting work is very predictable in appearance. To overcome this block walls are normally plastered to disguise them.

Cement is also used to factory produce window cills, lintols and even floors. These products are referred to as being made of precast concrete.

Lime:

Lime is one of the most economical and useful naturally occurring earth materials. It can be employed in a variety of ways in building. Used with sand it makes a mortar that is superior to its cement based counterpart. This is because it dries more rapidly and continues to breathe, cleansing the air that passes through it. Used for plaster it does the same thing. Used with water it makes economical whitewash or colourwash. Being hygroscopic, it also performs well as a regulator of the internal moisture content of spaces.

Oil, Coal and Gas:

Oil, coal and gas are earth substances that were millions of years in the making. Longevity is part of their nature. A whole range of organic chemicals are derived from these substances. 'Organic' means that the substance referred to contains carbon, a very abundant element that abounds in the natural world. Many organic chemicals are used in producing building materials, insulation, furnishing materials, cleaning products, pest control and decorative products.

The synthetics and chemicals produced by the transmutation of oil, gas and coal have difficulty in participating in the natural balance of the living world, in other words they are difficult to recycle. Their

Concrete is made by mixing cement, sand, water and crushed stone together and allowing this mix to set.

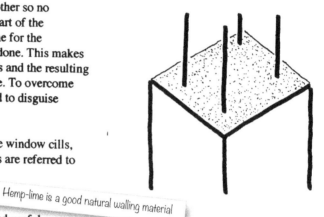

Hemp-lime is a good natural walling material

Reinforced concrete has steel bars in it to give it tensile strength.

Concrete is a naturally cold material that conducts heat very well.

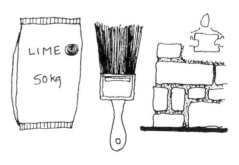

Lime is a beneficent earth material used for ... paint, mortar, plaster ...

production also involves the use of large amounts of energy and this produces emissions and particles that are released into the air. These are also unsuited to the earth's recycling system. Because they are slow to break down they lodge themselves in the life system and upset its balance.

Organic chemicals are usually combustible, insoluble in water and are either liquid or solids with low melting points. Many of these are volatile, that is, they evaporate even at room temperature, releasing vapours and gases. An accumulation of vapours from volatile organic chemicals can be harmful to life.

The worst organic chemicals are formaldehyde, organochlorines and phenolic compounds and the most hazardous exposure comes from decorating and pest control substances, preservatives and from the use of plastics. The very word preservative describes a substance deliberately made not to be part of the natural recycling system of the earth. Formaldehyde is used in certain types of wood sheeting materials, in furnishing fabrics, rugs and carpets, cosmetics and deodorants. It irritates the skin, the eyes, the nose and the throat and is associated with breathing difficulties, headaches, fatigue and nausea. It is the cumulative effect from many products containing this substance which is harmful to life. Organochlorines are potent and persistent chemicals which are also harmful. The body is unable to recycle these substances and they accumulate and cause illness. They are found in PVC, in pesticides, solvents and cleaning fluids. Phenol is a common disinfectant. It is also a strong irritant. Phenol compounds are found in cleaners, air fresheners, polishes and hygiene products. Phenolic synthetic resins containing formaldehyde are used in hard plastics, insulation, paints, fabric coatings and varnish. These cause skin rashes, nausea and breathing problems.

The extensive use of these types of substances make people sick and even contribute to their deaths. The inbuilt defence systems that we all have are constantly under strain to cope with the impact of these substances on our bodies. While our bodies do warn us that some things are going to be bad for us, we can mentally overide these signals and continue to expose ourselves to their injurious effects.

The use of plastics cannot reasonably be avoided in any building project. Their selection and use should however be confined to essential items such as electrical insulation and products where no alternative is readily available. Plastics dominate the field of damproof courses. They are also used to prevent moist air from passing into walls.

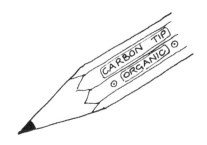

Organic means 'contains carbon'.

Many organic substances are used to produce building materials ... all of which are difficult to recycle.

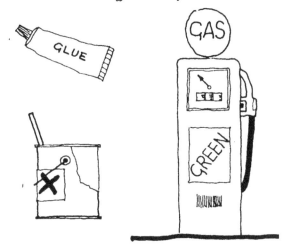

Beware of organic chemicals used in the production of building materials ... especially paints and adhesives.

Use your Senses to tell you what might be bad for you.

Watch out for certain insulations, board materials and varnishes that might contain formaldehyde.

Over exposure to some organic chemicals make people sick.

Constant over exposure can be more serious!

Take extreme care with paints and finishes and use all petrochemical based materials with extreme caution.

These are called vapour barriers. Similarly, plastics are used in moulded sections for gutters, fascias, soffits and so on. Plastic in these situations will expand in the heat of the sun and may be broken down by the effects of ultra violet light. Plastic might, at best be described as a dead material. Avoid it.

Metals:

Steel, aluminium, stainless steel, iron and copper are all metals that are commonly used in buildings. Generally energy intensive in their production, the use of metals should be confined to places where they are most useful - in pipes, taps, nails, bolts, locks and rainwater goods.

Too much metal in a house can cause disruption of the natural electromagnetic radiations. It can also attract manmade radiation in alarming amounts. Steel reinforcement is used inside concrete to give it tensile strength. Steel is also used alone to make building structures as it has good ability to bear compressive and tensile loads. Rust is the way in which steel is naturally recycled. Steel is also used for lintols and beams in loadbearing structures. Lead is used in roofing to form junctions as it is very flexible. Care should be taken where rainwater is being collected that it does not become contaminated by lead. Zinc is used as a rust inhibitor over steel cladding.

Water:

Water is an essential material for many building processes. All forms of load bearing structures use water in their creation. Concrete also requires the use of large amounts of water. Water that is introduced into the building process must evaporate before the building can be considered dry. This can take a considerable time. Any water that remains within materials which have had large amounts of water added to them, will contribute to that materials ability to conduct heat. This ability will make a material cold. Generally water attracts water. Water is essential for life and it also assists in the breaking down or decay of substances.

Water is also an important heat storage and distribution medium and is an vital part of all types of central heating systems.

Air:

Besides water, air is another important natural building material. Air has a good heat storage capacity and is a vital part of many modern insulating products.

Air also plays an important role in cleansing the interior of a building by carrying away waste products such as

Metals provide essential fixing components for sheltermakers - wherever possibly such fixings should allow for buildings to be dis-assembled at the end of their useful life

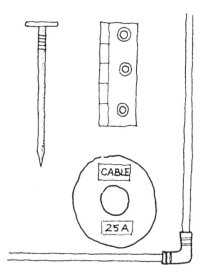

Metal is used in building for nails, fasteners, nuts, bolts, pipes, locks, hinges, reinforcment, wires ...

Avoid using too much metal in your building or you will turn it into a giant antenna!

Are you receiving me ?

carbon monoxide, skin particles, vapours, odours and so on.

Reeds, Rushes and Straw:
Reeds, rushes and straw have always been used both in wall and in roof construction. Their large air content gives them good insulating abilities. Decay in these can be accelerated by the presence of water. Protected from the rain, the natural insulating abilities of these materials can be well exploited.

Cloth and Wool:
Cloth and wool lend softness and warmth to interiors. Wool has natural insulating abilities derived from its natural oil content and its ability to trap air. Wool in its natural state is waterproof and can be used to weave tent coverings. Cloth can be used in screens and for wall coverings. Cloth impregnated with oil was commonly used to make windows before glass become readily available. Canvas can be used to make light coverings for frames and can be treated to make it waterproof.

Products Generally
Apart from the selection of particular materials for your home you will also be selecting particular products such as windows, doors, heating units, insulation, sanitary fittings, taps, paints and so on. These will be produced by various manufacturers and wherever possible you should choose items that are readily available locally. Some items will have to be ordered specially however, either direct from the manufacturer or from an agent.

The products you select for use should be examined beforehand wherever possible. This can normally be done at builders merchants, shops, showrooms and in buildings that are under construction or even completed. Catalogues for most building products are readily available and these normally contain a wealth of information on sizes, weights, performance and price. Information of this nature should be stored in your *Materials & Products File* along with any samples you obtain.

Comparing building products is an essential exercise if quality and value for money are to be properly assessed. Many products are made to conform to Standards such as the British or Irish Standard - B.S. and I.S. - or else have obtained an Agrement Certificate. If such is the case, these products have been tested by a relevant authority, have been considered to properly conform to their standards and carry a mark indicating this. Availability is another important consideration when selecting products. It is no

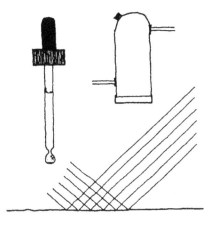

Use as little water as possible to make your building fabric ... though, water is good for ... storing and moving heat and reflecting solar radiation.

Air is an excellent insulator ... if you can stop it moving!
Air is also an excellent way of keeping an internal environment clean.

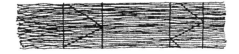

Reeds, rushes, straw and wool are all excellent insulators.

use selecting a product if it is not easily obtainable in the area where you wish to build.

Cost is obviously another important factor. Where a low-cost and possibly inferior product is being selected for use on the basis of economy, you should bear in mind that it might need replacing at some time in the future. It is important to remember that some products are easier to replace than others. For example, if you opt for cheap windows and these need to be replaced it could cause significant disruption in the home. On the other hand, if you opt for a low-cost flooring product such as plywood, this can fairly easily be upgraded at a later date by laying a higher quality finish over it. Generally, the most realistic cost savings can be achieved in the area of finishing materials and products. It makes no sense to skimp on structural materials, windows, insulation and external roof coverings.

Labour is always a significant proportion of building costs. When choosing products bear in mind the amount of work involved in using these. Even if you plan on doing a significant amount of work yourself, it is important to be aware of the amount of time you will need to devote to this. In all creative projects, the time required for finishing inevitably is greater than one imagines. However it should be said that this time is always well spend and yields enormous pleasure over a long period.

Wherever possible standard products should be selected for use rather than having products made to order. This is particularly true of items such as windows and doors.

Products

Concrete Blocks:

Concrete blocks are used to build walls. They are made either solid or hollow and are available in a range of standard sizes. The most commonly used block is the 100mm one. The overall measurements of this block are 100mm wide, 450mm long and 225mm high. Hollow concrete blocks are 225mm wide and are the same length and height as solid ones.

Concrete blocks are factory made by mixing sand, cement and aggregate together and pouring the mixture into a mould and leaving it to set. Blocks are very heavy, weighing up to three stone each when dry. Blocks are not waterproof and they absorb moisture. They are very efficient conductors of heat making them very cold to the touch.

Select products for use in your building that are available locally.

Check out all products before purchase!

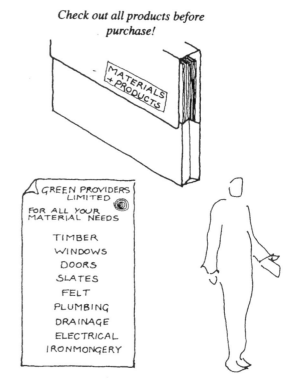

The Cost of Construction is made up of: The Cost of Materials & Products Plus The Cost of Labour

Economise wisely! Don't skimp on -Plumbing, Heating & Ventilation, Electrical Services, Windows, Foundations

Use standard items wherever possible, especially ... windows and doors.

Because they weigh so much, buildings made from concrete blockwork require very substantial foundations. In addition to this, because any movement in a block wall can cause cracking, it is critical that no settlement occurs in these foundations. This is particularly important where foundations are laid over any type of artificial fill.

Concrete blocks are delivered to building sites on pallets. The trucks making these deliveries have are very heavy in themselves and are made heavier still by the loads they carry. They are usually equipped with off-loading mechanisms. It is important, in any building project involving blockwork, that the truck making the delivery can get as close to the location of the work as possible on a reasonably substantial road surface. As many as 2500 standard blocks might be required for an average size dwelling.

Decorative type concrete blocks are designed to be left bare when constructed. Care needs to be taken with this type of blockwork as any mistakes made will remain exposed to view forever. It is also necessary to avoid cutting such blocks to make them fit. This requires that the overall size of the building be made to conform to an exact number of blocks. Needless to say, this is very difficult.

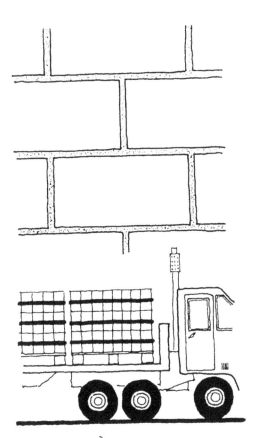

Concrete Block Transportation System

Reinforced Concrete:
The use of reinforced concrete in house construction is normally confined to the creation of foundations and floor slabs. Where it is used for foundations the concrete is poured into a prepared trench and the sides of the trench act as the formwork to hold the concrete until it sets. Steel bars are usually set into the trench beforehand and the concrete mix is poured is over them. The steel reinforces the concrete and allows it to withstand tensile loading. Concrete in many ways is ideal for foundations as it will conform to the shape of the trench easily, can be made level before it sets and provides a good base for building off. Best of all, the foundations will be covered up after they are made and you will never have to see them again!

Reinforced concrete is also used for making ground floor slabs. It is normally laid onto a bed of compacted stones, called hardcore, that has been smoothed over with a layer of sand. Before a concrete ground floor slab can be laid any pipes that need to pass through it have to be installed. These pipes might be drainage pipes from sinks and toilets and the water supply pipe coming into the house.

Concrete, even though it can be made waterproof, is best considered as not being so. Because slabs are more or less in direct contact with the ground they have to be protected from any possible moisture penetration. Usually, plastic

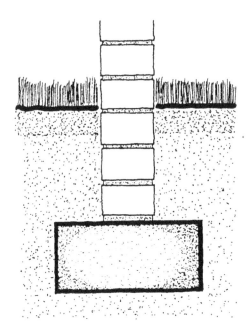

The proper place for concrete is ... under the ground!

sheeting is used to do this. This plastic sheeting -
usually called the damp proof membrane or DPM - is
laid on top of the sand and the concrete is poured on
top of this. Where the damp proof membrane has a joint
in it, or it is interrupted by a pipe going through it, there
is a likelihood of damp penetration unless extreme care
is taken.

To 'pour' a concrete ground floor slab, a mould is
required at the sides of it to contain the wet mix until it
has set. Sometimes this is done with temporary wooden
formwork or shuttering and sometimes the outside
walls are built up off the foundations as far as the top of
the proposed slab and these are used to contain the wet
mix. Steel reinforcing bars are laid in over the hardcore
beforehand.

As concrete dries and sets, a considerable amount of
the water used in making it has to evaporate. The bulk
of this evaporation takes place very quickly after
pouring but for it to completely dry takes a
considerable time. Concrete is a naturally cold material
and it conducts heat very well. If a floor slab is heated
from within the house, it will continually conduct heat
away to its colder side. Oftentimes, insulation is placed
under ground floor slabs to minimise this heat loss.

Because it is laid onto the earth, reinforced concrete
ground floor slabs can trap the natural emissions of
radon gas that normally are blown away by the wind
when they emerge from the ground. Instead, these
emissions, where they occur, are trapped by the
concrete lid that they encounter. The radon gas will
then find its way through cracks or holes in the
concrete slab and penetrate the house where it may
become trapped inside the building. Radon gas is a
natural radiation that occurs particularly where there is
granite present. If trapped inside a building however,
radon gas can be a serious hazard to the occupants. It is
only by constructing a complicated and expensive
mechanically ventilated radon sump under the slab that
concrete slabs can be safely used in radon prone areas.

Apart from its use to make foundations and floor slabs,
reinforced concrete is also used to make ring beams.
Ring beams are bands of reinforced concrete that are
made on top of concrete block walls, directly under
where the roof rests. The purpose of these ring beams is
to tie the entire wall structure into a 'ring' so that the
loads coming onto the wall from the roof can be
transferred efficiently to the ground. These loads come
onto the wall at an angle and tend to push the wall out
at the top. The ring beam resists this tendency because

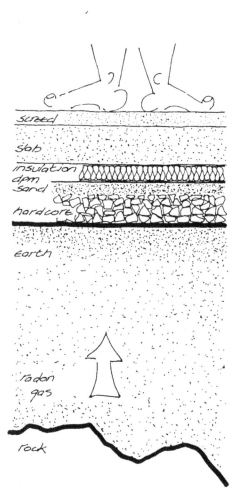

*Beware of radon gas penetration
through concrete ground floor slabs!*

it spreads the load away from the point of contact and ensures the structure is stable. Ring beams are cast on top of prepared walls with temporary shuttering at the sides to contain the concrete until it has set.

Another use of concrete in home building is for the making of hearths for fireplaces. Even in dwellings largely constructed from timber, an incombustible material such as concrete will be required when a conventional fireplace is being provided.

The appeal of reinforced concrete as a building material partly lies in its ability to take almost any shape. Once a mould is made for the wet mix it can be poured into this and left to set. Concrete slabs are also a convenience for builders, giving them a hard and even surface off of which to work. To employ reinforced concrete in situations other that for foundations, floor slabs, ring beams and hearths, temporary support for the wet concrete is needed. This can be expensive and requires a certain amount of skill to construct. Wet concrete is extremely heavy and consequently requires very strong supporting formwork to hold it. Columns and beams all must have formwork made for them to support the concrete until it is dry and hard. This hardening process can take quite some time to be complete.

Precast Concrete:
Because of the problems associated with containing wet concrete until it has set, many concrete products are premade in factories using moulds. These kind of concrete products are known as precast concrete. They include concrete window cills, lintols, fire hoods, kerbs and even floor slabs.

Concrete Roof Tiles:
These are factory made, with a colour additive included in the mix. They are available in a variety of shapes. They are quite a heavy but economical form of roof finish, though are not very attractive.

Clay Bricks & Blocks:
Originally developed commercially as a cheap walling material, clay bricks nowadays are quite expensive. One third the size of concrete blocks - 75x225x100mm - a standard brick can be comfortably held in one hand. Quite a degree of skill is required to lay bricks as they are normally left exposed to view.

Because they are kiln-baked and all the water has been driven from them, clay bricks are quite a warm material with good heat storage capacity. It is ironical that they are often used on the outside face of a building when their

Concrete slabs are a convenience ... for builders.

Beware of concrete ring beams ... these can be prone to condensation.

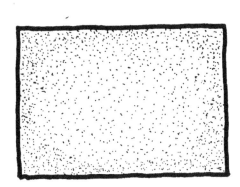

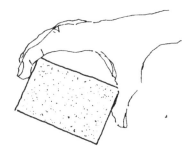

Bricks Are:
Warm
Breathable
Manageable
Attractive
Versatile
Small
Light

heat storage ability makes them better suited for internal use. Installed in the floor or as a wall in a sunspace, bricks will absorb a considerable amount of solar heat. Similarly, when used in a fireplace or stove they will warm up readily and radiate out their heat. Bricks can also 'breathe' and are hygroscopic, making them very suitable where a breathable construction is being designed.

Different qualities of standard bricks are available varying in colour, texture and in the way they have been manufactured. These variations are reflected in their cost. 'Overburnt' bricks or 'seconds' are sometimes available direct from the factory at a reduced cost. 'Specials' are also made allowing cills and decorative effects to be achieved though these are expensive. Firebricks are made from special clays to withstand high temperatures. They are used for firebacks and as linings for fireboxes.

Hollow, extruded clay blocks are also manufactured. Where internal walls are built from these, the air within them can be warmed to create warm walls that provide radiant heat to the interior of a building.

Clay Roof Tiles:
Although they are more expensive than concrete varieties, clay roof tiles will enhance the appearance of a building considerably. They are available in a wide range of colours and shapes and are relatively light also.

Decorative ridge tiles, hip tiles and edge tiles are also manufactured. These can be used to excellent effect and can even be employed decoratively where concrete tiles provide the main roof covering. Flat clay tiles can also be used as an external wall finish.

Other Clay Products:
Chimney pots, flue liners, pipes, kerbs, pots and decorative edgings are all clay products that are generally available.

Sanitary fittings, sinks, shower trays are all made from clay.

Clay Tiles:
A huge variety of clay tiles is available on the market. These range from glazed tiles suitable for finishing walls to the popular quarry floor tiles. Ceramic tiles are often used to face brick stoves.

Clay roof tiles being laid on traditional Latvian log house - Co. Mayo, Ireland

Slates:

At one time a very common roofing material, nowadays natural slates are quite expensive. They are available however and if used they will give your roof an excellent appearance especially if some red clay ridge and hip tiles are combined with them.

Reconstituted natural slates are also made. These are produced by mixing ground slate with a synthetic resin. Less expensive than the real thing, they offer a good alternative. Fibercement slates are also made. These lack the body and texture of natural or reconstituted varieties and are somewhat bland in appearance.

Slated roof on modern 'cottage' dwelling

All types of slates are suitable for use as a wall cladding also. Slate is oftentimes used as a hardwearing floor finish and to make both internal and external cills for windows.

Dampproof Courses and Membranes:

In loadbearing construction and where concrete ground floor slabs are created, the possibility of water making its way into the structure has to be prevented at all costs. This is normally done by using dampproof courses and membranes - DPCs & DPMs.

These are made in a range of widths, lengths and thicknesses. Because they play such a vital role in keeping a building dry, quality products should always be selected.

Vapour Barriers:

Vapour barriers function to prevent airborne moisture from passing through timber framed external walls to the exterior of the building. They are in fact, plastic sheets which are placed immediately behind the internal wall finish. If vapour barriers are being used a good quality product should be selected. Plasterboards are also manufactured with an in-built vapour barrier in the form of a thin aluminium foil covering.

Breathable felt sheathing on EconoSpace prior to installation of cedar external cladding

Vapour barriers are extremely difficult to install correctly as the theory of their use requires that a complete seal be made, with no gaps or tears occurring in them.

Flashings:

Flashings are strips of metal, usually lead, that are used to seal junctions between roofs and chimneys, to form roof valleys and to protect awkward junctions from water penetration. As such junctions are oftentimes visible, a quality product should always be chosen.

Composite materials and patented products, for use as flashings, are on the market and these should always be chosen with care.

Windows:

Windows should be selected for their durability, appearance, airtightness and for the quality of the ironmongery they are fitted with. It is essential to examine windows at first hand before making a final selection. Manufacturers catalogues will list the standard sizes that they produce and wherever possible these sizes should be adhered to when selecting windows for your particular design. Standard sizes are generally cheaper and more readily available than 'specials', that is windows made up specially to a particular size. Small manufacturers and joinery shops oftentimes make windows to order. Small operations of this type rarely produce catalogues of course. However a personal visit to the workshop will reveal much and such a course might prove the most economical and satisfying way of obtaining the windows for your building.

Windows are one item in a building that should not be selected solely on the basis of cost. It is far better to select a superior product as replacing windows is a disruptive and expensive business.

Timber windows have very good insulating qualities. Kiln dried, pressure treated softwood is well suited to making window frames. Cedarwood, though commonly used, is too soft a wood for this purpose. Hardwood frames in mahogany, teak or iroko are also common, though the use of these rainforest timbers may not be desirable. Softwood windows from a reputable manufacturer will be found more than satisfactory in use.

Carefully consider the type of finish you wish to have on your timber windows. A decision to use a breathable paint will involve repainting every 4-5 years. A stained finish will also involve restaining at similar intervals though this is a less precise job and so is quicker to carry out.

Aluminium windows should not be considered unless they incorporate a 'thermal break' within the frame. This is an insulating material that is packed into the hollow frame to prevent condensation. Without it, the cold inside face of the frame will develop condensation especially in kitchen and bathroom areas. Aluminium windows are oftentimes 'anodised', a process whereby the outer face of the window frame is coated with a colour. This is usually dark brown, though other colours can also be produced. PVC coated aluminium windows are also manufactured.

Timber windows are warm ... but, avoid using tropical hardwoods and, use breathable paint or stain ... and insist on good catches, latches and hinges.

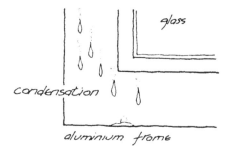

Beware of aluminium windows ... these can be prone to condensation.

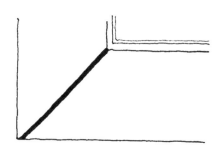

PVC windows are very chunky in appearance ... but if you are going to use them, make sure that the corner joints are well made.

For all types of windows make sure that the catches, latches and hinges are neat and strong.

Only very few openable windows are needed in any home ... and, consider using trickle ventilators for the small amounts of fresh air that are needed for ventilation purposes.

PVC windows are made of extruded plastic sections with a steel core to stiffen the plastic. These sections are usually fairly bulky in size. To make up a complete window, straight PVC sections are miter cut to form corners. These joints are then welded to seal them. If PVA windows are being considered for use close examination should be paid to these joints to ensure that a complete seal is achieved. Should such joints leak, the steel core is liable to rust. Coloured PVA windows are prone to fade in direct sunlight. Further effects of sunlight cannot be discounted on these type of frames.

For all types of windows the ironmongery controlling the opening and closing of the windows needs careful examination. Hinges, catches and clasps should be of obvious robust quality and be neatly incorporated into the frame. The catch should hold the window tightly shut so that no draught whatsoever can penetrate to the interior of the building. 'Tilt and turn' windows have become very popular, though it is impossible to make small adjustments to the amount the window is open. If fresh air is being brought into the building through independent ventilators, windows will function to light the interior and to provide a means of escape in the event of fire. Otherwise the window will remain closed the majority of the time. If there are several windows in a room it is really only necessary that one of them be openable. Some manufacturers produce windows with 'trickle ventilators' - an adjustable slot allowing fresh air to come through the frame without the window itself being open.

Double glazed windows have superior insulating qualities to single glazed ones. Because double glazing units are economical to produce in large sizes, this has tended to make for large areas of plain glass without dividing 'mullions'. Such windows can look very bland. Some manufacturers incorporate false mullions into double glazed windows to overcome this. If you are thinking of using this type of effect it is wise to take a good look at a sample window before you finally make up your mind.

Patent glazing is a form of window framing that used long sections of aluminium or timber and large areas of glass. It is normally used in roof areas to provide economical rooflights. It should be remembered that the heat losses from roof glazing can be considerable and that this type of glazing is very difficult to screen or insulate from the cold night sky. Patent glazing can also be used vertically and is an economical way of providing the large glazed areas needed to capture solar heat.

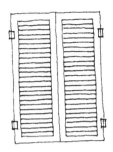

Double glazing gives excellent insulation ... also, consider installing timber shutters internally for night-time use.

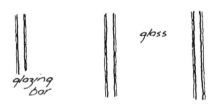

glass

glazing bar

Patent Glazing is an economical way of creating large areas of glass to capture solar radiation.

Salvaged Georgian window being installed in EconoSpace

Glass:

Glass for building comes in several qualities. Ordinary glass or float glass is brittle but relatively cheap. Tempered or safety glass is up to five times stronger than float glass and disentigrates into harmless pieces if broken. Laminated glass is made up of several layers of toughened glass with tough plastic sandwiched between them. The plastic holds the glass together if it gets broken.

Because it is not robust, glass has to be set into a frame when it is being used. These frames can be of metal, wood or plastic. The type of glass that is chosen for any particular window or door depends on the location and the likelihood of breakage in normal usage. As a general rule ordinary glass should never be used in internal glazed doors as this is far too dangerous. If you want to put your mind at rest about the glass in your house for once and for all, select tempered glass for use. If the worst happens and a window or glass panel gets broken, no one will get badly cut. Laminated glass is ideal for use where there are large expanses of glass. It is also used in skylights for safety reasons. Georgian wired glass is glass that has a fine wire mesh incorporated into it. This prevents the glass from falling apart it it gets broken. It is normally used in skylights or for glazed panels in firedoors.

Glass for windows is normally made colourless and clear which means that you can see through it. It is also made very flat so that what you see through the window will not be distorted. Obscure glass is glass that has some kind of decorative pattern in it that obscures the view through it. Coloured glass is made by the adding mineral oxides or other substances during manufacturing. Coloured glass colours the light passing through it and it is especially useful in locations where it is not important to actually see through the glass but where light is important - on a stairway for example. Coloured light can be used to create interesting spatial effects and feelings. Decorative stained glass panels in windows and doors will enhance any design.

Glass allows almost all the solar heat radiation that strikes it to pass through it. Once this heat radiation is inside the glass and it strikes an object, the heat will be released. This low temperature heat can then only escape through the glass by being conducted away, not by transmission. For this reason windows are double glazed - interposing a layer of air between them. Building Regulations often require that double glazed units be installed in new buildings.

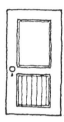

Safety glass should always be used in doors and rooflights ... or in situations where the glass might get broken and cause injury.

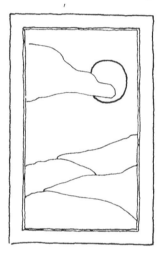

Coloured or stained glass can be used to create interesting and pleasant natural lighting.

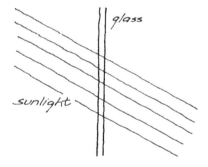

When sunlight passes through glass it releases its heat energy which then cannot escape again.

Special coatings are available for double glazed units that provides the inner surface of the glass with low-emissivity. What this means is that heat trying to escape through the window will be reflected back into the building. This type of glass is claimed to be as efficient as triple glazed units.

Other Glazing Materials:
Extruded plastic glazing materials are readily available. These range from simple corrugated perspex sheets to sophisticated triple layer products that are lightweight and clear. These types of products can offer good economies where an undistorted view is not critical - in overhead lights, for covered drying, play and parking areas, for simple greenhouses and so on.

Doors:
Doors can be broken down into two categories - external and internal doors. As with windows, doors are made in timber, aluminium and PVC and manufacturers produce catalogues illustrating their standard products. Alternatively doors can be made up specially.

Timber doors are more robust than either aluminium or PVC varieties. They are also more visually pleasing. Well seasoned softwood is frequently used for doors and hardwood types are also available. The type of finish chosen for timber doors, especially external ones, should be carefully considered.

External doors, especially your front door, will be a very conspicuous part of your home and so should be carefully chosen. A heavy timber door should be hung with strong hinges and fitted with a good lock which will hold the door tightly closed. This, of course, is true of aluminium and PVC doors also. The type of lock you wish to use should be suited to the type of door you wish to use. Some types of locks require the door to be drilled and morticed in order to properly fit them. It is worth giving external locks some thought, both from the security point of view as well from the point of view of casual coming and going. If you wish to use an automatic closer on external doors, to prevent excessive heat loss because of doors left open, make sure the door you choose can take such a closer. A good draught seal around any external door is very important, particularly at the bottom.

Glazed panels and letterboxes can be incorporated into external doors though oftentimes these are better located to one side or above the door. An old fashioned knocker can easily be installed in a timber door to good effect.

Where large glazed areas are created for trapping solar radiation, some form of shutter or screen should be installed to prevent heat being lost at night.

EconoSpace with salvaged windows and door

Handmade half-door in EconoSpace

Internal doors are subject to far less wear than external doors though a solid door is always preferable to a lightweight one. Internal doors are nearly always made of wood, either solid timber or a material such as Medium Density Fibreboard (MDF). Hollow doors, usually called flush doors, are faced with plywood and are quite lightweight. A wide range of styles are available from these plain 'flush' doors to elaborate panelled doors.

Internal doors play a large part in creating the style of your interior and they should be chosen with this is mind. Similarly, the type of locks you choose will be important. How your internal doors are finished is also critical to your internal decor. Also, the doorframe and the 'architrave' - the board that masks the joint between the doorframe and the wall - should be chosen to match the style of door you are using.

Different types of doors can be used in different parts of the house. For example, bedroom doors can be less elaborate than the doors in the more 'public' parts of the house. Double doors, that is doors comprising two panels that are hinged separately, give a generously wide opening allowing rooms to be opened up to hallways or to other rooms. Double doors are also effective as front doors, where one of the panels can function to cater for everyday traffic.

Sliding screens are large doors arranged so as to slide open. They can be arranged to be completely concealed when they do this. Japanese style sliding screens are made of paper and wood and are therefore very light. So light, in fact that they simply glide on a grooved track in the floor and require no sliding mechanism. This would not be possible with heavier sliding screens and a sliding mechanism would be needed at the top to support these.

Sliding doors are a convenient way of connecting living spaces with a verandah or patio space. Where these are being chosen, quality should be sought, particularly in the door's draught excluding ability and its locking capability. Safety glass should also be used. This is true of all doors, whether internal or external, that contain glass panels.

EconoSpace with salvaged glazing units in purpose made frames

Glazed sliding doors

Rainwater Goods:

Gutters and downpipes are known as rainwater goods. These are items that can have very little attention paid to them even though they are a very prominent part of any building. Plastic, aluminium and cast iron rainwater goods are available in standard lengths and sections in a variety of styles.

Plastic RWG have the advantage of needing no painting and of being efficient in terms of carrying water off the roof down to the ground. Plastic gutters, downpipes and brackets should be chosen for their strength and for the quality of their appearance. Aluminium 'seamless' gutters are frequently used, though aluminium is very soft and can be bent or dinged very easily. Aluminium downpipes can also be noisy in use. Cast iron is superior in every way to plastic or aluminium though its expense will deter most people from choosing it.

Galvanised iron gutters and downpipes are produced for agricultural buildings. These can offer a low-cost alternative to the domestic varieties. Galvanised iron, due to its zinc coating, needs to weather for several years before it can be painted.

Insulation:

One of the most critical choices that will be made in regard to products will be the selection of insulation. Choices range from treated cellulose to fibre glass to natural cork. In making your choice, the long term efficiency of the material will be an important factor as will be its cost. Because it is normally incorporated into the structure, installing a quality product is very important. Insulation as we know it, is a relatively new concept in dwellings and many products are synthetically produced and may have adverse effects on the internal environment of the home.

Of the natural insulations available, cork is the most well known. Made from the bark of the cork oak tree, cork insulation products are expensive, however desirable they might be. Cellulose fibre, another wood based insulation product, is cheaper than cork and offers the best opportunity of using a natural material. Essentially recycled newsprint that has been treated against fire and rodent attack, cellulose fibre is available as a loose-fill or in board form. The loose-fill variety is sprayed into a suitable wall cavity or attic space. This type of insulation provides better insulating performance in comparison to a similar thickness of fibreglass wool.

Perlite and vermiculite are other natural insulating materials that are both very fire resistant. However they

Wherever possible, rainwater should be harvested and stored ... if this is to be consumed both the roof covering, the rainwater gear and the storage vessels should not add any toxic substances to the water

A thatched roof requires no rainwater gear but care should be taken to direct runoff away from the building

Insulation Types

Cellulose Fibre
Cork
Air
Reeds, Rushes & Straw
Corrugated Cardboard
Wool
Feathers
Sawdust
Timber
Perlite
Vermiculite
Fibreglass
Mineral Wool
Urea Formaldehyde
Expanded Polystyrene

Make sure that your chosen insulation will do you no harm!

The best insulating materials have a low density ... with lots of air in them.

Insulating materials are not in themselves heatstores.

are not readily available commercially. When thinking of insulation it is important to remember exactly what makes a material an insulator - the fact that it does not conduct heat very well. Usually this means that the material has a low density and that it contains a lot of air. It is the air in fact that contributes most to insulating ability. Thus, corrugated cardboard, animal fleece, reeds, rushes, newspapers and feathers are all good insulators. If you are on an extremely tight budget you could insulate your building with flattened cardboard boxes salvaged from the supermarket!

Fibreglass, rockwool or mineral wool are all names applied to the commonest of the synthetic type insulation products. Manufactured from glass or mineral fibres and combined with synthetic resins, these products are available in rolls or in board form. Because their fibres are irritating to the skin, fibreglass insulating materials need to be carefully handled and should not be inhaled. Obviously it is important that once installed, loose fibres cannot penetrate into the interior of the dwelling. Fibreglass is fireproof but care needs to be taken that it does not get wet.

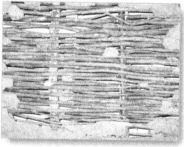

Expanded polystyrene, styrofoam and aeroboard are all names for the same thing - a synthetic, lightweight, water resistant material available in board form. Styrofoam is much used to insulate block cavity walls as it can withstand the dampness it is likely to encounter there. 'Green' varieties of styrofoam are now produced that are supposedly CFC free in themselves and in their manufacturing process. Fire is a major hazard with this material as toxic gases are given off when it burns.

Urea-formaldehyde foam and urethane foam are synthetic products also prone to give off toxic vapours when burned. Whatever the insulating merits of such materials their basic nature has to be suspect. It is important to remember that some heat storage capacity is an important part of any building. Insulation has no ability to hold heat, all it does is impede its passage to the cold exterior.

Plasterboard:
Plasterboards come in a variety of sizes up to 3000mm long and 1200mm wide. They also come in various thicknesses from 10mm up to 20mm. Plasterboards can be cut very easily with a fine tooth saw where full size boards cannot be used. Boards are faced with paper which can be painted directly or they can be finished with a thin 'skim' of wet plaster. They are normally used for finishing walls and ceilings.

Clay plaster - mixed by hand, or foot - and applied to wattles or lathes, will prove far superior to any plasterboard

100

Plasterboards with an integral vapour barrier are also made. This consists of an aluminium foil backing that functions to prevent airborne moisture from passing through a wall to the outside of the building. Aluminium also acts as a reflector, preventing heat from escaping.

Decorative Plaster:
A wide range of moulded decorative plaster products are available. These can be applied to walls and ceilings to enhance their appearance.

Metal Decking:
In its commonest form metal decking is known as corrugated iron. Popular for use in agricultural buildings, for sheds and outhouses, it offers a very cheap way to clad walls and roofs. Corrugated iron is produced with a galvanised zinc finish to inhibit rusting. This can be painted, but only after it has weathered for several years. The biggest drawback with corrugated iron is the fact that it is prone to pick up electromagnetic radiation and to cause disturbance within the internal environment because of this.

Aluminium decking is also made and this is available in a variety of colour finishes. More expensive than corrugated iron, aluminium does not attract or transmit electromagnetic radiation. All metal decking needs to be used very carefully to avoid setting up condensation problems. If it is used purely as an 'overcoat' for a building however these problems can easily be avoided. All metal deckings are made in a range of standard lengths and widths.

Paper:
Paper has all sorts of uses in building. It is a good insulator, can be used as a wall covering, can be used in lightweight screens and so on. Heavy gauge papers are used to make building papers which control the passage of moisture in an out of wall constructions. These allow water vapour to pass through them but inhibit the passage of liquid water. Paper is traditionally used in Japan to make internal sliding screens.

Felt:
Felts are products that combine some form of fibrous material with bitumen to make flexible and waterproof sheets. Produced in rolls, felt is used as an underlay beneath roof coverings or as a protectiive covering for timber frame buildings. Exterior grade roofing felts are also made. These are used on flat roofs.

A tin roof is a viable option for cost-conscious sheltermakers

Traditional Mongolian yurts are clad with felt ... this modern yurt is clad in heavy duty canvas

Paints and Finishes:

It is important to remember that internal paints, polishes and other finishes are all materials that you will surround yourself with in your completed home. Oftentimes these substances can emit powerful toxins which can pollute the indoor air.

Wherever possible, choose paints and finishes that have been produced naturally and that give off a pleasant smell. Natural paints and finishes will complement the natural materials that you might otherwise be using. Avoid products that carry any type of warnings on their labels.

Carpets, curtains and other fabrics that you choose should all be scrutinised carefully to ensure they are not harmful. Be particularly vigilant that foam filling in soft furniture is fire resistant.

Appliances:

The selection of appliances such as boilers and so on will be dealt with in the Building Services portion of Volume 2. In general however, it should be remembered that any appliance you install will become part of the internal environment of your home and therefore needs careful scrutiny before a final selection is made.

Selecting Materials & Products

As you begin to examine materials and products you will find yourself drawn to particular ones which you will want to use. Any relevant information that you can gather on these in the form of catalogues, notes, clippings and samples should be stored in your *Materials & Poducts File*. Prices should also be obtained for these and their availability in your area should be confirmed.

All this information will form the basis of the Specification for your home, that is the list of materials and products that you specify for use. This is a vital part of any building project and it will ultimately form the basis of the overall cost of the project. At this stage it will be possible for you to compare various items as to their probable cost. Roof coverings, for example, can be directly compared as to their purchase price. Also, an estimate of how much the roof covering for your building will cost can be calculated by using your floor area estimates.

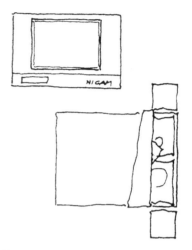

Make sure to select paints and finsihes that are not harmful.

Choose appliances and furnishings as carefully as you would choose materials and products.

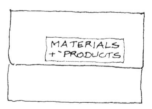

Your Materials & Products File will form the basis of the Specification for building your home.

It is vital that these types of exercises are carried out early in the project and that decisions in principle are made as to what materials and products you want to use. If the creation of a house is compared to the preparation of a meal, you will get some idea of what this is all about. To prepare a meal, you need to know what is available in the shops and how much everything costs. You also must decide on a menu and select the ingredients to make the dishes you have decided on. You also need to know how much of everything you need. So you make a shopping list, go out and buy everything, take them home and prepare them. If you are cooking on a tight budget you will select your ingredients carefully and keep waste to a minimum. You will also know that the time you spend putting the meal together will make the difference between success and failure.

Now designing a house is not a lot different. You decide on your menu (the type of house you want). You find out what ingredients (materials) are available and you find out how much these cost (your budget). You make your shopping list, buy everything and put all the ingredients together (build). If you are on a tight budget the more carefully you shop the further your money will go.

This is, of course, a highly simplified way of looking at this question but it is nonetheless accurate. In the case of the meal, if someone else is doing the cooking and shopping, the shopping list, the menu and the budget take on added importance. With building the same thing applies - if someone else is building the house they must have a good list of materials and have decided how much of everything is needed. This is why this exercise of deciding on materials and products is so important.

Another important reason for the close examination of materials and products is because the selections you make will decide how your building is going to be put together, or how it is to be constructed.

Summary

Choose building materials and products that will be good for your health.

Use your senses to guide you.

Use materials and products that have not demanded a lot of energy to produce.

Choose materials and products that can be reused or recycled.

Select materials and products that are available locally.

Economise wisely.

Choose appliances and furnishings as carefully as you would choose materials and products.

The materials and products used in sheltermaking should pose no threat to life inside or outside the building

32 Sheltermaker Design Programme
Choosing A Construction Systems

The topic of *Construction* draws together issues covered in *Structure, Environment, H&V, Timberfile* and *Materials & Products*. If these are the 'ingredients' then *Construction* is the recipe itself.

The sequence of decision making in regards your individual project will have begun when you declared your preferences in regards to *Environmental* and *H&V* issues. These decisions are now applied in the selection of a construction system that suits those particular choices.

For example, if you have decided to create a healthy internal environment, to gather and store solar energy, to have high levels of insulation and to use natural materials then your *Construction* options will probably be to build a breathable timber frame on-site; to treat the timber frame with Borax preservative; to use an ample thickness of cellulose or wool insulation or hemp-lime or clay-straw; to gather solar energy; to use wood as the primary [back-up] fuel; to use softwood windows and doors along with natural roofing, paints and finishes.

If these are the 'ingredients' for the meal you wish to prepare then the 'cook' - whether it be you or, more likely, someone else - will have to be skilled in that type of cooking. This is the key issue of natural/sustainable/eco-building - who will/can build it? To put it another way - if you wish to eat healthily you do not go to McDonalds or Burger King for dinner or invite a fast-food chef to prepare you a healthy banquet. The right person for the construction job, when they can be found, might be very expensive, in which case self-building might become an option. To do this a person needs to obtain some training and, when construction gets underway, they must have the time to carry out the work.

All of the required *Materials & Products* with which to build naturally are available on the open market but finding the person/persons to put these together (affordably) and a *Supervisor* to 'sign off' on mortgage certification and draw-down payments are the biggest challenges facing those wishing to build naturally. If these realities are faced now, then the likelihood of finding the right personnel for the planned work will be increased considerably.

The *Construction chapter* details the various 'issues' concerning the topic. Read this, paying particular attention to the details of your preferred construction system. You should also begin enquiries as to who might build and supervise your project when it goes on-site. Outline your preferences on the *Construction Worksheet.*

Next: SDP33 - Services: Plumbing, page 140

Construction

Construction is the process of deciding how your chosen building materials will be joined together to form foundations, walls, floors, roofs, chimneys, doors, windows etc. This process has several functions. Firstly, these materials must be assembled so that the building will stand up and, secondly, this construction must be made warm, dry and weatherproof. A further aim of the construction process is the health and safety of the building occupants. These aims - structural stability, warmth, dryness, weather-tightness, health and safety - are covered by Building Regulations which all new buildings and extensions have to meet. Apart from the need to comply with the Regulations it is assumed that the designer shares the aim of building safely, and healthily.

The topic of construction is revealing in terms of what our homes really mean to us - a particular attitude will have already been declared by selecting particular types of materials from which to make your home. This selection process will in itself have been indicative of the types of internal surfaces that you wish to surround yourself with. In other words, the selection of a particular construction system for your home will stem from choices that are rooted in the sensuous attitude you have towards your home. If you want warm, natural materials as internal surfaces then you have to select a construction system that will allow that. Similarly in terms of heating and ventilation, you have to select a construction system that will allow you create the type of internal environment that will be healthy, warm and clean.

It is vital that construction is seen in the context of particular materials that one wishes to choose and particular design aims that one has declared previously. Otherwise, a decision will be made based on a purely mental approach to the problem and the building that will result will inevitably be dissatisfying when one tries to live within the construction. Homes are for living in and living is a sensuous experience.

The aim of studying the construction process is to decide how your selected Materials & Products can be assembled to meet your design aims and to create a structurally sound, warm, weather-tight, dry and healthy building.

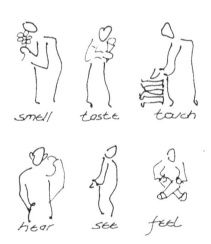

smell   taste   touch

hear   see   feel

By selecting particular Materials & Products with which to construct your home, your sensuous attitude towards the type of building enclosure and internal environment you intend to create, will have been made clear.

Building Regulations

The Irish Building Regulations came into force in 1992. Their purpose is to promote good practice in the design and construction of buildings in the interest of the health, safety and welfare of those who live and work in buildings, to provide for the special needs of the disabled and to provide for the conservation of fuel and energy and the efficient use of resources.

The Regulations set out the basic requirements to be observed in the design and construction of buildings. They apply to all new buildings and to extensions, material alterations and certain changes of use of existing buildings. The detailed technical content of the Regulations is provided in 12 Technical Guidance Documents published by the Department of the Environment. These are intended to assist building designers in the proper application of the 'functional requirements' of the Regulations.

The 12 Technical Guidance Documents are as follows:

A - *Structure*
B - *Fire*
C - *Site Preparation & Resistance to Moisture*
D - *Workmanship*
E - *Sound*
F - *Ventilation*
G - *Hygiene*
H - *Drainage & Waste Disposal*
J - *Heat Producing Appliances*
K - *Stairways, Ramps & Guards*
L - *Conservation of Fuel & Energy*
M - *Access for Disabled People*

The 12 Technical Guidance Documents set out the various requirements under the Building Regulations and also give guidance on the measures necessary to comply with them. While this guidance cites examples of how the various Regulations can be met, flexibility is allowed for in that individual solutions can also be applied as long as these meet with the basic requirements of the Regulations.

The primary responsibility for complying with the Regulations rests with the parties directly concerned - meaning the building owners, designers and constructors. In effect, Local Authorities will monitor the application of the Regulations primarily by inspecting buildings under construction. A "Commencement Notice" must be submitted not less than a week and not more than three weeks in advance of building work commencing so that the Authorities

Building Regulations are intended to promote good practice in the design and construction of buildings.

BUILDING REGULATIONS, 1991

TECHNICAL GUIDANCE DOCUMENT A STRUCTURE

INTRODUCTION

This document has been published by the Minister for the Environment under article 5 of the Building Regulations, 1991, for the purpose of providing guidance with regard to compliance with the requirements of Part A of the First Schedule to the Regulations. Where works are carried out in accordance with this guidance, this will, prima facie, indicate compliance with these requirements.

This document should be read in conjunction with the Regulations.

Guidance contained in this document with respect to the use of a particular material, method of construction, standard or other specification does not preclude the use of any other suitable material, method of construction, standard or specification.

TECHNICAL SPECIFICATIONS

Building Regulations are made for specific purposes i.e. health, safety and welfare of persons, energy conservation and the special needs of disabled people. Technical Specifications (including Harmonised European Standards, European Technical Approvals, National Standards and Agrément Certificates) are relevant to the extent that they relate to these considerations. Technical Specifications may also address other aspects of performance not covered by the Regulations.

The references in this document to named Technical Specifications, or to materials and methods which are likely to be suitable for the purposes of the Regulations, are not exclusive and other materials and methods may be suitable in particular circumstances. A reference to a Technical Specification is to the latest edition (including any amendments...

MATERIALS AND WORKMANSHIP

Under Part D of the First Schedule to the Regulations, building work must be carried out with proper materials and in a workmanlike manner. Relevant guidance is contained in Technical Guidance Document D.

Part D of the First Schedule to the Regulations defines "proper materials" as materials which are fit for the use for which they are intended and for the conditions in which they are to be used, and includes materials which:

(a) bear a CE Mark in accordance with the provisions of the Construction Products Directive (89/106/EEC); or

(b) comply with an appropriate harmonised standard, European technical approval or national technical specification as defined in article 4(2) of the Construction Products Directive (89/106/EEC); or

(c) comply with an appropriate Irish Standard or Irish Agrément Board Certificate or with an alternative national technical specification of any Member State of the European Community, which provides in use an equivalent level of safety and suitability.

The purpose of Building Regulations are basically the same everywhere - to promote good practice in the design and construction of buildings in the interests of the health, safety and welfare of those who live and work in them. Refer to your local Planning Authority for details of the Regulations in force in your area.

If you wish to design and build sensibly and carefully, you will be working within the aims of the Building Regulations - and probably exceeding their requirements!

can, as necessary, exercise their monitoring powers.

In terms of individual house designs, the requirements of the Regulations in regards to *Structure, Heating & Ventilation* were discussed in *Volume 1*. Further information on complying with the Regulations is contained in this *Part* and in subsequent *Parts of Volume 2*. However, it is important that these Regulations do not become intimidating to you, or cause you unnecessary worry. In essence, if you want to build soundly, you will be building in accordance with the Regulations. In fact, in many cases you will be going beyond their requirements.

At this stage of the design process the critical decision is the one to be made in regards to the type of structure and materials you wish to surround yourself with in your home. Once that decision is made, compliance with the Regulations is relatively straightforward and is dealt with at the Working Drawing stage of the design process.

Structures

All building structures can be described as being:

Loadbearing
Frame
Or
A combination of:
Loadbearing & Frame

Loadbearing structures are structures created with heavy materials such as stone, brick and concrete block. Frame structures are structures created with a steel or timber 'frame'. Structures created using a combined system would generally consist of loadbearing walls and a frame roof. Generally speaking all buildings consist of foundations, walls, floors and a roof. This *Part* covers each of these areas individually.

Foundations

All building structures require some sort of foundation to support them. The type of foundation required for your building will depend on the chosen structural system and on the type of ground on which the structure will stand.

Foundations can be made from concrete, stone or even wood. They function to spread the weight of the building over as large an area of ground as possible.

Loadbearing structures are normally built on continuous

Note
It has been pointed out that all structures are, in fact, Loadbearing. This is correct. In these Handbooks however, I have intended Loadbearing to mean 'masonry' ... i.e. heavyweight construction.

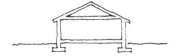

Generally, all building structures consist of foundations, walls, floors and a roof.

All structures require some form of foundation under them to spread their weight over a reasonably large area. Normally foundations are buried in the earth to protect them.

foundations called strip footings. Framed structures only need foundations where the frames come to the ground - pad foundations. Pad foundations are the easiest type of foundations to construct. Strip footings are a little more difficult requiring more excavation and are most suited to level sites. However, load bearing structures can be constructed on pad foundations with a little ingenuity. This has the advantage of keeping the walls mostly out of the ground where they are subject to damp penetration.

The size and depth of all foundations depends on the weight of the building they will be supporting as well as on the nature of the soil in which they are placed. Most ground can easily carry the weight of a house without any problem.

The layer of earth on which foundations rest is called the Bearing Stratum. This can be anywhere in the ground below the topsoil which comprises the first six inches. Normally foundations are placed deeper than this to protect them from frost damage and the effects of soil erosion due to rain and water percolation. The top of foundations are normally covered by eighteen inches to two feet of soil. The foundations themselves are usually a foot deep, meaning that foundation trenches or holes need to be dug about 3 feet or 1M down into the ground. The width of foundations depends on the width of the wall or post that the foundation is carrying. Three times the width of the wall or post is normal.

Foundation holes and trenches should be kept dry before the foundation material is placed in them. This can be done more easily for holes than for trenches. If there is seepage into the trenches from the surrounding ground, the reason for this should be discovered. Any flow of water through the ground in which the foundations are placed will erode the bearing stratum. Any flow of this nature needs to be permanently diverted around the excavations before the foundations are laid.

Settlement

Settlement is the slow compaction of the ground under the weight of a building. Ground that has been 'made-up' using rubble or fill is particularly prone to this. Settlement is a problem almost entirely confined to modern loadbearing structures, that is, buildings constructed from concrete blocks or bricks. Such buildings, because they have no tensile strength, are

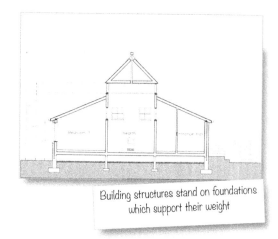

Building structures stand on foundations which support their weight

Foundation holes and trenches should always be kept dry before the concrete is placed in them.

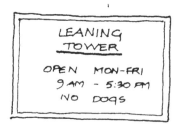

Beware of building on fill or made up ground ... settlement can easily occur.

very stiff and brittle and will crack if there is any movement in the foundation.

Foundations for loadbearing structures are regularly made larger than is necessary to transfer the massive load of the building safely to the ground. The reason for this relates not to whether a building will stand up or fall down but to finishes. If walls are plastered internally and/or externally, any slight settlement will cause cracks to appear. Internally this can be unsightly. Externally it can lead to water penetration as well as being unsightly. To counteract settlement, massive foundations are used.

With more flexible structures, such as those created using timber, settlement is far less common because these buildings are physically not as heavy as loadbearing ones. In an extreme case where there is settlement in the foundations of a frame structure this can be absorbed by the structure very easily without causing cracking.

Concrete Foundations

Concrete is the most commonly used foundation material. It is very suitable for this job as the supporting formwork for the wet concrete can be the foundation trench or hole itself. For strip footings on ground that is not level, the foundation trench has to be stepped to keep the bottom of it consistently below the natural contours.

Pad foundation holes are prepared by digging holes of appropriate size and depth. The advantage of pad foundations - apart from the fact that there is considerably less excavation to do and concrete to use - lies in the fact that the tops of the foundation pads do not have to be made level with each other. Any difference in level between the various pads can be allowed for in the construction of the walls or posts that will be resting on top of these. In contrast, stepped strip footings involve more work than level ones and consequent higher costs. Avoiding making steps in a foundation can involve considerable excavation - and consequent higher costs.

Stone Foundations

Stone is also a good material to use for foundations. All ancient buildings were constructed in this manner. Modern loadbearing construction using blocks however needs a level, rigid base such as is created using concrete. Stone foundations are ideal though for timber frame structures. Also, naturally occurring on-site rock can be used to provide support for frame structures. Trying to remove rock from a site in order to lay concrete foundations is a little absurd!

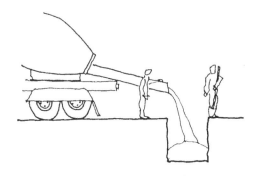

Concrete is the preferred material for creating foundations.

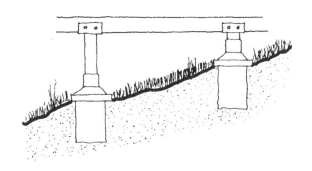

The advantage of pad foundations - apart from the fact that there is considerably less excavation to do and concrete to use - lies in the fact that the tops of the foundation pads do not have to be made level with each other.

Modern loadbearing structures - that is, those made of stone, bricks or blocks - require rigid, level foundations.

The notion of a 'foundation stone' is a very ancient one and the practice of laying one for a new building is still sometimes carried out. The Greek builders of old referred to the foundation stone as the 'omphalos', the centre, and the proper placing of this stone was critical to the nature of the building that was being created. Consequently the laying of this was enshrined in ritual and the propitiation of the deities was sought in so doing

Omphalos
The Foundation Stone

To create stone foundations, stones are packed into the foundation holes and finished off with a carefully chosen capstone. The stones should be packed carefully so that when the load comes onto the capstone they will not sink. Compact the soil at the bottom of the foundation hole with a ram before you fill it. In any event, this should be done for all foundation trenches and holes. Where you wish to build a loadbearing wall off a stone foundation you should use stone for the walling material, not concrete blocks. This will give sufficient flexibility to absorb any movement or unevenness. Holes or trenches for stone foundations need only be around 600mm below ground level.

Wood Foundations

Timber can also be utilised to construct foundations. If this is being done, naturally durable or pressure treated wood should be used. Timber used in this situation is normally "piled", i.e., driven down into the ground to allow beams to be placed across the tops.

Large timber sections can also be laid in trenches to provide continuous footings for walls. A railway sleeper is in fact a wood foundation that carries the weight of the track and the weight of the train also.

Appropriate for timber frame structures rather than for loadbearing concrete blockwork, timber piles are particularly useful where a boathouse or jetty is being built directly in the water or on waterlogged soil. Where solid ground is being built on, stone pad foundations offer the best 'natural' foundation.

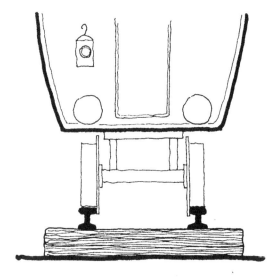

A railway sleeper is a wooden foundation.

Walls

External walls are the primary means of separating the outside world from the internal world of the home. As such, they must allow for the passage of light, air and persons through them as well as functioning to protect the internal environment that is created within. This requires that they be water resistant, have insulating

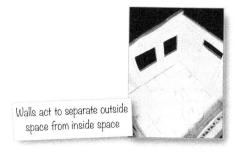

Walls act to separate outside space from inside space

110

qualities, be resistant to wind, weather and so on. External walls also function to carry building loads down to the foundations from whence they can escape into the ground.

Internal walls function to separate spaces within a building. As such they must fulfil a role in containing noise as well as accommodating door openings etc. Occasionally internal walls will also play a loadbearing role.

The choice of walling for your home needs to be made by paying careful consideration to the type of internal environment you wish to create. Such consideration is covered in detail in *Volume 1*.

Strip footings are generally used as a base for the construction of loadbearing walls, while pad foundations are used as a base for frame structures to rest on. Loadbearing walls fall into two broad categories - solid or cavity.

Solid Walling

Solid walls can be constructed from stone, concrete blockwork or brick. Such walls are built directly off the top of a foundation. A problem that solid walls oftentimes must contend with is damp. Insulating solid walls from excessive heat losses can also be problematical.

Rising damp describes the action of ground moisture rising through solid walls, much like blotting paper soaking up ink. This action, and the water and minerals that are drawn up from the soil by it, will eventually saturate the wall and decay will set in. Rain can also saturate a wall and cause dampness in it. The design and construction of any solid wall therefore must make provision to avoid dampness of any sort occurring in it, either from rain or from rising damp. Solid walling is also prone to high heat losses. This is especially true if a highly conductive material such as concrete blocks is used in the construction.

Essentially an outmoded form of construction, solid walling might be encountered however by those bold enough to attempt a restoration project on an old building. The use of solid walling in a new building cannot be recommended.

Where solid walling is encountered in a renovation project, plasterboards or wallboards fixed to battens on the internal face of the wall will serve to alleviate heat loss problems. If the house is to be heated with a convective

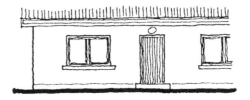

External walls must accommodate the passage of light, air and people ... be water and wind resistant ... be insulating, stable and strong ...Internal walls generally function to divide up internal space.

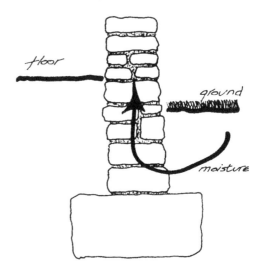

Rising Damp describes the action of ground moisture rising through walls, much like blotting paper soaking up ink.

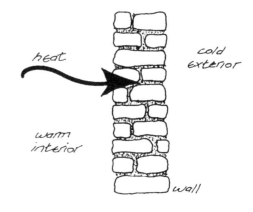

Solid walling is prone to high heat losses.

heating system care has to be taken however to install the dry lining without the battens being subject to dampness from condensation. The risk of condensation can be reduced by good ventilation to the inside of the building, though such ventilation will also carry away heat.

Pressure treated wood will prevent decay in wood likely to get wet though the fumes from the preservative will penetrate the living space. Providing for a flow of air behind the dry lining will reduce the risk of condensation occurring between the battens and the cold wall surface though unless the moist internal air is allowed to escape from the building by ventilation condensation will be impossible to prevent. If insulation is installed behind the dry lining the risk of condensation will increase. The effects of this condensation will remain undetected until the dry lining is removed and mould growths are discovered on the wall surface.

Often, vapour barriers are installed behind the wallboard or plasterboard to prevent the passage of moisture through the wall. Foil backed plasterboard will effectively do this as well as reflecting heat back into the room. It is difficult to make this sort of vapour barrier absolutely airtight, though for the theory of vapour barriers to be correctly adhered to it is essential to do this. Plastic sheets are also used as vapour barriers. Problems of condensation are associated with moist air and convective heating systems. A radiant heating system will produce less warm air and less risk of condensation therefore.

Cavity Walls

The cavity wall was developed about two hundred years ago as a means of preventing damp penetration into buildings. Solid wall construction is prone to this problem of dampness, mainly through the effect of capillary action - the drawing of water upwards through the porous wall material. This dampness comes from two sources, from the ground and from rain. The dampness drawn up from the ground by a wall will contain minerals which are present in the soil. These minerals contribute to the decay process.

A cavity wall is in fact two walls that are constructed side by side. A gap of up to six inches is left between these. The principle of the cavity wall is based on the belief that rain falling on the outer wall will not be able to cross the gap to the inside wall and make it wet.

Walls in buildings contain holes which allow for the passage of light, air, people and belongings.

THE FIRST CAVITY WALL

1792

112

Rising damp in a cavity wall is dealt with by installing a waterproof layer into the wall. Such damproof courses - DPC's - are placed above the level of the finished ground and these prevent the passage of moisture upward into the wall.

Normally the two walls of the cavity wall are referred to as "leaves". The dry leaf is the inner leaf of the wall. The wet leaf is the outer leaf of the wall. Cavity walls are a development of modern building methods. The theory of their construction and performance is based on a technical approach to the problem of water penetration into buildings. The reasoning behind the design of the wall is easy to understand and accept, however the proper construction of such a wall is difficult enough to achieve in practice. This is especially true where a cavity wall is constructed out of concrete blocks.

Normally, 4inch/100mm blocks will be used with a gap of 4 inches between them. This will make a wall of 12 inches thickness. Four inches is very thin for a wall of any height so each leaf of the wall has to be supported to stop it falling over. This is achieved very cleverly by joining the two walls together effectively making one wall of 12 inches thickness. While this solution admirably solves the problem of stability it also contradicts the theory of the cavity wall which is based on the idea of wet and dry leaves. This contradiction is minimised in practice by joining the two walls as little as possible and so minimising the risk of the water in the wet leaf crossing over the gap or cavity and wetting the dry leaf.

The joining of the two leaves of the wall is achieved by wall ties that are either metal or plastic. Of these, the metal variety are more robust, though their presence in a wall is bound to conduct heat out of the inner wall. The plastic variety are prone to damage during construction. The ties are built into the wall as each layer of blocks is constructed. They are spaced in a staggered fashion about eighteen inches apart. Both types of wall tie are made to throw off any water that might try to flow across them towards the dry leaf. Such water will in theory drip off the wall tie and fall harmlessly down the cavity without touching the inner leaf of the wall. In practice wall ties can easily catch mortar that falls from above while the remainder of the wall is being constructed. When this mortar dries it effectively bridges the cavity and can conduct dampness into the dry leaf. Such dampness will appear as a damp spot on the wall.

Before the days of insulated cavity walls, cavity walls were constructed with a two inch cavity. When such a wall was being constructed a 2"x1" lathe was placed in the

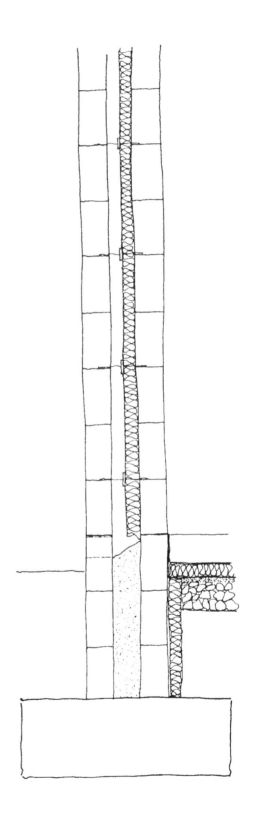

cavity to catch the mortar droppings and to protect the wall ties. The lathe was moved up each time a new layer was completed and was then rested on the new wall ties that were inserted. This practice has been discontinued in part because of the extra time it takes in construction. The other reason is because with insulation on one side of the cavity the lathe cannot be manouvered as easily as it might be.

It is this kind of practical reality that the theory of the cavity wall must confront. The question of what happens to the drips of water that will fall of the clean wall ties is also covered by the theory of the cavity wall. "Weep holes" are left at the bottom of the cavity so that any water dripping off the ties can get outside easily. To make a bottom to the cavity the gap between the two leaves is filled from the foundation up to the desired level. This needs to be at least six inches above the finished ground level. To assist with throwing the water out of the wall the bottom of the cavity is sloped down to the weep holes. These are simply open vertical joints left in the blockwork or brickwork. Weep holes also perform a further function in that they ventilate the cavity helping to dry off the inside of the wet leaf.

In practice, the bottom of the cavity, as construction proceeds, will catch the bulk of mortar droppings that fall down while the wall is being built. Such droppings will block up the weep hole exits. They will also bridge the cavity, though because the droppings will be below the level of the damproof courses this cannot in theory conduct water to the dry leaf. If bricks or blocks are temporarily left out of the wall above the level of the bottom of the cavity, any mortar droppings that do fall down can be cleaned out afterwards - except the drops that fall onto wall ties! Such cleaning of the cavity is almost never done. Likewise, the construction of weepholes is neglected.

The failure to properly adhere to the theory of the cavity wall leads to frequent problems of dampness at the bottom of such walls. What happens is that the accumulated debris at the bottom of the cavity remains constantly damp. It is for all intents and purposed part of the earth and is consequently soaking up as much water as it can from the ground. Without any weep holes to bring some air into the cavity this damp area never dries. Also the inside of the wet leaf does not get a chance to get dry either.

Ventilation bricks or grilles will provide good ventilation to a cavity for the purpose of drying off the inside of the wet leaf. These can be inserted into the

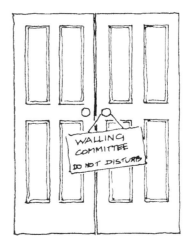

The Cavity Wall was developed about 200 years ago.

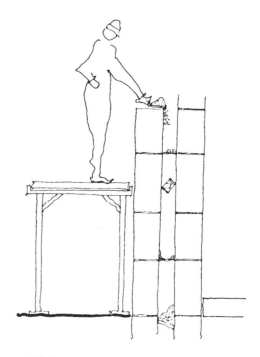

While the theory of the cavity wall is sensible ... to achieve this in practice is, however, difficult.

114

wet leaf of the wall above damproof course level. Second ventilation openings will also need to be located at the top of the cavities to allow the drying air to escape. The number and location of such ventilation openings will depend on the prevailing site conditions.

Cavity walls that use brick on the outer leaf have a better chance of drying naturally because they are more porous and allow drying air to actually pass through them very slowly. Concrete blocks are far denser than bricks and are more difficult to dry in this way. They are also unsightly and this fact combined with their wet quality usually means that blockwork is plastered over. This has the twofold effect of protecting the blocks from the rain as well as covering up the blocks. In reality, the external plaster is relied upon to keep the outer wall reasonably dry and usually no ventilation is provided to the cavity.

Brick will also prove to be a superior material when used on the inner leaf of cavity walls. The ability of brick to retain some of the heat passing through it will allow the inner leaf of the wall to warm up and so allow for a warmer wall surface. Plasterboard, wallboard or timber sheeting on battens facing a brick wall will allow a layer of air to be warmed up forward of the brick wall. This will contribute to the creation of warm internal surfaces. Insulation behind the brick inner leaf of a cavity wall will allow the brick to retain its heat.

Openings In Cavity Walls

Incorporating windows and doors into cavity walls needs considerable care to ensure that the dry inner leaf does not get wet. The door or window frame is oftentimes placed forward of the dry leaf to allow a window cill to be used inside the window. This strategy places the frame in line with the cavity and means that the joint between the frame and the wall can act as a path for moisture penetration. This possibility is resisted by the use of damproof courses - DPC's - that surround the window frame. These DPC'S also perform the function of separating the inner and outer leaves of the wall where the cavity is closed off at the edges of the opening.

Cills are used at the bottom of window openings to close off the cavity and these must also be wrapped with a damproof course where they touch the internal dry leaf. At the top of openings, whether they are window or door openings, lintols must be used to bridge the opening and support the walls above it. Concrete or steel lintols can be used for this purpose. Here again, where the inner and outer leaves of the wall meet, DPC's have to be used to prevent water getting into the dry leaf.

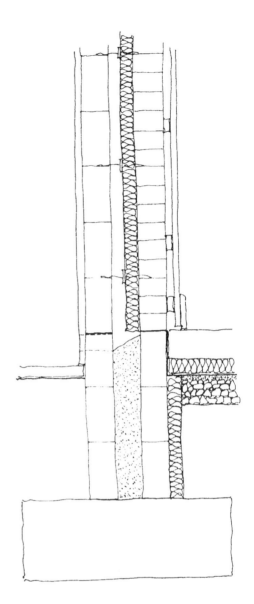

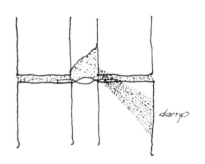

The failure to realise cavity wall theory in practice, leads to frequent problems of dampness in such walls.

Sometimes solid wall technology is employed for these purposes. In other words the sheer thickness of a solid wall is used to prevent rain penetrating through to the inside surface of the wall. This can be an easy solution to the problem of inserting lintols or cills into cavity walls but it carries with it a host of other potential problems especially when solid concrete lintols or cills are used. The most serious of these problems is "cold bridging". Cold bridging is what happens when a piece of solid wall is inserted into a cavity wall and then acts as a means for the heat on the inside of the building to pass directly to the outside. While the amount of heat lost in this way might be small the fact that the lintol or cill would oftentimes be considerably colder than the dry leaf makes it a potential site for condensation. This is especially true in rooms that can produce a lot of moisture, such as bathrooms and especially kitchens. Cold bridges can be avoided by using two lintols above wall openings and by placing insulation behind solid concrete cills.

As with solid walls, door and window frames need to be a tight fit to the cavity wall that they are in. The best way of doing this is by building these elements in. When this is not done and the frames are inserted when the walls have been completed, a tight fit is very hard to achieve. To overcome the problems associated with this - potential water and air infiltration into the building interior - the external plaster is usually carried right up to the window frame to cover the gap. Sometimes a sealant is used for this purpose especially when no external plaster is being used as would be the case with a brick external leaf. If the theory behind the construction of openings in cavity walls is understood and carried out in practice satisfactory results can be obtained. This is true of all aspects of cavity wall design. Care is essential to the process and this means that the construction of cavity walls is necessarily a slow process.

Ideally cavity walls should be built with a lime/sand mortar though cement and sand is the more normal type of mortar used. This is easier to prepare and stays workable for longer than the traditional lime/sand mix.

Cavity walls are very vulnerable to water penetration during construction. Such water would come from rainfall and would tend to soak in to the blocks. This water, added to the water trying to evaporate from the mortar, adds up to a considerable amount of moisture. All this water must be dried off after the roof has been put on. Where external plaster is applied to a wet cavity

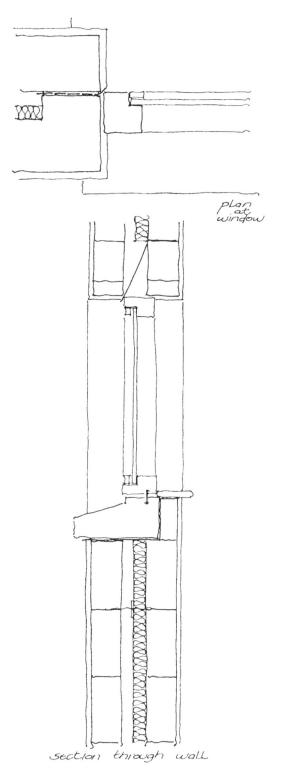

plan at window

section through wall

To create a Cavity Wall in accordance with the theory behind its construction, is, by necessity, a slow process.

116

wall, the dampness already in the wall finds it even more difficult to escape.

Building in dry weather will overcome some of these problems though this is not always possible because creating loadbearing walling is a slow process. Where a building is damp on completion the best way of drying it is by letting the air pass through it. Cavities should also be well ventilated. Leaving gaps in the outer wall immediately above the bottom of the cavity will serve well for this purpose as well as providing a means of cleaning out debris before the wall is closed up.

Concrete is the favoured material for the type of beams used over window and door openings in block cavity wall construction. They are usually called 'lintols'. These can be cast 'in situ' or they can be precast. Extreme care must be taken when installing lintols to ensure that no cold bridging occurs. Cold bridging happens when part of the construction is directly exposed to moist heat on one side and to cold on the other side. Such exposure can result in condensation occurring.

Condensation

Any given quantity of air contains a certain amount of moisture. The measurement of this is referred to as 'humidity'.

The warmer that quantity of air gets the more moisture it can hold. This moisture is in the form of an invisible gas, water vapour. Very warm air can hold lots of water vapour, but when that air cools down its water vapour cools down too and as a result turns back into water.

This phenomenon can be seen in a kitchen where the kettle has just been boiled. The air has been filled with water vapour and where the air has been cooled off - by being close to the cold glass in the window for example - its water vapour turns back to water and runs down the glass. This phenomenon also occurs on cold wall surfaces - especially where a 'bridging' of the cavity occurs.

Insulation and double glazing can be employed to alleviate the problems of surface condensation in buildings. More importantly, the main sources of water vapour - cooking and boiling - must have their emissions controlled by extracting them out of the internal environment.

In conventional cavity wall construction insulation is placed within the cavity against the inner wall. It is

The best way to dry out a wet building is to allow plenty of air to blow through it.

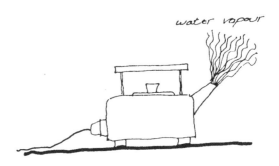

water vapour

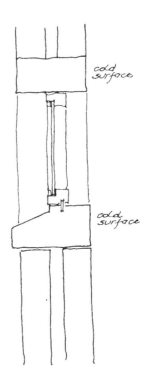

cold surface

cold surface

117

important that this insulation does not bridge the cavity and that special wall ties are used to hold the insulation tight to the inside wall. The function of the insulation is to retard the escape of heat from inside the house. In performing this task the inner block wall warms up and so reduces the risk of surface condensation.

Concrete Ring Beams

Ring beams are bands of reinforced concrete that are made on top of concrete block walls, directly under where the roof rests. The purpose of these ring beams is to tie the entire wall structure in a 'ring' so that the loads coming onto the wall from the roof can be transferred efficiently to the ground. These loads come onto the wall at an angle and tend to push the wall out at the top. The ring beam resists this tendency because it spreads the load away from the point of contact and ensures the structure is stable. Ring beams are cast on top of prepared walls with temporary shuttering at the sides that contain the concrete until it has set.

A major problem with ringbeams is the danger of creating a cold bridge and setting up condensation problems. Care must be taken when casting the beam not to infiltrate the cavity.

Insulation & Cavity Walls

One of the main problems associated with cavity walls is their vulnerability to heat losses. While a brick inner leaf to such a wall will provide some heat retention abilities it is difficult in practice to fully insulate the inner leaf. This is mainly because cavity walls rise out of the ground and so are in constant contact with a potential source of cold. This cold source will draw the heat from the wall.

It is possible to largely isolate a cavity wall from ground contact by building it on piers that rise from pad foundations. The walls are built off beams or lintols that are placed across the piers leaving them clear of the ground. This reduces ground contact between the cavity wall and the ground to a minimum. The benefits of this both in terms of reducing rising damp and in providing effective ventilation to the cavity are considerable. Such an approach will also allow the inner leaf to be more effectively insulated so that it can better retain heat. Bricks used in the inner leaf will retain heat far more effectively than concrete blocks. The ability of brick to breathe is also far superior to that of the concrete block.

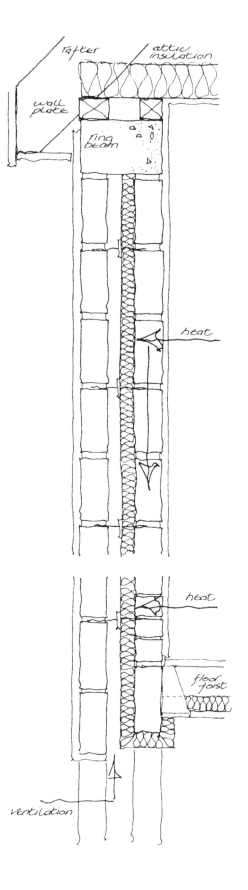

118

Modifying Solid or Cavity Walls

When solid or cavity walls need to be modified or removed subsequent to their initial construction, the work involved can be quite difficult and time consuming. The removal of these kind of walls or the making of openings in them, creates considerable debris and dirt and requires considerable energy also. Where such walls are supporting other elements of the building such as floors or other walls, these elements have to be supported in some other fashion when the wall is removed. There is no technical difficulty in this but the process requires care. Lintols or beams are used to do this and these can be of steel, concrete or wood.

Making openings in existing solid or cavity walls creates less debris than total removal does, but requires more care. The portion of the wall remaining over the new opening has to be supported by a lintol which can be inserted only after the opening has been made. In making new openings in cavity walls considerable care has to be taken to make sure not too much debris falls into the cavity. Pieces of debris could easily lodge somewhere in the cavity and provide a passage for damp to cross to the dry leaf. Also, damproof courses have to be inserted around the new opening to protect the dry leaf.

Fireplaces

Where a conventional fireplace is to be incorporated into a design, a masonry hearth and chimney has to be constructed to carry away the smoke etc. Such a chimney has to be constructed on a solid foundation.

A practical and more efficient alternative is to consider installing a metal fireplace with an insulated metal flue.

Timber Frame Construction

An alternative to concrete block cavity walling is to use timber frame construction. This is the oldest type of building construction and is considerably easier to make than any form of solid wall. It is also faster, dryer, healthier and potentially cheaper than solid or cavity wall construction. In terms of longevity, one of the oldest houses in the world is a Japanese timber frame house. It is 2500 years old and is still standing. Components of ancient timber buildings that are discovered in the earth testify to the proliferation of timber use throughout history. Timber frame construction accounts for the majority of domestic building in the world.

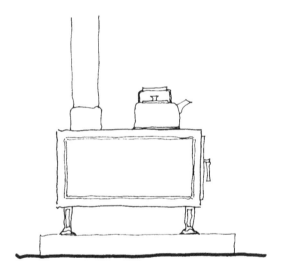

Timber Frame Construction is the oldest form of building construction and is considerably easier to make than any form of solid wall.

119

One of the most significant comparisons that can be made between timber frame construction and cavity wall construction is the differences in the amount of water used in the building process. Timber frame construction considerably reduces the volume of water needed to created a building. This makes for a far drier completed building, speeds up the construction process and surrounds the occupants of the building with a warmer and more pleasant walling material thereby creating a more satisfactory internal environment.

Timber frame construction allows a building to be constructed largely above the ground. The advantages of this are considerable as the ground is a continual source of cold and damp. It also allows a building to be constructed on even the most difficult site.

Types of Timber Frames

Timber frame construction methods vary from region to region but are basically similar to each other wherever they are built. Several types exist - the Segal Frame, the Post & Beam Frame, the Platform Frame and the Balloon Frame. Timber frames can be considered as being self supporting timber skeletons that are then covered over with a weatherproof 'fabric'.

All timber frame types conform to the principles of gravity in that they provide easy paths for the gravitational energy passing through them to find its way into the ground. Such frames are very fast to erect and are incredibly strong once they are completed. The principles of Structure are detailed in *Part VII Volume 1 Structure* [Volume 1, pages 153-177].

The principle type of wood used for timber frames is softwood. Hardwood is sometimes used and is crafted according to the old methods of jointing, such as the mortise and tenon. Such hardwood frames would be left exposed internally on completion of the building. Softwood frames are nailed or bolted together and are usually, though not always, covered up afterwards to conceal the fixings that are holding them together.

The Cruck Frame

In its originally constructed form, a Cruck Frame was made from the trunk of a single tree. This trunk was sawn in half lengthwise and the two halves were then laid on the ground in the shape of a pointed arch. Fixed together at the top by lashing or by timber pegs the frames were then stood upright with the "feet" being

Timber frame construction considerably reduces the volume of water needed to create a building ... it also allows a building to be constructed largely above the ground.

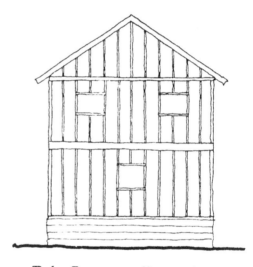

Timber Frames are self-supporting skeletons that are then covered with a weatherproof building fabric. These are very fast to erect and incredibly strong.

dropped into prepared foundation holes. A minimum of two frames were needed to make a three dimensional structure. In such a simple building the two cruck frames were connected together by a beam at the ridge and by further beams lower down the crucks.

Before the frames were stood into their foundation holes their feet were charred to protect the wood from decay. These early cruck frame buildings were more like upturned boats than they were like conventional buildings and there was no differentiation between the roof and wall surfaces in them.

Later developments in this method led to the frames being stood onto low foundation walls that rose above the ground and to the introduction of vertical walls. All this was accomplished within the shape provided by the tree trunks - a naturally strong shape that could easily accommodated gravitational flow through it. The vertical wall elements in these late Cruck Frame buildings were made in such a way that they carried no weight other than their own weight down to the ground.

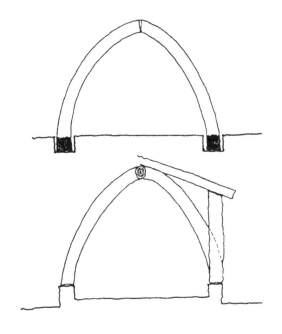

The Segal Frame

A modern version of the Cruck Frame can easily be utilised to make timber frames for building. Rather than using tree trunks, large flat sections of timber - up to 8x2 inches in section - are bolted together flat on the ground in the desired shape. A double layer of timber is used to form the roof shape of the frame and to support the floor. A single layer - or column - is used between these to form the vertical part of the frame. Diagonal bracing is incorporated into the frame shape to provide rigidity. Such a frame can be up to two stories high.

To make a building, two or more frames are erected on prepared foundation pads that rise at least six inches above the ground to protect the bottom of the frames from ground based moisture. Any differences in the levels of the tops of the foundation pads can be adjusted by trimming the legs of the frames. Once erected, the frames are fixed together with further sections of timber - again usually 8x2 inch sections - to make a rigid three dimensional framework.

This modern version of Cruck Frame construction has the advantage of being easily assembled on site. Once the timber sections have been laid out on the ground in the correct shape they can be clamped together, drilled, bolted and then erected onto prepared foundation pads.

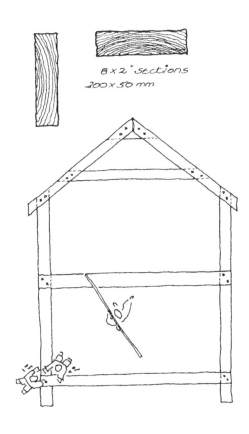

8 x 2" sections
200 x 50 mm

A hard, flat work area is the best for assembling Segal frames. This area can be marked out with the frame shape in chalk and the timber sections laid over these marks before they are drilled and bolted. Ideally such a work area should be covered over with a simple roof if there is a possibility of rain during the construction period. Such protection will allow the assembly work to continue as well as protecting the timber from getting unnecessarily wet.

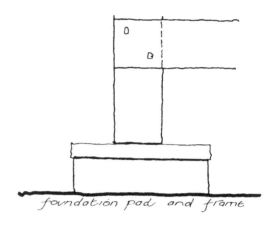

foundation pad and frame

Finished frames can be set aside until all frames have been completed and are ready for erection. This may have to be in the open. Remember, the covered area will have to be big enough to allow the frames to be taken out in one piece! These frames are also very heavy. At least four people will be needed to carry one. More people will be needed when the frames are being erected, but this can be organised to be done in a day of house raising.

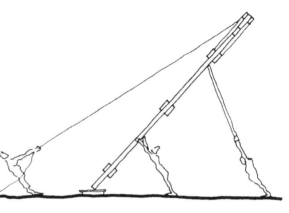

Segal Frames are the basis of a system of self-building known as The Segal Method. This was the creation of the architect, Walter Segal. A Trust exists which provides information on the Method:

Post & Beam

A post and beam structure is a frame structure that consists of rectilinear shapes that provide paths for gravitational energy - weight - to flow through. Because these paths are relatively indirect and contain right angles around which the energy must flow, post and beam structures must be made very strong at these angles where the 'weight' is most likely to get impatient and try to break out.

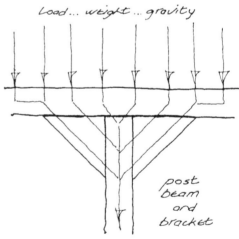

Load... weight... gravity

post beam and bracket

A post and beam structure consists of just that - posts or columns - and beams. The beams are attached to the columns which carry the building weight down to the earth. The beams must be made sufficiently deep to accommodate the loads passing through them. Also, the junction of column and beam must be strong enough to allow the building weight to flow smoothly into the column. Brackets or braces are used to do this.

Post and beam structures are used in housing as they give the rectilinear form most often found in rooms. It is not hard to imagine making a pitched roof on top of a structure of this kind. Stacking two post and beam sections one on top of the other and placing a pitched roof over this gives us the familiar cross section called for in many housing plans.

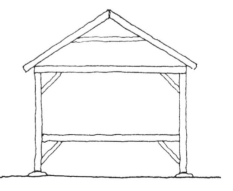

Two variations of post and beam structures are the balloon frame and the platform frame. These frame types differ from the post and beam frame in that the members making up the frames are more closely spaced.

Balloon Frames

Balloon frames are frames that are erected on-site, all the timbers being nailed together. This method utilises 100x50mm section timbers - 4x2's. These run from the base of the structure to the eaves. The timbers are usually spaced about two feet apart with intermediate spacer pieces fixed between the timbers to prevent bowing. An intermediate floor can be fixed to the walling timbers and diagonal bracing is inserted at the corners of the frames. The roof sits on top of the frame and is fixed to it.

A certain amount of skill is needed to erect a Balloon Frame, in comparison to the Segal Frame which can be easily tackled by self builders.

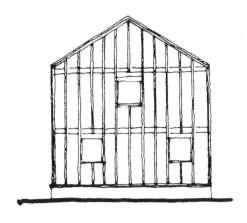

Platform Frames

Platform frames consist of rectangular wall and floor panels made from 100x50mm sections of timber. These timbers are usually spaced 400-600mm apart and fixed top and bottom to other 100x50mm sections, called top and bottom plates. The horizontal loading affecting platform frames is dealt with by facing the frames with plywood which provides diagonal paths for them to follow. Alternatively, timber braces can be installed at the corners.

Platform frames are probably the most popular form of timber frame construction in use. Often produced in a factory, platform frames are fast and easy to erect. The frames required to build a house can be brought on-site ready made. These frames can then be nailed together very quickly to form a complete structure. This allows for a rapid construction time and ensures that the building is enclosed as quickly as possible. Window and door frames can be factory fixed further speeding up the on-site work. Platform Frames can also be constructed on-site either in position or by preassembly in a covered work area.

By utilising preassembly methods economies of time and materials can be achieved in platform framing. This contributes to a rapid building process allowing a sealed building to be erected in only a few days. The advantages of this are enormous especially where rain is frequent - situations where otherwise the building fabric would get wet before it could be properly sealed against the weather.

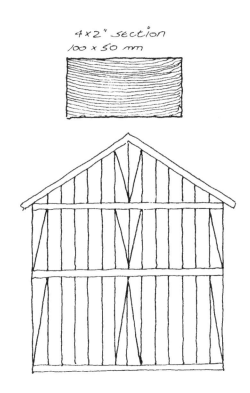

4x2" section
100 x 50 mm

Where plywood sheeting is used, platform frames normally accord with the standard plywood panel size of 8x4 feet. What this means is that wall panels are made 8 feet high and the vertical timbers in the walls are made at 2 feet centres. This allows whole sheets of plywood to be used, saving time and keeping costs down. Where an 8 foot high panel is not sufficiently high for the space being created increments of 1 foot or 6 inches can be used. Factory made panels are always plywood faced. Similarly, floor panels are generally faced with plywood and are sized accordingly. If a wood floor using tongued and grooved boards is required it is probably more economical to use the plywood faced floor panels and lay the timber boarding over these afterwards.

In regards to construction methodology, ground floor wall frames sit on base plates. These can either be a 100x50mm section atop the dry leaf of a cavity wall or it can sit on top of a timber beam that is spanning between piers on pad foundations. It really is important to keep wood as far away from the ground as possible. Even the dry leaf of a cavity wall will be damp below damproof course level. While the damproof course will separate the timber from the damp - and in theory keep it dry - it is better to have the frames sitting on a beam that is clear of the ground. Where a suspended timber floor is being used, this is laid first and the wall frames will sit on top of this. The roof sits on top of the frames and is fixed to them through another section of 100x50mm timber called a head binder. The roof over platform frame buildings is usually made with lightweight trusses.

Window and door frames can be installed in factory made frames allowing a tight fit to be achieved. This is essential if cold air infiltration is to be properly controlled. Such openings are made in the frames by interrupting the vertical timbers where necessary. Timber lintols and cills are fixed to the top and bottom of these. In the case of frames made on-site, windows and door frames can be inserted afterwards. Because timber frame is essentially a dry building system, the insertion of these is far simpler than in cavity wall construction. Internal walls in all timber frame buildings are made using either 75x50 or 100x50 sections. These can be faced with plasterboard, plywood etc. as required.

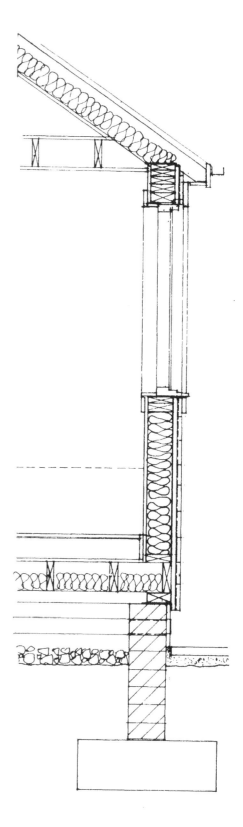

Walls In Frame Buildings

All timber frame buildings are similar in their standing
state and give a sound basis for making a warm and
pleasant home with a healthy internal environment. All
timber needs to be kept out of direct contact with water to
avoid setting up decay. Such water can come from sources
like the ground or from condensation. Avoiding contact
with the ground is not difficult to achieve - the building is
simply raised above it. This has many advantages apart
from avoiding contact with the potentially wet ground. For
example natural emissions of Radon gas can dissipate
naturally. A sloping site can be built over without
resorting to fill to level out the ground. A suspended
timber floor can be installed on the ground floor. The
advantages of this are many, plus the fact that the ground
and vegetation can remain largely undisturbed.

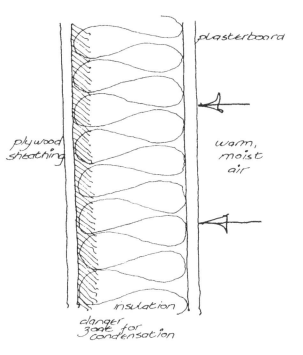

Wetness from condensation is a different matter from
defending against ground based moisture. Condensation is
caused by a build-up of moisture in the internal air of a
building. Such moisture comes from people breathing,
from cooking, washing activities and so on. Moisture
build-up in the internal environment can be controlled by
ventilating the inside of the building - allowing fresh air to
come in and warm moist air to go out. When a building is
heated by conventional radiators this is not usually done
because the air has been heated at great expense.

Warm moist air will try and escape to the outside of a
heated building whatever way it can. It will do this by
rising towards the roof and also by passing through the
fabric of the building. As such moist air makes its escape
it cools down. This reduces the amount of water vapour
the air can carry and some of this vapour turns back to
water - condensation. Where cold unventilated areas exist
within the building fabric the water so produced cannot
dry and therefore might set up decay. This problem is
particularly acute where insulation has been introduced
into the depth of the timber frame - presenting on one side
a warm face and on the other a cold face to the escaping
moist air. The existence of insulation within the frames of
all timber frame buildings is hazardous and might result in
the construction of ideal decay conditions. Extreme care
therefore must be taken with this type of construction.

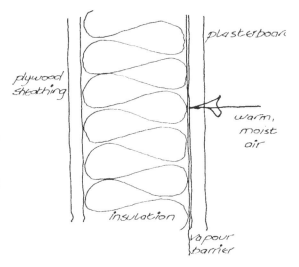

Conventionally, this problem is tackled in several ways,
none of which are particularly good for the occupants of
the building. One method is the use of vapour barriers.
Vapour barriers are water and air proof sheets that seal the
timber frame/insulation from the inside of the building.
The theory of vapour barrier is that moist air cannot pass
through them - meaning that condensation cannot take

place within a wall because the moist air cannot get into it. These barriers are usually placed in walls - the part of the building fabric where the greatest risk of condensation is perceived to lie. Roof areas are normally left free of them as it is accepted that the warm moist air has to escape, somehow! Roof areas are usually draughty and as draughts are in fact good ventilation the risk of condensation is considered minimal in a roof space - as long as it is not tightly sealed.

Vapour barriers are either made of plastic or of aluminium. They must be continuous to work effectively and this is almost impossible to achieve in practice. Any hole or gap in the vapour barrier will be like a slow puncture in a tyre - air will escape through it, carrying with it moisture which might condense within the wall wetting the timber. This is why timber is preserved! If vapour barriers worked it would be sufficient to apply them and not to preserve the wood at all.

The theory of preserving timber is that if it gets wet and cannot dry then it will not decay. The chemicals used to achieve this 'preservation' by their very nature are harmful. Any fumes the chemical preservatives give off that penetrate the interior of the building will be harmful. A natural preservative such as Boron however will not do this. The best preservative though is conscious design - keeping the timber out of the ground and away from damp or wet surfaces.

The first step in eliminating vapour barriers has to be a reduction of the condensation risk. This is done by creating warm internal surfaces. This accords with the needs of our bodies also - if the internal surfaces are warm and the internal air is not constantly being filled with moisture that cannot escape, there will be no condensation.

The easiest way to achieve warm internal surfaces is to create a layer of trapped air around the internal spaces. This 'dry lining' will act more or less like your clothing does in keeping your body warm. The layer of trapped air is created by placing insulation in a continuous layer on the outside of the timber frame. All types of timber frame structures can be sheeted over with plywood and insulation run continuously across this. This will leave an air space surrounding the internal spaces which will act as an insulator.

What is being created is a timber frame, sheeted in plywood with insulation wrapped cozily around this.

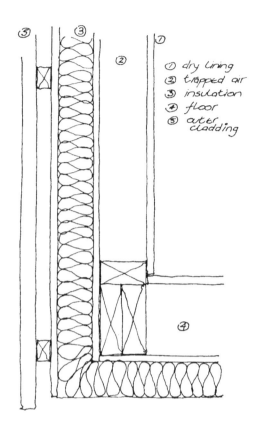

① dry lining
② trapped air
③ insulation
④ floor
⑤ outer cladding

The best timber preservative is conscious, good design ... keeping the timber out of the ground and out of contact with damp or wet surfaces.

To eliminate Vapour Barriers from timber frame construction first requires that the condensation risk be reduced.

The building is raised out of the ground and the timber ground floor also has its wrapping of insulation under it. Windows and doors interrupt the walls in places and these are a tight fit and minimise air infiltration through them. Controlled vents allow fresh air into the building and a vent in the roof allows stale air to get out. The internal walls are timber or plasterboard sheeted.

In terms of the external cladding - a timber frame can be finished with wood, slate, metal decking, corrugated iron etc. This is attached to battens fixed over a layer of felt.

While timber frame buildings will be warm in themselves, no real thermal capacity exists in the materials of the building to retain heat. This means that when the heating is turned off the building cools down fairly rapidly. Thermal capacity can be installed in a timber frame building by filling in the hollow walls. Dry stacked bricks could be used to do this, or timber. The warm air making its way to the outside through the wall will give up its heat to the filling in the wall. When the heating is turned off the thermal capacity of the filling will allow the walls to stay warm. Thermal capacity means weight. If thermal capacity is being added into a timber structure remember that the load of this has to be transferred effectively down to the ground.

External Finishes for Timber Frames

The wrapped timber building with its walls that breathe and its ventilation system that channels air in and out is like a neat package. This package is quite delicate and needs some external protection. This protection can be provided in many ways. Bricks, concrete blocks, timber sheeting, metal decking or plaster are all options that can readily be used for this.

All external finishes to timber frame structures should be regarded as further layers of the building. A 50mm gap should be left between the insulation and the outermost layer. This forms a cavity and, as with the conventional cavity wall construction, care must be taken to keep the layers as separate as possible. This will prevent moisture from penetrating the cosy building fabric. A layer of roofing felt is oftentimes used behind lightweight external cladding.

If timber cladding or slating is not an acceptable external finish an appearance to plastered blockwork can be achieved by using expanded metal and plastering over it.

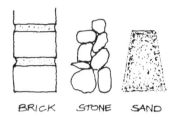

BRICK   STONE   SAND

While timber frame buildings are warm in themselves they contain no appreciable Thermal Capacity.

This timber framed building sits on wooden foundations, has clay plastered clay-straw walls finished with clay paint

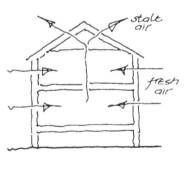

stale air

fresh air

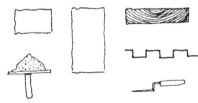

The external appearance of a building is really a window dressing exercise. If the outside layer is regarded as being made to look almost any way you want a great sense of freedom will be sensed. What is important is that the wrapped box is made properly. After that the outer layer - or external finish - is very much a matter of taste.

Part Timber Houses

In this type of construction - 'Timber & Brick' - the dry inner leaf of the cavity wall is replaced by a timber framed wall. The advantage of doing this lies in getting rid of the concrete block wall on the inside of the house. A timber frame wall is a far warmer element for an interior feeling in a house. Normally such a wall is finished by covering it with plasterboard slabs which are then painted - a process similar to how upstairs 'stud walls' are normally made. Alternatively other finishes, such as wood panelling, can be applied to the timber frame wall.

There are risks however in mixing what are essentially 'wet' and 'dry' forms of construction. These risks derive in part from the fact that the blockwork/brickwork outer leaf must be stabilised off the timber frame by using wall ties similar to those used in the all block wall. The introduction of these ties are potentially hazardous for the timber in the frame wall. A second threat is from moisture rising from the ground and entering the bottom of the timber frame - the timber frame normally sits on top of a few concrete blocks built up off the foundation. The threat of damp penetration here is minimised by the use of a DPC under the timber.

In part timber house construction the timber frame and the roof are erected very quickly - within a matter of days - and the roof is also completed. The outer concrete block wall is then erected - usually a matter of a few weeks. Part timber houses are normally the work of specialist firms. The frames are premade in a factory to suit the particular design then transported to the site and lifted into place. Entire floors can be pre made, ready to walk on. In a part timber, factory based construction, the insulation is placed within the thickness of the timber framed wall, immediately behind the plasterboard or other internal finish. To combat the likelyhood of condensation occurring 'vapour barriers' are introduced into the construction behind the finished inside face of the wall.

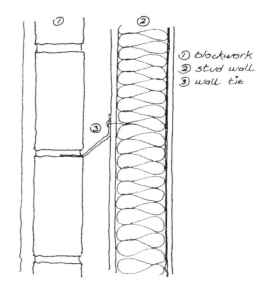

① blockwork
② stud wall
③ wall tie

Certain risks arise in the mixing of wet and dry forms of construction, for example, with Timber & Brick.

In Ireland many timber framed houses are clad with a veneer of concrete blocks, an unnecessary, costly and risky procedure

128

There are many advantages to enlisting the help of a specialist firm in the creation of your timber/part timber home. It is advisable to examine the exact system that is being offered - normally vapour barriers and preserved timber come as standard with such services.

Concrete Floors

Concrete floors are laid onto a prepared surface consisting of "hardcore". Hardcore can be anything from discarded broken bricks to rubble or quarried chunks of rock. This is laid in a six inch layer directly onto the ground after the topsoil has been removed. The hardcore is well compacted and is then covered with a two inch layer of sand called "blinding". The blinding will stop the wet concrete from running through the hardcore.

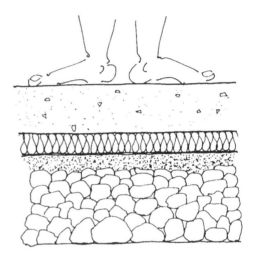

Because the concrete will virtually be in direct contact with the ground a damproof membrane - DPM - must be laid under concrete slabs to prevent dampness from seeping into the slab and consequently into the house. This damproof course, or membrane, is laid on top of the blinding. Concrete slabs are usually laid so that the top of them is finished level with the damproof course in the dry leaf of the wall. If this is done the damproof membrane under the slab can be turned up between the slab and the wall and then joined with the DPC in the wall. This ensures that the floor slab and the walls above DPC level are protected from direct penetration by moisture. While it is very easy to draw DPM's and DPC's and to overlap and join them on paper, in reality complications can arise at corners and other junctions/changes of direction giving rise to damp penetration.

Concrete floor slabs are normally made four inches thick though six inches is also common. Steel reinforcement is not normally used except for the introduction of a layer of steel mesh close to the top of the slab. The rising walls of a load bearing structure are usually used as the permanent formwork for a concrete ground floor slab. Solid internal walls are built directly off the finished slab which might be thickened up where such walls occur. This can be done by making a depression in the hardcore that coincides with the line the wall will take allowing the slab to carry the weight of the wall without cracking.

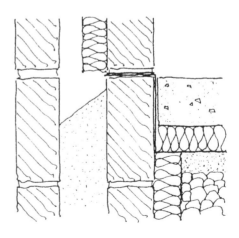

Any pipes that need to pass through the slab such as the incoming water supply pipe, electrical cables or drainage pipes need to be installed before the concrete is poured though it is best to avoid this as the damproof membrane must inevitably be interrupted to install them.

Concrete slabs are normally finished with a two inch layer of sand/cement screed which can be finished very smooth. Pipes and cables are oftentimes embedded in this screed. This practice is very risky in respect of water pipes as they can leak.

Concrete floor slabs are inherently cold and will contribute to heat loss from the building. They are also very hard underfoot. The problem of heat loss through a concrete floor can be alleviated somewhat by putting insulation under it before the wet concrete is poured. Rigid insulation is needed for this and it should be laid above the dampproof membrane.

Concrete floors act as lids on the ground interrupting the natural emission of Radon gas from the earth. Where a slab has a crack in it or a pipe or cable passing through it, Radon gas can pass into the building through these openings. All solid floors carry with them risks of Radon gas penetrating the interior of the building. This risk can be minimised by good internal ventilation, though once a risk is identified in a particular geographical area it is far safer to construct a suspended timber floor and so relieve the problem completely.

If nothing else is an indictment of concrete floors the threat of Radon pollution must surely be. In domestic scale construction the suspended timber flooring is a healthier and warmer alternative to concrete any day. That something so obvious would need constant reiteration is strange. In truth, concrete slabs are a convenience for builders and this is the reason behind their proliferation.

With the increase in popularity of underfloor heating, the concrete slab is being touted as the best way of exploiting such radiant systems. In truth, a concrete slab provides too massive a heat store to be an effective heating element.

Suspended Timber Floors
A suspended timber floor will provide a warm, dry and pleasant surface for living on. Such floors are made using beams called joists with a finishing layer over these which can be anything from plywood to tongued and grooved boards. Both ground and intermediate floors can be made in this way.

The size and spacing of floor joists depends on the distance they must span. In practice, joists that are

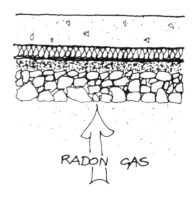

Concrete floor slabs act as lids on the ground interrupting the natural emission of Radon Gas from the earth.

The benefits of suspended timber floors for a buildings' occupants cannot be over emphasised. The model clearly shows how such a floor floats above the ground allowing for a warm, dry, and sensuous feeling to be created.

150x50mm or 6x2 inches, are the commonest section that is used. This depth of section is easily managed by one or two people. A 6x2 joist carrying a normal domestic loading will span 3200mm between supports. A section 150x63 will span 3700mm. Such joists would be placed 300mm apart and would have "bridging" placed between them - short sections of joist 300mm wide. This bridging counteracts the tendency of the joists to turn.

Oftentimes the sizes of the ground floor spaces in a domestic scale two storey building are controlled by the effective span of the joists that form the ceiling of the space and make the floor above. Commonly 3600mm is regarded as an effective distance between supports.

If larger spaces are to be made on the ground floor, beams can be introduced on which the joists can rest. Such beams will be deeper than the joists they carry and so will stand down into the space and interrupt the line of the ceiling. As long as the beams are carefully placed and their location thought out such an effect on a ceiling can be incorporated into the overall design.

Beams for this purpose are best made from timber. These can be solid or hollow. Hollow beams have the advantage of being light and strong. These are made from solid sections of timber and plywood. Solid sections of timber or laminated timber beams can be left exposed for effect.

Timber ground floors are not subject to the same requirements in terms of clear spans as upper floors are. A timber ground floor can be supported underneath wherever necessary. It is common to support suspended ground floors off a 100mm concrete slab, resting the joists on bricks and timber wall plates. A wall plate is a section of timber to which floor joists are fixed. Good ventilation is essential to suspended floors. If the underfloor area is not open ventilation grilles have to be provided. It is far more effective to leave a generous clear space between the earth and the bottom of the timber ground floor. This eliminates many of the problems of cold and damp associated with the ground.

The clear space under a suspended timber floor will allow the free ventilation of that space. Moisture or Radon gas emerging from the ground will quickly be blown away. If the rising walls of the building are not built clear of the ground, ventilators have to be installed which allow air to blow under the floor and do the same job. This is not nearly as effective as an open system. A further disadvantage of closing a building in underneath is that pipes coming in or going out of the building are effectively isolated.

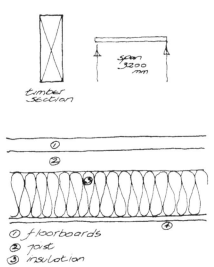

timber
section

span
3200
mm

① floorboards
② joist
③ insulation
④ ceiling

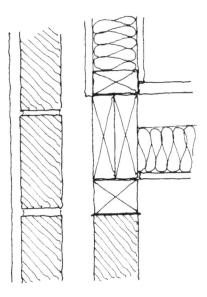

Timber ground floors should be insulated against heat loss. This is best done under the bottom of the joists providing a continuous and effective insulating cover. If this insulation can be made continuous with the wall insulation an effective overcoat will be made for the building.

Suspended floors allow the natural slope of a site to be spanned over without recourse to fill. This can considerably reduce construction costs. Underfloor heating can also be installed in suspended floors.

Timber Roofs

Solid or cavity walled buildings require timber roofs to enclose them. The simplest roof form is the pitched roof. These are made with rafters - beams that make paths for the weight of the roof to follow across to the walls. This ensures that the various roof loads are swiftly dispatched to the foundations. When block construction is used a timber 'wall plate' is fixed atop the wall and the roof rafters are then fixed to it.

Rafters are allowed to overhang the walls they cover to give protection against rain. They are normally spaced at two foot intervals. The ends of the rafters have a board fixed to them which is called the fascia board. The gutter is fixed to this. The fascia board usually has a groove cut into it near the bottom to throw water off of it. The underneath of the rafters are also closed in. The boards that are used to do this are called soffit boards. These usually have some holes left in them to allow air into the roof space to ventilate the roof timbers. Roofing felt is laid over the rafters and allowed to sag between them. Timber battens are then nailed across the rafters. The final roof covering is then attached to these battens by nailing.

Load bearing walls have little or no ability under tension loading. For this reason, a pitched roof needs to be triangulated to present a vertical load to the wall on which it rests . If the roof tends to push the wall out at the top it will set up tension loading in the wall. This risk is eliminated by tying the arms of the roof together. Such a tie is known as a collar. All pitched roof construction is based on triangulation and on making effective paths for the roof loads to follow across to the walls. The weight that a roof must carry can be considerable if concrete roof tiles, natural slates or sods are used.

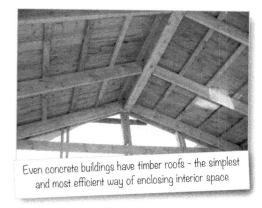

Even concrete buildings have timber roofs - the simplest and most efficient way of enclosing interior space

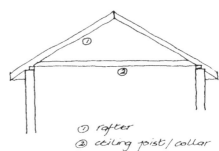

① rafter
② ceiling joist / collar

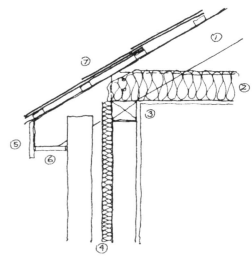

① rafter
② collar / ceiling joist / insulation
③ wall plate
④ cavity and insulation
⑤ gutter and fascia
⑥ soffit
⑦ slates, battens and felt

Where a roof has to span a large area purlins are usually used to support the rafters at their mid point. Purlins are heavy sections of timber that run at right angles to the rafters and stop them from sagging. A typical purlin might be 75x175mm in section. Purlins are themselves supported on struts that are usually 100x50mm sections. These rest on 100x75mm sections that run along the top of the ceiling joists. In this kind of roof the ceiling joists a play role in carrying the weight of the roof. For this reason these joists must occasionally rest on internal walls that can support them. Ceiling joists can also be supported from above by attaching them to the rafters. The 100x50mm sections of timber that are used to do this are called hangars.

The pitch of a roof depends on the covering that is used. Slates and tile roofs should have pitches greater than 20 degrees. Roofs can also be made considerably steeper than this.

The rafters, purlins, collars, struts and ceiling joists of a roof are fixed together using nails. Where the ceiling joists and the rafters meet the wall they rest on a wall plate. This is a section of 100x75mm timber that has been fixed to the wall using bolts. The wall plate sits on the inner leaf of the cavity to make sure it stays dry. Roofing felt is placed over the rafters and this is allow to slightly sag between them. Felt is the last line of defence against water penetration. Any water getting under the outer roof covering will run down the felt and be carried outside. The felt is fixed down with 2x1 inch battens. These are fixed to the rafters and at right angles to them. The distance these are apart will depend on the roof covering being used. Slates and tiles are fixed to such battens completing the roof covering.

The attic space formed by such a roof would usually not be intended to be used except to house the cold water tank and as a storage space. The collar would likely be too low for a person to pass under without stooping. Such an attic is just waste space created by making a pitched roof.

When a pitched roof is finished with a vertical wall this wall is known as a gable wall. If the end of the roof is pitched and there is no vertical wall it is said that the roof is hipped.

The type of roof that has rafters, purlins, collars, hangars, struts and ceiling joists is known as a cut roof. What this means is that it is assembled on site and the timbers used in it are cut to fit.

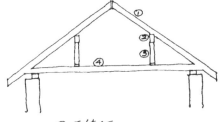

① rafter
② purlin
③ strut
④ collar / ceiling joist

Canvas Roof

Thatch Roof

Slate Roof

Tin Roof

An empty attic space is always well ventilated by holes in the soffit and sometimes even the cavity in the wall is open to the attic. This allows lots of air to circulate through the attic keeping the timber dry. Attic insulation is really better laid across the top of the ceiling joists leaving air pockets between the joists and the ceiling and the insulation above. Air that cannot readily move is a good insulator. If hardboard is nailed to the top of the joists insulation can be laid on top of this in a continuous fashion. This will allow the insulation to work best. If it is stuffed between the ceiling joists it simply will not work as well.

If access to the cold water storage tank has to be maintained a raised walkway should be installed that is kept clear of the insulation.

Roof Trusses

An alternative to making a cut roof is to use premade roof trusses. These are triangulated frames that are made using light sections of timber. The timbers are fixed together using gang nails. Gang nails are flat plates with protruding teeth which are fixed to the timber in a factory. The advantage of using lightweight roof trusses lies in the speed and ease of construction which they allow.

As with a cut roof, the attic space created when using lightweight roof trusses is not usable. In fact the space inside the roof is very difficult to negotiate.

Lightweight trusses are fixed to wall plates and are normally spaced 600mm apart. Standard size trusses are made which can be bought directly off the shelf.

Attic Rooms

Advantage can be taken of attics to provide usable living space. This is done by carrying the outside walls up reasonably high to allow clear head room under the collar of the roof. The distance from the top of the floor joists to the underside of the collar will need to be 2400mm. The space in an attic room will have to have this height over a minimum of half the floor area. The remainder of the floor area can have a lower ceiling height than this - in other words a sloping ceiling. This should not be lower than 1500mm over half the room area. Attic rooms can gain a lot of storage space under the sloping sections of the roof. A careful cross section should be drawn of any attic room you are making to ensure that you have sufficient height in it.

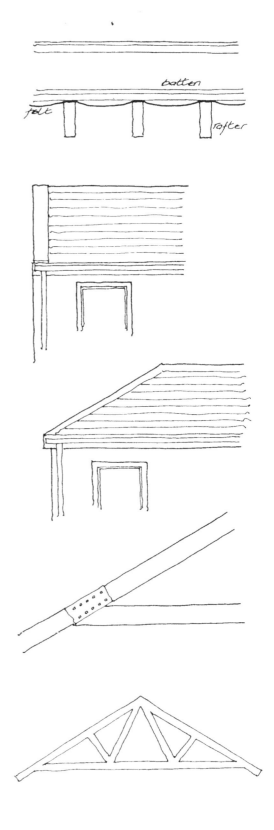

A roof with attic rooms should be made with gable walls rather than a hipped roof. This will allow light to be brought in through windows in these gables as well as allowing the attic space to be as big as possible. Additional light can be brought in to attic rooms through rooflights. These are fixed into the plane of the roof and can be openable. These should be located to allow a person to see out through them. High heat losses can however result from such rooflights. Insulated shutters should therefore be installed.

Dormer windows can be made in attic rooms to allow vertical windows to be made in the sides of the roof. Dormers create awkward junctions that have to be waterproofed and this can be difficult to do.

If insulation is fixed between the rafters in an attic room situation care must be taken that the roof timbers gain sufficient ventilation.

Sod Roofs

Sods can be used as a effective roof covering. Used this way, the full benefit of the material can be exploited. These are, that it is cheap, readily available, is a good insulator, has grass growing out of it and it produces oxygen!

Sod roofs can be laid to pitches of up to 45 degrees as long as the sods are prevented from sliding off the roof by holding them at the edge. A sod roof is laid over a roof membrane that is specially made to fit over the entire roof and has no joints. Any chimneys or pipes that come through the roof can be catered for in the making of the membrane. This membrane will prevent the passage of moisture from outside the building but it will allow airborne moisture - water vapour - from within the building to escape. Such a membrane, because it comes in one piece, is easily laid. These membranes are designed to prevent root penetration through the roof and can be produced in sheets of up to 500 square meters.

The sods - around three inches deep - are laid over a three inch layer composed of soil and gravel. This layer is for root ventilation. Both these layers are laid over a further layer of two inches of gravel. This eight inches of earth roof will have up to a foot and a half of grass growing on it as well as sustaining wild flowers, bees, birds and insects. The air trapped between the blades of grass act like a fur coat keeping you warm inside your house. Sod roofs also cut down the convection heat losses from your house. In hot weather the sod roof keeps the house cool.

A sod roof is a practical alternative to other roofing systems and is no heavier than a roof made with concrete tiles. The growth of grass will be self regulating. The main thing to watch out for is to buy a first class roofing membrane. Once this is covered over with sods you want to be able to forget about it. The membrane you get should preferably be specifically for the purpose of making sod roofs. The membrane should prevent water penetration but allow water vapour from inside the building to pass through it unhindered. This is very important. No gutters or downpipes are required on a sod roof.

Sod Roof

Internal Finish

Gypsum plaster is often used to cover internal wall surfaces. There are two basic ways to do this, either wet or dry. Wet gypsum plaster is normally applied to solid wall surfaces such as concrete, concrete block and even brick. It can be finished very smooth. Internal plastering is a highly skilled job and the material itself is tricky to work with. Wet plastering introduces a lot of moisture into a building and this moisture has to evaporate before the building can be considered dry. Air is the best way of drying out plaster. Leave windows open so that there is a flow of air through the house. Closing up the house and heating it to remove the moisture will only cause problems with condensation. You must get the water out of the house altogether and free flowing air is the best way to do this. A freshly plastered house should not be lived in until it is perfectly dry.

When wet applied plaster dries its surface will produce dust which can irritate the throat and lungs as well as getting into everything else in the house. Again, you need to get rid of as much of this dust as you can before you move in.

An alternative to using wet plastering is to use plasterboard internally. Plasterboard is gypsum plaster that has been mixed and set in the factory and faced on either side with paper. Plasterboards can either be fixed to solid walls with dabs of mortar or fixed onto timber studding using nails. Where plasterboard is fixed onto timber studding against a solid wall it is known as dry lining. Where plasterboards are used on both sides of timber studding it is known as a stud wall. Where dry lining is used it is important to allow for air to circulate between the plasterboard and the solid wall. This air movement will keep the timber studs properly ventilated.

Wet plastering introduces a lot of moisture and dust into the interior of a new building.

Clay plaster finish with ochre paint

Plasterboards come in a variety of sizes up to 3000mm long and 1200mm wide. They also come in various thicknesses from 10mm up to 20mm. Plasterboards can be cut very easily with a fine tooth saw where full size boards cannot be used.

Plasterboards usually have at least one coat of wet plaster applied to them after they have been fixed. This covers over the joints between the sheets and gives a smooth consistent finish. Even though less water is used in the process than with wet plastering, the introduction of any amount of water into a building means that this water has to be gotten rid of before the building is habitable. As with wet plastering, surface dust is also a problem with this technique.

Wallboards are plasterboards that are made with tapered long sides. When these sides are butted these tapered sides form a shallow trough which can be filled with a small amount of wet plaster bringing the surface of the joint level with the surrounding boards. Wallboards can be decorated directly as one of their paper surfaces is of a high quality to receive paint.

More care must be taken erecting wallboards than with wet plastering but the low water content of the procedure makes it very desirable to use. If the joints in wallboard are made dry - by using a wooden coverstrip, the use of water can be avoided completely. Dry jointing will require that you take care in positioning the joints so that their appearance is neat and not too clumsy looking. Extreme care in workmanship will also be needed.

If you want a smooth wall or ceiling surface that you can paint over the wet jointed wallboards are the best way of getting it. The amount of water used can be very small. The only problem that you are likely to have doing it this way is the dust created when the joint filler is smoothed off with sandpaper after it has dried. If the room has a good through draught blowing across it when the sanding is being done the dust residue can be kept to a minimum.

All types of gypsum products have a good ability to absorb and release water vapour. This is of benefit where a natural internal environment is being created.

Oftentimes plasterboards and wallboards are made with an aluminium foil backing that acts as a barrier to the passage of air through external wall of a building to the outside. This is done in an effort to prevent condensation occurring in the vicinity of the timber studding to which the boards are fixed. Foil backings also act to cut down the amount of heat passing through a wall.

Sensuous interior finishes allow us to be intimate with the buildings we occupy. Clay plaster finish with ochre paint.

The interior of buildings is where the Mysteries of Life reside ... it is critical therefore that our choice of internal finishes acknowledge this.

Generally gypsum plaster is for internal finishing and decorative use. If gypsum plaster is used in its dry state this will keep down to a minimum the amount of water introduced into the building process. Precast moulded pieces can be used to good effect in taking the bare look off of large flat wall and ceiling areas. Gypsum contains no toxins and is safe to use.

One of the main complaints about stud walls is the difficulty of putting a nail into it to hang a picture on the wall. This problem can be overcome by the use of a picture rail from which anything can be hung.

Gypsum plaster including wallboards and plasterboards perform excellently in fire. Depending on the thickness of plaster or board used, walls and ceilings can be fireproofed to the standards normally required by local fire regulations.

A common complaint about internal stud walls is that they transmit noise from room to room too easily. This is true and it happens because these walls are for all intents and purposes hollow, so when they are banged the boards on the surface act like the skin on a drum - they amplify the sound. This problem can be overcome by deadening the ability of the wall to act in this way. This can be done by using thick slabs that will not vibrate when they are struck or by filling the hollow of the wall with a sound deadening material. Something as simple as newspapers or cardboard will do this adequately. Conventional insulation could also be used.

Choosing A Construction System

The choice of construction system for your home will be a matter of balancing the requirements of your Brief with your budget, with your builder and with your site. Of all these requirements it is the demands of your Design Brief that must be adhered to most rigorously. This is because such demands as 'warm internal surfaces' can only be met by using timber framing. Similarly, a desire to build inexpensively will require that you get involved in the construction yourself - this would also point to timber frame as the system offering the best option to you. Generally, opting for concrete cavity walling will be a wholly mental approach to what is essentially a feeling process. Such a selection would normally exclude you from the construction process also.

A yurt displays its bare bones and delicate skin

A sensitively finished interior will constantly delight

Your choice of Construction System will be a balance of your design requirements, your budget, your builder and your site.

Hand-built with love and dedication

The nitty gritty side of your chosen construction system - the *Building Regulations, Working Drawings, Costing* etc. - will be covered in subsequent *Parts* or indeed can be gleaned from other sources. What is critical at this point in the design process is to declare your preference in choosing Materials, Products and a construction system that will allow you to easily assemble these to create the type of home you most want for yourself.

Recapturing time is one of the primary objectives of the sheltermaking process

Summary

Construction deals with the assembly of your chosen materials and products to create a sound, warm, weather-tight, dry and healthy building.

If you wish to design and build carefully you will be working within the aims of the Building Regulations.

Generally all building structures consist of foundations, walls, floors and a roof.

Timber Frame Construction is the oldest form of building.

Your choice of Construction System will be a balance of your design requirements, your budget, your builder and your site.

Sheltermaking fosters deep connections and fills us with hope

Sheltermaking is all about building our homes and nurturing our lives

Sheltermaking is an ancient and revered tradition, remnants of which reside in our genes and can easily be awoken and nurtured.

Traditional turf house with thatched roof Co. Cavan, Ireland

Like its companion *Services*, Drainage & Electrical, *Plumbing* can be thought of as a kind of 'insert' into the 'body' of the building design. What this means is that the pipes, tanks, panels and wires associated with these *Services* are inserted, or, threaded through, the building fabric occupying little space but nonetheless carrying out vital functions. While the relative 'smallness' of these hardly affects the building size at all, minimising pipe and cable runs is important for various reasons. This has an effect on the layout of the various *Spaces* in the design and consequently this must be taken into account before the building 'plan' or layout, is finalised.

Plumbing covers all aspects of delivering water to the various parts of the building that require it. Information on your particular requirements will be contained in your *Brief*. It is a good idea to extract this information before going any further. This will be stored in your *Space Plans*, your *Space Analysis Sheets* and, if you intend to have a 'wet' heating system, in your *H&V* File. Print the *Plumbing Worksheet* and list on this *Spaces* that require hot & cold water supplies. Include the *Boiler/Heat Pump Room*, if are going to have some form of central or underfloor heating. Create a *Plumbing* File to keep the *Worksheet* in.

The critical things to take into account when designing a *Plumbing* System are:
1) Consumption of hot and cold water.
2) Wherever hot water is required should be close to where it is being produced.
3) Central heating systems require extensive pipework and the installation of radiators which can be intrusive unless 'designed in'. If this is your chosen system you need to examine your *Space Plans* and consider where in each *Space* radiators are going to be installed. Also, bear in mind that the principle set out in 2) above applies to central heating systems.

Read the Plumbing chapter, noting as you proceed various items particular to your design - for example, you wish to use solar panels to produce some of your hot water, or, you wish to harvest rainwater to provide for some of your consumption. Enter this information onto the *Plumbing Worksheet*. Also, begin gathering information on the various products available - particularly their likely cost.

Finalising a *Plumbing* system is a post-planning, *'Working Drawing'* exercise - in other words it happens at the 'detailed design' stage of the project, just before you go on-site to build. It is work that should be discussed/agreed at that stage with a plumber - preferably the one who will carry out and maintain the installation. At this point of the design exercise meeting the demands set out in *Items 1-3* above will suffice to ensure that the building layout or plan, shortly to be created, will facilitate that detailed design and installation. If you intend to have some form of boiler or heat pump, make sure that you have a *Space* designated for that.

If you are working on replanning, upgrading or extending an existing house you will need to gather information on the existing system. Refer to the *Surveying* chapter in *Volume 1* for information on how to do this. In the case of wishing to install solar hot water panels the orientation of the existing roof will also be required.

As piped-in water supplies become more expensive and more degraded with chemical additives, collecting rainwater becomes more and more attractive. A 'collector area' for rainwater is essentially a roof delivering water to gutters and downpipes which discharge into a storage tank or tanks. Such tanks can stand above ground and should be of such quality that they do not contaminate the stored water which can therefore maintain its potable quality. Equally, roof coverings and rainwater goods should not contaminate rainwater as it is being delivered into storage. Alternatively stored water can be used exclusively for use in toilets, in the garden, etc.

Next: SDP34 - Services, Drainage, page 156

Rainwater storage tanks used to shelter a vegetable garden

Plumbing

A safe and reliable source of fresh water is essential to any home. Sources of water for domestic use include the public mains supply, springs, wells, and, boreholes. Plumbing is the word used to describe matters dealing with the supply, distribution and use of water within buildings.

Most of the world's water cannot be used because it is saline or locked in glaciers and ice sheets. Only a very small percentage of the remaining water is present in rivers and lakes or in the ground - groundwater.

Water contains such things as minerals, salts, trace metals, nutrients, bacteria and organic matter. Groundwater chemistry depends mainly on rock type. Limestone makes water hard with high concentrations of calcium and bicarbonate. Such water is referred to as being 'hard'.

Public water supplies are sterilised - using chlorine or chlorine and ammonia - before being passed on to the consumer. Flouride may also be added.

Water from a spring or well that is intended for domestic consumption should be subjected to biological and chemical analysis before consumption. It might also be advisable to have any piped-in water supply so analysed.

The main chemical indicators of water pollution are ammonia, nitrates, chloride, potassium and manganese. Bacteriological examination tests for the presence of faecal bacteria in the water.

Some purification is oftentimes necessary to remove impurities and to reduce the hardness of water from springs and wells. Filters can remove lead, aluminium, and other metals as well as chemicals from the incoming supply, though to get inert, chemical free water, a battery of filters would be needed

Filters, if used, need to be well maintained as bacteria can reproduce within them. Silver is oftentimes used for this purpose as it inhibits bacteria growth.

Domestic Water Supply Sources:

Public Mains
Springs
Wells
Boreholes

Most of the world's water is saline or locked in glaciers and ice sheets.

Water Can Contain:

Minerals
Salts
Trace Metals
Nutrients
Bacteria
Organic Matter

Chlorine
Ammonia
Flouride

Potassium
Manganese

Water filters need to be well maintained otherwise bacteria can reproduce in them!

Group Water Schemes

In many cases a public or 'group water supply' is available to the consumer. In such cases the Local Authority or other body will administer the scheme. It should be remembered that water received in this way is metered and paid for on the basis of consumption.

Group water supply schemes usually run under the public road and the water is piped into individual properties in a plastic supply pipe. This is normally carried in a 750mm deep trench to the house or to where the supply is required. Stop valves or stopcocks are normally provided both at the road as well as where the trench meets the house. This ensures that the supply can be cut off when necessary - for maintenance, repairs etc.

A water meter might also be installed by the Council close to the road.

Where land is being selected as a potential building site, the availability of water should be carefully investigated. Where a mains supply does exist it should be confirmed that access can be had to this.

Wells

If no piped supply exists on-site, a water diviner can locate a groundwater source and a well can be made.

Any on-site water supply should be located upslope of any likely sources of contamination. Such sources could be nearby septic tanks, slurry pits, factories etc.

The type of well you end up with depends on the depth of the permanent water table on-site - in other words how deep down the natural water level is.

The water table level can be discovered by digging a deep hole on-site. Such an excavation can yield information not alone on the water table but also on general soil conditions, percolation etc.

In the case of dug wells and boreholes, a submersible pump is normally used to take water from the well and deliver it to the dwelling. A 13mm pipe is used for this and stopcocks and isolating switches are used to cut off the supply where and when required. Alternatively, a bucket/winch can be utilised where the well is shallow! Similarly, a wind pump will prove very effective in pumping water either from shallow or deep bore wells.

Water received from a Group Water Scheme is usually metered and paid for on the basis of consumption.

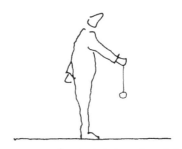

When a building site is being selected, the availability of water should be carefully investigated.

Any on-site water supply should be located uphill from any likely source of contamination.

143

An old fashioned dug well can be used if the permanent watertable level is less than 4.6m (15ft) below ground level in a dry summer.

A bored well is suitable if the watertable is more than 4.6m (15ft.) below ground level in a dry summer. Some people believe that the water from such wells is from too deep in the ground and is too rich in minerals etc. for safe consumption.

Up to 1M of rainfall can occur each year. This can be a valuable source of water for non-drinking use - for example it can be used for toilets and for watering the garden, washing the car and so on. Soft rainwater is also valued for hair washing purposes.

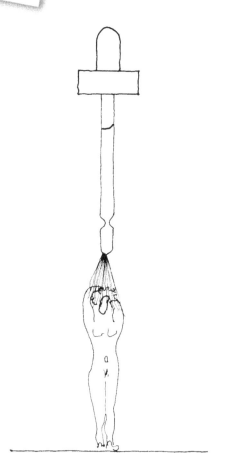

Harvesting rainwater is becoming more and more important as piped-in supplies become more and more polluted by such things as fluoride.

Rainwater is perfectly healthy for drinking!

Need & Consumption

A water allowance of 230L/50 gal per person per day should be allowed for in calculating daily water needs.

In practical terms, any well or borehole should be capable of providing 1/6th of your total daily water need in any one hour. For example, the water yield necessary for a 5 person household is 5x50 gal = 250 gals. Therefore any well or borehole should have a minimum yield of 250/6 = 41 gal per hour.

Toilets use up to half of the incoming water in any home.
Baths and showers use one third - 33%
Drinking and cooking accounts for 5-10% of total use.
Laundry takes up 8% and dishwashing, 5%
In the garden 2% of the water supply is used.

Flushing the toilet uses between 2 and 4.5 gals or 9-20L per flush. You can cut this by up to 30% by using a brick or bottle in the cistern. New toilets use 6L or 3 gals. per flush.

A shower delivers 20L of water per minute - a water saving shower head can halve this. Alternatively, an egg-timer fixed to the wall of the shower will ensure that shower time is kept down, thus saving water!
Taps - their delivery varies from 10 to 20L per minute.
A washing machine uses 110-220L of water per load.
Front loading machines use 40% less water than top loaders.

Care should be taken in the selection of all machines, appliances and fittings that utilise water to ensure that consumption, and therefore waste, is kept to a minimum.

All water using appliances should be carefully selected to ensure that consumption and waste are minimised.

Other Water Uses

Apart from the use of water for cooking, washing and toilets, water is also a major component of heating systems. Because it can move easily and can carry a lot of heat, water based heating systems are very common. Central heating and underfloor heating systems are based on the distribution hot water through pipes. These can either be copper or plastic.

Water in heating systems is normally sealed which means that the same water is used over and over again within the system.

Apart from its 'practical' applications, water can provide a pleasant and soothing feature in a conservatory or garden. Fountains, pools and even lakes are possible to the imaginative and daring! Water in front of a sunspace/solar collector will greatly assist in the gathering of solar radiation as well as allowing for deep reflection.

Flowing water has well known psychological benefits and can also provide a useful source of power either for practical or frivolous purposes.

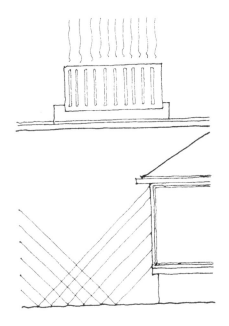

Plumbing - The Regulations

Refer to the Regulations pertaining in your area

Building Regulations require that dwellings be provided with a bathroom containing either a bath or shower and a washbasin. Kitchens must be provided with a sink of adequate size and a draining board. Hot and cold running water must also be provided to these fittings.

'Sanitary conveniences' - meaning toilets or urinals - must be located in a space dedicated to that purpose, or in bathrooms.

Any space containing a sanitary convenience must be separated from any area where food is prepared or cooked by a properly ventilated lobby.

A washbasin must be provided close to a sanitary convenience and this must be provided with hot and cold running water.

All sinks, washbasins, toilets, etc. should be designed and installed so as to be easily cleanable.

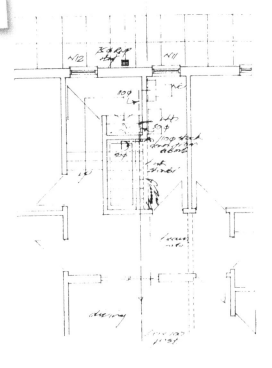

Plumbing Systems- Cold Water

The simplest plumbing system is one which relays the incoming cold water directly to where it is needed - i.e. to taps, toilet cisterns etc. This type of system is known as a direct system.

Direct systems are not permitted where the incoming supply is from a County Council main as they can reduce pressure for consumers further down the 'line'.

Where the water supply is from a private well, a direct system can be used, though the efficiency of the system will depend on the number of draw-off points and on the pressure available. If the pressure is excessive, damage can be caused to taps and valves.

A more versatile plumbing system is known as the indirect system. In this, the incoming water supply is piped into the house usually in a one inch plastic pipe, called the 'supply pipe' - this would be coming from a mains supply or from a private well.

In the case of a County Council mains supply, it is permitted to take only one tap off this supply pipe - the kitchen tap. The kitchen supply is taken directly off the supply pipe as, in theory, the water will be fresher than water taken from the tank in the roof. In the case of a private well, it is desirable to only draw water from the supply pipe for use in the kitchen. The remainder of the incoming water is then piped in a 'rising main' to a high level storage tank usually located in the attic. It is from this tank that all other points in the house requiring cold water are fed. These would be - toilets, sinks, bidets, showers and the hot water cylinder.

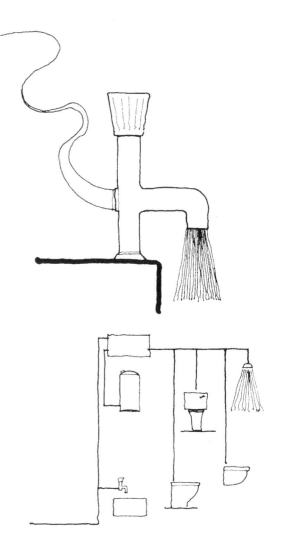

Plumbing Systems - Hot Water

Commonly, domestic hot water is produced by heating cold water within a copper cylinder. This is done either by using an electric element or by utilising heat generated by a boiler that is then fed into the cylinder. A draw-off pipe takes hot water from the cylinder and delivers it to taps, shower heads and so on.

The production of hot water by electrical means is carried out with an immersion heater. This is an electrical element that is inserted into the copper cylinder.

Where a boiler of any sort is being installed this can also be used to produce hot water by directing hot water into the cylinder. This is usually done 'indirectly' using a coil within the cylinder. High recovery cylinders are those

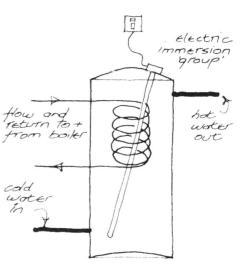

146

which 'recover' hot water quickly after a hot tap has been run.

Pipes carrying hot water should always be insulated to reduce the heat loss from them. Cold water pipes should also be insulated as they can be subject to condensation. This is particularly true of copper pipes.

Normally plumbing pipes are carried in floors and walls and are concealed wherever possible. The practice of locating water pipes within concrete floors is a bad one as leaks can prove to be disastrous.

In principle plumbing 'runs' should be kept as short as possible which means that kitchens, utility rooms, boiler rooms and bathrooms should be located either side by side or one above the other. In many ways the ideal setup is to have the boiler located centrally with short radial arms extending out from it.

Once the basic principles of plumbing are understood, specific reference should be made to publications devoted to the topic. And remember, it is a plumber who will know how to make a system work best.

Apart from the simple hot and cold water systems described, which are quite straightforward and simple to understand and install, more sophisticated plumbing arrangements can be utilised. A pressurised system, for example, eliminates the need for a storage tank because the incoming water supply is pressurised and then distributed in this pressurised state to all taps etc. Such systems are more complex and expensive both to install and to service. The benefits are that constant pressure is maintained and there is no need for a high level storage tank.

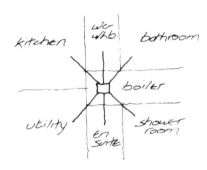

Cardinal Rules:

All hot and cold water pipes should be insulated.

Water pipes should never be buried in concrete floor slabs.

Plumbing runs should always be kept as short as possible

Central Heating

Central heating uses hot water to distribute heat to the various parts of a dwelling that require it. The water used for this is heated by some form of boiler and is usually then circulated by means of a pump through a series of pipes. Radiators are installed within these pipe runs and when the circulating hot water fills the radiator it sets up a convection current which heats the air around it. The word 'radiator' is a bit of a misnomer as these units provide heat primarily by means of convection. This means that it is the air that is being heated, not the fabric of the space. Reference should be made to *H&V chapter, page 262, Vol. 1.*

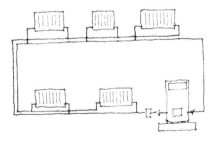

There are many forms of central heating systems, the 2-pipe system being the most common. In this a flow pipe carries hot water from the boiler and a return pipe carries the cooled water back to the boiler, with the assistance of a pump, to be heated again. Variations in pipe size, boilers, radiator type are possible. Sealed or open systems can also be installed. In an open system, a small header tank of water is located in the attic and this maintains the correct water level within the system by topping it up when there is evaporation. In a sealed system there is no header tank and the system is pressurised. This allows for smaller pipes, higher temperatures and more efficient radiators to be used though a 'low water content' boiler is required to make the system operate efficiently.

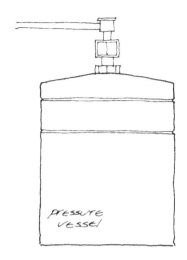

pressure vessel

Obviously the more sophisticated a system gets the more expensive it becomes and possibly it becomes more difficult to service and maintain. Simplicity always has a great appeal, of course.

Temperature control with central heating can be in the form of room or radiator thermostats. Temperatures can be preset and maintained, time settings can be made to turn the system on and off automatically and other sophistication enjoyed.

Central heating boilers should be located as close to the centre of the system as possible thereby avoiding long pipe runs. The hot water cylinder should also be sited nearby. The boiler is sized according to the calculated heat losses. Boilers can either be of the solid fuel 'back boiler' type or can be automatic units fuelled by oil or gas. Radiators are sized according to the heat losses from the spaces where they are located.

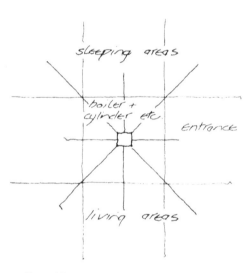

Central heating boilers should be located as close to the centre of the system as possible.

As with all aspects of building services, experts will help you fine tune your basic design intentions. Computer programmes are oftentimes used for the purpose of sizing systems also. Once your intentions are clear to yourself, the help you need will be found quite easily.

Underfloor Heating

Underfloor heating is a form of central heating that utilises lower temperatures. Instead of conventional radiators the floor itself is heated up and radiates out its heat to its surroundings. This provides for a far gentler form of heating, lower air temperatures and a more benign heated environment.

As with central heating, the boiler in an underfloor system should be located centrally allowing for 'loops' to be sent

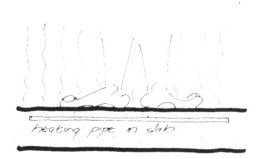

heating pipe in slab

148

out in various directions. These loops are connected to a manifold which maintains the desired temperature in that particular loop. These temperatures can be adjusted and set as desired.

Because the water temperature in an underfloor system is much lower than in a conventional central heating system condensing gas boilers can be used very effectively.

Normally concrete is the preferred 'medium' for underfloor heating though suspended timber floors can also be fitted with the system. This overcomes some of the time lag problems encountered with concrete slabs.

.

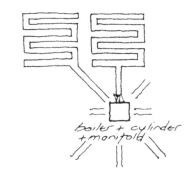

Pipes & Components

Copper and plastic are the principal piping materials in present use both for heating and for plumbing while steel is used in radiators and boilers.

Copper piping is not suitable for use below ground and strictly speaking it should not be buried in concrete floor slabs either. However, where this is unavoidable, the pipes should be lagged with newspaper for protection.

Joints are formed in copper piping either using soldered or compression fittings. Soldered joints are simple to install and are relatively cheap. Difficulties however can be encountered with leaks in a system that is solder jointed. Compression fittings make for a very versatile and long-lasting copper piping system.

Plastic piping can either be jointed using a jointing piece with solvent or compression fittings can be used. Plastic and copper systems can also be intermixed.

Boilers, taps, sinks and all other plumbing fittings should be chosen with care. Decisions and choice will relate to many factors - who is doing the work; funds; personal preference; availability, and so on. An abundance of colourful literature will be available to the designer, detailing in intimate detail the performance and promise of these products. Common sense will be your greatest ally in finding your way through this information.

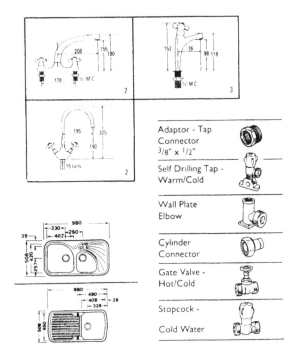

Adaptor - Tap Connector 3/8" x 1/2"

Self Drilling Tap - Warm/Cold

Wall Plate Elbow

Cylinder Connector

Gate Valve - Hot/Cold

Stopcock - Cold Water

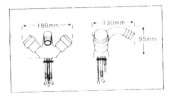

Solar Water Heating

Each year the sun pours 10,000 times more energy onto the planet than is currently used. This energy is very useful for the generation of low temperature heat and is especially good for the production of hot water.

The average home requires up to 3000kWh of energy per year for heating water. On average 1000kWh of solar energy per year falls on an inclined, south facing surface of 1 sqm. Usually it is possible to collect between one quarter and one third of this. In practical terms, there is sufficient solar radiation available in these latitudes, to provide up to 60% of a houses' annual hot water needs.

Radiation comes from the sun in the form of electromagnetic waves. These are invisible to the naked eye and lie in the infra-red portion of the spectrum. Of this radiation, 60% of it is 'diffused', meaning that it passes through cloud cover before reaching the ground. The balance, 40%, falls directly on the earth. This is what we call 'sunny'.

To collect the available solar energy in order to heat water requires some form of 'solar collector'. There are many different types. Choice of type comes down to selecting the most suitable technically for the requirements and restrictions of the application. Reliability of course is essential. The chosen type should also be long lasting and easy to maintain. Basically there are two forms of solar collectors - flat plate collectors and evacuated tube collectors.

The sun annually provides 10,000 times more energy to the planet than is currently consumed.

Flat Plate Collectors

More commonly known as 'solar panels', flat plate collectors were originally developed for use in sunny and warm climates, like the Mediterranean. A typical panel consists of a glass fronted insulated box containing a matt black metal panel or matt black pipes full of water. When solar radiation falls on the panel, the black surface absorbs the radiation in the form of heat. The water within the panel or pipe then begins to heat up while the insulation ensures that as much heat as possible is retained. Water is drawn off the panels either by natural convection movement or more commonly by pumping it to a storage tank. This warm or hot water is normally used for washing purposes.

Solar panels will operate in almost any daylight conditions. Sunlight filtered through cloud cover or reflected up from the ground will still produce results. In summer, 4sqm of a good type of panel, mounted at

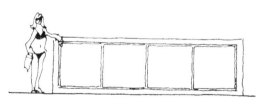

150

between 30deg and 60deg to the horizontal and facing south-east to south-west should produce most of the hot water required by the average family home. This would be 40-50% of its hot water needs over a year - 100% on a good day and 10% on gloomy days. The collector should be mounted in an unshaded position tilted to face a little west of south. Other orientations between SE and SW and tilts from 10-50deg cause only minor reductions in the overall energy collected however. The panels can be mounted on the roof or on a specially made frame located as close as possible to the hot water tank.

Solar panels are particularly cost effective for swimming pools or situations where large quantities of warm, rather than hot water are required.

The benefits of solar panels are considerably reduced when conditions become unfavourably cold, cloudy or windy. In higher latitudes, the best overall performance is achieved by using the collector to preheat cold water before it is fed to the existing hot water tank where some other form of heating is used to bring the tepid water up to usable temperature. A separate, insulated, solar tank is oftentimes used for this. Such a tank would have a capacity of around 50l or 10gal.

Where solar heating systems cannot satisfy the total demand for hot water throughout the year they are usually used to pre heat the water before it enters a conventional water heating system. The water heated in the panel is piped from the collector to a storage tank circulating either by means of natural convection - thermosyphon - or by using a pump which is more common. A direct solar water heating system heats water, holds it in the solar store and passes it on to the domestic hot water tank. In an indirect system there is no direct contact between the heat transfer fluid and the domestic hot water system. The solar water/fluid is circulated from the storage tank through a heat exchanger coil immersed in the hot water cylinder. Anti-freeze and corrosion inhibitors can be added to water based indirect systems or special oils can be used instead of water. This reduces the risk of corrosion and increases efficiency.

For maximum efficiency as a heat collector solar panels should be designed so as to maximise the sunlight absorbed and to minimise the heat losses due to convection and conduction. The amount of heat absorbed depends on maximising the incoming radiation reaching the absorber - affected by the orientation of the panel and by the type glazing used.

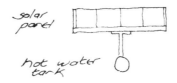

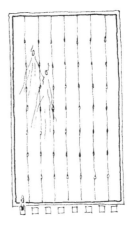

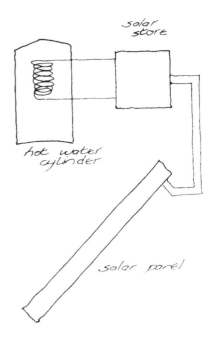

151

Another critical factor is the absorber plate efficiency. This is affected mainly by the material of the absorber and its surface finish. The water flow rate is also a factor in maximising efficiency.

Heat loss from solar collectors depends on the absorber surface finish and on the type and thickness of the panel insulation and glazing. Matt black is an excellent absorber surface, but at high temperatures this results in significant heat losses from the front of the collector. Coatings called 'selective surfaces' are now often used on absorbers to increase efficiency - thin films of semiconductor materials such as black chromium, black nickle, oxidised stainless steel or black copper oxide. These have a high absorbance of solar radiation but are poor emitters of thermal radiation, so heat losses are greatly reduced. Double glazing of panels used for space heating applications are recommended where there is a high winter demand.

To get the most from a solar panel installation some form of control system is required. A solar controller - a piece of electronic gadgetry - compares the temperature of the collector with that of the system circuit and signals a small pump when to start and stop. This prevents a reverse flow from taking place when the panel might begin to draw warm water back from the storage tank and radiate it out to a cold night sky. Systems operating on the thermosyphon principle do not need pumps or controllers but need large bore pipes, valves and careful pipe routing. All indirect systems should be filled with a special antifreeze solution to prevent winter freezing, otherwise the system should be drained and used only in warm conditions. Airlocks can sometimes present a problem, especially after a system has just been filled with fresh water. Automatic bleed valves or manual bleed valves will solve this problem.

Once again, if you wish to utilise such a system, expert advice taken at an early stage of the design process will prove to be invaluable. Such advice can oftentimes be obtained simply by reference to specialised published information.

Surface Absorbances For Solar Heat

Percentage indicates amount of available radiation that is captured:

Whitewash; white paint; polished aluminium - up to 20%

Light coloured paints; polished copper - 20-40%

Medium shade paints; aluminium paints; light red bricks and tiles - 40-60%

Black and other dark paints; asphalt; bituminous felts; slates - 80-100%

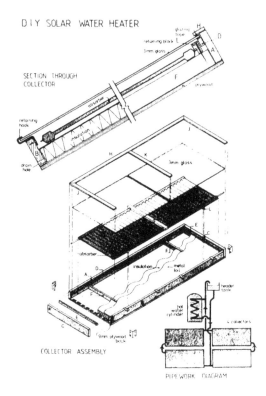

DIY SOLAR WATER HEATER

SECTION THROUGH COLLECTOR

COLLECTOR ASSEMBLY

PIPEWORK DIAGRAM

ASSEMBLY

1. Screw and glue together frame (A,B,C and C).
2. Screw and glue frame onto backing ply.
3. Attach corner plates.
4. Fix parts F, insulation and metal foil.
5. Mount absorber with retaining blocks.
6. Drill pipe entry holes and fit pipes. (N.B. After tightening fittings onto pipe, absorber cannot easily be removed again).
7. Fit glazing stops D and E, and central support G.
8. Fit glass retaining hooks.
9. Glaze with putty or glazing tape and screw on parts H, J and K cover strips.
10. Drill drain holes.

The Simplest Flat Plate Collector

A conventional radiator, of around 1sqm in area, painted matt black, fronted with glass and contained in an insulated box will function as a basic solar collector. The efficiency of such an arrangement can be quite high, though the large water content makes the collector slow to respond to changes in radiation levels. This will cause some loss of performance in winter conditions but is thought to have little effect on the annual total energy collected. The radiator needs tapped connecting holes at all four corners to allow for a diagonal water flow internally. The panel is connected to either the HW cylinder or to a dedicated solar tank. Condensation can be a problem with this type of panel, though efficient ventilation will overcome this. More suitable as a source of summer hot hot water, this simple type of solar panel can be made very economically.

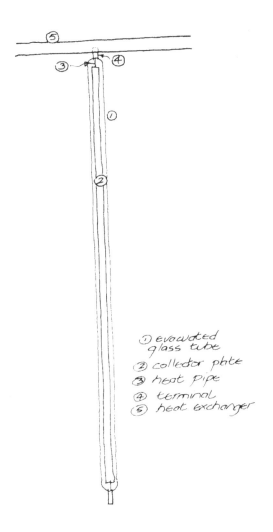

Evacuated Tube Collectors

Evacuated tube solar collectors are the latest development in efficiently collecting solar radiation. They are designed for high performance, converting direct and diffused solar radiation into heat. This provides either hot water for washing or even contributes to low temperature space heating systems.

These collectors consist of a 65mm diameter, 2m long, glass tube that has been evacuated. Within the tube there is a black copper absorber plate. Attached to the back of this plate there is a stainless steel heat pipe connected to a terminal protruding from one end of the tube. The vacuum within the tube eliminates convection and conduction losses and also protects the plate and the heat pipe from damage in adverse conditions.

The tubes operate with very high efficiencies particularly under poor solar conditions and can respond rapidly to changes in radiation levels thus making good use of short sunny periods. They are frost resistant, lightweight and easy to transport and assemble. An average family would need 30 tubes to provide for their hot water needs.

The tubes work by having a collector plate with a special selective coating that converts the maximum amount of solar energy into heat with few losses. Attached to the back of this plate is a heat pipe that is a super efficient conductor of heat. A special fluid within this pipe evaporates when heated and transfers the heat

1) evacuated glass tube
2) collector plate
3) heat pipe
4) terminal
5) heat exchanger

153

to the top of the heat pipe where a stainless steel terminal attaches to a manifold heat exchanger. When the vapour within the heat pipe comes in contact with the 'cold' manifold heat exchanger the vapour condenses, gives up its heat and the fluid returns to its original position. This cycle is repeated over and over again and all the while heat is being carried away to the HW cylinder or to a solar water tank or some other storage system.

More sophisticated and expensive than flat plate collectors, evacuated tubes are simpler to install and to maintain. They should be located with a southerly aspect, inclined to the horizontal. They can either be mounted on the roof or on a special framework. This should be convenient to the hot water tank.

This type of windmill is perfect for pumping water either from a well or from storage tanks

The Plumbing File

The Space Plans already assembled can provide the basis for displaying your plumbing requirements. Use photocopies of the plans for this, indicating the type of units that require connection to hot and/or cold water, possible radiator locations etc. It is useful, for clarity, to use coloured markers to indicate hot and cold supplies. These plans should be stored in the *Plumbing File*.

Details of sinks, WC's, showers, taps, boilers, radiators etc. should also be assembled along with relevant pricing information.

When the building layout is being organised your marked up Space Plans will form the basis of the overall Plumbing Layout. Possible locations for back boilers, boilers, hot water cylinders, solar collectors etc. should be considered at this stage and this information stored in the *file*.

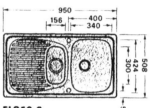
EL950-2
Overall size 950 × 508. Cut out size 930 × 488 × 13mm corner radii. Main bowl size 340 × 424 × 160. Half bowl size 156 × 300 × 125. Suitable for 600mm wide sink base

Summary
A house requires a reliable source of clean, drinkable water.
Domestic water consumption should be carefully controlled to avoid waste.
Building Regulations require that houses contain a bathroom and kitchen supplied with hot and cold running water.
Solar Energy can provide a large portion of domestic hot water requirments.

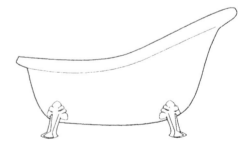

Rainwater storage tanks

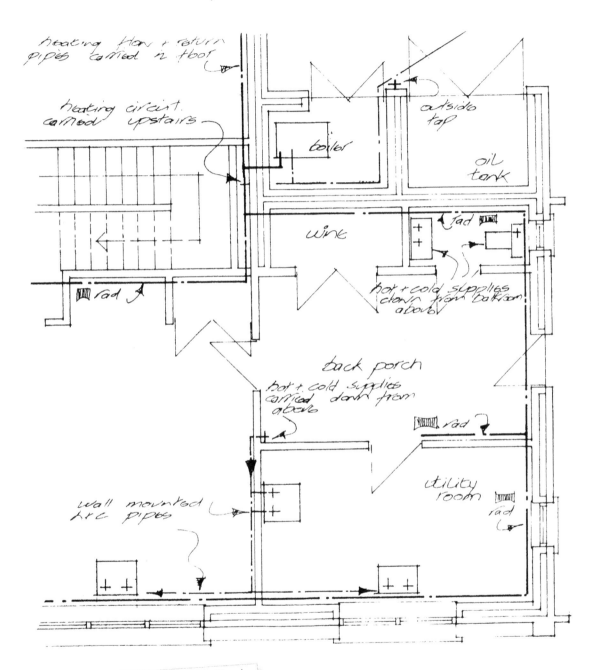

heating flow + return
pipes carried in floor

heating circuit
carried upstairs

boiler

outside
tap

oil
tank

rad

wine

hot + cold supplies
down from bathroom
above

rad

back porch

hot + cold supplies
carried down from
above

rad

wall mounted
h+c pipes

utility
room

rad

A plumbing layout is overlaid on a building plan
... pipe runs should be kept as short as possible
and concealed while remaining accessible

155

Drainage is the 'other side' of *Plumbing* because it carries waste water away from where it has been used and delivers it to some form of treatment system for cleansing. It is this latter aspect of *Drainage* that requires most consideration at this stage of the design process. *Drainage* also covers rainwater disposal.

Drainage requirements mainly affect the outside of the building where pipes, manholes and so on need to be buried in the ground. Prevailing site levels become critical in many cases, especially where a site slopes. The ability of the installed treatment system to properly cleanse waste water are critical in the protection of the wider environment. Because a *Drainage* system is essentially hidden and the effects of system malfunctions may take place away from view, it is critical to install a system that is certain to work properly. Clearly, the minimisation of the volume of waste water produced reduces the 'work' the system has to do in achieving this.

Read the entire chapter. Print the *Drainage Worksheet* and note on this what type of system you wish to use. If you already have a site the system information can be 'keyed' into this when the *Site Analysis* is being carried out. Any specific requirements of the *Local Authority* for that area should also now be assembled. *Percolation* and *Water Table Tests* should also be carried out as detailed in the *Manual*. Check with your *Local Authority* the exact form of the *Tests* required in your area. If you are going to acquire a site its drainage capability should be considered before purchase. Enter *Percolation* and *Water Table Test* results onto the *Drainage Worksheet*.

The option of installing a compost toilet should be investigated as a means of by-passing the difficulties of disposing of septic tank effluent. This will be a matter for the *Local Authority* or other regulatory body to decide on.

Where the drainage system in an existing house is being altered or extended thorough survey information of the existing system will be required in order to formulate realistic proposals.

Next: SDP35 - Services - Electrical, page 167

Drainage

Drainage systems take the waste water from a house and dispose of it via pipes either to a public drain or more likely to a septic tank. The outlet from the septic tank is then either connected to a percolation area, a reed bed system or some form of treatment plant.

The drainage requirements of sinks, wash-hand-basins, showers, washing machines, baths etc. usually involves connecting these units to a two inch waste pipe. This pipe incorporates a simple trap to prevent smells from the drain escaping back into the building. Toilets are normally connected to 4in. pipes.

Drainage systems always have a vent pipe which protrudes above the eaves of the house. This allows smells originating from the system to be vented off at high level.

Rainwater is always kept separate from the so called 'foul' system. Caught in gutters and gulleys, rainwater is simply piped to 'soakaways' where it seeps back into the ground.

Soakaways are holes in the ground about three or four feet deep that have been filled back with stones. The pipe from the rainwater system - usually a 4in pipe - will discharge over the top of these rocks and so the water will return to the ground. It is important to ascertain the permeability - the grounds' ability to absorb water - before deciding how deep or shallow the soakaways should be. Their location is also important of course.

Rainwater can also be held above ground for use in watering plants and for other non-consumptive applications.

Some distinction is usually made between the 'greywater' and the 'foul' elements of drainage waste. Greywater is water flowing from baths, sinks, showers etc, while foul water is that coming from toilets.

The overall aim of any drainage system is to ensure the effective and speedy removal of waste from the house. This aim also includes the disposal of the waste in a way that is non polluting.

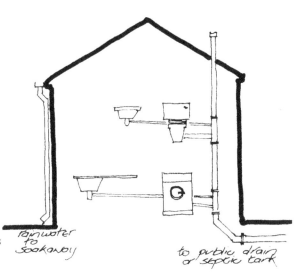

Rainwater is always kept separate from the foul drainage system.

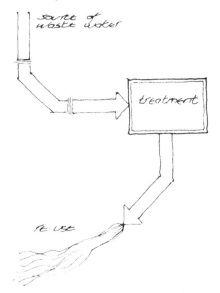

The overall aim of a drainage system is to ensure the effective and speedy removal of water-borne waste from the building and to dispose of it in a safe and non-polluting manner.

Drainage Systems

In practical terms, from the point of view of the occupancy of the house, the prevention of foul air entering the building is a major priority. Ready access to pipework via rodding points etc. is also critical. Protection against extremes of temperature, protection against corrosion and the restriction of the likelihood of siphonage are also important. Siphonage is where the water 'trap' on a unit is sucked away leaving the unit open to smells from the system. Proper venting of pipework prevents this occurring. All units requiring connection to a drain must be 'trapped' with a satisfactory water seal and means of access. The minimum depth of these seals should be: 75mm for traps on pipes up to 50mm dia and 50mm for traps on pipes over over 50mm dia.

Waste pipes are themselves connected either to a 'stack' or they discharge over a gully located outside the building. A 'stack' is a vertical pipe, 3 or 4 inches in diameter that has a number of units connected directly to it. A stack itself is normally carried internally and runs underground out of the building to meet the external drainage system.

In a two pipe system - that is, a system consisting of two stacks - the waste pipes from toilets are routed to one stack while the pipes emanating from sinks, whb's, baths etc. are conveyed separately to another stack - this is the so called 'greywater'.

As with the single pipe system, ground floor sinks, showers etc. are usually connected directly to gulleys which are themselves then linked up with the stack/s carrying waste from upper floors.

A two pipe system is relatively costly and involves using a large number of pipes in comparison with a single stack system. On the positive side, such a system allows greywater to be recycled independent of the foul waste, though this is a facility also obtainable in a single pipe system where all the waste is emanating from the ground floor of the building.

The stack diameter required is all systems is 100mm/4". The bend/s at foot of stack/s where it/they emerge from the building should have a large radius - two 135 degree bends can be used.

In both two pipe and single stack systems the pipes emerging from the building normally run underground in 4 inch pipes. Where kitchen or other waste is likely

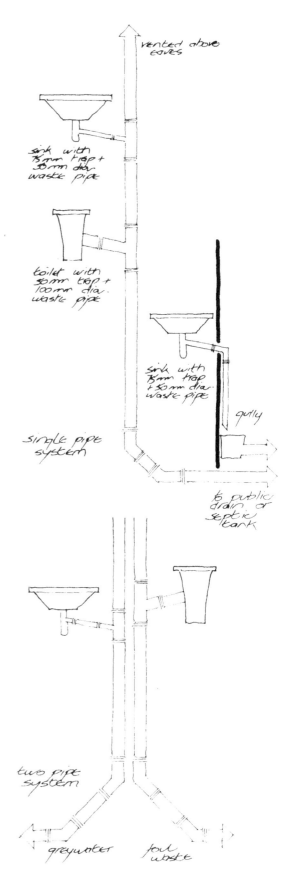

vented above eaves

sink with 75mm trap + 50mm dia waste pipe

toilet with 50mm trap + 100mm dia. waste pipe

sink with 75mm trap + 50mm dia. waste pipe

gully

single pipe system

to public drain or septic tank

two pipe system

greywater   foul waste

158

to contain grease or chemicals interceptor traps can be fitted to trap these substances and prevent them from contaminating the system. Such traps - or gulleys - are fitted immediately outside the building where the contaminated waste is emerging.

Where gullies and stacks meet, manholes are created allowing for access should problems of blockage etc. arise. Where underground waste pipes change direction either a manhole or an armstrong junction is installed to ensure that any blockage can be gotten at and cleared by rodding.

Where ground floor appliances are connected to a stack rather than to a gully, the vertical distance between the lowest branch connection and the bottom of the first manhole should be at least 450mm.

The 4 inch pipe/s carrying waste/greywater run either to a septic or some other form of tank. Septic tanks are then connected to percolation areas, reed beds or a mechanical treatment plant. Greywater waste, if it is being treated separately, is routed to a percolation area, reed bed or mechanical treatment plant.

Underground waste pipes must be laid to falls of at least 1 in 80, more usually 1:40.

Generally, in any drainage system appliances need to be closely grouped to be economical. What this means is that bathrooms, kitchens and so on should either be side by side or one above the other.

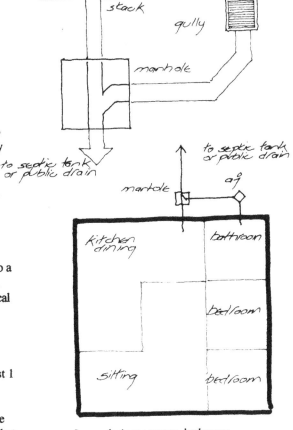

In any drainage system, bathrooms, kitchens, utility rooms etc. should be closely grouped.

Compost toilets offer a viable and waterless alternative to 'wet' toilets ... and produce a valuable compost into the bargain!

Drainage Pipes

In regards to drainage pipe material uPVC is most commonly used. These can handle wastes up to 80degC while modified uPvc can handle 90degC. Joints are usually push-fit 'O' ring fittings or solvent cement joints. Remember that plastic pipes need to be able to expand so they should be mounted to allow for movement! Cast iron, spun iron and vitrified clay pipes can also be utilised.

Gulleys, manholes, armstrong junctions and so on are also manufactured in plastic and will give adequate service. Where vehicular traffic is likely to cross a manhole or other junction, cast iron covers should be utilised. Junctions can also be constructed in rendered blockwork.

Septic Tanks

Septic tanks function to allow settlement of solid waste and do not adequately treat sewage. The main treatment of the sewage effluent occurs when the effluent enters the ground. It is the soil which are relied upon to render the effluent harmless. As the effluent moves through the granular material of the surface it is subjected to various physical, chemical, and biological processes which remove many of the chemicals and break them down into simpler usually less harmful substances. Where the liquid effluent emerging from the septic tank passes through the ground too quickly the necessary breakdown does not take place and the groundwater is contaminated.

Septic tank effluent is highly polluting if it directly enters water because it contains bacteria and viruses as well as nitrogen and phosphorus. The most serious type of water contamination resulting from insufficiently treated septic tank effluent is Ecoli, a faecal coliform bacteria present in the gut of warm blooded animals. The presence of this is water is an indicator of the possible presence of pathogenic microbes which could cause diarrhoea, hepatitis, dysentery, typhoid fever and gastroenteritis. Farmyard waste can also contribute to the presence of Ecoli in groundwater.

A septic tank is a settlement tank wherein the settled solids form a sludge on the floor of the tank. Anerobic digestion of the solids within the tank results in their breakdown and partial liquefaction with the evolution of gas. A scum forms on the liquid as maturing occurs. An outlet pipe from the tank discharges liquid effluent when the tank contents rises above the level of the discharge pipe. A properly operating tank will reduce the suspended solids and the BOD level. BOD stands for 'biochemical oxygen demand' - this is, the amount of oxygen required to promote proper breakdown of the effluent while it is within the tank.

Further treatment of the emerging effluent is carried out either within a percolation area, a reed bed or a mechanical treatment plant. When properly installed and functioning these systems will discharge treated effluent that will not contribute to polluting water sources.

The septic tank should be at least 1.5m/5ft. deep below the level of the drain connected to the building being served. There should be at least 300mm airspace under the tank roof and the inlet and outlet pipes should extend 450mm below their respective inlet/outlet

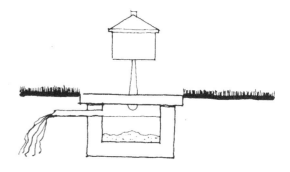

Septic Tanks function by allowing solid waste to settle in the bottom of the tank. They do not adequately treat the sewage entering them.

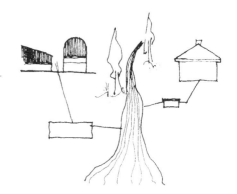

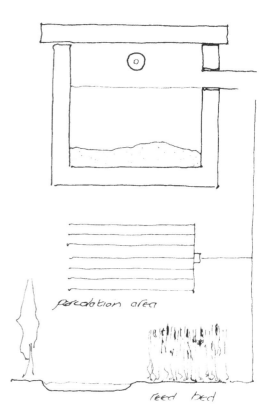

percolation area

reed bed

160

levels. When in use a scum should form on top of liquid in the tank within 1 month. If not, pig manure or well rotted farmyard manure can be used to promote the necessary breakdown.

The size of septic tank required is based on the number of persons likely to be using the system . The tank will provide 12 months sludge storage if all the household waste is routed to the tank. If greywater is to be recycled separately a longer storage period will result.

No. of persons: 1-4 2720l / 600gal.
                5-9 3750l / 825gal.

The length of septic tanks is generally three times width and consist of two interconnected compartments, the first containing sludge and the second containing effluent.

Tanks may be installed 24ft. from house being served and not less than 60ft. from the nearest point of any adjoining dwelling. The drainage to the septic tank from the building will be vented at the house to release foul smells from the system.

A septic tank should be desludged when the depth of sludge in the first compartment is greater than 18in/450mm. 75mm of sludge should be left in the bottom to reseed new sludge.

Septic tanks are connected to percolation areas, reed beds and treatment plants via 100mm pipes.

Percolation Areas

A Percolation Area is designed to receive septic tank effluent and to discharge it uniformly through the soil. The size of percolation required for any system is based on the likely volume of effluent it will have to handle and on the 'percolation' of the ground where it is to be located. It is desirable that the highest level of the water table within such ground should be below the bottom of the percolation medium.

Percolation Tests

In order to ascertain the percolation ability of the soil a percolation test must be carried out. This is done by excavating a test hole 300mm square and 450mm deep below the bottom level of the first percolation pipe. The sides of the holes should be scratched to allow water to percolate out of the sides of the hole as well as exiting through the bottom. 50mm of coarse sand or fine gravel

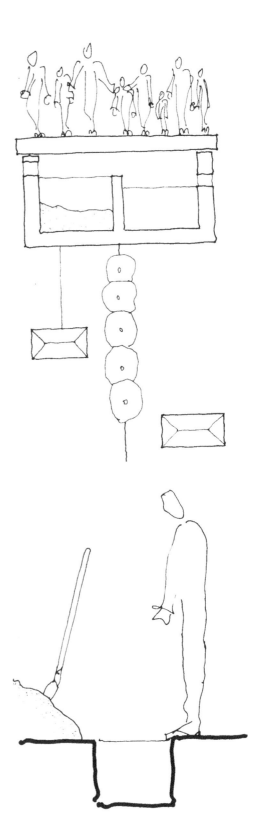

161

should also be placed in the bottom of the excavation. The hole is then filled with clear water to a depth of 300mm and the hole covered. The hole is refilled the next day with water to depth of 225mm and the time for this to completely soak away is observed. The time in minutes is then divided 9 (9" = 225mm) to get the average time for the level water to drop by 1 inch.

The test hole is then covered for a further 24 hours and the test repeated three further times, on successive days. The average time resulting from the four tests is then obtained by totalling the four test results and dividing this total by four. This average is then given the value 'T'.

The length of distribution pipe required for that particular location is then ascertained in accordance with the following table:

T in mins.	Pipe length in M
1	17
2	21
3	26
4	30
5	35
10	47
15	56
30	78
60	105

The required length of piping is then divided into at least three equal lengths.

Test failures may be due to to presence of impervious soils. This will appear in the average by making T greater than 60. In such instances it is necessary to replace unsuitable soil with fine gravel or course sand.

A further cause of test failure may be due to a high water table level on-site. A further test should be carried out to ascertain this:

Water Table Tests

Excavate a trial hole 1mx1mx2m deep. Cover this for at least 48 hours. Examine the hole after this period. The depth of water should not exceed 600mm after this time. Should it be the case that the water level is above the 600mm level after the 48 hour period has elapsed it may be necessary to install land drains may reduce site water table level. Alternatively, the percolation area can

2.4   Percolation test:

The purpose of this test is to determine the percolating p of the percolation area required is obtained from Table 1

2.4.1   Test procedure: The test holes which are 0.3m × below the proposed depth of the invert level of the perc approximate dimensions, about 50 litres of water will b

2.4.1.2 The bottom and sides of the holes should be scra remove any smeared soil surfaces and to provide a nat water may percolate.

2.4.1.3 Clear water shall be poured into the excavation

2.4.1.4 Additional clear water shall be added as nece: 300 mm until the subsoil has become swollen and satu

The need to saturate the soil as described is to simulate surrounding the trenches in the percolation area.   Th on the soil type and its moisture content at the time considerable moisture before saturation is reached

2.4.1.5 Thereafter, the time required for the water expressed in minutes divided by 4 is the time fo: value "t".

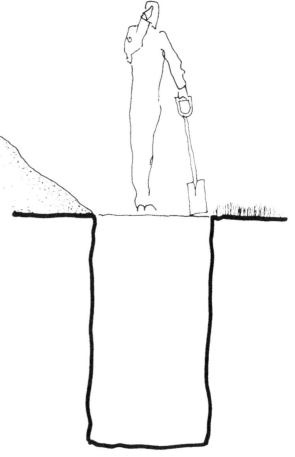

be built up sufficiently to allow the system to function properly.

Ideally, one should be building on a site where percolation can be obtained without encountering the expense of importing soil and building up ground. A further thing to avoid is underlying rock - the presence of this will easily be ascertained by excavating for the above tests.

Percolation Area Construction

A Percolation Area consists of distribution pipes laid 2m apart in lengths not exceeding 60ft. No part of the PA can be within 60ft. of any adjoining house; within 60ft of any road boundary or fence or within 10ft of adjoining boundaries. Furthermore the PA cannot be:
Within 100ft of any stream, river, lake or private well.
Within 200ft of any public water supply source well etc.
Within 300ft of any seashore or lake or river bathing area.

The distribution pipes are 75mm in diameter and are laid in sections of 300mm, open jointed with 6mm gaps. The pipes are laid in trenches 750mm wide and are surrounded by at least 150mm of course gravel for the full width of the trench. The gravel should be 40-28mm in size and is covered with plastic sheeting. The distribution pipes are vented at each end, 9" above ground level. These pipes should fall no more than 1:200.

In order to accommodate a proper drainage system using a Percolation Area the following guide, as to necessary site size, should be used:

A site with 3 free boundaries should be not less than 1000m2 one quarter acre.
A site with two free boundaries should be a minimum of 2000m2 or one half acre.
A site with no free boundary should be a minimum of 4000m2 or 1 acre.

Constructed Wetlands

Where it is impossible to install a conventional Percolation Area, or, where this is not desired, a Reed Bed systems can also be used. Reed Beds or 'Constructed Wetlands' accept the effluent emerging from the septic tank and carry it through a specially constructed wetland consisting of selected water plants, microscopic organisms, aerobic and anaerobic substrates and a meandering water column. Such a system can remove nutrients, organic compounds and metallic ions and increase oxygen and pH levels in a variety of waste waters.

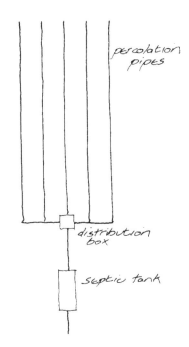

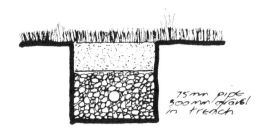

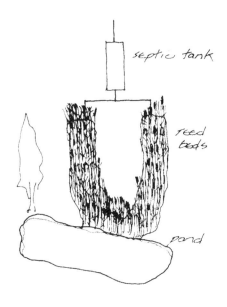

163

Most constructed wetlands/reed beds are marshes -
these are artificially made and consist primarily of
cattail, bulrush, rushes or reeds. Wastewater treatment
efficiencies are very good especially for BOD's and
fecal coliform bacteria. Further advantages of such a
system lies in the fact that a habitat for wildlife is also
being constructed and that a pleasant landscape feature
also results.

A typical system consists of a Marsh-Pond-Marsh
configuration. The first marsh accepts the effluent from
the septic tank and consists of a shallow basin with
densely growing marsh vegetation - typically cattails,
bulrush, reeds or rushes in 100-200mm of water. This
marsh functions to reduce BOD and to remove
suspended solids, metals and pathogens.

The Pond, with a depth of 500-1000mm of water,
functions to further reduce BOD. and most significantly
for nitrification and denitrification purposes. Duckweed
grows on the surface of the Pond. Pondweeds may also
be planted in shallow portions of the pond to further
promote treatment.

The 'emergent' Marsh consists of a shallow basin
growing marsh vegetation - cattail, bulrush, reed or
rushes in 100-200mm of water. The outlet from the
emergent marsh carried 'clean' water which can be
directed as wished, either into the ground or flowing to
an existing watercourse.

In the creation of Constructed Wetlands an impervious
membrane is required to line the bottom of the Marshes
or the Pond. This can consist of clay or, more normally,
plastic.

Reed Beds can be used to treat all the wastewater
emerging from a building either 'combined' i.e. foul and
greywater mixed or, alternatively, separate beds can be
created to treat these individually.

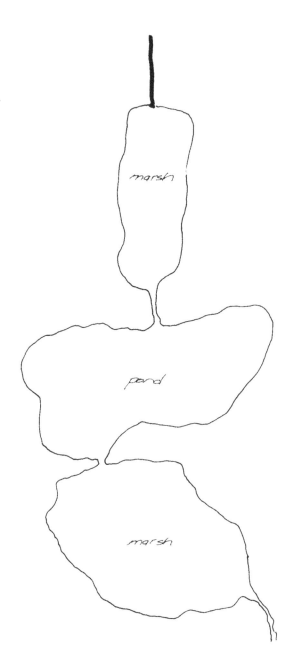

Treatment Plants

Where neither a Percolation Area nor a Constructed
Wetland is to be used to treat effluent a mechanical
treatment plant will be required. Such units rotovate
sludge to reduce BOD. They are most suited to tight
urban/suburban sites where no alternative to their
installation is possible.

Rainwater

Rainwater and surface water are never piped to Septic tanks or any other form of drainage system. Such water is normally piped underground to 'soakaways' from whence it can percolate bach through the ground. Rainwater can also be held above ground for various used. Care should be taken that roofing materials, lead flashings etc. do not contaminate this.

Rainwater Gear

Rainwater Gear - RWG - consists of metal or plastic pipes and gutters. Installing seamless aluminium gutters is an on-site operation. Aluminium is however probably too soft a material for this purpose. Plastic and galvanised RWG will give better service.

Critical factors in selecting and sizing RWG -
The roof area to be drained and the gutter flow capacity. The distance of any gutter angle (i.e. bend) from the outlet is also important. Downpipes are connected to gullies which themselves are connected to soakaways.

Drainage File

The type of drainage system that you wish to use should be contained in your *Drainage File*.

If you must use a Septic Tank and Percolation Area details of this should be on the File as well as the Requirements of the Local Authority.

If a main drain runs near to your site and you are connecting to this, you should have its location marked on a map and have some idea of how deep it is under the road.

If you are considering using a Reed Bed and/or recycling 'greywater' details of how you are going to do it should be collected and stored in your *file*.

Information on gutters, downpipes, gullies, armstrong junctions etc. can all be on this *file*.

In addition, Space Plans should have noted on them requirements in regards to drainage. All sinks, showers, baths, toilets etc. will require a pipe running from the receipticle to the outside of the building to carry away waste water.

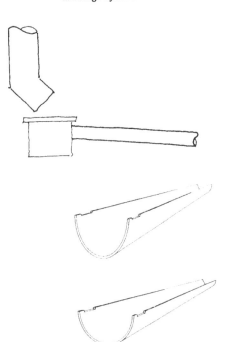

Rainwater should never be piped into a septic tank ... or into any form of foul drainage system.

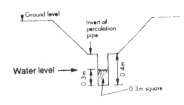

Percolation Test Hole

Summary

Domestic waste water is disposed of via pipes connected to public drains or to a septic tank.

Rainwater and domestic waste water must always be disposed of separately.

A distinction can be made between 'foul' waste water and 'greywater' and the means of their disposal can differ.

Septic tanks must be connected to a percolation area, a treatment plant or to a reed bed to properly treat the effluent flowing from them.

All waste water disposal must be carried out in a way that is non-polluting.

A compost toilet facilitates the retention of valuable nutrients on-site

A drainage layout is overlaid on a building plan ... pipe runs should have their diameter and the 'fall' they are to be laid at indicated on the drawing

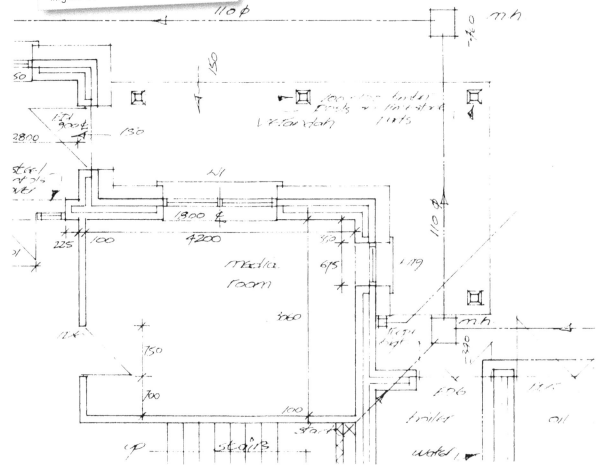

35 Services - Electrical

Key issues concerning domestic *Electrical* services are:

1)   Consumption

2)   Health

The issues surrounding consumption are obvious. These will become particularly clear if you opt for an 'off the grid' system! The issues surrounding health will be there whether you are making your own electricity or 'buying it in'. In particular, bedroom areas are those in most need of protection from the 'negative' effects of the electromagnetic radiation that accompanies electricity flow in cables. The location of the electrical distribution box and/or meter box needs careful consideration and should ideally be isolated from living and sleeping areas. Phenomena such as 'dirty electricity' also need to be thoroughly investigated as part of the design exercise as this can be detrimental to health. Dirty electricity is electricity which instead of having a smooth and consistent wave profile has acquired 'spikes' in its waveform as it made its way through the grid to the location where it is going to be used. Such spikes can be detrimental to health. Properly, all forms of electromagnetic radiation likely to impact a building need careful attention, particularly where it might be planned to broadcast wi-fi within a building or it is planned to use handheld phones.

Read the entire chapter and print the *Electrical Worksheets*. Outline on the *System Worksheet/s* the lights, switches, sockets, appliances and so on that each *Space* will require. Phone, internet and TV outlets should be included. If you have developed *Space Plans* you can even position these on your drawings.

If you intend to install some generating capacity of your own - photovoltaic cells, a windcharger or turbine - you will have to carefully calculate your anticipated consumption. You can do this using the *Consumption Worksheet*, which can also used where a conventional supply is to be installed. You will need to use several *Worksheets* to detail everything, so number these *Sheet 1, Sheet 2*, etc. Use the *Consumption & Supply Worksheet* to calculate your total daily consumption, the cost of this and the cost of installing an alternative energy supply. You should also obtain some costs for alternative energy equipment - particularly for the storage element which tends to be expensive. This is why 'consumption' is such a critical issue. It is worth noting the table on page 175 documenting the 'thirst' of many appliances.

An *Electrical* File should be created to store the *Worksheets* and any other relevant information, such as catalogues.

Electrical installations take up minimum space in a building and consequently have little effect on the evolving layout or plan. What might have an effect however is space for battery storage and a back-up generator. If you are 'going down that particular road' update your *List of Spaces/Space Analysis Sheets* to accommodate such storage space, if necessary.

Reading *Electrical Layout* on page 175 will give you an idea of what 'happens' when its time to incorporate *Electrical* system information into the *Working Drawings* for the building.

Where you are working on replanning, extending or renovating and existing building a thorough survey of the existing system will be required. Refer to the *Surveying* chapter for information on doing this.

Next: SDP36 - Planning Regulations, page 178

Being off-grid allows one to focus on consumption and connects one to nature

Electricity

All physical matter is composed of atoms. Atoms are made up of small particles called protons, neutrons and electrons. Electrons and protons are separated by an energy field that holds them apart. These particles are said to be negatively and positively charged respectively.

The separation of positively charged protons and negatively charged electrons within atoms creates a tension within the atom. This tension is known as an electrical field.

If electrons begin to move within a substance, that is they begin to detach themselves from one atom and grab onto another, that movement is called electricity. Electricity is therefore the flow of negatively charged electrons through a substance. When electrons begin to move, that is when electricity flows, an electrical field enshrouds that flow. A second field also enshrouds such a flow. This field is called a magnetic field. Electrical and magnetic fields, considered together, are called electromagnetic fields.

Natural electricity occurs in a form known as direct current. Direct current describes the way in which the electrons flow - in one direction only. All matter contains some form of natural electrical charge. Our brains are electrically operated and our cells are all electrically charged.

The natural electricity in the environment is all the time trying to earth itself, that is, it is trying to escape into the ground. Natural electricity can build up in the atmosphere and finally "earth" itself in the form of lightning. Any materials that impede this flow of natural electricity can cause an electrical charge to build up on that material. Clothing made from synthetic fibres oftentimes does this, holding the natural electrical charges produced by the body. Such a build-up is known as static electricity. Generally, the use of synthetic materials will lead to static electricity build-up. Such a build-up can cause disturbance to the balance of natural electromagnetic radiation.

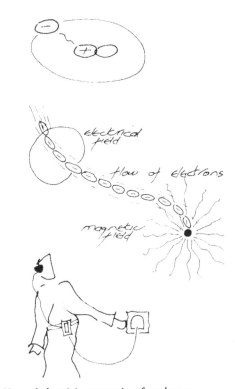

Natural electricity occurs in a form known as direct current - DC

Electromagnetic Fields

Flowing electricity is always accompanied by electric and magnetic fields. Where electricity is flowing in a wire these fields can be imagined as a sort of wrapping on that wire. Electromagnetic fields, as they are called, accompany any movement of electricity whether natural or manmade.

Human bodies use minute electromagnetic charges to carry out the functions of living. Our brains are electrically operated and our cells all contain electrical charges. Human metabolism is geared to the background levels of electromagnetic radiation reaching the earth from the sun and the planets. The earth also emits electromagnetic radiation. This electromagnetic field pulses at the rate of 7.83 beats per second. Our bodies electric system also pulses at about the same rate.

Electromagnetic fields move in straight lines at the speed of light and come in many different forms. These are distinguished by the length of the waves by which they move. This movement is called radiation because of the way the fields radiate out from their source. All this is, of course, invisible and therefore mysterious. For example light is an electromagnetic radiation. The wavelengths of light vary within a range from violet light to red light. Electromagnetic means a mixture of electric and magnetic. So, light is a radiation that is a mixture of electrical and magnetic energy. When this mixture strikes a surface it makes the surface visible to our eyes which are tuned to receive those wavelengths of electromagnetic radiation. The light that is reflected from an object determines the colour of that object. For example, a tomato reflects the red radiation striking it and this is what gives the tomato its red colour. Materials which absorb all the light radiation falling on them are black, in other words they reflect no light away from themselves but absorb it all.
Radio and microwaves are also electromagnetic radiations. So are X-rays, gamma rays, infrared and ultraviolet rays.

Natural electromagnetic fields reach the earth from the cosmos. The sun is the main source of such fields. Radiation is mysterious in that it can travel through the vacuum of space without difficulty. We are sensitive to and need electromagnetic radiation in order that our bodies can tune in to the natural world and function as they were intended to. We depend on these energies for our health of mind and body and we are sensitive to any unusual exposure artificial or natural. People also emit electromagnetic energy as do plants and animals.

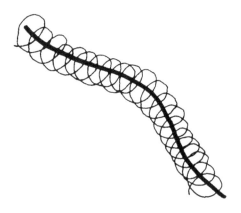

Flowing electricity is always accompanied by electric and magnetic fields ... electromagnetic radiation

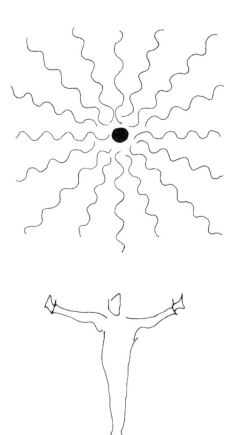

We are all sensitive to and need electromagnetic radiation so that we can tune in to the natural world ... an upset of this natural balance can be serious for our health.

Any upset in the balance of electromagnetic radiation surrounding us can be very serious for our our health. For example, if your body never got any sunlight it would almost definitely get out of balance - in other words you would get sick. The effects of the moon on the body are also well known. These are also caused by electromagnetic radiation. We normally use our senses to tune in to the electromagnetic world, using our eyes, our ears and most of all our sixth sense.

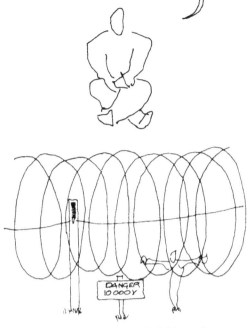

Where natural electromagnetic radiation is generally not harmful to people, manmade electromagnetic fields can be extremely hazardous. Hazardous fields are created when alternating current is passed through wires at high voltage or pressure. Such fields can impact our bodies with high dosages of electromagnetic radiation that are far in excess of what occurs naturally. The effects of such exposure are normally dealt with by our immune or defence systems. Stress is a normal feature of the human reaction to an excess of artificial electromagnetic radiation. Such radiation can exist in large amounts around high tension cables, transformers and even domestic appliances. Microwaves, cathode rays, radio waves also surround us from a variety of sources.

Man-made electromagnetic fields can be hazardous to people.

Much of the disturbance caused by an excess of artificial electromagnetic radiation is due to the use of high voltage alternating current. This is normally conducted into buildings from the national grid - the wires that deliver electricity to you directly from the power station. To make the electricity reach you it is sent down the wire under high pressure - voltage - much like water under pressure in a hose. High pressure is used to limit the losses that inevitably occur when electricity is moved from one place to another.

High-voltage Alternating Current (AC) produces very strong electromagnetic fields.

When that electricity reaches you it has been reduced somewhat in voltage at a local transformer but it is still dangerous. In fact it could quite easily kill you. As the electricity runs around your house in wires and is consumed by electrical appliances and so on, electromagnetic fields surround the electricity. These will effect you if you are within their range. For example, in sleep, our bodies renew themselves and are particularly prone to being disturbed by strong electromagnetic radiation. Such disturbance might only mean that you wake up not feeling rested. But you will be stressed. Your body has been disturbed in sleep and has not been able to properly renew itself. For this reason care has to be taken when locating conventional wiring in your design, especially in bedroom areas. Some experts recommend in fact that the electricity supply to bedrooms be turned off when you go to sleep! Generally, care should be taken where equipment with large motors and so on are located.

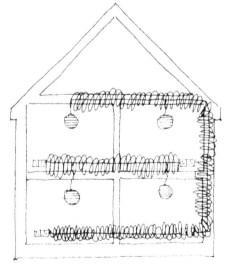

The electricity flowing around you house is surrounded by electromagnetic fields.

Manmade Electricity

Electricity can also be produced artificially. Windmills, dynamos, turbines and photovoltaic cells are all used to make electricity. Some of the electricity generated in this way is direct current, similar to the natural form of electricity. When electricity is made in large amounts commercially it is made in the form of Alternating Current. Alternating current is different to direct current in that the electrons responsible for the electricity flow move back and forth rather than flow always in the one direction. Alternating current is the preferred form of electricity in large scale production because it can be generated more efficiently than direct current and it can be transmitted over large distances with little loss of power.

The generation of electricity on a large scale is a very inefficient process. Waste heat and exhaust gases are produced by power stations. These stations have to be operated in response to consumer demand which peaks at certain times of the day. What this means is that everyone wants to consume electricity at the same time - at lunch or dinner time. Because alternating current cannot be stored, to meet the peak demand the electricity has to be generated as it is needed. When the demand drops, the production must also drop. Shutting down and starting up generating equipment like this is not an efficient use of this equipment. Power stations have to be made large enough to cope with these peak demands, another inefficiency.

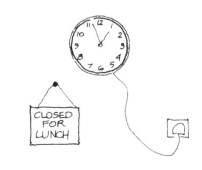

Oil, coal, gas or turf is oftentimes burned to make electricity. The power of flowing water is also harnessed to do the same job. Nuclear power is also used. All these types of power stations cause serious disruption to the natural balance of the planet when they operate.

Such facilities are set up to serve people and their needs for electrical power. In other words, power stations are there to supply a demand made by consumers who finance the operation of these stations. Any increase in overall demand is met by the construction of new power stations. Increased demand of course does not lead to increased efficiency, but rather to more waste. Improvements to the efficiency of many domestic appliances and artificial lighting can vastly reduce domestic electricity consumption.

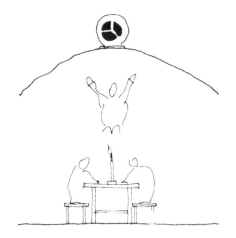

172

Photovoltaic Cells

There are several alternatives to obtaining an electricity supply from a national grid. Windmills, turbines and photovoltaic cells can be used for this. Of these photovoltaic cells probably offer the most viable alternative.

Photovoltaic cells are made from thin layers of silicon that become electrically charged when light falls on them. This electricity can be drawn off and used or it can be stored in a battery. The electricity is in the form of direct current. This type of current is ideal for operating artificial lights. Household appliances are also produced that work on this type of direct current, low voltage electricity. This would allow an entire house to be operated on this type of current. Where appliances are not obtainable that use direct current, the electricity being produced by the cells can be converted into normal alternating current operating at 220V.

Photovoltaic cells contain no moving parts, are lightweight and small and can supply all your normal domestic needs without getting hooked up to the national grid. Washing machines, fridges, computers, televisions and so on can all be operated from this source. The number of cells needed will depend on your electricity requirements. Additional cells can easily be added in to such a system. If all domestic appliances are operating on the direct current available from the cells, the electromagnetic radiation caused by the flow of electricity through the wires in your home will be very minor compared to those produced by conventional alternating current.

Because photovoltaic cells depend on sunlight to work there is always the possibility that your demand for electricity might not coincide with its natural production. Special storage batteries can overcome this, by keeping electricity in reserve. Where this is not sufficient - say, in dark midwinter conditions - a small wind generator can augment the supply. More than anything, photovoltaic technology and the consideration of its use to power our homes, will bring under serious consideration the amounts of electricity we consume.

Photovoltaic systems are rapidly becoming a viable economic alternative to conventional power. In situations where the conventional supply has to be brought a long way to the new building, the cost of installing a photovoltaic system will immediately become competitive with the cost of installing the conventional supply.

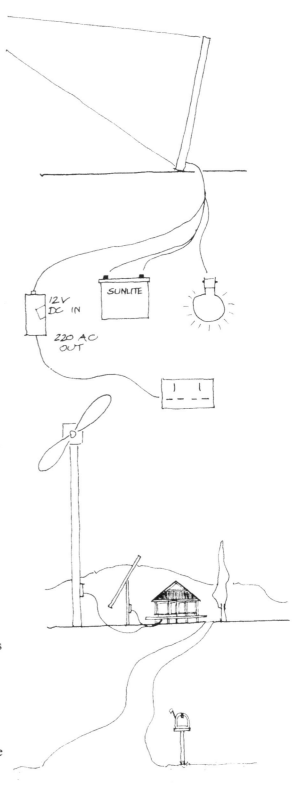

173

More than anything, photovoltaic systems reduce the likelihood of people being overexposed to large doses of electromagnetic radiation. Also, the way in which these systems work is very much in balance with the balance of nature itself.

Solar cells, as they are also known, have to be located facing south. They can easily be attached to the walls or roof of a building or be fixed to a small freestanding mast.

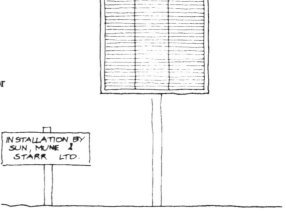

Windpower

Electricity generating companies are increasingly regarding large scale windmills as an alternative to conventional methods of power production. On a domestic scale, small wind generators can provide for your home needs. Again, use of such a system will bring you to a closer awareness of the balance of nature. The wind needed to power a wind generator will not blow consistently so reliance on the battery storage capacity will be greater than with a photovoltaic system which waits, not on the wind, but on daylight to begin functioning.

Wind generators have to be shut down if wind speed gets too high and of course they have moving parts and therefore need servicing. Their best use seems to be on a large scale or as a back up to a photovoltaic system.

The work that windmills can do, as opposed to the electricity they can generate, should not be ignored. Water pumping can be done directly with a windmill without the use of any electricity at all. The fun aspects of these machines should not be forgotten either. A simple sail mill will simply give pleasure for those watching its lazy movement. Detachable sails can be installed on such equipment so that it can be shut down easily if the wind gets too strong.

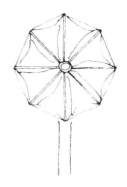

Windmills need to be carefully sited to take best advantage of the local wind conditions. If a wind system is to be part of your design you should carefully consider the location of the equipment in relationship to house.

Water Turbines

Flowing water can provide a consistent source of power to operate a turbine that will generate electricity. Such turbines can produce conventional alternating current. The application of such systems on a domestic scale will very much depend on the existence of a body of water with a suitable flow on your site. As with wind generators, turbines contain moving parts and so need to be maintained.

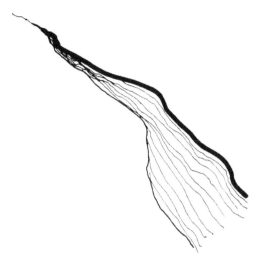

Electrical Layout

Whichever type of electricity supply you choose, the means of representing it on paper will remain the same. If alternatives to mains electricity are being considered, the amounts of power that you realistically need should be given careful thought. This should hold true even when considering a conventional system, of course! The use of a photovoltaic or wind system should be discussed with an expert at an early stage of your design.

The individual Space Plans in your *files* can be used to begin laying out the electrical services. This is done by simply marking onto the plans the positions of socket outlets, switches, lighting points and so on. If symbols are used to do this the information can be displayed simply and clearly. Information on telephone and TV outlets can also be marked onto the room plans. Any of your furniture and equipment that is electrically operated will need a power supply brought to it. You will also need outlets for casual use, such as plugging in a vacuum cleaner, bedside lights and so on. Extract fans, attic lights and so on should not be forgotten! Remember that some lighting points will also be required outside. Also, if you are using a conventional outside supply, the electrical company will require a meter box to be located on an outside wall where the meter can be read. The incoming supply first runs to this box and is then routed to the distribution board within the house. The distribution board is the place from which all the cables run to the various points within the house that require an electrical supply. In the event of a fault the board will close down part or all of the system as a safety measure. If this happens you may have to make your way to the distribution board in the dark to switch the electricity back on again. It should be located in a place that is easy to get at and at a reasonable height above the floor.

While the location of all electrical points can be marked easily onto the plans, the height of these above the floor has to be indicated by a figured dimension. Some thought needs to be given to what these heights should be. Socket

The amount of electrical power that you are likely to consume in your home should be given careful consideration at all stages of the design work.

Appliance	Power Rating (in Watts)	Normal Monthly Use (in Hours)
Water heater (quick recovery)	4500	82 9
Water heater (standard)	3000	113 3
Lights	1200†	160
Refrigerator/freezer (frostless)	425	317
Air conditioner	1300	80
Range	11.720	60
Clothes dryer	4800	17
Food freezer	300	250
Refrigerator	235	161
Television (color)	300	125
Dishwasher	1190	24
Television (b/w)	255	114
Frying pan	1170	14
Heater (radiant)	1300	10
Iron (hand)	1050	10
Coffee maker	850	9
Broiler	1375	6
Radio	80	90
Washing machine (automatic)	375	14 6
Toaster	1100	2 7
Vacuum cleaner	540	5 6
Food wastes disposer	420	5
Clock	2	750

outlets are normally required to be located at 450mm above floor level. Switches for lighting points should, of course, be located at a convenient height for normal use. 1400mm above the floor is normal for this. The connection of a light switch to the lighting point itself is shown by a straight line. Where this lighting point is located on the ceiling it is marked on the plan in the position desired and the symbol used for it will indicate that it is in fact ceiling mounted and not on the floor! Where wall lights are being used and the switches for them are located somewhere else in the room again a line is used to show the connection between the switch and the light. Alternatively, wall mounted lights can incorporate a switch in which case the symbol used will indicate this. Where lights are required that can be operated by different switches, for example, a landing light that can be switched on and off either from upstairs or downstairs, both switches are shown with lines running to the lighting point.

It is generally not necessary to concern yourself with showing the actual cable runs on your drawings, though some thought should be given to this. This is particularly true where a solid wall encloses the interior of the building. To accommodate the cable runs, chases or shallow channels must be cut in the wall to allow the cabling to be concealed. This, needless to say, is a messy job. Cables installed this way are enclosed in plastic or metal conduit.

In a timber framed building, cables can easily run within the timber frame construction and therefore be neatly concealed. It is also possible to provide holes or notches in the timber studding through which the cables can be threaded prior when the wiring is being installed. Such holes would be made at an early stage of the construction. Where insulation is to be installed within the timber framing it will effectively surround the electrical cables. This can easily cause a heat build-up if the cable used is not heavy enough to deal with the flow of electricity through it. Metal conduits can also be used in timber frame walls to protect the cables. Also, where vapour barriers are installed these have to be broken to allow sockets and switches to be mounted on the face of the walls. Any breaking of the vapour barrier negates the whole theory behind their use.

As with timber framed walls, electrical cables can also be threaded through timber floors. Again, holes or notches can be left to facilitate these runs. In general, wiring should always be installed where it can be gotten at if this should be necessary.

Electrical Points

Socket Outlets
Light Points
Light Switches
Telephone Points
TV Points
Electrical Appliances
Extract Fans
Outside Lights
Meter Box
Distribution Board

key to symbols

Light switch connected to:

ceiling light

wall light

twin switched socket outlets

cooker point

extract fan

telephone point

boiler

heating system control gear

TV point

bathroom wall mounted heater

distribution board

176

If each space in your design is examined you can decide the exact number and location of electrical, TV and phone points that you need. These can all be joined up when the overall plan is finalised.

It is a good idea to gather information on the type of sockets, switches and so on that are available. You can do this by visiting a local electrical supplier and asking to see their range. Catalogues should also be readily available. Fittings need to be selected so as to blend in with the overall effect you are creating in your building. Where socket outlets can often be concealed, light switches cannot be so these need to be carefully selected. The prices of the various types of fittings can also be found out at a supplier. Light fittings can also be looked at and priced in the same way. High efficiency lights will be more expensive that conventional ones, but savings will be made in the amount of electricity that you use. Dimmer switches are also a good way of controlling degree of artificial light in an interior. As you make your mind up about the various fittings you wish to use put this information into your brief document under an independent Electrical File. The electrical work will be considered as an individual item when it comes to pricing the construction.

It is easy to get carried away marking in electrical points on your drawing. Every point has to be paid for of course, so keep a check on the number of points you are showing. Whatever type of electrical services you chose to install, whether a conventional supply, wind power, photovoltaics or some combination of all of these, it is worth discussing your proposals with an expert before you finalise your layout.

If a conventional mains supply is to be installed in your house, it is preferable if that installation is laid out so as to avoid the creation of closed wiring loops. A radiating system, with wiring radiating out from a central point will avoid the creation of a cage effect, completely enclosing the occupants in large doses of manmade electromagnetic radiation.

Electrical File

Details of the electrical points required in all the spaces in your home should be recorded on the Space Plans or on tracings/photocopies of them. A simply notation using symbols for plug outlets, switches, light points, audio/video outlets, TV points, telephone and so on should be used to do this. The height off the floor of these items should be noted on these layouts - this is why it is a a good

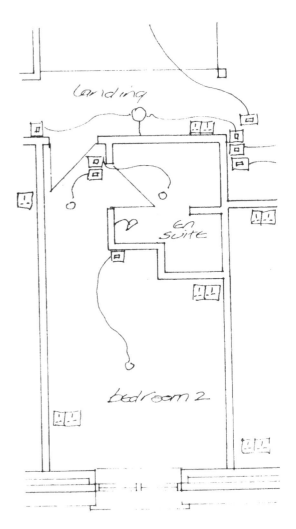

Avoid creating closed wiring loops when laying out the electrical system.

idea to keep this information on a separate sheet from the actual plan layout. The connections between light switches and the lights they operate can be simply indicated by a line.

Any outside lights or electrical points should be borne in mind. Also the requirements of the ESB as far as a meter box is concerned.

Catalogues of lights, outlets, switches should also be on this File.

If some alternative to the ESB is being considered - such as Photovoltaic Cells - details of this should be on the File as well as any special requirements of the system. This type of information can be gotten from any company that installs such systems. The same is true if Wind Power or Water Power is to be utilised.

Final Electrical Layout drawings are done at the very end of a project. As with plumbing, the experts are the people who do the work - the electricians. Final layouts should be agreed in consultation with a competent tradesman.

All conventional electrical installations have to meet the standards of the electrical supply authority and should always be carried out by qualified persons as certification is normally required before a regular supply is connected.

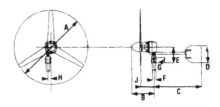

DIMENSIONS	A	B	C	D	E	F	G	H	J
Inches	72	21.4	47.5	16.7	15.9	3.54	5	3	14
mm.	1828	542	1205	425	403	90	127	77	355
SHIPPING SPECIFICATION (2 CARTONS)									
1 Carton		560 × 480 × 330 mm				Weight 47 Kg			
1 Carton		1330 × 450 × 250 mm				Weight 15 Kg			

Summary

Electricity is a natural occurence.

The flow of electricity is always accompanied by electrical and magnetic fields - electromagnetism.

Manmade electricity is generally far more powerful and dangerous to life than natural electricity.

You can generate electricity with photovoltaic cells, wind generators or water turbines.

The electrical layout of your home should take account of the effects of electricity on the body.

The subject of *'Planning'* is a rendezvous with the Real World. To understand the implications of this read the entire *Planning* section of the chapter. If you are designing for a jurisdiction other than the Republic of Ireland you will need to investigate the local regulations and assess their requirements.

It is important to understand how the *Planning* system has evolved and to develop a strategy to negotiate your way around the obstacles which it might place in your path. Generally speaking, avoid 'going against' specific planning policies as set out in any local *Development Plan*. Also bear in mind that *Planners* are primarily concerned with the general location of dwellings and with how a building looks on the outside. This leaves immense room to manoeuvre your way through what is essentially a cumbersome and paper-bound system. Also, check if your *Local Authority* publishes *Design Guidelines* that you must pay heed to.

If you intend to build 'under the radar' as it were, it is important not to over-expose oneself, quite literally! It is usual that neighbours are the first respondents to unapproved construction, contacting the local planning department who then obliged respond officially. So, if you are following this route make sure that your neighbours are on-side. Also bear in mind that the market value of property partially derives from the paperwork which supports it - in other words some form of permit or permission to build at that location. Selling a property without such documentation will limit the asking price as well as limiting the range of likely buyers. The lesson to be learned from this? Do not over capitalise. Keep any buildings small and simple and construct these in such a way that they can be deconstructed and re-erected elsewhere, or the materials salvaged for re-use.

If you already have a site, carry out the *'Planning Assessment'* exercise as set out on page 184. Create a *Planning* File to store this along with details of your *Planning Approval/Permission* if this is already in place. If you intend to purchase a site it is important to carry out the planning assessment exercise before you buy!

In the case of designing an extension you should check what information, if any, relating to your building, is held on file in the *Planning Office*. This can have a large bearing on how one approaches a *Planning Application* for an extension. Oftentimes extensions can be made without the need to apply for permission as long as the extended floor area falls within set limits - refer to Exempted Development on page 186.

Planning Permissions are granted for specific designs - what you are granted permission for is what you are supposed to build. If you vary too much from this problems might ensue, particularly with 'signing off' on mortgage draw-down payments.

Next: SDP37 - Building Regulations, page 188

Planning & Building Regulations underlie the 'certification' of buildings thereby 'securing' their value against debts undertaken in the construction process

Planning

The regulatory elements of Planning that need to be considered in any design and building project do not relate directly to individual need but to the so called common good. These elements are documented and laid out in the local Developmen Plan.

The Development Plan

This is a document prepared by the Planning Office of the relevant Local Authority which sets out development objectives and lays down guidelines and standards as to how these objectives might be achieved. A Development Plan strives to control development by adherence to these guidelines and standards.

Development Plans are reviewed every five years or so. Before a new one is approved a Draft Copy is made available to the public and submissions can be made as to its contents. These submissions, usually objections, are taken into consideration by the Local Authority before the final draft of the new Development Plan is passed and becomes the functioning instrument of planning control.

The Planning issues relevant to your building project do not relate directly to individual need but to the so-called Common Good.

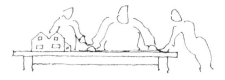

All Planning Applications are considered in the light of the current Local Development Plan

Planning Authorities consider all applications for building and development projects in relationship to the guidelines and standards laid down in its current Development Plan. These guidelines and standards range from being very general to being very particular and do not in themselves provide ready made design solutions. Rather, they act as an influencing force that strives to harmonise development and make for a better built environment. Generally, the objectives of any Development Plan can be considered worthwhile.

Development Plans recognise the importance of proper housing development and try to facilitate this in every possible way. While this may not be recognised by many people it is nonetheless true. It should be remembered that planners do not design buildings but merely consider other peoples designs when they are submitted to them for Planning consideration. What planners do is to provide the context in which development takes place. It is left to the individual designer to create building designs that recognise this and use it as a positive influencing factor on the evolution of an individual design solution.

In truth, it is the recognition by Planning Authorities of the importance of housing development that has allowed the spread of insensitive and unimaginative designs. Because Local Authorities recognise the general housing need and the importance of housing development they make every effort to facilitate it. It is the exploitation of this fact that has led to what is called planning blight. Planning blight is very much a misnomer and should be more properly called design blight.

The lack of imaginative solutions to what is quite a simple and straightforward design exercise - the design of a house or houses and small ancillary buildings - is the cause of this design blight. Planners are not designers but rather they consider other peoples designs in relation to the objectives of the Development Plan. Because of this their influence on design has been minimal. It is building designers who are at fault here not planners.

Stringent guidelines and standards have had to be introduced into Development Plans because design standards have dropped so low. It is in an effort to improve overall standards that modern Planning Regulations exist at all. The way that Development Plans have evolved is very much in response to the

Development Plans recognise the importance of proper housing development and try to facilitate this.

The Planning Issues

1. When do I need planning permission?
Generally, you need planning permission for any development of land or property unless it is specifically exempted from this need. The term development includes the carrying out of works (building, demolition, alteration) on land or buildings and the making of a material (i.e. significant) change of use of land or buildings.

Planners themselves do not design buildings but provide the context within which development takes place.

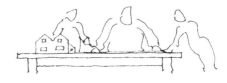

Planning Blight should be more properly called Design Blight.

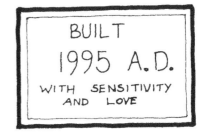

BUILT
1995 A.D.
WITH SENSITIVITY
AND LOVE

Refer to the procedures and regulations pertaining in the area where you are building

reality of the built environment. These plans have had to become more stringent and more direct in demanding particular kinds of solutions to design problems. This can be seen in the new demand for vernacular design. These demands would not exist at all if proper design solutions were regularly submitted to Local Authorities.

The aims of the Local Authority in relation to housing development will be clearly expressed in the Development Plan. This document may be consulted in the Planning Office or in the Public Library. If it is remembered that all planning applications are judged in the light of these objectives individual design solutions can be made that harmonise with these objectives.

Planning Permissions

The majority of building projects are subject to Planning Permission being obtained from the relevant Local Authority. These permissions can be divided into two categories, Outline Permission and Planning Permission.

Outline Permission sanctions development in principle on a particular site. No design is submitted with the application but only an verbal outline of the development that you wish to undertake.

Planning Permission sanctions development for the particular design submitted with the application.

In a case where Outline Permission has previously been granted for development on a particular site, an application for Planning Permission on that site is classified as Planning Approval.

Where development has taken place without Planning Permission being obtained an application for retrospective Planning Permission is called Retention.

Similarly, where Planning Permission has been obtained but the development is substantially different from the design that was submitted with that application, an application for Retention must be made for the revised design.

Planning Applications should be very carefully considered before they are submitted to the relevant Local Authority. All applications must be accompanied by a copy of a public notice that indicates the intention to seek Planning Permission. This can either be in a newspaper circulating in the area or a notice erected at the property in question.

County Development Plan : Applicants are advised to refer to the County Develop
    (i) clearly states the POLICIES of the Planning Au:
    (ii) contains comprehensive guidelines on Desig:

Large-Scale Developments : Applicants considering large-scale developments
    Planning Authority in the preparation of the applic

Dwelling House : E.S.B. Connection : Applicants are most strongly urged t permission to establish :
    (i) that the site can be provided with a service,
    (ii) that the terms quoted for such a service have been agro

Extension : Where an application relates to an extension to an existing deve
    (i) new works are to be clearly identified by means of colour le
    (ii) the detailed drawings (layout, plans, elevations, sections) proposed).

Effluent Disposal :
  Public Sewer: Submit detailed layout and longitudinal-section drawings as to s
  Septic Tank: The provision of the septic tank and percolation area are to Ireland standard recommendations S.R.6:1991 (Available fr 8370101).
    Soakpits are not a satisfactory alternative to percolation a

Development Contributions: Where public services (e.g. water/sewerage/rr development then it is the normal practice of th: towards the CAPITAL cost of such infrastruct The current contributions for a residential uni:

with above rates being subject to review. T payable to the Sanitary Authority. Cor development.

Most new buildings require Planning Permission from the Local Authority before construction can take place.

MINIMUM DOCUMENTS TO BE LODGED WITH AI

1. PUBLIC NOTICE must be given for all planning applications and MUST state :
  ★ "Kilkenny County Council" as a heading;   Rate
  ★ Applicant's name:
  ★ Clearly Define whether { Permission / Outline Permission / Approval } is being sought;
  ★ The Location of the land;
  ★ The Nature and Extent of the Development.   Con

Public Notice shall be given both by (a) a Notice erected on the site and (b) by advertisement in a newspaper
(a) On-site Public Notice MUST be
  Conspicuous, visible and legible from Public Road - further details are prov
  Maintained on-site for not less than 1 month after lodgement of applica:
  become defaced or illegible within the period.
  Two copies of the site notice must be lodged with the application docu:
  The position of the notice must be indicated on the accompanying pla
(b) Newspaper Public Notice. (2 copies to be submitted)
  (i) must be published in a newspaper circulating in the area and whi:
  The following newspapers ONLY are acceptable to Kilkenny County C:
    Kilkenny People   Munster Express (up to Th
    Irish Independent   Irish Times Irish Pri
  (ii) the full page of the newspaper must be submitted (with the pla within two weeks of the date of publication of the newspaper
Applications for Developments involving an Environmental Impact State
Government (Planning and Development Regulations 1994
Applications for Developments involving application to the Environment
and 18(1)(i) of the Local Government (Planning and Development) Regul:
Applications for developments comprising of industrial activity or storage
should refer to Article 18(1)(H) of the Local Government (Planning and D:

2. APPROPRIATE PLANNING FEE — See notes on application form

3. APPLICATION FORM — This must be completed in full.

4. SITE LOCATION MAP — An extract (not less than A4 size) from appropr: (the number of the O.S. map is to be stated) on which the overall site of th the applicant (and/or the site owner) has an interest are to be outlined in of on-site Public Notice must be shown

5. SITE LAYOUT DRAWING: (Scale 1 : 500) to show, but not be limited to:
  Site Boundaries, (shown in colour)   Water Supplies;
  Existing Structures;   Effluent Disposal Syste:
  Proposed Development;   Parking Facilities;
  Adjoining Public Road(s)/Footpath;   Development(s) on adjoi
  Access from Public Road;   Other features in the :cc
  structure (or part thereof as appropriate)

A Planning Application should be very carefully considered before it is submitted to the Local Authority.

Planning applications must be processed by the Local Authority within two months of the application being made.

The planning submission is available on request for public viewing during this period. Representations can be made by anyone wishing to object or query a particular application. Such representations, which should be made in writing and refer to the application by number, will be taken into account by the Planning Officer when a decision is being made on the application.

A Grant of Planning Permission or Outline Permission can be exercised within a five year period from the date of issue. In the case of an Grant of Planning Approval this must be exercised within the five year period dating from the issue of the original Grant of Outline Permission.

An application for Planning Permission requires that Plans, Cross Sections, Elevations, A Site Layout & Details of Materials, Construction & Drainage are submitted as well as a Site Location Map.

Conditions & Objections

When a decision is issued by the Planning Office after two months there may be attached to it certain Conditions which must be complied with if the permission is to be exercised. Conditions oftentimes refer to such matters as siting, external finishes and sewage disposal. An applicant who objects to the decision itself or to any of the Conditions that might be attached to it may appeal the decision within four weeks of the decision being issued. A third party objecting to a planning decision may appeal within three weeks. Planning Appeals are made through an independent authority.

During the period when a Planning Application is being considered by the Local Authority, third parties may make submissions directly to the Local Authority in respect of the Application and such submissions may be taken into account by the Planning Officer when arriving at a decision. Such third party submissions must by made in writing and consequently appear on the Planning File for inspection by the applicant.

Where insufficient documentation is submitted with a Planning Application the Local Authority may make a

---

Planning Applications must be processed by the Local Authority within a period of two months.

LOCAL GOVEMENT (PLANNING AND DEVELOPMENT) A

NOTIFICATION OF DECISION TO GRANT PERMISSION /OU~
~APPROVAL (SUBJECT TO CONDITIONC

COUNCIL OF THE COUNTY OF KILKEI

To: Tish Warn
    Silk   Vale
    Maynooth.
    Co. Kildare

A Grant of Planning Permission or Outline Planning Permission can be exercised within a five year period from the date of issue.

COND NO 5	All surface water run-off from roofs, shall be collected and disposed of wi by means of soakpits or in the event being proposed full details of same sh agreed with the Planning Authority. Si not be allowed to discharge onto the publ properties.
Reason:	To avoid interference with other proper! to the public road with consequent traff
COND NO 6	The fence which fronts this site shall be approved fence not more than 1 metre in along a line not less than 3 metres from th The area between the new road bounda shall be suitably structured, set level w topped surfaced with these works being such a manner as to ensure the existing not adversely affected.
Reason:	In the interests of traffic safety.
COND NO 7	The entrance gates shall be set back not than 4.5 metres from the new roadside recess space 9 - 11 metres wide along boundary. The full area of the splayed suitably structured, black-topped surfa with the public carriageway with thes constructed in such a manner as to en drainage system is not affected. The splayed recessed access shall not exce where of block work shall be neatly exposed to public view.
Reason:	In the interests of traffic safety
COND NO 8	The area to the rear of the dwc view through the provision of maintained and renewed as r eastern and south western h building line.
Reason:	In the interests of res

request for Additional Information. Such a request effectively stalls the planning process in regards to time. When the Additional Information is submitted the two month processing period effectively commences again.

Planning Assessment

If you own a piece of property or land or are considering ownership it is a good idea to check if any Planning Applications have been made in respect of the property or site. You do this by visiting the Planning Office. The key document you need for this is the Ordnance Survey Map that includes your property or site. If all you have is a portion of this map you need to know the number of the larger map it comes from.

The Planning Office will have a complete set of Ordnance Maps for the area of its jurisdiction and the Planning Official will be able to pull out the relevant one when you quote the map number. From this the site you are interested in can be identified. If a Planning Application has ever been lodged in respect of that site the site will be outlined and a number will appear against it. This number is the number of the Planning File. You are entitled to consult the Planning File which will contain any application as well as any other correspondence in relation to the application or the site. You may transcribe information from the Planning File and copy any drawings on it, though these may not be traced, only roughly copied.

Existing Planning Permissions

If a Planning Permission exists for a site you have an interest in it will be in respect of a particular building and design. The drawings for this will be contained on the file. If the Planning Permission is to be exercised the building that is erected must confirm with these drawings and any Conditions attached to the Permission . If any changes are to be made to the permitted design or in respect of the Conditions attached to the Planning Permission a new application will have to be made.

While changes are oftentimes made without resorting to re-application and such altered designs are constructed without interference from planning officials, when such a property is being sold, the discrepancy between what is built and what is on the drawings will be revealed and will delay any possible transaction until the proper permission has been obtained. This involves an application for Retention of an Existing Building which means that a set of drawings must be prepared in respect of the altered

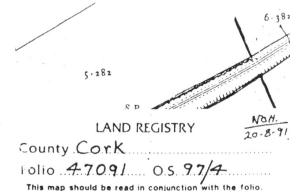

LAND REGISTRY

County .Cork..........................

Folio ..4.7.0.9.l..... O.S. 9.7/4...........

This map should be read in conjunction with the folio. (Plan No. on 1st page)

This map does not show appurtenant or servient rights.

It is not conclusive evidence as to the boundaries or extent of the land. (See Section 85 of the Registration of Title Act 1964)

Where a boundary has been transferred from a smaller scale map, accuracy is limited to that of the smaller scale.

This map, subject to the provisions of the L.R. Rules, is acceptable for subdivision purposes.

```
Reference No. in Planning
Register: 6/287
-----------------------------------
Column 1 - Conditions
-----------------------------------
and shall be maintained to
form a feature of the proposed
development.


(5)
All planting to comply with
the specifications of the
landscaping scheme agreed
shall be maintained by the
developer and if any plant
should die it shall be
replaced within the next
planting season.


(6)
Entrance shall be recessed a
minimum of 4.5m from existing
front boundary fence and side
walls shall be splayed  at an
angle of 45 dgs. and walls
and piers shall not exceed a
height of 1m over the level
of the adjoining public road.


(7)
Side walls and piers of
entrance shall be of natural
stone or sod and stone
construction.
```

design. If this is in any way unacceptable from a planning point of view alterations may have to be made to the building to correct this. This procedure is one to avoid at all costs. This can be done by building in strict accordance with the submitted design.

If there is an existing building on the site and drawings exist on the file in respect of it, these should be checked to ensure that what is built is the same as what is shown on the drawings. This may not be possible to do by reading the drawings in the Planning Office. You will need to obtain a set of drawings of your own so that you can take them out to the property and check them against what is actually built. The drawings will contain the name of the person or firm that prepared them. Take a note of this and as well as the Project Title and Number. Contact the person or firm yourself and try and obtain a set of drawings from them. It is probably best to do this by a letter followed up a day later by a phone call. The letter should clearly indicate the Project Title and the Drawing Numbers that you wish to obtain and why you wish to obtain them. It should also state that you are willing to pay for these. With the follow up call you should find out if the original drawings are still in existence and whether or not you are going to get them. It is important to remember when trying to obtain information that you are asking busy people to give time to your particular problem. It is essential for you to know exactly what it is you are looking for and to state this clearly. Generally you will find people willing to help as long as they don't have to drag information out of you or become embroiled in solving what is essentially your problem.

Existing Outline Planning Permissions

If only an Outline Permission exists for the site, information on this will also be on the Planning File. Outline Permissions do not involve particular designs but rather are an indication of what is generally acceptable from a planning point of view. It is usual when Outline Permissions are issued for Conditions to be attached to them in respect of the design and the location of any building that might be proposed for that site. These Conditions will be a reflection of the planning aims outlined in the Development Plan and are general guidelines that should be carefully studied.

10 NO CONDITIONS ATTACHED TO PLANN

COND NO 1 The development shall be connected to in a technically satisfactory manner to ac the requirements of Kilkenny County C

Reason: In the interests of public health and f occupants of this development.

COND NO 2 The developer shall provide and arra indefinite maintenance of an adequa

Reason: In the interests of public health and occupants of this development.

COND NO 3 Upon commencement of development shall be paid to Kilkenny County Cou. contribution towards the capital cost ass of public water supply which facilitate: proposed development. This charge is subject to review.

Reason: To ensure that an equitable contributi of public services which facilitate the

NOTE: In addition to the above c connection fees in general are curre Connection Fee
Where road crossing is required additional fee
National Road (Realigned)
National Road (Unrealigned)
Regional Road - £350 / County Roa

COND NO 4 The proposed septic tank and effluent c constructed and laid out in accordance National Standards Authority of Irelar "S.R.6:1991" as published by Eolas.

Reason: In the interests of public health and to the occupants of the development.

Footnote: It is emphasised tha alternative to percol used.

185

Exempted Development

Certain types of building development are exempt from Planning Permission. The purpose of exemptions is to avoid controls on developments of a minor nature, such as small extensions to houses. Certain types of structures intended for agricultural or forestry use are also classified as exempted development.

Small scale domestic extensions, including conservatories and sunspaces, do not require Planning Permission if the extension is to the rere of the house and does not increase the original floor area of the house by more than 23 square meters; does not exceed the height of the house and does not reduce the open space at the rere of the house to less than 25 square meters.

The conversion for use as part of a dwelling of an existing garage, store, shed etc. attached to the rere or side of a house is normally exempted development, subject to the 23 square metre limit mentioned earlier.

A garage, carport, shed, kennel etc. can be built without Planning Permission as long as it does not extend out in front of the building line of the house and does not exceed 4 meters in height if it has a pitched roof. A 3 metre limit applies for any other type of roof and a floor area limit of 25 square meters applies. Such structures, where they are built to the side of an existing house, must match the finish of the house and may not be used for commercial purposes or for keeping pigs, poultry, pigeons, ponies or horses.

A front porch can also be built without Planning Permission as long as it does not exceed 2 square meters in area and is more than 2 meters from any public road or footpath. Where the porch has a tiled or slated pitched roof it must not exceed 4 meters in height or 3 meters for any other type of roof. A front porch within these limits is the only type of development allowed to extend beyond the line of the front wall of a building and still remain exempted.

All building development, whether exempted or not, must comply with the Building Regulations.

Certain types of building development are exempt from Planning Permission.

Can I build an extension?
Small scale domestic extensions, including co do not require planning permission if the ext rear of the house and

• does not increase the original floor area o more than 23 square metres (where ther earlier extensions, this threshold is a cum

• does not exceed the height of the house,

• does not reduce the open space at the r to less than 25 square metres.

Can I convert my garage to domestic
The conversion for use as part of a dwellir living room or bedroom) of a garage, stor attached to the rear or side of a house is development, subject to the 23 square m

Can I build a garage?
You can build a garage, carport, shed, gre domestic pets, etc., as long as it does not of the building line of the house and does in height, (if it has a tiled or slated pitched (if it has any other roof type). The floor i exempted development is 25 square metr may not be lived in, used for commercial keeping pigs, poultry, pigeons, ponies or h sheds, etc. to the side of the house must the house. You cannot reduce the open s rear of the house below 25 square metre:

Can I build a front porch?
You can build a porch without planning as it does not exceed 2 square metres i than 2 metres from any public road or t porch has a tiled or slated pitched roof i metres in height or 3 metres for any ot front porch within these limits is the on development allowed to extend beyond the building (the building line) and still r

Can I erect walls, fences and gates
Capped walls made of brick, stone or blo finish, railings and wooden fences can be e they do not exceed 1.2 metres in height i

The EconoSpace has been designed to meet Exempted Development parameters

Planning File

The assembly of a *Planning File* involves the collection of notes from, or copies of, relevant sections of the local Development Plan; obtaining copies of the Planning Application form and Site Notice; collecting data on previous applications on any site you own or are interested in purchasing etc. etc.

This *File* will become vitally important as you enter into the Planning stage of the project.

Summary

Planning Regulations exist to cater for the so called Common Good.

Local Planning objectives are published in the local Development Plan.

Generally, all new buildings require Planning Permission though certain types of developments are exempt.

SITE NOTICE

1. Must be of durable material

2. Must be **securely erected in a conspicuous position easily visible and public road**

3. Must be shown on a plan accompanying the application

4. Must be headed "**Application to Planning Authority**"

5. Must state:

    (a.) Applicant's name
    (b.) whether application is for **permission, Outline Permis**
    (c.) nature and extent of development including number of
    (d.) that the application may be inspected at the **Planning**
County Council, Town Centre, Tallaght, Dublin 24

6. Must be erected on or before the day the application is submitted ar for at least one month after the making of the application

Applicants are advised to ensure that all of in relation to the erection and maintenance fulfilled, as failure to do so will result in a de the application

---

Comhairle Chontae Dhún Laoghaire-Ráth an Dúin
Halla an Chontae,
Dun Laoghaire,
Contae Átha Cliath.
Fón: 205 4700
Fax: 280 3122

Dun Laoghaire-Rathdown County Council
County Hall,
Dun Laoghaire,
Co. Dublin
Tel. 205 4700
Fax: 280 3122

PLANNING APPLICATION FORM

PLEASE READ INSTRUCTIONS AT BACK BEFORE COMPLETING FORM. ALL QUESTIONS MUST BE ANSWERED.

1. Application for Permission ☐ Outline Permission ☐ Approval ☐ Place ✓ in appropriate box.
Approval should be sought only where an outline permission was previously granted.
Outline Permission may not be sought for the retention of structures and continuance of uses.

2. Postal address of site or building ....
(if none, give description
sufficient to identify) ....

3. Name of applicant (Principal not Agent) ....
Address ....
.... Tel. No. .... Fax: ....

4. Name and address to which ....
notification should be sent .... Tel. No. .... Fax: ....

5. Brief description of proposed development ....

6. Name and address of ....
person or firm responsible
for preparation of drawings ....

7. State applicant's legal interest or estate in site or property ....
(i.e. freehold, leasehold, etc.) ....

8. If applicant is not the owner, state name & address of owner. ....

9. Area of Site .... sq. m. Floor area of proposed development .... sq. m.
Floor area of development proposed to be retained within the site .... sq. m.

10. Does the proposal involve demolition of any habitable houses? Yes ☐ No ☐

11. Method of drainage .... Source of Water Supply ....

12. In the case of any building to be retained, please state present use of each floor or use when last used. ....

13. Gross floor space of proposed development .... sq. m. | Newspaper Notice
No. of dwellings proposed (if any) ....
Class(es) of development ....
Fee Payable £ .... Basis of Calculation ....
If a reduced fee is tendered details of previous relevant payments and

If you are designing for a jurisdiction other than the Republic of Ireland you will need to investigate the local Regulations and comply with their requirements.

Building Regulations cover the 'technical' aspects of building and, as such, are dealt with at the *Working Drawing* stage of a project. This was referred to in item *19* of the *Design Programme* where you were asked *'Who will oversee the technical aspects of the design and construction process?* This will most likely be a technician or an engineer who can also prepare the *Working Drawings*, supervise the construction and 'sign off' on mortgage draw-down payments. If you are planning on using 'alternative' materials such as hemp-lime, straw or even breathable timber frame and you intend to get a mortgage it is essential that the technical/supervisory person is brought on board at this stage. If that is not feasible or possible it can be left until later - bearing in mind that 'alternative' construction and conventional mortgaging may not make happy bedfellows.

If you are building 'under the radar' it is still important to take on board the intention of building regulations, particularly in respect of energy efficiency, hygiene, sanitation, fire safety and so on.

Next: SDP38 - Site Analysis, page 196

If you are self-building you may need to engage a professional to certify that your building satisfies the requirements of Planning & Building Regulations

Building Regulations

Building Regulations are a set of legal requirements the purpose of which is to promote good practice in the design and construction of buildings in the interest of the health, safety and welfare of people who use buildings.

The Regulations, insofar as they affect the design and construction of dwellings, comprise a set of requirements addressing the following:

Part A: Structure
Refer to *Part VII Structure Pages 22/23* (Volume 1, Pages 174/5)

A1; (1) A building shall be so designed and constructed that the combined dead, imposed and wind loads are sustained and transmitted to the ground -

(a) safely, and

(b) without causing such deflection or deformation of any part of the building, or such movement of the ground, as will impair the stability of any part of another building.

(2) In assessing whether a building complies with sub-paragraph (1) regard shall be had to the imposed and wind loads to which it is likely to be subjected in the ordinary course of its use for the purpose for which it was intended.

A2; A building shall be so designed and constructed that movements of the subsoil caused by subsidence, swelling, shrinkage or freezing will not impair the stability of any part of the building.

A3; A multi-storey building shall be so designed and constructed that in the event of an accident the structure will not be damaged to an extent disproportionate to the cause of the damage.

A4; "dead load" means the force due to the static mass of all walls, permanent partitions, floors, roofs and finishes including all other permanent construction and services equipment affixed to the building;

"imposed load" means the load assumed to be produced by the intended occupancy or use of the building including distributed, concentrated, impact, inertia and snow loads and the force due to the static mass of moveable partitions, but excluding wind loads;

"multi-storey building" means a building comprising or including five or more storeys, a basement storey being regarded as a storey;

"windload" means all loads due to the effect of wind pressure or suction.

All building development must comply with the Building Regulations.

Regulations vary from country to country and from place to place. It is critical that one appraises oneself of the particular Regulations pertaining at the location where you intend to build.

Part B: Fire

B1; A building shall be so designed and constructed that there are adequate means of escape in the case of fire from the building to a place of safety outside the building, capable of being safely and effectively used.

B2: For the purpose of inhibiting the spread of flame within a building, the internal linings -

(a) shall offed adequate resistance to the spread of flame over their surface; and

(b) shall have, if ignited, a rate of heat release which is reasonable in the circumstances.

B3; (1) A building shall be so designed and constructed that, in the event of fire, its stability will be maintained for a reasonable period.

(2) (a) A wall common to two or more buildings shall be so designed and constructed that it offers adequate resistance to the spread of fire between those buildings.

(b) A building shall be subdivided with fire resisting construction where this is necessary to inhibit the spread of fire within the building.

(3) A building shall be so designed and constructed that the unseen spread of fire and smoke within concealed spaces in its structure or fabric is inhibited where necessary.

(4) For the purposes of sub-paragraph 2(a), a house in a terrace and a semi-detached house are each to be treated as being a separate building.

- B4; The external walls and roof of a building shall be so designed and constructed that they afford adequate resistance to the spread of fire to and from neighbouring buildings.

B5; A building shall be so designed and constructed that there is adequate provision for access for fire appliances and for such facilities as may be reasonably required to assist the fire service in the protection of life and property.

For all buildings, other than agricultural buildings and houses under 3 stories, a Fire Safety Certificate is required before development takes place. Such a Certificate is obtained from the Local Authority and certifies that the submitted design complies with the above Fire Regulations.

1997 Update:

Part B: Fire - A first floor (escape) window should have an unobstructed opening not less than 850mm high and 500mm wide. The opening section of the window should be secured by means of fastenings which are readily openable from inside. The bottom of the window opening should be not more than 1100mm and not less than 800mm (600mm in the case of a rooflight) above the floor of the room in which it is situated. In the case of a dormer window or rooflight the distance from the eaves of the roof to the cill or vertical plane of the window should not exceed 1.5m, measured along the roof.

(It should be noted that if a dwelling contains a third floor Fire Safety Certification is required.)

Regulations change from time to time, so make sure you are working to the Regulations current in your area.

Even if you are building 'under the radar' it is wise to comply, as far as is practical, with Building Regulations

Part C: Site Preparation & Resistance to Moisture

C1; The ground to be covered by a building shall be reasonably free from vegetable matter.

C2; Subsoil drainage shall be provided if necessary so as to prevent the passage of ground moisture to the interior of the building or damage the fabric of the building.

C3; Precautions shall be taken to avoid danger to health and safety caused by substances (including contanimants) found on or in the ground to be covered by a building.

C4; The floors, walls and roof of a building shall be so designed and constructed as to prevent the passage of moisture to the inside of the building or damage the fabric of the building.

C5; "contaminant" includes any substance which is or could become flammable, explosive, corrosive, toxic or radioactive and any deposits of faecal matter or animal matter;

"floor" includes any base or structure between the surface of the ground or the surface of any hardcore laid upon the ground and the upper surface of the floor and includes finishes which are laid as part of the permanent construction;

"moisture" includes water vapour and liquid water.

Part D: Materials & Workmanship

D1; All works to which the Regulations apply shall be carried out with proper materials and in a workmanlike manner.

D2; "proper materials" means materials which are fit for the use for which they are intended and for the conditions in which they are to be used, and includes materials which:

(a) bear a CE Mark in accordance with the provisions of the Construction Products Directive (89/106/EEC); or

(b) comply with an appropriate harmonised standard, European technical approval or national technical specification as defined in article 4(2) of the Construction Products Directive (89/106/EEC); or

(c) comply with an appropriate Irish Standard or Irish Agrement Board Certificate or with an alternative national technical specification of any Member State of the European Union, which provided in use an equivalent level of safety and suitability.

Part F: Ventilation

F1; Adequate means of ventilation shall be provided for people in buildings.

F2; Adequate provision shall be made to prevent excessive condensation in a roof or in a roof void above an insulated ceiling.

1997 Update:

Part F: Ventilation - the following words should be added to item F1: '... including adequate provision for the removal of water vapour from kitchens, bathrooms and other areas where water vapour is generated.'

Part G: Hygiene

G1; A dwelling shall be provided with -

(a) a bathroom containing either a fixed bath or a shower bath, and a washbasin, and

(b) a kitchen containing a sink of adequate size and a draining board, and

(c) a suitable installation for the provision of hot and cold water to the bath or shower bath, washbasin and sink.

G2; (1) Adequate sanitary conveniences shall be provided in a building in rooms provided for that purpose, or in bathrooms, and every room or bathroom which contains a sanitary convenience shall be separated by means of a properly ventilated passage or lobby from any place where food is prepared or cooked.

(2) Adequate washbasins shall be provided in -

(a) rooms containing sanitary conveniences; or

(b) rooms or spaces adjacent to rooms containing sanitary conveniences.

(3) There shall be a suitable installation for the provision of hot and cold water to washbasins provided in accordance with sub-paragraph (2).

(4) Sanitary conveniences and washbasins shall be of such design and be so installed as to allow for effective cleaning.

G3; "sanitary convenience" means a water closet or a urinal.

Part H: *Drainage & Waste Disposal*

H1; (1) A building shall be provided with such a drainage system as may be necessary for the hygienic and adequate disposal of foul water from the building.

(2) A building shall be provided with such a drainage system as may be necessary for the adequate disposal of surface water from the building.

(3) No part of a drainage system conveying foul water shall be connected to a sewer reserved for surface water and no part of a drainage system conveying surface water shall be connected to a sewer reserved for foul water.

H2; A septic tank shall be -

(a) of adequate capacity and so constructed that it is impermeable to liquids;

(b) adequately ventilated; and

(c) so sited and constructed that -

(i) it is not prejudicial to the health of any person,

(ii) it does not pollute, so as to endanger public health, any water (including ground water) which is used as a source of supply for human consumption, and

(iii) there are adequate means of access for emptying.

H3; "combined drain" has the same meaning as in Section 10 of the Local Government (Sanitary Services) Act, 1948 (No. 3 of 1948);

"drain" in relation to a building means any pipe, forming part of the drainage system of the building, which is either -

(a) wholly underground, or

(b) a continuation, in the direction of the flow, of part of a drainage system that has been underground, and includes a "combined drain";

"drainage system", in relation to a building, means the system of pipes and drains used for the drainage of the building, including all other fittings, appliances and equipment so used but excluding subsoil water drains;

"foul water" means any water contaminated by soil water, waste water or trade effluent;

"sewer" has the same meaning as in the Local Government (Sanitary Services) Acts, 1878 to 1964;

"soil water" means water containing excreted matter, whether human or animal;

"surface water" means the run-off of rainwater from roofs and any paved ground surface around the building;

"trade effluent" means effluent from any works, apparatus, plant or drainage pipe used for the disposal to waters or to a sewer of any liquid (whether treated or untreated), either with or without particles of matter in suspension therin, which is discharged from a premises used for carrying on any trade or industry (including mining), but does not include domestic sewage or surface water;

"waste water" means used water not being soil water or trade effluent.

Part J: Heat Producing Appliances

J1; A heat producing appliance shall be so installed that there is an adequate supply of air to it for combustion and for the efficient working of any flue pipe or chimney.

J2; A heat producing appliance shall have adequate provision for the discharge of the products of combustion to the outside air.

J3; A heat producing appliance and any flue pipe shall be so designed and installed, and any fireplace and chimney shall be so designed and constructed, as to reduce to a reasonable level the risk of the building catching fire in consequence of its use.

J4; "heat producing appliance" means an appliance (including a cooker and an open fire) which is designed to burn solid fuel, oil or gas and includes an incinerator.

Part K: Stairways, Ramps & Guards

K1; Stairways, ladders and ramps shall be such as to afford safe passage for users of a building.

K2; In a building, the sides of every floor and balcony and every part of a roof to which people normally have access shall be guarded to protect users from the risk of falling therefrom.

K3; In a building, the sides of every vehicle ramp and every floor and roof to which vehicles have access shall be guarded against the risk of vehicles falling therefrom.

K4; The requirements of this Part of the Building Regulations apply to stairways, ladders and ramps which form part of a building.

Part L: Conservation of Fuel & Energy

L1; A building shall be so designed and constructed as to secure, insofar as is reasonably practicable, the conservation of fuel and energy.

1997 Updates:

Part J: Heat Producing Appliances - Item J4 now becomes item J5. Item J4 now reads - A fixed oil storage tank which serves a heat producing appliance shall be so located as to reduce to a reasonable level the risk of fire spreading from the building to the tank.

Part L: Conservation of Fuel & Energy - Item l1 is now extended to include the following - 'This shall be achieved by -

(a) limiting the heat loss, and, where appropriate, maximising the heat gains through the fabric of the building

(b) controlling, as appropriate, the output of the space heating and hot water systems; and

(c) limiting the heat loss from pipes, ducts and vessels used for the transport or storage of heated water or air.

A revision to the permissable U-values was also made. The current standard is as follows:

Pitched Roof: insulation horizontal: 0.16 $W/m^2/°C$; insulation sloped: $0.2W/m^2/°C$

Flat Roof: $0.2W/m^2/°C$

Walls: $0.27W/m^2/°C$

Ground Floors: $0.25W/m^2/°C$

Windows, External Doors, Rooflights: 2.2 $W/m^2/°C$

Part M: Access for People with Disabilities

M1 Adequate provision shall be made to enable people with disabilities to safely and independently access and use a building.

Complying With The Building Regulations

The primary responsibility for compliance with the Building Regulations rests with designers, builders and building owners. Building Control Authorities - normally part of the Local Authority - have powers to inspect design documentation and buildings as well as powers of enforcement and prosecution where breaches of the Regulations occur. Penalties, fines and imprisonment can be imposed where the Regulations can be shown to have been breached!

The individual designing for his/her own needs will inevitably want to comply with the Regulations and need not fear such threats. It should be borne in mind that all regulations to do with house construction emanate from the proclivity of speculators, landlords and others willing to exploit housing need. In most cases the individual designing for their own needs will, in fact, wish to exceed the requirements of the Regulations. The steps necessary to meet the Regulations will be covered under *Planning & Working Drawings*. The Department of the Environment also publish Guidance Documents illustrating how one can comply with Regulations.

When development commences - including Exempted Development - a 'Commencement Notice' must be sent to the local Building Control Authority. This will allow the Authority, if it so chooses, to inspect the development at any stage of its construction. In any event it is wise to keep a photographic record of work as it proceeds and to consider engaging the services of a qualified person to monitor the work and to then furnish a Certificate of Compliance with the Building Regulations when work is complete.

Building Regulations File

This *file* should contain notes on the particular Regulations that will be relevant to the building that you are designing. It is a good idea to note against particular Spaces particular requirements of the regulations.

Summary
Building Regulations are legal requirments governing various aspects of building design and construction which must be complied with when carrying out any building work.

38 Site Analysis

Detailed *Site Analysis* is the final piece of the house design 'puzzle'. In some ways the site is, in fact, the 'board' on which the house design 'game' is played. Imagine your *'Space Plans'* laid out on this 'board' then moved around to satisfy the demands of your *Brief*, particularly in relation to access, the gathering of solar energy, drainage, views, exposure to weather, neighbours and so on. The laying out out of your *Spaces* in this way, to satisfy all the varying demands of your design intentions, is actually what the 'planning' of a house is all about. Where this exercise is carried out against the 'background' of the site, the design can forge the necessary connections to the 'outside' world which will surround it.

The *Site Selection & Analysis* chapter is clear and self-explanatory. Read this and then follow its directions. Print the *Site Analysis Worksheet* and paste onto this a copy of your site map. Record information about your site onto individual copies of this.

If you are working on an existing building the procedure is the same, with your site map showing the existing building.

Generally speaking, as much time as possible should be spent examining a site, even one that a person might be familiar with. Spending time on a site at night is a good exercise before a person might commit to purchasing it. It is also worthwhile to develop an ideal plan then to investigate a variety of sites seeking out the one that mosts suits that particular design.

Next: SDP39 - Brief Appraisal, page 211

Establishing site boundaries

Site Analysis

The design and form of any building will be greatly influenced by its location. The physical conditions of the site will have a major bearing on the way the plan develops and should be assessed and understood from the outset.

If no site exists it is as well to choose one rather than to go through the final design exercise on paper only. Choosing a site in this way allows one a lot of freedom! Such factors as cost and availability can be ignored and one can choose freely without the restrictions these considerations normally impose.

If you have a particular site under consideration for purchase it is desirable to undertake an initial design exercise before the deal is finalised. This will allow you to assess the suitability of the site to the type of building you wish to put on it.

Whether you already own a site or not the process of analysis is the same. This begins by acquiring a map of the property in question. Normally this will be in the form of a scaled Ordnance Survey map. Such maps are usually at a scale of 1:2500 or 1:1250.

A map of this scale will indicate a site of half an acre to one acre as being the size of several postage stamps. North will be at the top of the sheet and usually ground levels will be indicated along the major roads. Bench Marks might be shown by an arrow indicating an actual mark that exists on the side of a building or other permanent fixture. Such Bench Marks and levels are related to sea level at some place within the country. This will be indicated at the bottom of the map as will the date of the survey.

The design of any building is always greatly influenced by its site.

If you are considering buying a site ... carry out a preliminary design exercise before you sign anything.

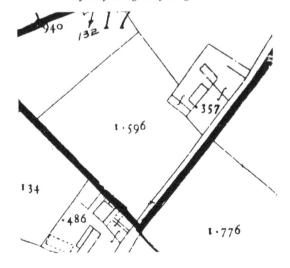

Apart from information on orientation and and levels Ordnance Maps give an interesting overview of the land surrounding the site you are interested in. Field patterns, earthworks, ruins, houses, roads, woods, public buildings, rivers, areas liable to flooding, pylons and streams all appear on these maps. This information will provide a context for the site you are interested in.

Every site will have a history stretching back into antiquity. It is as well to be aware of this. The Ordnance Map will give an indication of how the land was divided up into fields and roadways and generally how the buildings were oriented in the area. A map is an ariel view and when it is read in an historical perspective a sense of the place you are choosing to build will be more clearly seen. In an extreme case your site may be the location of an ancient battle or some other dreadful event. It is as well to know these things before you purchase. Generally of course no such thing will have happened on your land though other less traumatic events will have occurred there. A map will be your key to discovering these things as well as leading you to information contained in books and in the stories and legends of the area. Ancient placenames, which often appear on maps, can also yield up interesting facts.

Any factories, quarries, dumps or other such developments in the area likely to cause irritation, annoyance or danger should be noted by scouting the area. A visit to the Planning Office and an examination of their map will also be a worthwhile exercise. This will allow an overview of the planning situation to be obtained before committing yourself to purchase.

Once the site has been placed in historical and geographic context it can be examined in detail itself. This is done by spending time on the site and by recording facts and impressions about it. The best way of doing this is by recording the information onto an enlarged map of the site. You can do this easily by having the portion of the Ordnance Map containing your site enlarged on a photocopier. This can be done with reasonable accuracy. If the enlargement allows the entire site to be shown on an A4 sheet this will be easy to manage on site when the information is being recorded. Information on enlargement ratios is contained in *Part VI S…* Refer to Volume 1, page 153 *[Volume 1 Pa…*

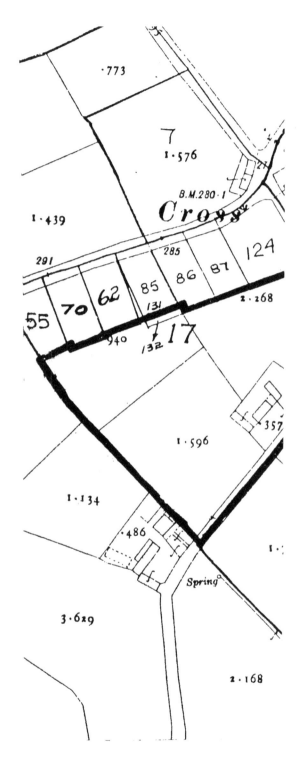

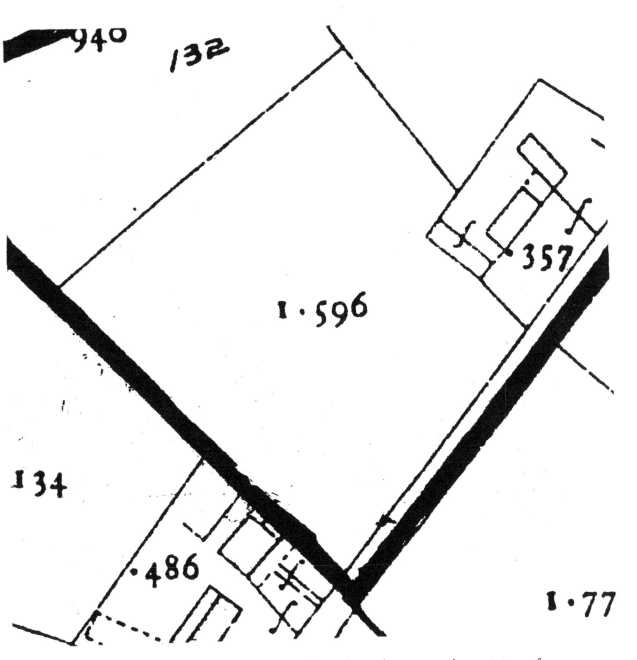

Bring plenty of photocopies with you to the site and use separate sheets to record separate types of information. These should cover all aspects of the site and its immediate surroundings.

You will not be able to complete a comprehensive survey in one visit and you should not try to. Rather you should make several visits at various times of the day and night. You should also try approaching the site on foot and even on a bicycle. With this type of survey or analysis you are attempting to become aware of all the aspects of the site and its location that will affect you and your family and, of course, the layout and style of the building that you will subsequently design. The importance of completing these exercises cannot be stressed enough. It is far better to encounter a problem with a site at this early stage rather than to discover it when your house is built and you have moved in.

Headings for your *Site Analysis Sheets* might be as illustrated on the following pages ...

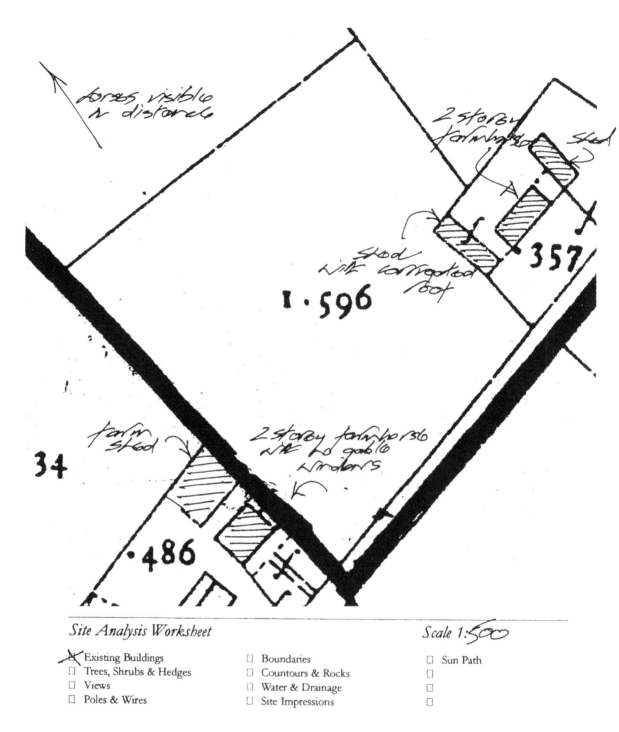

Site Analysis Worksheet   *Scale 1:500*

☒ Existing Buildings   ☐ Boundaries   ☐ Sun Path
☐ Trees, Shrubs & Hedges   ☐ Countours & Rocks   ☐
☐ Views   ☐ Water & Drainage   ☐
☐ Poles & Wires   ☐ Site Impressions   ☐

Existing Buildings

Note all buildings on the site, their location, condition and size. How to do this is described in *Part VI, Surveying* [*Volume 1 Pages 115 - 151*]

Also note the buildings on adjoining sites. Make particular note of any shading that might be caused by these and any windows that overlook your land. Note whether these buildings are one or two storeys and the type of exterior finish on the walls and roof.

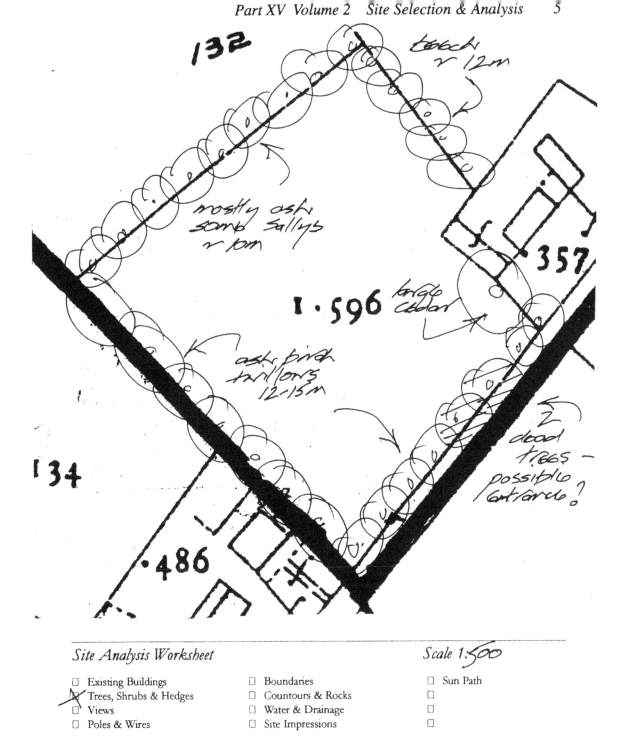

132

beech r 12m

357

mostly ash some sallys r 10m

1·596

large cedar

134

ash birch willows 12-15m

2 dead trees - possible entrance?

·486

Site Analysis Worksheet   *Scale 1:500*

☐ Existing Buildings	☐ Boundaries	☐ Sun Path
☒ Trees, Shrubs & Hedges	☐ Countours & Rocks	☐
☐ Views	☐ Water & Drainage	☐
☐ Poles & Wires	☐ Site Impressions	☐

Existing Trees, Shrubs & Hedges

Locate these on the enlarged site plan, noting their approximate height, type and the degree to which they obscure views, provide screening, shading and so on. Note the general condition of all growth, especially trees. Trees and tall shrubs are good indicators of the prevailing wind direction and strength. If these are noticeably leaning this means that the wind blows regularly and strong. This fact must be taken into account when making your design.

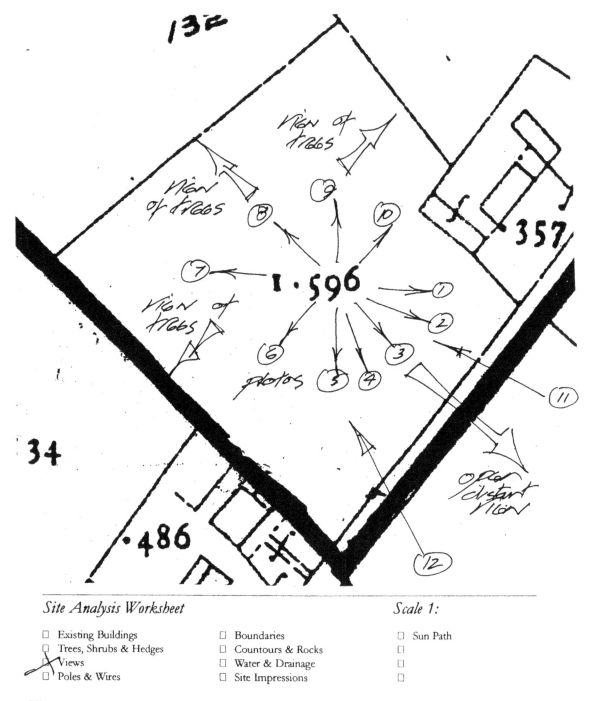

Site Analysis Worksheet

Scale 1:

- ☐ Existing Buildings
- ☐ Trees, Shrubs & Hedges
- ☒ Views
- ☐ Poles & Wires
- ☐ Boundaries
- ☐ Countours & Rocks
- ☐ Water & Drainage
- ☐ Site Impressions
- ☐ Sun Path
- ☐
- ☐
- ☐

Views

Note the views that exist from various parts of the site and support this with photographs. Record the position and direction of the photographic views on a site plan.

Try taking some panoramic shots by panning the camera through a wide arc from a fixed spot. You can use a tripod to do this though hand held shots will work just as well. Make sure the shots you take overlap sufficiently to allow them to be joined together when printed. Take 'outward' as well as 'inward' views from selected spots. Take plenty of photos!

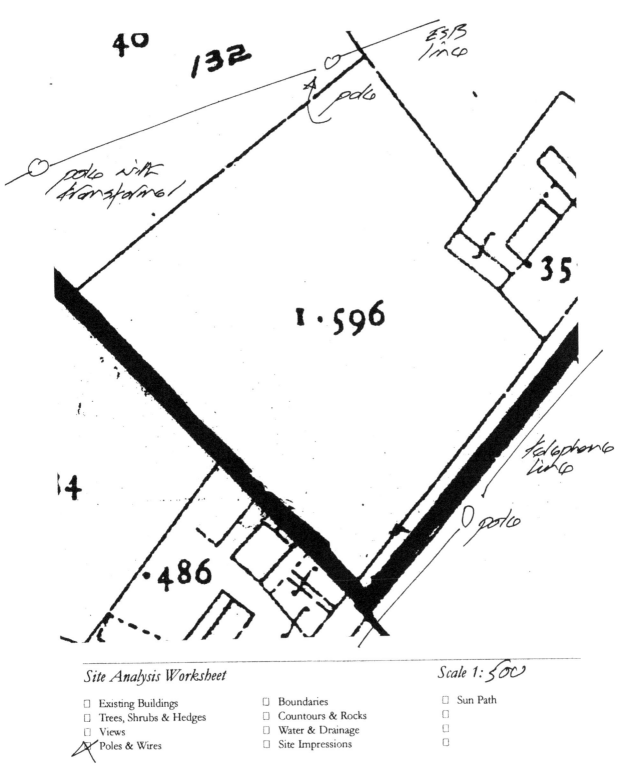

40

132

ESB
line

pole

pole with
transformer

35

1·596

telephone
line

pole

14

·486

Site Analysis Worksheet   *Scale 1:* 500

☐ Existing Buildings   ☐ Boundaries   ☐ Sun Path
☐ Trees, Shrubs & Hedges   ☐ Countours & Rocks   ☐
☐ Views   ☐ Water & Drainage   ☐
☒ Poles & Wires   ☐ Site Impressions   ☐

Poles & Wires

Locate these and try to identify what they carry - telephone or electricity. The proximity of these services to the site will have an effect on the cost of hooking into them. Especially note high tension cables and pylons.

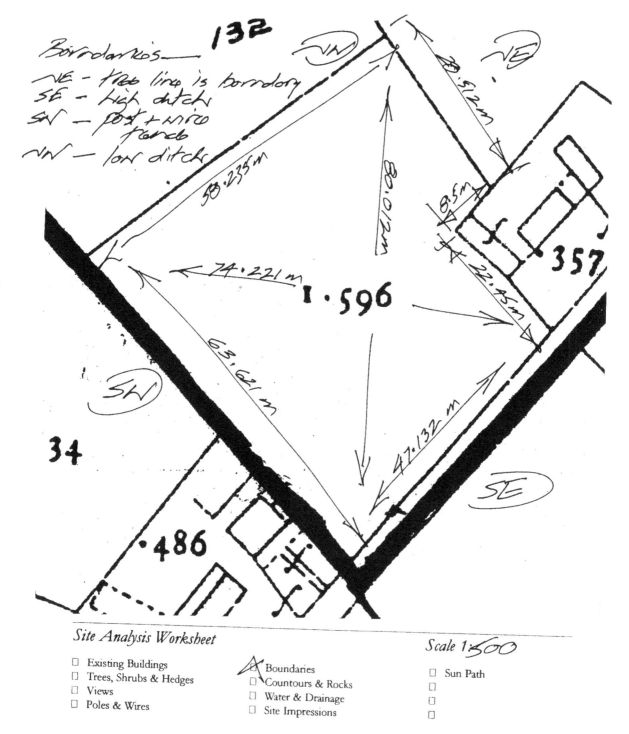

Boundaries— **132**
NE - tree line is boundary
SE - high ditch
SW — post + wire fence
NW — low ditch

34

1·596

·486

357

NW

NE

58·235 m

80·220 m

74·221 m

63·621 m

47·132 m

8·5m

22·45m

36·912m

SW

SE

Site Analysis Worksheet

- ☐ Existing Buildings
- ☐ Trees, Shrubs & Hedges
- ☐ Views
- ☐ Poles & Wires

- ☒ Boundaries
- ☐ Countours & Rocks
- ☐ Water & Drainage
- ☐ Site Impressions

- ☐ Sun Path
- ☐
- ☐
- ☐

Scale 1:500

Boundaries

Note if these are clearly defined and their condition. Refer to *Part VI, Surveying* [*Volume 1 Pages 115 - 151*] for guidance on how to do this. It is also a good idea to measure the boundaries.

Especially note the road boundary if there is one. Make sure that access can be had from the road safely and that this access will be safe when exiting from the site also. Consider heavy vehicles getting onto the site during construction.

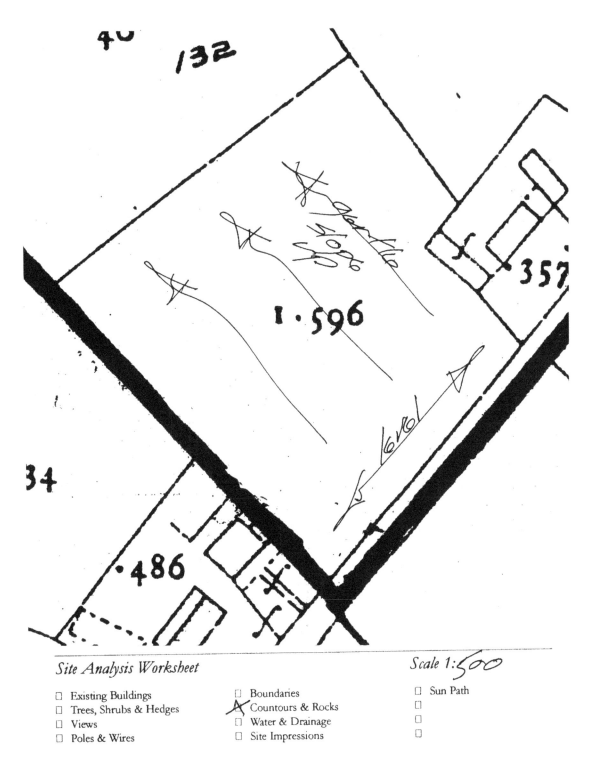

Site Analysis Worksheet

Scale 1:500

- ☐ Existing Buildings
- ☐ Trees, Shrubs & Hedges
- ☐ Views
- ☐ Poles & Wires

- ☐ Boundaries
- ☒ Countours & Rocks
- ☐ Water & Drainage
- ☐ Site Impressions

- ☐ Sun Path
- ☐
- ☐
- ☐

Contour & Rock Survey

Note the general contours of the land, where the highest and lowest points are and where any rock outcrops occur. Examine the site from adjoining lands and roads and evaluate to what degree it is overlooked. Check the lowest parts of the site for signs of waterlogging. It is worthwhile to do this during a rainy spell.

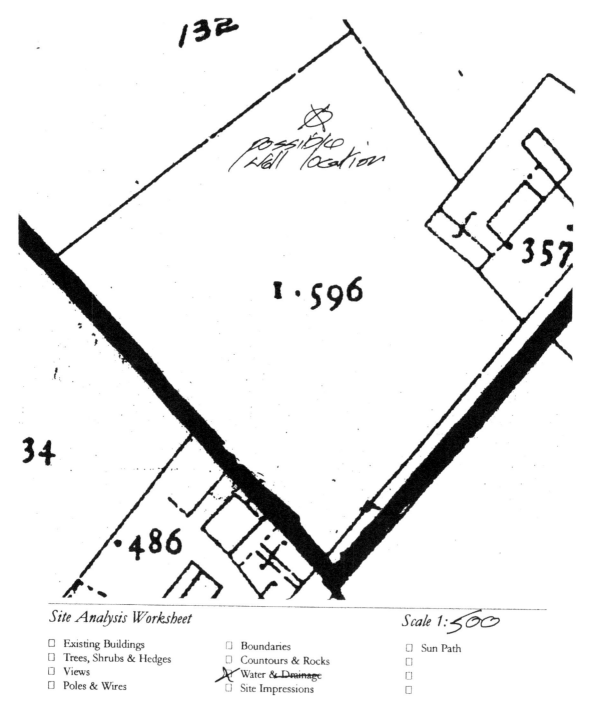

Site Analysis Worksheet

Scale 1:500

- ☐ Existing Buildings
- ☐ Trees, Shrubs & Hedges
- ☐ Views
- ☐ Poles & Wires

- ☐ Boundaries
- ☐ Countours & Rocks
- ☒ Water & Drainage
- ☐ Site Impressions

- ☐ Sun Path
- ☐
- ☐
- ☐

Water & Drainage Services

Locate these if they exist. Normally they will run under the nearest road and their presence will be indicated by manholes and gullies. If you are in doubt ask local advice. This is a good way to get to know your potential neighbours.

If there is a well on the site make an examination of this and arrange for an analysis to determine the purity of the water. If the well is to supply the proposed building it will be necessary to determine the potential flow of water from it also. Again local knowledge will be invaluable in this regard.

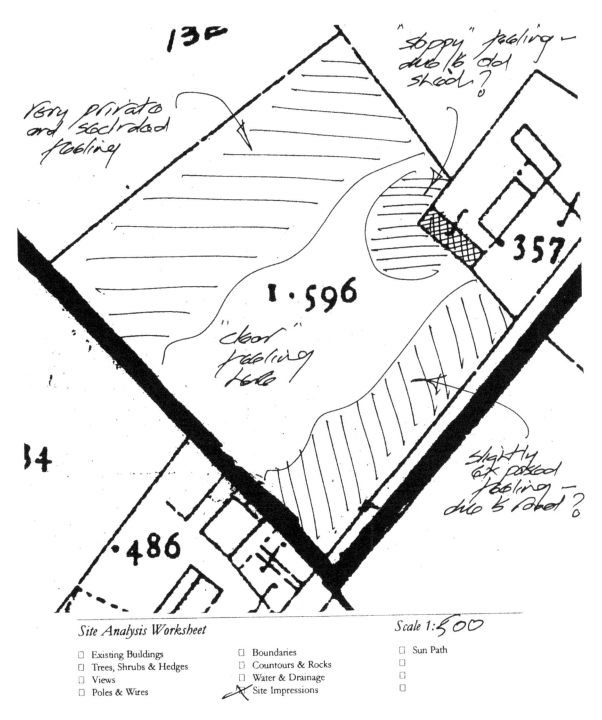

Site Analysis Worksheet

Scale 1:500

- ☐ Existing Buildings
- ☐ Trees, Shrubs & Hedges
- ☐ Views
- ☐ Poles & Wires
- ☐ Boundaries
- ☐ Countours & Rocks
- ☐ Water & Drainage
- ✗ Site Impressions
- ☐ Sun Path
- ☐
- ☐
- ☐

Site Impressions

For this you will have to rely on your intuition. Note which parts of the site feel best and which places you find yourself drawn to. Everyone in the family should do this. Take your time with this aspect of the site analysis and repeat the exercise several times at various times of the day and night as well in varied weather conditions.

Children are very good at doing this type of work. They should be encouraged to express their feelings on where the house or building should be located.

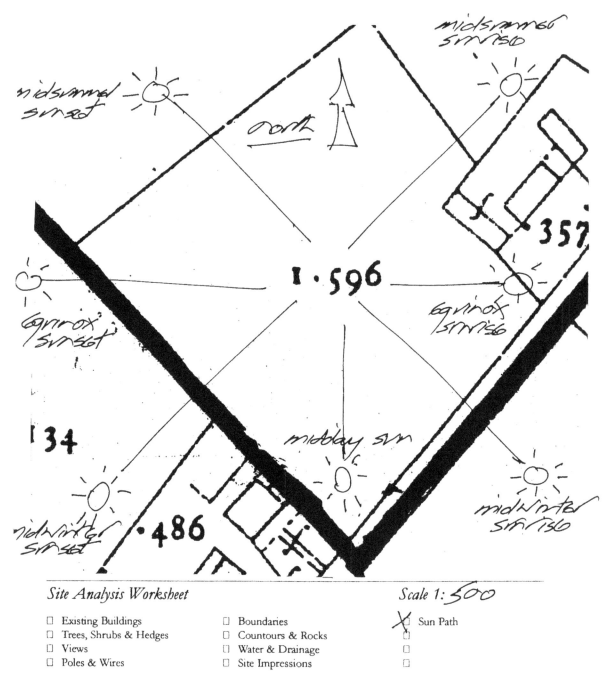

midsummer sunrise

midsummer sunset

north

equinox sunrise

equinox sunset

1·596

357

134

midday sun

midwinter sunrise

·486

midwinter sunset

Site Analysis Worksheet   *Scale 1:* 500

☐ Existing Buildings   ☐ Boundaries   ☒ Sun Path
☐ Trees, Shrubs & Hedges   ☐ Countours & Rocks   ☐
☐ Views   ☐ Water & Drainage   ☐
☐ Poles & Wires   ☐ Site Impressions   ☐

Sun Survey

Use a copy of the OS map to do this. Pick a spot on the site where you think the house might be. Using this point as the centre construct a circle with as large a radius as will fit on the page. Mark the North & South points as well as those indicating East & West.

Following the diagram on *Part V, Space Mock-Ups, Page 13* [*Page 95, Volume 1*], set out the rising and setting points of the sun at various times of the year. It is a good idea to use several sheets for this.

Remember that at midwinter the sun rises a mere 15 degrees above the horizon at noon! If this winter sun is to be obstructed you should be aware of it from the outset.

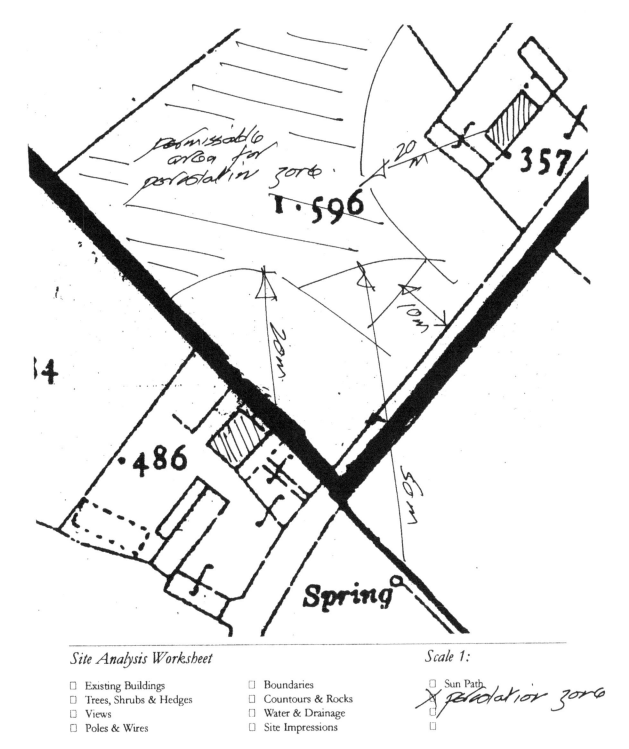

Site Analysis Worksheet   *Scale 1:*

- ☐ Existing Buildings
- ☐ Trees, Shrubs & Hedges
- ☐ Views
- ☐ Poles & Wires

- ☐ Boundaries
- ☐ Countours & Rocks
- ☐ Water & Drainage
- ☐ Site Impressions

- ☐ Sun Path
- ☒ *Percolation zone*
- ☐
- ☐

Drainage

Note from the OS map any wells or springs that are indicated on the site or nearby. Any Percolation Area that is proposed will have to be 60m from this and 20m from any dwelling.

If there is a farmyard nearby try to ascertain where the runoff from this goes. If it flows under or across your site you may have a pollution problem.

Dousing

It is generally accepted that natural forces criss-cross the earth, forming a network of natural electromagnetic radiation. Such radiation, particularly strong in some cases, is considered disturbing to people. An example of this would be where radiation is produced by the crossing of underground water courses. Such radiation can be discovered by a competent douser and this exercise is recommended to be carried out at an early stage. If something feels wrong with the site but you cannot pinpoint why, it is worthwhile having the site doused to discover the cause.

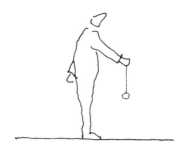

A modern version of natural electromagnetic radiation is produced by power lines, microwave transmissions and so on. These should be similarly assessed to ensure that their subtle radiations do not cause disturbance to humans or indeed animals. The effects of these radiations is hard to analyse but it is accepted that they are disturbing if not outrightly harmful.

The collection of this type of information will yield up an immense amount of data on a site. It is critical not to be afraid to look closely at what you are proposing buying. Do not be swayed by extraneous matters like the fact that sites are scarce or that your partner has his/her heart set on that particular piece. Be realistic.

Spending time on a site is the best way to get to know it

It is also a good idea to duplicate your likely living patterns by checking out such things as the shops, schools, community facilities etc. that you might use when/if you decide to buy. Try driving to/from work or picking up the kids from school and bringing them to the site. If there is any sort of drawback it is best to become aware of it from the beginning and to make a reasoned assessment of the value of the site in terms of your needs right from day one.

Summary

The design of any building is always greatly influenced by its site.

If you are considering buying a site carry out a detailed Site Analysis and a preliminary design exercise ... first!

39 Sheltermaker Design Programme
Brief Appraisal

Before the all-important *Layout* exercise begins it is necessary to review your *Brief* and to put your files in order.

Devising a building layout - a plan - is a creative exercise carried out within the parameters and conditions set out in your *Brief*. As such, it is partially based on fixed criteria such as floor area and the site conditions. The layout will also be influenced by more abstract considerations to do with feelings and your sense of how things should be. To allow you focus on this critical 'living' aspect of the design you must have the 'fixed' aspects clearly set out in your files to support the creative journey you are about to embark on. How to do this is explained, in depth, on pages 212-218. Read these now and update your *Brief* accordingly.

Particular attention needs to be paid to the *Plumbing, Drainage, Electrical* and *H&V* Files and to the details of the systems you intend to use. Where these take up a relatively small amount of space in themselves they are easy to overlook as one rushes ahead to create a 'plan'. Each of these aspects of the building has its own demands, particularly in regards to the location of critical things such as boilers, meter cupboards, distribution boards, stoves, battery storage, percolation areas, etc. While these items are oftentimes too small to appear on drawings, at some stage they will have to be introduced into the design equation. It is better to do this while the design is still 'elastic'. What this means in practical terms is for you to have a clear idea of the nature of the systems you intend to employ even if the details of these systems are not complete.

If you are working on an existing building your situation is similar. In order to be freely creative you will need your files to be up-to-date. Don't be fooled into thinking that you 'know' the building you are working on. Unless this knowledge is backed up by facts, figures, drawings, etc. you will end up in a muddle! Extending an existing building is, in many ways, harder that designing one from scratch.

Next: SDP40 - The Sun Path, page 219

Layout

You are now at the stage in the design process where you have a comprehensive *Brief*, a detailed concept of each *Space* you want to create, an idea of the kind of *Materials* and *Structure* you are going to use, a clear impression of the *Site* on which the building will be placed, an awareness of the *Planning & Building Regulations*, an overall *Budget* for the project and you have decided on the type of *Services* that will be required. As well as this information you will have developed a clear impression of the design theme/s and the style your building have. Your house at this point has become highly individual.

Within your *Brief* you will have answers to all the questions that are now going to arise. The *Layout* or plan of the house is going to be a balanced mix of answers to all these questions.

If you do not have a site, either choose one in an area that you would like to live or simply create one on paper. This is a wide-ranging freedom that you can enjoy without actually buying a site. If you are designing a house for a piece of land that is not actually yours you can still get hold of the Ordnance Survey map for it and work as if it was yours. Estate agents usually have photocopies of the relevant parts of the maps for the sites that they are selling. You can obtain one of these easily enough by asking for it.

There is never only one design solution to any building layout. The possibilities are not infinite but they certainly are numerous. It is very easy to follow a particular line of reasoning in a design approach and for this to become final in your mind. If such an approach creates limitations as your work through the design you may become stuck. When you get stuck like this you may not readily see the way out of it. The best thing to do in those situations is to step back and try looking at everything another way. Remember, the *Brief* is a document full of facts and figures about the house you are designing. It is your friend. You can always extract yourself from a tricky design, go back to the *Brief* and start again.

The State of Your Brief

Completed:
Space Analysis & Space Mock-Ups
H&V System Concept
Materials & Products Selected
Construction System Selected
Services Systems Selected
Planning Investigated
Building Regulations Assessed
Site Analysis Completed
Design & Style Selected

Your Brief will now be able to provide all the answers to all the questions that will arise as the Layout proceeds from here on in.

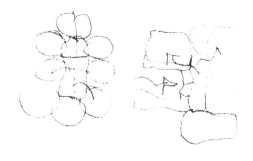

There is never only one design solution to any building Layout exercise.

The importance of assembling a clear *Brief* cannot be overstressed. Everything you can think of has been put in there, you have thought about it all, have made your decisions and you are using it as a guidebook that is helping you find your home. If any changes or insertions have to be made to the *Brief* make them now.

From your *Brief* you should know such things as, what *Materials & Products* are available; what skills and services you can call on and how much you have to spend. These answers should be all there in your *Brief* and you should be able to gain access to them very easily.

The design project will now have a life of its own. It is a good idea to take pause at this point to reorganise your *Brief*. Comb through your *Files* and weed out any irrelevant information. Make sure your information is clear and fill in any gaps or omissions that have not been taken care of yet.

All involved in the project should now get together and the *Brief* should be gone through. This is best done by reading aloud and making alterations as you go. The level of design that you are now embarking on is creative work. Everyone will want to be involved now that much of the drudge work is over. Two is the most people that should work on any design solution together. If there are more people than this involved make two separate designs. Design teams should be balanced to work well. If you are working a design through alone you will need someone to explain your design to occasionally otherwise you will become too involved and will not be able to remain objective.

Creative work of this nature is demanding. You will find that as much time will be spent thinking as designing but this is only as it should be. You are looking for something and if you remain aware of this, answers will present themselves in all kinds of places. Looking at existing buildings and spaces is very important now as well as looking at the details of how your favourite spaces are made. Looking at buildings under construction is very important also.

If insertions or deletions have to be made to the Brief ... make them now!

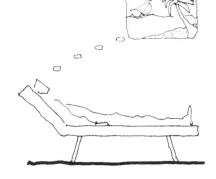

As the Layout exercise proceeds, you will find that as much time will be spent thinking ... as will be spent designing.

Reviewing The Brief

Before a proper, considered approach can be made to the question of *Layout* it is vitally important that the *Brief* be brought up to date. What this involves is a detailed review of each *File*.

At this point in the design process *Files* should exist for all aspects of the home you wish to create. *Files* that you should have are;

Space Files:

A *File* should exist for each *Space* in your home. These should detail items of *Furniture & Equipment*; a list of the Activities that will be carried on in the *Space*; an outline of the *Abstract Qualities* desirable in the *Space*; a decision on the *Location* of the *Space* in relationship to the other *Spaces* in the house and decisions on the *Surfaces* of the interior of the *Space*. A *File* should also be included outlining the details of the *Circulation Space* or *Spaces* in the house.

Further items in the *Space Files* will be *Space Plan Cards* including information on the size of the *Space*, its layout and the possible location of windows and doors. Cross Sections should also be included detailing the height of the space and its shape.

Budget File:

The *Budget File* will contain details of your *budget*; an estimated cost per square foot for your building; figures for building costs that have been gathered from builders and so on; prices for sites and site services such as hooking into the Local Authorities water supply, connecting to the ESB and getting Planning Permission; prices on windows, doors, timber, paint, boilers - all the items that will go into making your home.

How you are going to pay for your building should also be on this *File*. If you need a Loan, details of the repayments required should be included. If you are building out of Income, your resources should be listed and very careful note made of the costs of various materials and products.

To build cheaply is more time consuming that being able to spend freely. On the other hand building cheaply requires more resourcefulness, ingenuity and creativity. Such input into a building design can be most effective. One needs to be realistic though in terms of the time commitment one might be able to make in organising the building project.

MAIN BEDROOM 6:2

1 ACTIVITIES

1:1 SLEEPING
1:2 LOVE MAKING
1:3 TALKING / CHATTING
1:4 READING
1:5 RESTING
1:6 DRESSING
1:7 PHONE CALLS.
1:8 LISTENING TO MUSIC
1:9 STAR GAZING

2 FURNITURE & EQUIPMENT.

2:1 LARGE DOUBLE BED
2:2 2 NO BED SIDE TABLES
2:3 FULL LENGTH MIRROR
2:4 DESK / DRESSING TABLE
2:5 MIRROR OVER DESK.
2:6 BED SIDE LIGHT
2:7 BOOK SHELF / CASE
2:8 EASY CHAIRS
2:9 PAINTINGS
2:10 TELEPHONE
2:11 TABLE
2:12 MUSIC SYSTEM ?

3 ABSTRACT.

3:1 SUNNY MORNINGS ESPECIALLY
3:2 PRIVATE
3:3 QUITE
3:4 AIRY
3:5 SPACIOUS BUT NOT TO BIG

Heating & Ventilation File:

This *File* will contain information on the type of heating system you wish to install including catalogues, samples and so on.

Information on the degree and type of *Ventilation* the building will have should be on this *File* also.

Usually windows are used to ventilate the interior of a building but this is not always the most efficient method. Proper ventilators with adjustable vents offer a better alternative especially if a tightly sealed house is being constructed. Care should always be taken to provide openable windows or emergency exit routes in the event of fire.

Materials & Products File:

Details of the *Materials* you wish to use, catalogues and any other information relevant to this subject will be contained in this *File*. *Product* Information will mainly be in the form of catalogues, specifications and samples. Wherever possible such information should be backed up by first hand knowledge - in other words examining the products for yourself. This is especially true for windows. Window latches and hinges are very difficult to assess from photographs. It is better to visit the manufacturers showroom and try a window out before you finally select it for use.

If you are planning on having lots of built-in units in your home you should have some idea of who will make them - again catalogues may fulfil this role or even a drawing from a local joiner who will design and build units under your direction.

Manufacturers spend large sums on promotional material to bring you information on their products - get your hands on as much of this information as you can. Builders Providers, newspaper ads, the Golden Pages are all good sources of *Product & Material* information. The list of materials to be used on any building project is really an extended Shopping List.

Copies of prices of all *Materials & Products* should be kept in the *Budget File.*

It is very important to know about the availability of the particular *Materials & Products* you decide on. It is no use picking something and not being able to get it when you need it. Also, use the fact that you are a potential buyer to get proper service from suppliers, manufacturers etc..

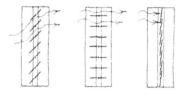

Calculated Building Elements U-Values:

external walls ~ 0.17 N/m²/°C

Roof ~ 0.2 N/m²/°C

Floor ~ 0.19 N/m²/°C

THE PREMIER SHEATHING AND SARKING BOARD FOR THE TIMBER FRAME AND CONSTRUCTION INDUSTRY

THE BENEFITS:
- ✓ Good vapour permeability
- ✓ High racking strength
- ✓ Weather resistant
- ✓ Breather paper not normally required
- ✓ Improved insulation properties
- ✓ Same nail gun settings as plywood
- ✓ Fewer nails are required than comparative boards
- ✓ Easy to cut
- ✓ Readily available ex stock
- ✓ Environmentally beneficial
- ✓ Virtually formaldehyde free
- ✓ Bitumen free
- ✓ No preservative treatment
- ✓ Uses forest thinnings and waste

APPROVALS:
- ✓ Produced to ISO 9001 and BS 1142
- ✓ A category 1 panel in compliance with BS 5268
- ✓ Conforms to BS 5250

TECHNICAL SPECIFICATION:

Thickness	9.2mm
Standard Size	2400x1200mm
Others by agreement	
Weight	6.8Kg/ m²
Density	720-750Kg/ m³
Bending Strength	22-30 MPa
Tensile Strength	10-16 MPa
Transverse internal bond	0.2-0.5 MPa
Racking Strength	1.73kn/ m²
Water Vapour Transmission Resistance	1.47 MNs/g
Wet cup method	
Thermal Conductivity	0.08 W/mK
Air Permeability	0.02-0.03m³/m²
Extractable Formaldehyde	<0.002mg/m³

Prices and details of timber availability and section sizes should be part of the *Material & Products File*. Alternatively, a separate *Timber File* might be created.

Construction File:

This *File* will detail the construction system the proposed building will use. This will either be masonry loadbearing construction or frame construction.

Loadbearing construction is the normal cavity wall type of construction while frame construction usually indicates the use of lightweight timber frames or Post & Beam construction.

Oftentimes timber frames sit on conventional loadbearing walls and have a loadbearing wall built in front of them to give protection from the weather. If this is not done the timber frame can have legs' which sit on individual pad foundations. The outside of such a frame can be finished in a variety of ways including weatherboarding, shingles, slates, tiles and sand/cement render on expanded metal.

All domestic roof construction is of the timber frame type. If you wish to have attic rooms the way the roof is made will have to accommodate this.

Any information on Local Builders, Timber Frame Erectors/Manufacturers that you gather will also be on the *Construction File*. Details of site conditions/levels might also be included.

Electrical Services File:

Details of the electrical points required in all the spaces in your home should be recorded on the *Space Plan Cards* or on tracings/photocopies of them. A simply notation using symbols for plug outlets, switches, light points, audio/video outlets, smoke alarms, TV points, telephone and so on should be used to do this. The height off the floor of these items should be noted on these layouts - this is why it is a good idea to keep this information on a separate sheet from the actual layout. The connections between light switches and the lights they operate can be simply indicated by a line.

Any outside lights or electrical points should be borne in mind. Also the requirements of the ESB as far as a meter box is concerned. Information on the initial ESB hook-up requirements should also be included. Catalogues of lights, outlets, switches should also be on this *File*.

Timber Supplies
Best price ~ £175/m³ delivered
All Swedish whitewood, graded + kiln dried

construction system
foundations – concrete strip footings
Rising walls: 300mm block-work to floor level
Floor: Insulated suspended timber floor with ply heating panels
Walls: 150mm timber frame with Panelvent breathable sheathing and cellulose insulation, block or render/expanded metal external skin.
Roof: cut timber roof or pre-assembled trusses + cellulose insulation + breathable felt + slates
Note: Form 'loft' spaces where height will permit
Timber frame: use manufacturer or build on site?

Electrical
Contact ESB re providing electrical supply on site to provide power during construction – essential if frame is to be built on site?
Contact West Wind Co. re wind generator. Where to locate this? what about batteries? – locate these under suspended floor?
Photovoltaics – locate panels below house on lower ground?

If some alternative to the ESB is being considered -
such as Photovoltaic Cells - details of this should be on
the *File*, as well as any special requirements of the
system. This type of information can be gotten from
any company that installs such systems. The same is
true if Wind Power or Water Power is to be utilised.

Plumbing Services File:

The *Plumbing File* will contain catalogues of baths,
sinks, wash-hand basins, toilets, showers, bidets, taps,
shower heads, washing machines and dishwashers, cold
water storage tanks, hot water cylinders and so on. All
these items can be selected and priced before your
design is finalised. Remember to check on availability
especially of non-standard items.

The type of pipework you wish to use should be noted
on the *File* - copper with soldered or compression
joints. Or perhaps you wish to use plastic. This *File*
will overlap to some extent with the *Heating &
Ventilation File* insofar as the hot water system may be
linked into the heating system.

If solar water heating in the form of panels or
evacuated tubes is to be used details of these systems
should be on the File.

Details of the water supply should also be available on
the *File*.

Drainage Services File:

The type of *Drainage* system that you must use will be
on the *Drainage File*. If you must use a Septic Tank
and Percolation Area details of this should be on the
File as well as the Requirements of the Local Authority.
If a Constructed Wetland system is proposed, details of
this should be available.

If a main drain runs near to your site and you are
connecting to this, you should have its location marked
on a map and have some idea of how deep it is under
the road.

If you are considering recycling 'greywater' details of
how you are going to do it should be detailed.

Information on gutters, downpipes, gullies, armstrong
junctions etc. can all be on this *File*.

evacuated tube
collectors:
? How many
? locate where
? use frame above roof
to mount tubes

water supply -
Have dowser locate source
Drill + have water tested
for mineral / metal
content.

Percolation Test Results
Test Holes 1 + 2
Average time "T" - 4 mins.
Conclusion: Percolation
Area will have to be
created from material
having 'T' value in 15-30
range.
Size: + 200 m² in excess
of Appendix C requirements

Constructed wetland ~
will Planners accept
this?
Contact "GS Wetland Systems"
to arrange site visit.
ASAP!

Planning File:

All information on the *Planning* Requirements relating to the area in which you wish to build should be included on the *Planning File*. Letters, maps, records of meetings, application forms, notes from the Development Plan are all items on would expect to find in such a *File*.

Site File:

Maps, measurements, notes on orientation, levels, boundaries, vegetation, access are all subjects for inclusion in your *Site File*. Photographs are also an invaluable addition to such information.

Design & Style File:

Photographs, magazine cuttings, sketches, newspaper clippings, notes, colour shade cards, fabric cuttings and so on are items for inclusion in this *File*. This information will illustrate the type of effect you wish to create in your design. Such details would relate to the inside as well as to the outside of your building.

In many ways it is this *File* that glues together all the disparate elements of the design for it contains information on the more personal aspects of your home. *Construction, Plumbing, Drainage* and so on, are really only the bare bones of your design. All these elements end up being covered in the completed building by the type of finish and style you wish to invest your building with.

Developing The Layout

When all the *Files* in your *Brief* have been thoroughly updated detailed work on the *Layout* of your building can proceed. This level of design is a little like juggling - keeping several balls in the air at once. This is why it is vital to have clear decisions and information in your *Files* and why you should be able to get at this information quickly and easily. For example, you need information on the *Furniture & Equipment* that you have decided to put in a particular place. No matter that you might change your mind now, that the process has begun. What is important that you have given the subject thought, you have expressed your attitude to the topic. Right down to the type of light switches you are going to use, you should be able to put your hands on a *File* and have answers to refer to. It is the creative interpretation of this raw information that will direct the course of your design. This is cake-making and you have assembling ingredients for your masterpiece.

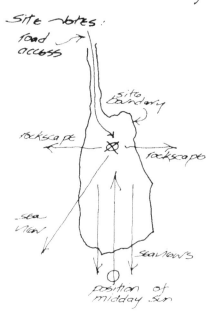

When all the Files in your Brief have been thoroughly updated ... detailed work on the Layout can proceed.

There is a strong connection between the path the sun takes around a house on its daily journey and the path of your life. Recognising this can be the key to forging a strong inner/outer connection that links the intimate world of the house to the outer world.

One begins exploring this by examining the way in which the sun moves around a point on your site. This can be marked on the ground as the 'centre' of your layout or plan. In other words, you pick a spot on the site where you want the house 'to be' and mark this with, for example, a timber post. You can then observe, using this marker, the direction of the rising, setting and midday sun. Moonrises and moonsets can also be observed and their directions recorded. Prevailing winds and views can also be noted in relation to this marker.

If you are working with an existing building you can observe sun path and note if it might cause shadowing on your proposed extension.

Such observations, seen as they are from a fixed point against the landscape, readily key one into the natural world. It is vital to integrate these observed connections into the design, otherwise the inner world of the house will be cut off from the outer world which surrounds it. This will starve the occupants of natural vitality and make the building difficult to live in fully.

'Living fully' is not an *'Activity'* listed on an *Analysis Sheet*. It belongs under the *'Abstract'* heading. It cannot be observed or analysed. It is an unfolding, the development of your life as nurtured within your design. This is the living of an unseen future, fed by the vitality of nature. This is the core of sustainability, recognising how we are part of the living world and depend on its sustenance for survival. Solar energy is the primary source of such vitality. Gaining heat and light as well are a bonus.

To a large extent, because it is unseen, we cannot clearly 'plan' for this future. However, it is most likely that a closer harmony with nature will be key to living this future fully. Observing how the sun moves around a fixed point on your site - the centre of your design - is the first step in forging this living connection and incorporating this into the layout.

Read *Pages 8-9* of the *Layout* chapter, then carry out the exercise of marking your 'point' on-site. This is a 'living' exercise - in other words you need to carry it out 'live' on-site. After your point has been established it can then be marked onto your site map. Give yourself time with this - perhaps choose several points and then select the one which feels the best. These are rituals and should be approached as such. You are seeking to enter the realm of aliveness which already exists on the land. If you do not have a site you could 'borrow' one. This might be a site that you are considering buying. If you are designing an extension to an existing building your *Site Analysis Worksheet* should show this.

Next: SDP41 - Circulation, page 226

Layout Form

Apart from the raw design information relating to your
own particular choices and wishes, the *Layout* or Plan
of your building will be influenced by the Sun & Moon
Paths and by the type of Circulation System you decide
to use.

The Sun Path is the primary influencing factor in the *Layout Form* of a sensitively designed building.
The Sun Path diagram therefore is an essential part of your Layout information. Properly speaking, as
with Life itself, the Sun is the source of all *Layout Forms*. The Moon & Planetary Paths, similar as they
are to the Sun Path, will then automatically be catered for.

By accepting the influencing force of the Sun on *Layout Form*, one automatically keys in to the source
of Life itself. By incorporating this awareness into the *Plan Form* of a home, one creates both a focus
and a receptor for life giving energy.

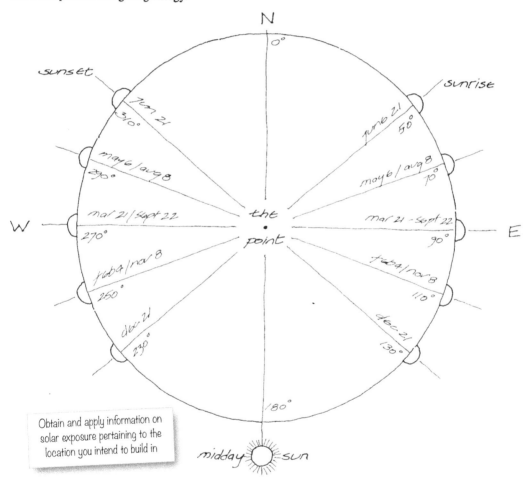

As will be seen from the Sun Path Diagram, it takes the form of a circle. At the centre of this circle is a
Point. This Point is the Point from which the *Plan Form* emerges. This keys the individual *Plan* both
into the small-scale world of the individual as well as into the infinite world of the Universe. It is this
consciously made interrelationship that connects the personal world and the natural world together and
makes a home into what it truly is.

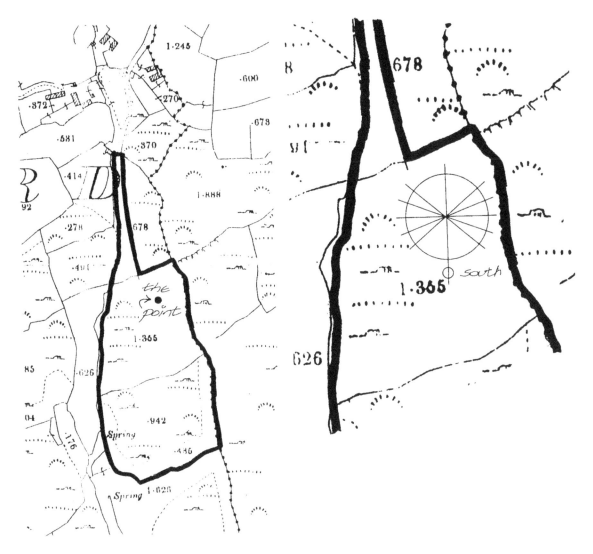

In physical terms, the Starting Point of the *Plan Form* of your home is where you yourself choose this Point to be on the physical Earth. That is, the Point you choose on your Site. From this Point the *Plan Form* of your home emerges and is connected to the wider scale of the Universe via the Sun Path that encircles it. This Point can be physically made by marking it with a rock, a stake or a fire.

The Starting Point of the *Plan Form* of your home can also be made on a Site Map. This will, of course, be necessary where no physical site exists, though the limitations of this approach should be carefully considered. These limitations can be compensated for by the physical act of choosing a Point anywhere on the Earth - your existing back garden; the forest; commonage etc. - and in this way the true meaning of creating shelter can be brought home to one.

In choosing a Point on the Earth to be the centre of one's world, the Elements of Earth, Air, Fire and Water that characterise Life can be unified and consciously viewed. The chosen Point represents Earth. The element of Air will exist all around this Point and it can be physically be represented with something like a flag. The Sun Path around this Point represents Fire. This can also be expressed by lighting a Fire. The element of Water can be made physically present and if this is done in the form of Water in a clay jar for example, a further unification of the Four Elements can be achieved. Such representation of the Four Elements and one's relationship to the wider world is crucial one to the development of an individual *Plan Form*.

When a Point has been chosen from which the *Plan Form* of your building will emerge, the way in which the Circulation to, from and within that *Plan Form* must be decided on. In its simplest form the home is a single space with the fire at its centre. Even within such a simple *Plan Form*, common in so called 'primitive architecture', a sophisticated *Layout* is employed designating particular parts of the *Plan Form* to eating, sleeping, dreaming, talking and so on. Generally in such single space *Plan Forms* the entrance faces East. The various living activities are disposed around the fire and the entrance according to the relative importance of these. The Circulation pattern follows this. In a more modern *Layout* individual spaces are dedicated to various activities necessitating a more sophisticated and conscious linking of Elements, Entrance and Activities. Nonetheless, the 'primitive' linking of the centre of the *Plan Form* to a single Point will prove to be the most successful and adaptable *Plan* Form that is possible to arrive at, allowing for the unification of the diverse aspects of the design by a central *Circulation* system.

By breaking up the *Plan Form* into individual *Spaces* it is very easy that a 'centreless' design will be arrived at. Extreme care needs to be taken that this is not the case as such a *Plan Form* will not properly relate the inner and outer worlds to each other. While such 'centreless' *Plan Forms* comprise the bulk of modern house designs and such homes provide adequate and comfortable shelter for their occupants, the absence of a proper relationship between the inner world of the home and the outer world of The World At Large can be pinpointed as the missing ingredient in making such house designs whole. Generally is is the absence of a unifying element - for this read proper *Circulation* - that creates this situation within buildings.

Because people are so adaptable and because we all recognise the deep and important need for shelter it is possible to make almost any enclosed space habitable. By creating an individual design however, the need for such extreme adaptability is removed, allowing the *Plan Form* to follow both physical as well as more abstract inner need. In arriving at a workable *Plan Form* it is the need to successfully connect the individual *Spaces* in the design together that holds the key to creating a properly integrated *Plan Form*. This connective tissue can be referred to as *Circulation Space*, that is, the *Space* through which one circulates on the way to and from the individual *Spaces* of the design. Such *Circulation Space* can also host particular activities though its main function is to facilitate the

When a Point has been chosen from which the Plan Form will emerge ... the way in which the Circulation to, from and within the Plan Form, must be decided on.

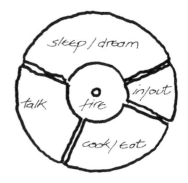

The creation of a Plan Form around a specific Point will prove to be the most successful and adaptable Layout that it is possible to arrive at.

It is very easy to create a 'centreless' design. Such a Plan Form will not properly relate the Inner and Outer Worlds to each other. Generally it is the absence of a unifying element within a design that creates such a situation.

vital flow of energies through the entire system that is being created.

Circulation Space, if not considered as a *Space* in itself, with particular *Activities* carried on there, can very easily become simply a corridor with no function whatsoever other in channelling people from one Space to another. Without a particular feeling or activity to enliven it, a corridor will be nothing more than a dead area with no life whatsoever. A corridor that hosts even a storage function will be more alive than a corridor with nothing but dead walls on either side of it. If *Circulation Space* is regarded in terms of an old fashioned 'Hall' with the function of unifying all the individual *Spaces* within the building one will come very much closer to creating a design that is dynamic, alive and exciting. If this *Circulation Space* or *Hall* also serves as the location of the Point from which the building relates to the Outer World then a balanced whole in terms of design will likely be achieved.

If a two-tiered design is being considered then the creation of a *Central Hall/Circulation Space* will become even more important. Historically, the creation of enclosed chimneys has had the greatest effect in modifying house design in recent times. Before the use of the enclosed chimney the *Central Hall* served not only as Gathering/Cooking/Eating Space but also as Chimney. Because of this, the upper floors of houses were left open to the *Central Hall* to allow smoke to percolate upwards and exit through the roof. The invention of the enclosed chimney allowed for the *Central Hall* to be floored over creating more floor space within the same volume as before. This also, of course, cut off the upper floor/s from the ground floor thereby elimination the spatial unity that had existed before. The enclosed chimney also propelled the fire to an outside wall and in this way the centralising and unifying effect of the fire was lost.

These changes in how houses are organised internally still affect our thinking today, though inventions such as central heating allow for the recreation of the *Central Hall* and the enjoyment of the unifying effects of this. It is vitally important therefore, if a two-tiered design is being proposed, that a *Central Hall/Circulation Space* comes under consideration.

Whether a single storey or a two-tiered design is being considered, it is worth noting that locating a fire at the Central Point of the design will allow one to fully exploit the unifying effect of this.

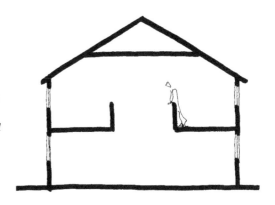

It is vitally important, if a two-tier design is proposed, that a Central Hall/Circulation Space is given serious consideration.

It is the notion of unification that is common to all design types - single storey, two-tier, or some variation of this, and it is in this regard that the strength of the *Sun Path Diagram/Central Hall* 'pattern' can be fully appreciated. What such a pattern allows is for a unification of the plan around a focal point that has a meaning beyond the enclosure that is being created. If this is not done, in some form or other, the building will lack centre and consequently fail to connect fully to the outside world of which it is undeniably a part.

In a single storey design the creation of a central focussing point is not particularly difficult to achieve. In a two-tiered design however, care needs to be taken that a focus that unifies both levels of the design, and also, connects these to the outside world, is more difficult to achieve.

Variations on the single storey/two-tier theme can also be explored. Half levels - that is adjoining floors that are separated by half a level - can provide a very workable design solution. However, where a small, tight plan is being developed, a solution that keeps all the accommodation on the same level will prove to be the most workable approach.

The decision in regard to building height - that is, the number of floors your building contains - must be made with proper regard being paid to the prevailing site conditions and to the attitude of the local Planning Authority. Also, it is vital to consider the living patterns that will ensue should you live on one floor and sleep on another. It is all to easy that the stairs becomes the most trafficked area of the building!

It is also worth bearing in mind that even where a firm decision to create a single storey design has been made, the incorporation of a parking/working area below the dwelling is always worth considering.

The commonest argument in favour of two-tiered design solutions is the one based on cost. By placing all the accommodation on a single level the area of the external 'envelope' - that is, the outside surface area of the building - increases. This is true. However, such a line of argument, based as it is on a single aspect - i.e. cost - is a very narrow way of looking at the problem. To properly consider this question a wider-ranging argument, including matters such as: convenience; ceiling heights; the feeling of space; flexibility etc. needs to be made. Remember, a sphere contains the largest volume for the least surface area. Now, while a sphere is both difficult to construct and to live in, the

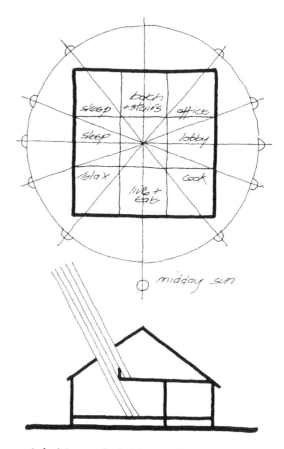

A decision on the height your building is going to be, must be made with proper regard being paid to the prevailing site conditions and to the attitude of the Local Authority Planning Office.

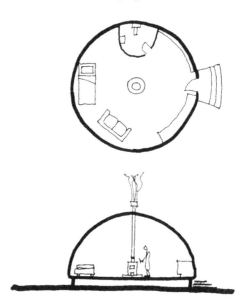

principle is worthwhile noting: by keeping as close as possible to a symmetrical 3-dimensional shape, you will maximize volume while keeping surface area to a minimum.

Arguments in favour of single storey and half-level design solutions need to be loudly made otherwise conventional thinking will have one trundling up the two-tier road. Consider - where a family home is being created and a Master Bedroom and 3 Children's Rooms are being included. Does conventional thinking not lead one to say - "the bedrooms are going upstairs". Now, if this attitude is not balanced by a counter argument that says, at the very least, - "why should that be?" - one will find oneself creating a design wholly based on the conventional thinking that places *Living* accommodation on one floor and *Bedroom* accommodation above it. While workable solutions to such a design strategy can be found, if alternative routes are not considered, exciting options will have been ignored.

Consideration of the long term use of space is vital at these early stages of the design process. It is all too easy to imagine life as being unchanging and to design with this attitude. Change, however, characterises life and if your building can accommodate change then change will be so much easier to both accept and to absorb. People are highly adaptable creatures and the buildings we create to live in must reflect this aspect of survival, otherwise our ability and willingness to adapt and change will be hampered and compromised.

Perhaps the most serious in-built self-restriction that you can foist upon yourself is to stratify the accommodation by placing *Bedroom Areas* above *Living Areas*. A further compounding of this approach is to amplify the mistake by connecting the two-tiers with nothing more than a staircase. There are many examples of this design approach that are lived in successfully. In order to properly evaluate such homes it is important to see beyond the gratitude usually expressed at the possession of almost any form of shelter. To look beyond such gratitude inevitably means to question it. It is this form of speculation that allows for the creative unravelling of the sleeve of gratitude and the ongoing freedom that inevitably derives from this sort of activity. There is no better place to begin unpicking this wretched garment.

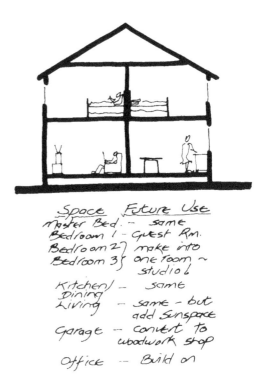

Space   Future Use
Master Bed. - same
Bedroom 1 - Guest Rm.
Bedroom 2 } make into
Bedroom 3 } one room ~
           studio
Kitchen/ - same
Dining
Living - same - but
        add Sunspace
Garage - convert to
        woodwork shop
Office - Build on

It is vital to consider the long-term use of Spaces, at this stage of the Layout process, if you have not done so before.

As with our bodies, good circulation is essential to maintaining 'aliveness' within a building. This is normally overlooked in house design yet people sense it by regularly complaining about 'dead corridors'. Indeed poor circulation can have just that effect in a building, causing some spaces to be starved of vitality. Such vitality comes from the people in the building - who move around within the circulation system charging it up as they go. Vitality also comes from the life outside the building which, if consciously drawn inside and allowed flow through the circulation system, will energise it too.

Endeavours in these kinds of directions will place their own demands on an evolving design. It's not as simple as it might seem. People who might 'charge up' a circulation space will have to be happy and meaningfully engaged with life if they are to have surplus energy to literally splash around. Also, they would have to have some empathetic connection with their surroundings - the spaces they are in. By the same token, hauling a few pot plants or creating a water feature won't necessarily make an indoor space feel 'natural'.

Read *Layout, Pages 10-13* to understand some of the implications of all of this circulation stuff. Refer to your *Circulation Space Analysis Sheet/s* and amend these if necessary. Remember, how the circulation space is designed and functions is key to creating a flexible and adaptable building. This is particularly true where work and/or food production are being designed in. The journey from a kitchen to a kitchen garden and back again might be a regular one which would immensely benefit from a careful 'circulation analysis'. Carefully locating work space in such a way that one can have a day or a weekend off might make an immense difference to the quality of one's life.

It's now a good time to review the location of external doors in all the *Spaces* in your design. These are the portals which allow life to flow in and out of the building. A critical function of circulation space is in forging the connection between the inner world of the house and the outer world surrounding it. This 'threshold' - usually at the front or back door - is the interface between the two worlds. If properly designed, one can move seamlessly back and forth across this interface, effectively integrating the life of the house into the life of the site. Having external doors in bedrooms creates lots of potential in such spaces - even though those of nervous disposition will inevitably point out how risky this is. But the option of turning a bedroom into a home office or a shop with a 'public interface' is too valuable an adaptation strategy to casually overlook.

Another aspect of *circulation* that also needs careful consideration is how people and goods will move back and forth between the inner world of the house and the wider world surrounding it. The location of neighbours, shops, churches, schools, fuel supplies, workplaces as well as the doctor, dentist and mechanic, should all be carefully considered and mapped. Consideration should also be given as to how such journeys should might be made without the direct assistance of fossil fuels.

If you are working on an existing building your approach to the layout exercise will have to be versatile and imaginative. The principles articulated above will be the same but with the addition of limitations imposed by the existing infrastructure which will inevitably restrict some design options. Care needs to be taken not to imagine deconstructing almost the entire existing building as a means of creating a fresh design. Unless you own a building outright and have not paid too much money for the privileged, tearing a building apart is a highly risky exercise. If you can identify and accept the key limitations of what you are working with this will be of great assistance as you craft your way forward.

42 Sheltermaker Design Programme
Developing A Layout

You have now arrived at the heart of the Sheltermaking Mysteries. Armed with your facts, figures and decisions, you are now ready to transform these 'ingredients' into a coherent design. This creative act needs to be appreciated as a life process. Logic, intuition, common sense, practicality, emotion, dream and reality all play their part. This requires that a balance be found between these elements allowing them to be integrated and harmonised. The challenges that will be encountered in reaching this objective will be demanding. However, the scope of the design process and its structured approach allow such complexity to be resolved more or less at the kitchen table. No matter how demanding this gets it is infinitely better than encountering these challenges while building and then having to live within the inevitable mistakes. The key to successfully transforming your *Brief* into 3-dimensional reality, is time. You must allow yourself time both to carry out the work as well as to feel everything through.

The layout emerges from the 'point' articulated in item *40*, beginning life as a *'Seed Plan'* before growing into a clearly defined series of interconnected *Spaces*. The fluency with which this can be achieved will depend on the clarity of your *Brief*, particularly the layout of your individual *Spaces*. If a set of *Space Plan Cards* have been developed as described in item *13*, then things can move forward fairly rapidly. On the other hand, if no *Space Plans* have been created they now must be developed. Refer to item *13* for guidance on how to do this.

Where one is working with an existing building, the survey plan of this will form the background for the new *Spaces* to be laid out on. In all other respects the *Layout* exercise, as described, should be followed.

The other critical element to formally prepare is the information on the *Plumbing, Drainage, Electrical* and *H&V* systems. As stated earlier, these aspects of the building design can be overlooked in the rush to create a 'plan'. This can be disastrous, particularly where the *H&V* system is concerned. It is imperative that all of these systems have been designed in principle before moving forward and that details of these are incorporated into all versions of the evolving layout.

We are living in an age when the current ways and patterns are being recognised as being deficient. The way forward is not clear. Obviously, changes are on the way. No one is quite sure what these will be. On a psychological level, the onslaught of bad news and dire prediction that we are fed daily threatens our very survival. Where the fear stirred up by this remain unconscious we are driven into a senseless denial, hypnotised by indecision. The house design process allows such unconscious fears to be uncovered and for life-based solutions to be developed to deal with them.

The Layout process is described in detail in the *Layout* chapter beginning on page 229. You should read through all of this material then begin the process for yourself, giving yourself plenty of time. Do not be deceived that *'Developing A Layout'* is the same as any other exercise in the design process. It is the **point** of the design exercise and as such it demands considerable attention. The diligence with which earlier exercises in the *Design Programme* have been carried out will very much assist the smooth and successfully completion of this important exercise.

Next: SDP43 - Costing Your Design, page 278

Imagine your site as the place you are going to plant yourself in order that your life can be fruitful

Circulation Space

As has been described earlier, *Circulation Space* is the connective tissue of the design. It is what ties the individual *Spaces* together and moreover, it is what gives the building 'heart'. It is no coincidence that 'heart' and 'hearth' are so similar.

The unification of the disparate *Spaces* within your design is a major function of the *Circulation Space*. This unification process is carried out by considering each *Space* you wish to create in relationship to its likely neighbours and to the overall Sun Path Diagram. In other words, the preference you have expressed in your *Space Analysis Sheets* under the heading of *Location* will now be acted upon. Furthermore, the preferred orientation of each of these *Spaces* will now begin to influence how your *Layout Form* will develop. Your *Analysis Sheet* entitled *Circulation Space* should also be consulted as to the *Activities* you may wish to carry on there.

The following design procedure can be carried out without prior work having been done in regards to the preparation of *Space & Activity Analysis Sheets*: the creation of *Space Plans* and *Mock-Ups*; *H&V Calculations*; *Materials & Products* selection; *Services Layouts*; *Planning & Building Regulation* matters; *Site Selection & Analysis* procedures and the compilation of a *Design & Style File*. However, if the design is approached in this way it should be borne in mind that the resulting design will need constant modification to adjust for these factors if and when they are taken into consideration. It goes without saying that this approach is not recommended unless ones aim is to replicate the type of design that these **Handbooks** are aimed at avoiding. In truth, even a short-cut approach based on these *Be Your Own Architect* principles will prove to be superior to most professionally designed solutions. Nonetheless, when the magic of designing *space* is felt, it is inevitable that one will want to get it right and common sense will take one to the proper starting place to follow the procedure through to its proper conclusion.

Circulation Space is the connective tissue that binds the design together.

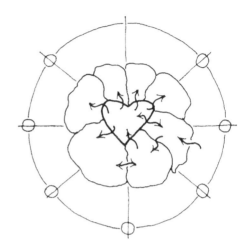

ESSENTIAL WORK TO BE
CARRIED OUT BEFORE
PROCEEDING PAST THIS POINT

Preparation of:

Space Analysis Sheets

Space Plans

Space Mock-Ups

H&V Calculations

Materials & Products Selection

Services Systems Concepts

Planning & Building Regs. Info.

Site Analysis

Design & Style File

Broadly speaking, the design procedure that will be followed from here onwards is largely intuitive. While specific tasks will be carried out in a specific order it is critical to the success of the design that a relaxed and loose approach is adopted. This is why it is so important to have a proper *Brief*. Think of the *Brief* as the raw material and yourself as the creator of a unique sculpture. The three dimensional form of this sculpture is now going to emerge under your expert hands using this painstakingly prepared raw material. The full excitement and magic of this process can be enjoyed to the fullest now. If there are any aspects of Fear lurking around they must be rooted out now, otherwise they will become in-built and appear as dark spots within your design. Again, the importance of preparing a clear *Brief* is being stressed.

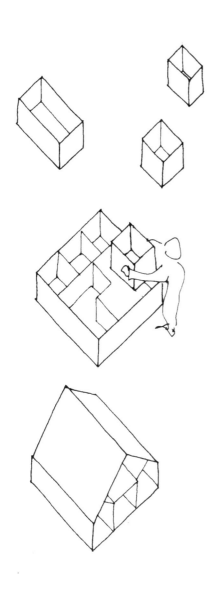

Seed Plan Prelims:

Levels: Generally 1 ~ with
lofts where
roof space will allow

Circulation Space Analysis:
Activities:
☑ moving from space to
   space
☐ connecting inside + outside
   together @ front +
   back doors
☐ Access to storage
☐ Display of paintings
Furniture + Equipment:
☑ Occasional tables (×3)
☐ Telephone tables + chairs
                    (×2)
☐ Paintings (see Inventory
                    for sizes)

Abstract:
☐ Lively
☐ View to outside
☐ Intimate
☐ "cloister" feel around
   courtyard "point".

Putting a house design together is a form of sculpting. To over-simplify the process - what you will be doing is assembling 3-dimensional objects in a particular way to satisfy your expressed desires. This assembly of what is really an Inner World will then be wrapped in a covering and enclosed from the so-called Outer World.

The question of the number of levels your building will have must now be decided upon. The design procedure follows on from here by preparing a *Seed Plan*. It is from this *Seed Plan* that the final design will emerge.

To allow the *Seed Plan* - and ultimately your home - to work, a clear notion of the type of *Circulation Space* you are creating is needed. It is this *Space* that will act to unify all the other *Spaces* in the design and allow the building to properly fulfil all its intended functions.

Seed Plans

Your *Brief* will contain a set of individual *Space Plan Cards* which will form the basis of the final *Plan* of your building. What needs to happen now is for these to be assembled in such a way that they accord with your expressed wishes. Furthermore, it is necessary for these *Spaces* to be oriented correctly.

Within this matrix will be the *Circulation Space*, the area that will unify the entire design and make it all work properly.

To guide you in how to put the *Space Plan Cards* together to achieve your stated objectives, you first make a *Seed Plan*. If you are planning on having a building with more than one floor, you will need to make 2 or more *Seed Plans*.

A *Seed Plan* is a simple arrangement of interconnected *seeds* which represent the various *Spaces* you wish to create. These are going to be 'cast' in various ways, joined together with connective tissue, modelled, sunlit and styled. Finally, the arrangement that satisfies you the most is going to be developed in detail to the point where it can be built and inhabited.

Space Ref.	Name	Area ~	Orientation
1.1	Front Door + Porch	6	Flexible
1.2	Back Door/Utility	15	Flexible
2.2	Kitchen/Dining	40	South + West
3.1	Pantry	6	(Internal)
4.1	Living Room	20	South + West
4.4	Children's Sitting Rm.	20	South
4.7	Study	10	flexible
4.9	Sunspace	25	East/South/West
4.10	meditation	10	flexible
5.4	workshop/boiler	25	flexible
6.1	Bedrooms (x3)	36	East/West
6.2A	Master Bedroom	30	East/West
6.2B	Guest Bedroom	12	East/West
7.1	Bathroom	7	flexible
7.2	Shower Rooms (x2)	8	flexible
7.5	Hot Tub	~	South (outside)
8.3	Circulation	~ 15% of Total	flexible
9.3	Decks	~	South + West
11.9	Courtyard	~	flexible
	Total	$\frac{260}{39}$ + 15% for circulation	

299 m² × 10.764 = 3218 sq ft

Reduce overall area by say 10% = ~ 270 m²
= ~ 2900 sq ft.

In terms of working materials to start this process you will need - greaseproof paper; soft pencils; an eraser; coloured markers or pencils and photocopied enlargements of the Site, and ... time.

Seed Plans are not drawn to scale but each *seed* should be drawn in rough proportion to the size of each *Space*. Tracing or greaseproof paper should be used to draw these.

In organisational terms, it is very worthwhile to note on each page you are going to use, the 'Version Number'. If this is done, you can allow yourself the freedom of making lots of sketches and then collating these according to the order in which they were produced. This will have many advantages as you can refer back to the work you have done.

Freedom of expression is the key to this exercise - you will need to be making many different versions of the *Seed Plan* and allowing yourself to become a little fevered, obsessed even, throwing aside one sketch in favour of another, charging onward towards your objective. To enjoy this level of creative freedom you really do need a strong *Brief* to support you! Without it you will be foundering with too many questions to answer, blurring the issues at hand.

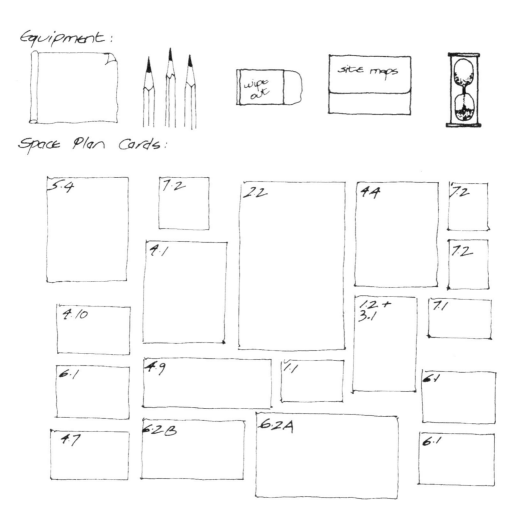

Making Seed Plans

The *Brief* will now provide the information relative to how the various Seeds go together - this will be noted under the heading *Location* in your *Space Analysis Sheets*.

For example, the Living/Kitchen/Dining area is to connect with the Central Hallway and the Utility Room/Back Door. The *Seeds* can be drawn to show this and the title of each *Space* written into the relevant *Seed*. The diagram can then be extended to include all the *Spaces* in the design. Do not be over concerned about getting the Orientation absolutely correct at this stage.

Liken this exercise to learning to ride a bicycle or learning how to juggle. You can get fancy after you learn the basics. Remember, a *Seed Plan* is the seeds of the design. This will ultimately grow into a final house plan which will satisfy all the conditions of the *Brief*.

It is crucial now to bear in mind the 'looseness' of the design process, to accept the likelihood of making mistakes, of getting lost, confused and even totally gummed up. This is all okay. In fact if you do not suffer some form of anxiety something is wrong. All the decisions you are now making are going to have a large bearing on how you will live your life within your self-designed accommodation. So, you are bound to be presented with choices and decisions that will be difficult. By having a comprehensive *Brief* at your disposal the 'physical' aspects of these decisions can be separated from the 'metaphysical' aspects thereby allowing properly balanced decisions to be made.

If you are planning on having more than one level in your building, begin by listing the *Spaces* you wish to have on the varying levels. Then create a *Seed Plan* for the ground floor accommodation. When this is working satisfactorily, you can make *Seed Plans* for the remaining floor/s in the design.

Ref.	Space	Located Next to / Close to:
1.1	Front Door	Kitchen-Dining / Living
1.2	Back Door	Utility / Pantry / Shower
2.2	Kitchen-Dining	Utility / Pantry / Living / Childrens Sitting / Shower / Sunspace / Deck
3.1	Pantry	Kitchen / Utility / Back Door
4.1	Living Room	Kitchen-Dining / Front Door / Shower / Deck
4.4	Children's Sitting	Kitchen-Dining / Bedrooms / Sunspace / Deck
4.7	Study	Front Door / Shower / Quiet!
4.10	Meditation	Shower / Quiet!
5.4	Workshop	Car parking / away from house
6.1	Bedrooms	'cluster' rooms / Bathroom
6.2A	Master Bed.	Deck / Hot Tub
6.2B	Guest Bed.	Deck / Hot Tub
7.1	Bathroom	Bedroom 'cluster'
7.2	Shower Room 1	Back Door / Kitchen-Dining / Living / Children's Sitting
7.2	Shower Room 2	Meditation
7.5	Hot Tub	Master Bedroom / Guest Bedroom

You are now on your own to a large extent. You have now to make the design yours. The sort of thing you should be doing is making lots of *Seed Plans* and getting a real feel for this. Also, you should be finding your own way to do this - if you are still working strictly by the book, loosen up! If something bothers you about the *Seed Plans* you are making find out what it is and rectify the problem. After you have become comfortable with the idea of *Seed Plans* and with representing these ideas on paper you can begin to add in more information.

Begin to take Orientation into account and create a *Seed Plan* that has all the *Spaces* correctly oriented. Never mind if this looks odd! This will inevitably happen if you have designated South as the preferred orientation for each *Space*. What is important is for you to see and grasp the possibilities and to make decisions accordingly. This is usually called 'Compromise', though this is a word that should be lightly spoken. Hold out for what it is you want.

Now begin to take account of the *Site* parameters - for example, where the vehicular Entrance/Exit should/can be. You can do this by placing a sheet of greaseproof over a copy of the enlarged Site Map.

Your intentions in regards to which portions of the garden should be visible from within your building can also come under consideration now.

In many ways, it is a good idea to develop your ideal *Seed Plan* without reference to a specific site. This will allow a clear pattern to emerge and a site can then be found to accommodate this. Generally speaking, a site should accessed from the East or North with open vistas to the South and West.

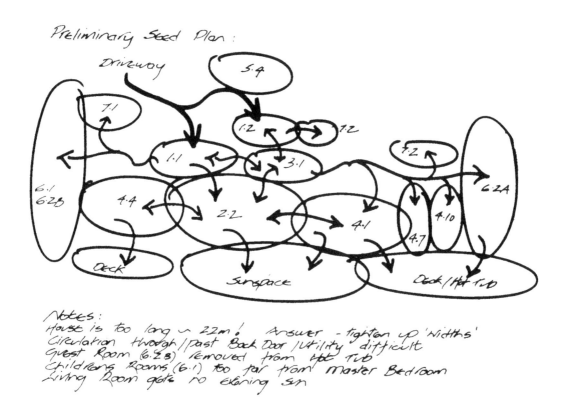

234

When you arrive at a version of the *Seed Plan/s* that satisfies you, refer to your *Activity Analysis Sheets* and mark out on a tracing of the Plan/s the 'activity path' necessary to carrying out this activity. Cooking/Washing-Up and Laundry are the activities that it is vital to get correct. If you find you are wandering all over the diagram in order to say, cook and serve a meal, this is what you will be doing in the finished building also. If you want to avoid this kind of exhausting effort, rectify the problem on the *Seed Plan*. This can often be done simply be rearranging the *Seeds*!

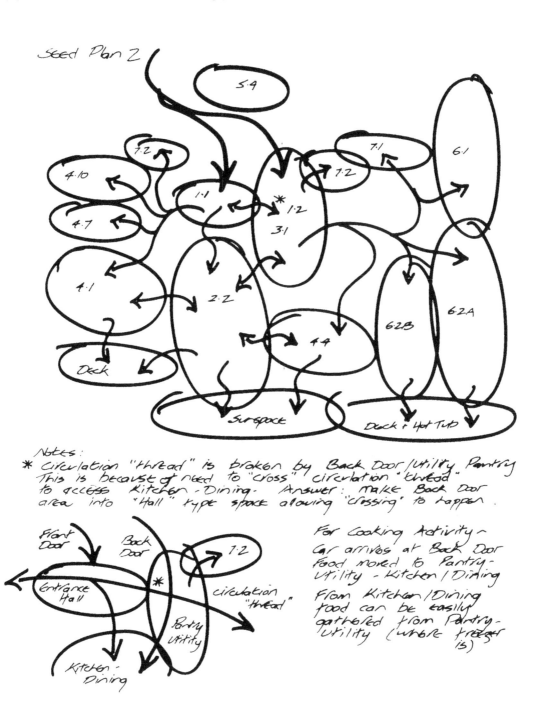

Notes:
* Circulation "thread" is broken by Back Door/Utility Pantry. This is because of need to "cross" circulation "thread" to access Kitchen-Dining. Answer: make Back Door area into "Hall" type space allowing "crossing" to happen.

For Cooking Activity ~ Car arrives at Back Door Food moved to Pantry-Utility - Kitchen/Dining

From Kitchen/Dining food can be easily gathered from Pantry-Utility (where freezer is)

There is never only one design solution to any building plan. The possibilities are not infinite but they certainly are numerous. It is very easy to follow a particular line of reasoning in a design approach and for this to become final in your mind. If such an approach creates limitations as you work, you may become stuck. When you get stuck like this you may not readily see the way out of it. The best thing to do in such a situation is to step back and try looking at everything another way. Remember, the *Brief* is a document full of facts and figures about the house you are designing. It is your friend. You can always extract yourself from a tricky design, go back to the beginning and start again. All this is far easier than constructing an ill-fitting design and forcing yourself to live in it.

The project will very definitely have a life of its own at this point. The level of design that you are now involved in is highly creative work. Everyone will want to be involved now that the worst of the drudge work is over. Two is the most people however that should work on any one design solution. If there are more than people involved make two separate designs. Design teams should be balanced to work well. If you are working a design through alone you will need someone to explain your design to occasionally otherwise you will become too involved and will not be able to remain objective.

Creative work of this nature is demanding. You will find that as much time will be spent thinking as designing but this is only as it should be. You are looking for something and if you remain aware of this, answers will present themselves in all kinds of places. Looking at buildings and *Spaces* is very important and looking at the details of *Spaces* and how they are made. Looking at buildings under construction is very important also.

Start writing notes to yourself. Writing things down puts information right on front of you where you will see it. Avoid clutter however and keep things organised. Obsession, not in itself a bad thing, should be balanced with - sleep; laughter and excitement.

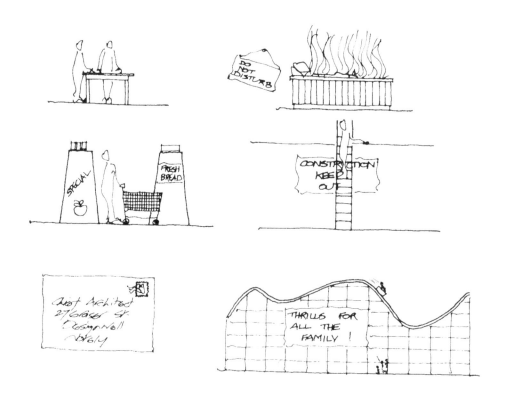

The *Seed Plans* can now be quite large as there will be quite an amount of information going on to these. Orientation will now be very important and from now on the top of any of the pages you draw on should have north at the top of the page. A final decision on orientation for each *Space* will provide you with possible window locations. Views should also be marked onto the *Seed Plans*. These will be in particular directions and should be drawn correctly relative to the direction of the view. Site Photographs are useful now in that you can look at a photograph of a particular view and relate it to the space it will be seen from. Remember to show the site access and the prevailing wind direction.

When Seed Plans have been developed to the point where they accurately reflect information on the *Brief* in terms of the location of rooms relative to each other, orientation, views and such matters, the *Space Plan Cards* can be laid out to this pattern.

It should be said that arranging the *Seed Plan* so that all conditions in the *Brief* are met is not always that easy. Some things in your *Brief* may have to change - for example if you want all rooms to get direct sun all day you will end up with a long narrow house. All in all, your *Seed Plan* should be a good balance between all the conflicting and harmonious aspects of your *Brief*. In this respect the design is very much your own.

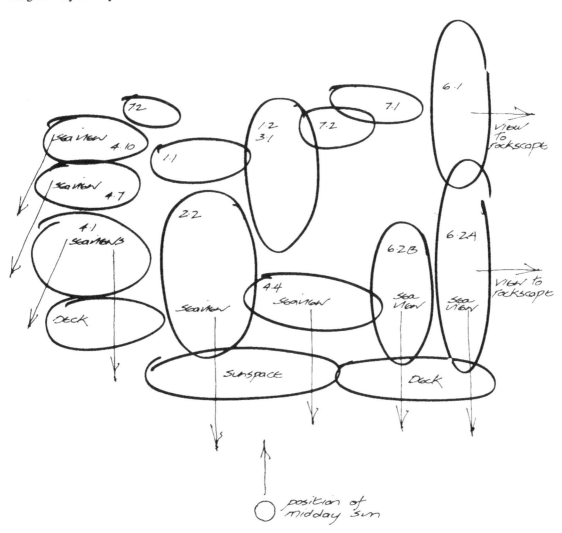

The requirements of the heating system are very important to take into account also. If there is to be say anything like a solid radiant heating system using a Finnish fireplace this has to be fairly accurately sized, a *Space Card* made for it, or check that it is included on some other *Card*. If open fireplaces or wood burning stoves are being used their location needs to be marked onto the relevant *Space Card/s*. These should be ultimately located on internal walls. Remember that if you have a two storey design the chimneys/flues for these will need to pass through the upper floor. Check on the process of delivery, storage and getting access to your chosen fuel. Fuel will have to be brought into the house and ash taken out. If you are going to use a boiler room or locate a solid fuel stove in a compartment to itself, make a *Space Card* for it and include it in your *Seed Plans*. You should be producing lots of these at this stage.

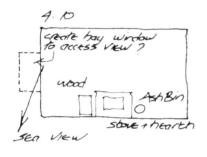

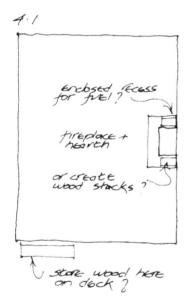

One of the critical issues in regards to installing a solid fuel appliance, be it a wood burning stove or a device that burns coal, is the matter of bringing fuel to the fire and disposing of the consequent ash. If this sequence of supply and waste removal is properly planned then the advantages of not using an oil-fired boiler can be capitalised on. This is particularly true if wood is the fuel of choice.

If you are designing for an actual site - one that you are definitely going to build on - you may not be able to make the orientations perfect due to the site conditions. For example if you want to collect solar heat but the views are to the north you will have to find an acceptable design solution to this problem. This is usually called compromise - you weigh up all the factors and decide which is the most important thing. Is the solar heat collection more important than the view? It is by weighing things up on their own merits that priorities can be decided. It also helps to remember that you are dealing with three dimensional space and that solutions will be evident from looking at the *mockups* and the *models*.

Seed Plans should now be accompanied by sketch cross sections of the *Spaces* you are including. This is particularly true where there is any change in level whatsoever. Cross sections will give you a clear idea of what your building structure is going to be like. Refer to *Part V - Space Mock-Ups* (*Volume 1; Pages 83 - 113*) for information on this. Your *Space Files* however, should already include 1:50 cross sections. This is further evidence of the importance of a well prepared *Brief*. If you can draw on this type of information easily and quickly your work will proceed without any interruption to the smooth flow of the current creative process. If you now have to start thinking about cross sections, work on the *Seed Plans* will have to be temporarily halted.

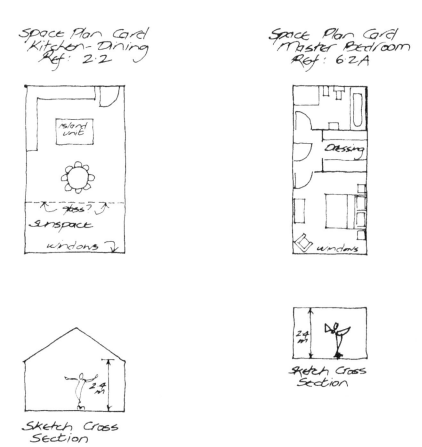

The cross sectional profile of any Space is critical to ensuring the 3-dimensional quality of that Space. It is very difficult to percieve such qualities by creating and reading drawings alone. Ideally, Space Mock-Ups should be made and drawings then made to represent these in 2-dimensions.

Developing The Seed Plan

When a satisfactory *Seed Plan* is completed, the relevant 1:20 *Space Plan Cards* are then laid out face down according to this pattern. Leave out the *Circulation Space Card* for the moment. By laying out the *Cards* in this way, a rough *Plan* will be made. If the *Cards* are laid out on top of coloured paper or card, this colour will indicate the *Circulation Space/s* left between the various *Spaces*.

Play round with the pattern and combine/recombine these until you feel in control. You must understand what you are doing and use this symbolic information as your signposting - not as a strict set of rules. Once you understand that the pattern is in you, will you be able to find it! You will probably now find yourself referring back to your *Seed Plan* collection, readjusting these, referring to you *Files* .. and having great fun.

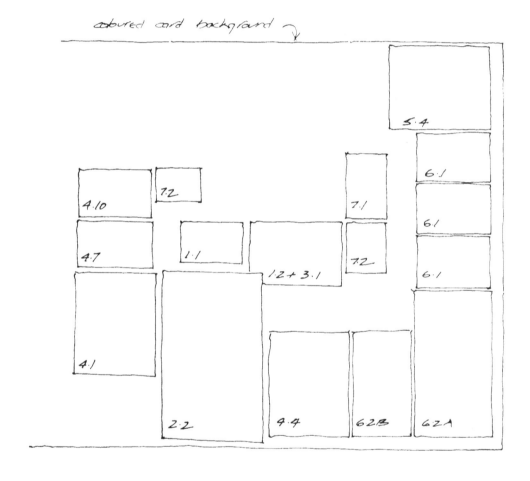

At this stage of the design process lots of rough Plans can be made using various patterns. It is important to get a 'feel' for this exercise - using the Seed Plan to guide you. You must begin to 'see' the Plan in front of you and have a clear understanding of exactly what you are doing. When this happens you will be in control of the design and what emerges will be a clear reflection of the house that is within you.

When turned over, all the *Space Plan Cards* will show layouts and indications of door and window positions. These will not all be in the right place for the particular *pattern* that is now developing. To correct this it is possible to create "mirror" images of particular *Spaces* therby allowing the original *Space Plan* to be utilised in a new way. (*See Page 27*)

Oftentimes however, an entirely new *Space Plan Card* will be required, one that is laid out using the developing *pattern* as a guide. This is how the evolving design moves from being an assemblage of individual *Space Plans* towards being a coherent and integrated *whole*. This movement - more a leap, really - allows every *Space* to adjust itself relative to its neighbours and to settle comfortably into a complete and harmonious whole.

This "leap" from *Space Plan Card Layouts* to *Plan* activates the chemistry of the design process bringing the design to life.

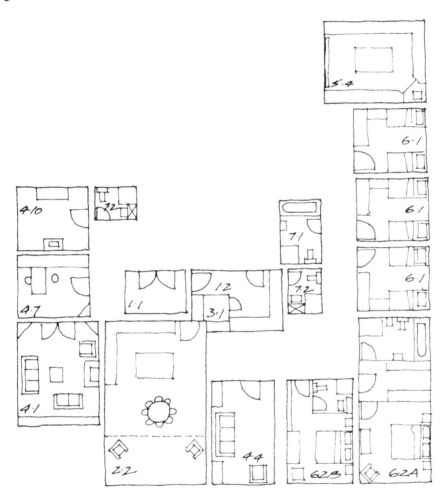

The trick of reading Space Plan Card Layouts is to keep seeing the Spaces within the Layout as being individual. In this way the scale of the necessary changes remains manageable. Such changes usually have to do with making an individual Space function better as part of the developing Layout. If one moves through the design from Space to Space in this way you will not be overwhelmed by the scale of the work involved.

241

Mirror images of *Space Plans* are made by tracing over a particular *Space Plan Card* then turning this over and reading it from the back. Photocopies can be made of the tracing and pasted onto card to create a new *Space Plan*.

There are always 4 possible combinations for reading any particular *Space Plan*. Sometimes one of these will naturally fit into your evolving *Plan*. However, bear in mind that once the design process has given way to *Plans* it usually make more sense to plan a particular *Space* to fit the place it occupies in the evolving *Plan* rather than to adhere to the original *Space Plan Card* configuration. The one thing to bear in mind is that the design has now come alive and as a result *Spaces* have a tendancy to grow! Keep tabs on both individual *Space* areas as well as on the overall area the evolving *Plan* covers.

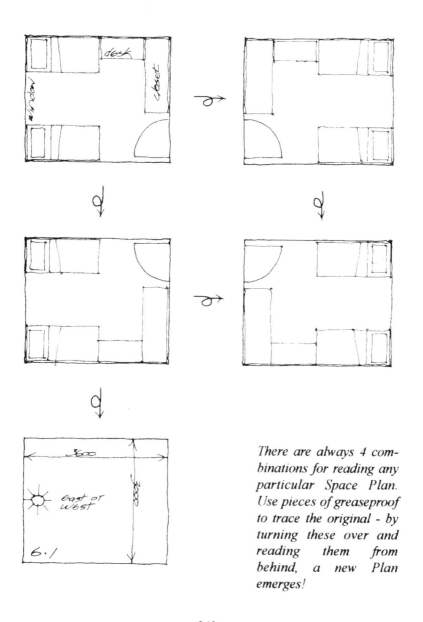

There are always 4 combinations for reading any particular Space Plan. Use pieces of greaseproof to trace the original - by turning these over and reading them from behind, a new Plan emerges!

Remember that if you are planning an upper floor you will need a stairs to access it. The stairs should be treated as a *Space* or as part of another *Space* - for example the *Circulation Space*. If not already done, a *Card* should be made to include the stairs now.

The space that a stairs occupies will depend on its width and on the height through which it must rise. Reckon on steps of 180 - 190*mm* high and on threads 240 - 250*mm* wide. To calculate the number of "risers" required to go from one floor to another divide the overall height - in *mm* - by 180, e.g. for a height rise of 3000*mm*: 3000÷180 = 16.666. If this result is adjusted downwards to 16 risers, each riser will be 187.5*mm* high.

The number of threads required in a stairs is always one less than the number of risers, in this case we will have 15 threads. Stair widths should be a minimum of 900*mm* and a 2000*mm* clear space overhead is required throughout the entire flight. Landings should be a minimum of 900*mm* wide.

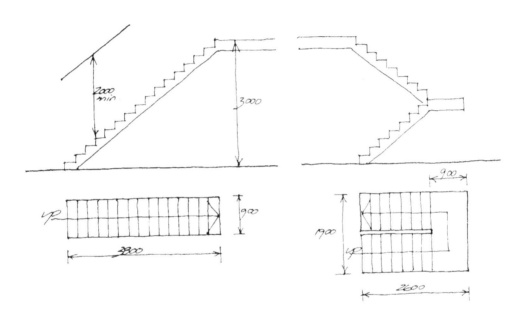

General Stair Rules

- [ ] All steps should have the same rise.
- [ ] All parallel steps should have the same thread.
- [ ] All tapered steps should have the same thread.
- [ ] Ideally, 2 X Rise + Thread = 600*mm* (or between 550 & 700*mm*).
- [ ] There should not be more than 16 Risers in any one flight.
- [ ] Stairs should have a handrail on at least one side if the stairs is 1000*mm* wide or less. If the stairs is wider, handrails are required on both sides.
- [ ] Handrails should be at a height of between 840*mm* and 900*mm*.
- [ ] Stairs rising through heights greater than 600*mm* must be guarded by a railing or balustrade.

Doors and windows should come under consideration now also. Openings for internal doors are normally 900*mm* wide and 2100*mm* high, though Bathroom door openings can be reduced to 700*mm*. Openings for Double Doors can range from 1200 - 1800*mm*. It is important to remember that when a door opens it swings through a wide arc. In the case of double doors this can demand a large amount of space. Sliding doors require much less space - and the open door can be concealed within a "pocket" in the adjoining wall.

Window sizes also need some attention at this stage. The choice here will relate to the height and depth of the *Space* being illumanated as well as on its orientation. Oftentimes the top of window openings are kept the same height as door openings - 2100*mm*. Where a *Space* has a lofty ceiling this may be too low however. Window cill heights will depend on the *Space Plan* and on whether or not furniture or radiators are being placed under windows.

At this stage you should have a good idea of the brand of windows you intend to use in the finished building. The choice of particular windows for particular *Spaces* should be made by reference to the catalogue illustrating this choice - it should be stored in your *Materials & Products File*.

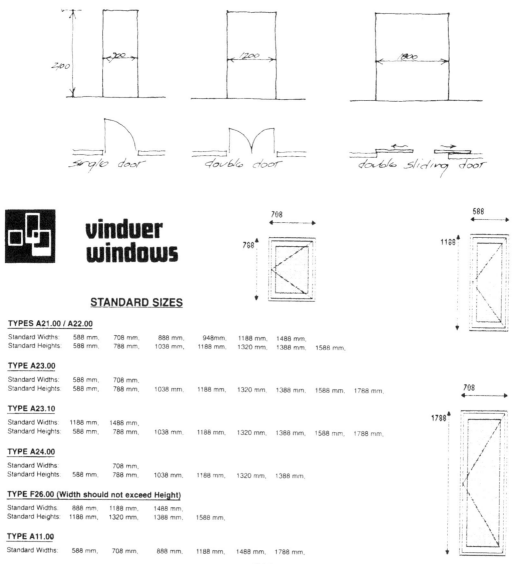

vinduer windows

STANDARD SIZES

TYPES A21.00 / A22.00

Standard Widths:	588 mm,	708 mm,	888 mm,	948mm,	1188 mm,	1488 mm,		
Standard Heights:	588 mm,	788 mm,	1038 mm,	1188 mm,	1320 mm,	1388 mm,	1588 mm,	

TYPE A23.00

Standard Widths:	588 mm,	708 mm,						
Standard Heights:	588 mm,	788 mm,	1038 mm,	1188 mm,	1320 mm,	1388 mm,	1588 mm,	1788 mm,

TYPE A23.10

Standard Widths:	1188 mm,	1488 mm,						
Standard Heights:	588 mm,	788 mm,	1038 mm,	1188 mm,	1320 mm,	1388 mm,	1588 mm,	1788 mm,

TYPE A24.00

Standard Widths:		708 mm,					
Standard Heights:	588 mm,	788 mm,	1038 mm,	1188 mm,	1320 mm,	1388 mm,	

TYPE F26.00 (Width should not exceed Height)

Standard Widths:	888 mm,	1188 mm,	1488 mm,	
Standard Heights:	1188 mm,	1320 mm,	1388 mm,	1588 mm,

TYPE A11.00

Standard Widths:	588 mm,	708 mm,	888 mm,	1188 mm,	1488 mm,	1788 mm,

When the leap from laying out *Space Plan Cards* to making the first *Plan* has been made what will be evolving is a complete and integrated 2-dimensional design. This will be very big however, given that the *Cards* themselves are 1:20 in scale. While the evolving *Plan* will be very clear at this scale it will be too big to comfortably tackle the next few steps in the design process. The answer to this is to scale down the cards to a managable size. This is done with a zoom photocopier.

A zoom photocopier will allow you to reproduce your original *Space Plan Cards* at a desired scale. I:100 is a very managable sizes to work with. To reproduce your *Space Plan Cards* to this scale follow this procedure:

Track down a zoom photocopy machine. These can be found in newsagents, photocopy shops, shopping malls, etc.
Place the *Space Plan Card* you wish to reduce in scale on the glass screen.
Set the zoom reduction control at 70% and make a copy.
Repeat this process for each of the *Cards* that you wish to reduce in scale.
Put aside the 1:20 scale originals.
Take the copies you have just made and copy each one using the same 70% reduction setting.
Now <u>discard</u> the 1st copies. This is critical if you wish to avoid being totally confused! If you want to reuse the paper rather than throwing it away, mark these 1st copies 'no scale' to distinguish them from the 2nd copies.
Set the zoom reduction control to 82%.
Using the 2nd copies make fresh copies of each *Space Plan* at the 82% setting.
Again, discard the 2nd copies, or mark them 'no scale' to avoid confusion.
Mark the 3rd copies '1:50 Scale'.

These drawings are now a managable size. They can be pasted onto light card, trimmed and used to create *Plans* that are not so big. They will also allow 1:50 scale *Space Models* to be created, so it might be an idea to make another set of these 3rd copies - showing the '1:50 Scale' title to avoid confusion!

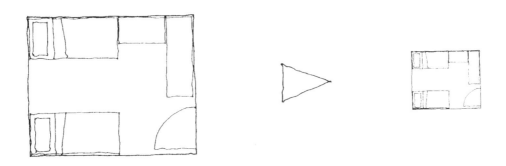

If your 1:20 Space Plan Cards are reduced to 1:50 Scale your Preliminary Plans will be more manageable in size.

To create 1:50 Scale Space Plan Cards from 1:20 Scale Originals:

Copier Setting 1st Copy	Copier Setting 2nd Copy	Copier Setting 3rd Copy
70%	70%	82%
Put aside originals	*Discard 1st copies*	*Discard 2nd copies*
		Mark 3rd copies: "1:50 Scale"

Creating Sketch Plans

The 1:50 *Scale Space Plan Cards* can now be assembled according to the pattern illustrated on *Page 26*. We will assume, for the purpose of this exercise, that no changes have been made to the individual *Space Plans*. (If you have made alterations or additions to your *Space Plans* and pattern this is good - just follow the procedure described here using the new *Space Plans* and pattern)

Each 1:50 *Space Plan* should be cut out of the photocopied page it is on and pasted onto an A3 page in the appropiate position according to the 1:20 pattern previously laid out. (*Refer to Page 26*) The A3 page should then be titled "*Version 1*" and photocopied several times.

To create your first Sketch Plan:

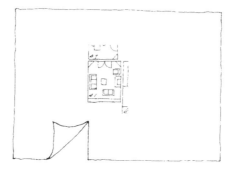

Cut each 1:50 Space Plan out of its photocopied sheet

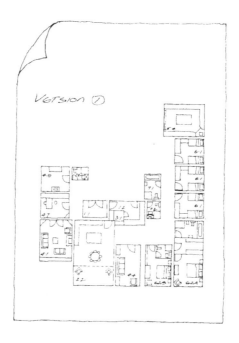

Paste the 1:50 cutout Space Plans onto a blank A3 sheet according to your evolving 'pattern'.
Title the sheet 'Version 1' and make several photocopies of it.

246

Using the photocopied *Sketch Plan Version 1*, identify problem areas and obvious changes, ideally using a red pen for clarity. Notes should also be written as to the nature of the proposed changes/modifications.

The design process now follow this procedure:

1. Checking that each *Space* is connected to everything else - to other *Spaces* and to the world at large beyond the 'walls' - according to the *'Location'* preferences expressed in the *Space Analysis Sheets* in your *Brief.* (Clearly, if you do have not this information available to you - because you have not done your *Analysis*! - you will have no signposting to follow and you will therefore be stuck.)

2. Checking that each *Space* will have the orientation chosen for it (that *Space Analysis* again!) and can enjoy whatever view is available. (from your *Site Analysis & Seed Planning*)

3. Refining the 'circulation' system to ensure free and easy movement within, as well as to and from, the building.

4. Refining individual *Space Plans* to accord with the evolving *Sketch Plan.*

5. Developing a 3D form to 'package' the refined *Sketch Plan*, taking into account your chosen *Materials & Products* and *Construction System.*

At this stage it is critical to understand that the design is going into free fall to some extent. It is the *Brief* that is going to slow your descent and provide a degree of control. If your *Brief* is not up to the job the consequences are clear. (If the parachute analogy is not appealing, think up one that is - bungee jumping ??) The point is that you now need to move beyond total control, that your *sheltermaking genes* now need to be activated, that you need to be flying beyond *rational* into a place where creativity takes over. I've described that as a 'leap' on *Page 26* and the words are probably worth repeating:

"This is how the evolving design moves from being an assemblage of individual *Space Plans* towards being a coherent and integrated *whole*. This movement - more a leap, really - allows every *Space* to adjust itself relative to its neighbours and to settle comfortably into a complete and harmonious whole. This "leap" from *Space Plan Card Layouts* to *Plan* activates the chemistry of the design process bringing the design to life."

Because this process of *'living your architecture'* is entirely personal - the 'life' referred to above is your life - the experience of each and every designer will be different. The best I can do is to describe the factors common to all successful layouts, to ask you to trust in this process, to swallow your fear and to take the leap into freedom.

While the design of individual *Spaces* occupied a large portion of the design exercises so far, the relegation of *Spaces* now to second place behind the 'pattern' should not to taken as an excuse to avoid creating *Space Plans*. Without the essential information on size and orientation these planning exercises will simply not work because there will be to many unknowns in the equation.

If major changes need to be made to your *Sketch Plan Version 1* make them now, before moving to the next phase. Title new *Sketch Plan/s, 'Version 2', 'Version 3'*, etc.

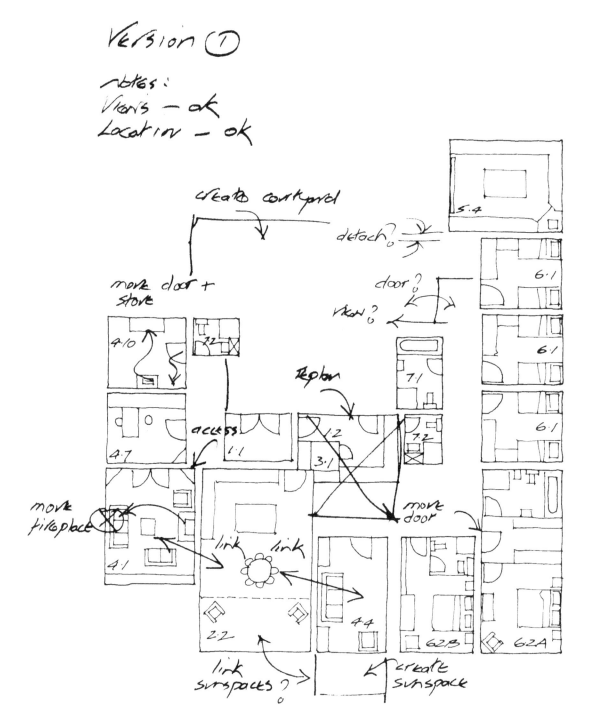

Required changes to Sketch Plan, Version 1:

4.10	*Alter door position and move stove*
2.2	*Create links to 4.1 & 4.4*
4.4	*Add Sunspace - link to Sunspace of 2.2?*
1.2 & 3.1	*Replan*
6.2A	*Move door*
6.1	*Provide door from Courtyard to Bedrooms? Create view to Courtyard?*
5.4	*Detach entirely from main house?*

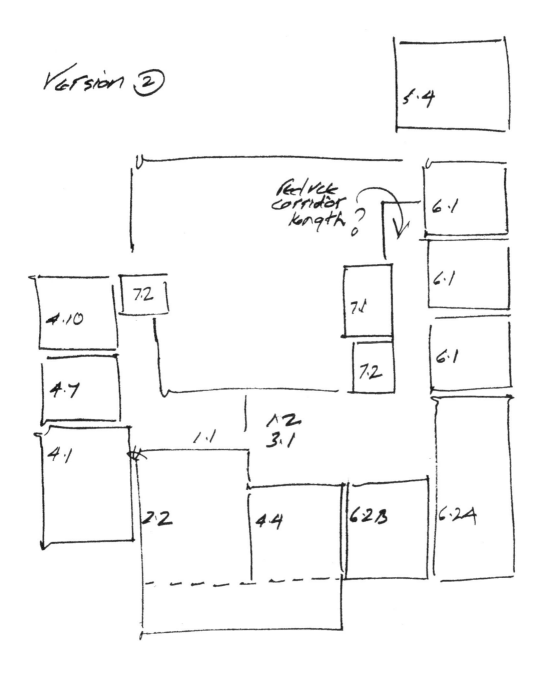

Version ②

5.4

feel vck
corridor
length?

6.1

6.1

6.1

7.2

4.10

7↓

7.2

6.1

4.7

↑2
3.1

1.1

4.1

2.2

4.4

6.2B

6.2A

This 'Version 2' Sketch Plan merely outlines the various Spaces. This allows each Space to be seen clearly in relationship to its intended neighbours and to the world outside the 'walls'. Orientation and access to views is also clear. The length of the corridor serving the Bedrooms, 6.1 is highlighted as something to change. This type of problem identification is essential at this stage of the design process, otherwise problems will be carried forward and will require solutions later on when correction will inevitably be more difficult.

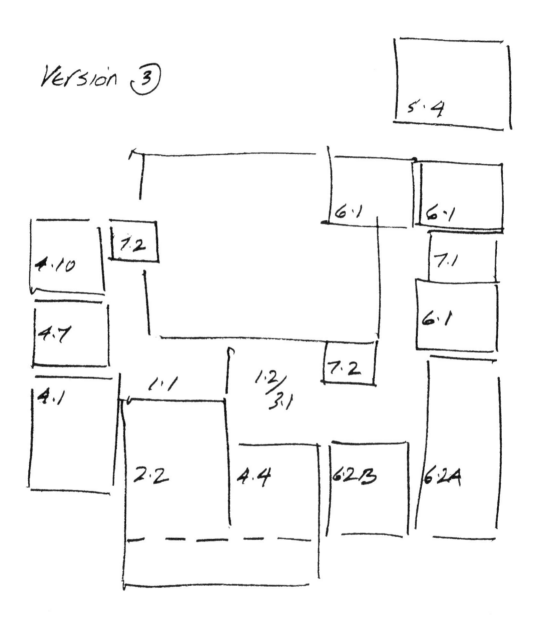

Version ③

5·4
4·10
7.2
4·7
4·1
1·1
1·2/3·1
2·2
4.4
6·2B
6·2A
7·2
6·1
6·1
7.1
6·1

The 'Version 3' Sketch Plan proposes a solution to the Bedroom corridor problem identified in 'Version 2'.
This involves moving the Bathroom, 7.1 across the corridor to free up the potential door access and the view
to the Courtyard. The last Bedroom, 6.1, has been repositioned to shorten the corridor. This means that this
Space and the other Bedroom adjoining it will have to be replanned internally.

250

The flow of movement within and outside the design is the next thing to be observed and refined if necessary. Again, bear in mind that the design has come to life and will have a tendency to grow if not kept under strict control. Also, you must see this process of imagining movement as a reflection of what will be happening in the real world when the design is constructed. If a muddled design is created you will not be able to move about within it with ease. You will have to adapt to the muddle! If the muddle is sorted out now and the flow of movement within the design is shaped to suit your preferred living patterns then, effectively you will be adapting the design to suit your way of life. This is the essence of *'living your architecture'*.

Using the latest *'Version'* of your *Sketch Plan*, make a tracing of it by overlaying the *Plan* with a sheet of greaseproof paper. Loosely draw in the primary circulation routes, starting with the route to and from the external doors. Next draw in the circulation routes within the *Plan* itself. These routes will begin to make 'life' of the design visible. This is akin to mapping the circulatory system of our own bodies. In the case of the evolving home design, rather than our lifes' blood, it is people that will be flowing through the *Plan*. Just as blockages in our bodily circulatory systems can cause severe illness, the circulatory system of your home can result in dangerous blockages. Clearly, the building will not get ill - but perhaps you might, or more realistically, you will not be able to be as active, or to move about as energetically as you might want to, within the finished building.

It is important to fully grasp the power of this idea. It is not one that is hypothesised in the world of Real Estate as we know it! Studies of 'primitive architecture' from around the world however illustrate examples of plans that are laid out to mimic the human form.

If the hypothesis that are homes are reflections of our *Selves* is accepted, then the importance of giving plenty of time to this stage of the design process will be appreciated. An effective *Brief* will now provide you with a strong framework from which to explore this idea of *'living your architecture'*. If you have not done your homework this process will be as confusing as staring at a piece of paper and trying to understand the nature of life itself.

The best that you can ever hope for in regards to understanding the nature of life is to *'know yourself'*. If the hypothesis that are homes are reflections of our *Selves* is accepted, it follows that *'self knowledge'* can result from the process of designing your own home. It is the life within us that guides us in this quest. This is an intuitive process, removed from the often callous processes suggested by the brain. So, one has to listen to one's inner voice here for guidance. All I can do is to suggest ways of you tuning in to that voice and of allowing it to infuse your evolving design with the spirit of your life.

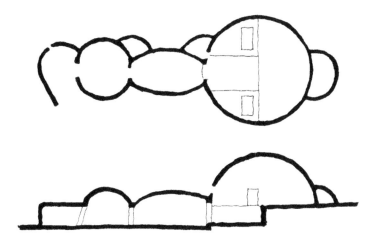

Plans in so-called 'primitive architecture' often mimic the human form:
Plan & Cross Section of Eskimo Igloo

251

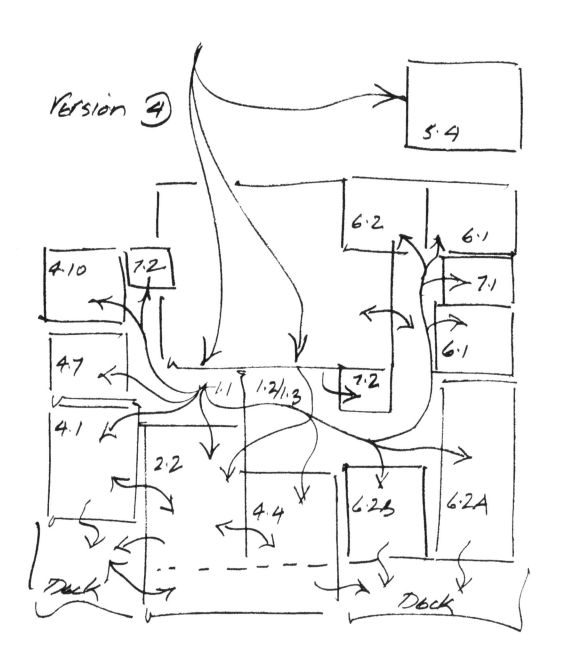

The 'flow' through the plan now begins to become clear. The Front Door area, 1.1, is the 'hub' of the action. The crossing of the route from the Back Door/Utility/Pantry Spaces, 1.2/1.3, by the path from Space 1.1 to the Bedrooms will need to be closely examined however. With the access to the 'outside' sketched in, the position of the Decks clarifies as does the possibility of providing a door to the Bedrooms, direct from the Courtyard.

Because the design has effectively come to life, a watchful eye must be kept on its tendancy to grow. A simple way to check on the current size of your plan is to outline it, break it into managable 'boxes' and calculate the areas of these. Here the rough total comes to 294.25m². This compares to the earlier estimate on *Page 16* giving a 'target' of 270m².

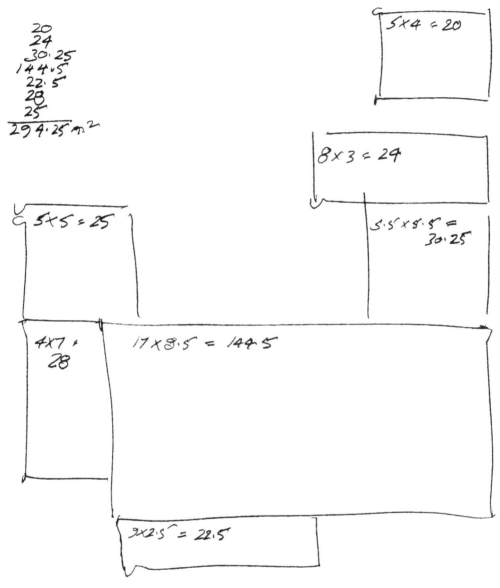

When it comes time to construct your building, the floor area that has to be enclosed will be the largest determining factor in calculating *Costs*. Obviously, the choice of materials and construction methods will have their profound effect on these calculations as will the cost of Labour. However if a cost per square foot or per square meter is used as a yardstick at this stage you will have a clear idea of whether your project is financially viable or not.

So, divide the estimated floor area into your Budget. This will yield up a cost per *sqm* or per *sqft*. By relating these figures to construction costs in your area the truth about the viability of your project will be told. If the news is bad - scale back now!

When the exercises described in *Pages 31-38* have been carried out, a new *Version* of the *Plan* can be drawn incorporating the changes, modifications, alterations and inspirations that will inevitably have accumulated within the design. The frustrations associated with this drudgery - and it is drudgery! - should not obscure the fact that this work is essential to the creation of a *workable* building. If the plan on paper cannot be made to work for the task/s set out in your *Brief* then you will be hostage to these inbuilt problems when you try to live within your design.

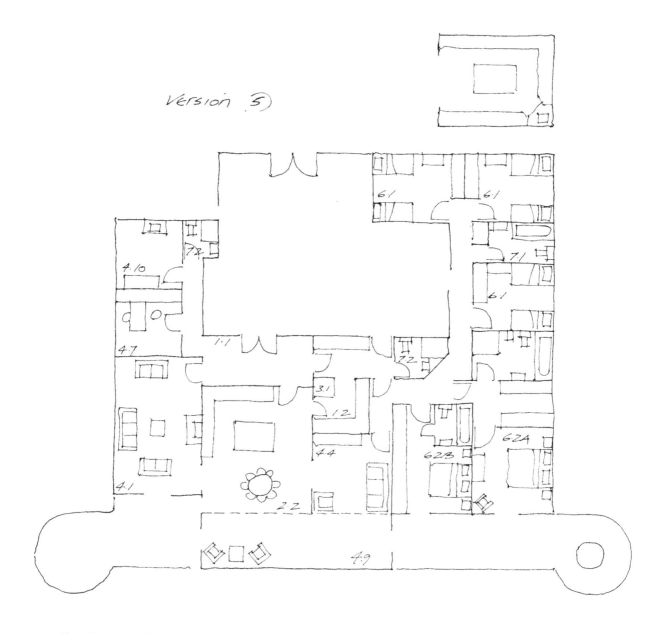

This 'Version 5' Sketch Plan is drawn to incorporate the modifications and changes noted previously. It is drawn as a 'composite' - that is, rather than being made up of Spaces 'stuck' together, it is drawn as a complete whole. This is done by tracing from Space Plan Cards and by creating new Cards that fit the shape of the evolving Plan. The difficult area of the Back Door/Utility Room 1.2 & Pantry 3.1, has here been replanned to fit the space available for it.

It is worth bearing in mind that human beings are usually willing to conform to the 'shape' a building sets out for them. By 'living architecture' one consciously shapes the building to conform to the 'shape' of your life - a complete reversal of the norm. If your evolving design cannot, at this stage, host your life as you wish to live it, or imagine living it, then you must correct this _now_. Let the challenges of this process be 'real', in other words, look at the evolving *Plan* as if it is a map of your life.

Because the future is unknown, all we can do is to move towards it. Creating a building that anticipates this unknown future is tricky! What will happen however is that the design will begin to reveal a future that you will recognise, confirming that you are moving in the right direction. When this happens you will know that the project is a real and vital part of your life.

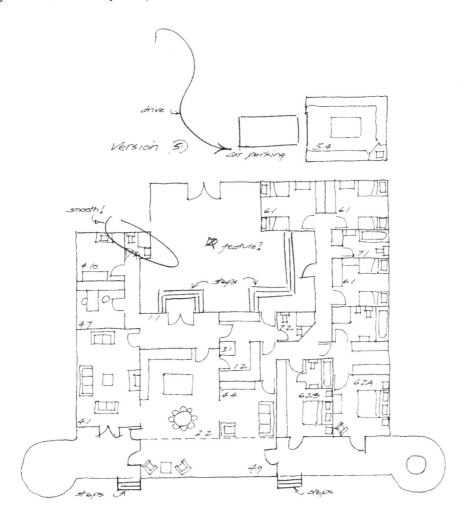

This Version 5 Plan essentially meets the requirements of the Brief. With the exception of the Shower Room, 7.2, alongside the Meditation Room, 4.10, the plan form is reasonably 'smooth' - an important consideration when it comes to Costs! Other notes have been made on the Plan which can be made part of new Versions. Inevitably, other refinements will need to be applied to individual Spaces as the dimension of height is added to the design equation. The question of the overall 'form' of the building will also have a bearing on individual Spaces and possibly even on the Plan itself.

Developing The Layout In 3 Dimensions

When *Seed Plans* and *Preliminary Layouts* have been made it will be readily visible that the project needs to develop a third dimension to make the design whole. The addition of this dimension of height will have the effect of not only giving your building and the spaces within it height, but it will also raise questions relating to *Materials*, *Structure* and *Construction*. These matters must be properly addressed in order that the project can be realised in the real world - that is, if you wish to make the building and to live in it you will have to deal with these matters at this point.

In addition to giving a dimension of height to your design you will also now have to consider cost and the construction methodology likely to be used to create your building. These are elements of the 'juggling' referred to earlier.

It should be stressed that the process of design from here forward will not be linear but rather will be broad and somewhat repetitive in some respects. This will not only allow for various options to be considered but will also have the effect of refining the design, reducing it to its essential parts. This 'loose' approach gives the designer a great deal of latitude. When the design has reached the point of satisfaction it can then be 'shrunk to fit'.

In regards to *Materials*, the selection of these will probably have already been made in general terms. That is, you should know from your *Brief* what your floors, walls and roof are likely to be made of. Also your choice of *Construction System* will have been given consideration. These choices will now have a bearing on the 3-dimensional form that your building will take, particularly if you wish to construct a two-tier building.

For example, you wish to create a two-tier design and you wish to use concrete block cavity walling and concrete block internal walls throughout. This decision will effectively demand that the position of your upstairs walls coincide with the position of your downstairs walls. This means that upstairs rooms and downstairs rooms must be of similar size.

If you are willing to have timber stud partitions on the upper floor you will gain a certain degree of flexibility as these do not require a wall to be constructed beneath them for support. The external walls on the upper floor however must conform to the position of the supporting walls below them.

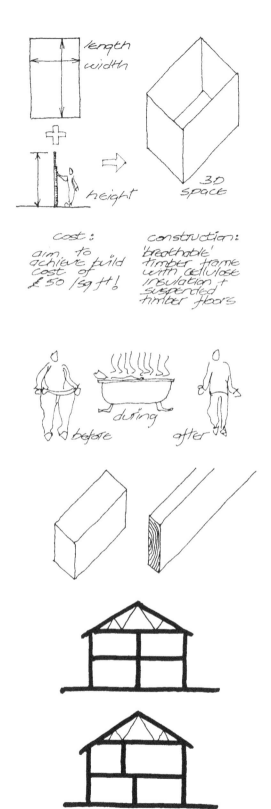

In contrast to block construction, with timber framing, a far greater degree of freedom can be had as to where walls are positioned on ground and on upper floors. This applies both to external walls as well as to internal partitions.

Where timber frames are to be clad externally in brick or block, and where such cladding is to be carried through to an upper floor, then, of course, a continuous supporting wall will be required under it.

It is possible to support brick or blockwork on a lintol or beam thereby eliminating a ground floor supporting wall but such construction will turn out to be costly and difficult to achieve.

In regards to floors - if you wish to have large *spaces* on the ground floor, these will have to be spanned over with joists to provide a floor to the rooms above. By reference to the Floor Joist Span Tables in the *Timberfile* it will be seen that to clear span a distance of 4 meters would require that 44x200 Strength Class B joists be installed at 400mm centres.

Roofs are generally straightforward as their triangulated form gives them considerable strength and quite large spans can be readily achieved. Alternatively, the roof can be broken into smaller components and a device such as a valley gutter used to form the joints between smaller roofs.

Generally, if timber framing is used with external cladding attached to this, any variety of shapes can be made to suit your design aims. If brick or blockwork is to be used, confining these materials to the ground floor will provide one with sufficient flexibility to satisfy most purposes.

If models are used extensively at this stage of the design process it will be possible to pinpoint structural difficulties. These can often be solved by modifying the model and the change can then be incorporated onto the drawings. A second reading of the *Structure* and *Construction* chapters in *Volume 1* is advised.

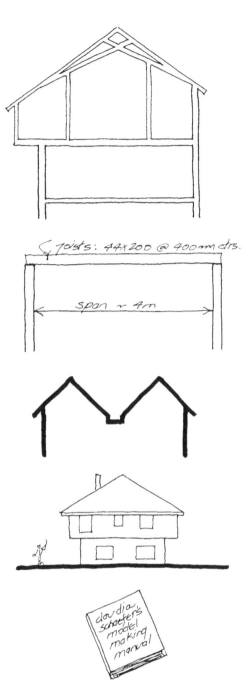

Making Models

Once the general *Plan Form* has been decided, 1:50 plans and cross sections should be created for all the *Spaces* in your design. The methodology for this is described in *Part V - Space Mock-Ups, (Volume 1; Pages 83 - 113)*.

Following this, 1:50 scale models for each *Space* must be made. These are constructed using 1mm white card.

To make a 1:50 *Space Model* you follow the procedure set out in *Part IV - Drawings & Models, (Volume 1; Pages 61 - 81)*. While this procedure describes how to make a *model* of a piece of *furniture*, making a 1:50 *Space Model* is exactly the same.

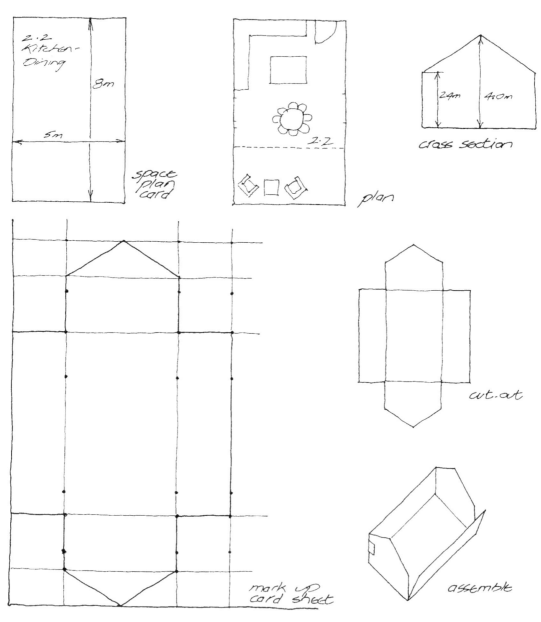

One variation that you might like to introduce to the procedure is to draw a plan of the *Space* within the *Space model*. This can be done by pasting a copy of the plan to the floor of the model before it is closed up.

The *Space Models* can be left open on top for convenience.

If you are having more than one level you should make a *Space Model* of the area the stairs will occupy. This should be sufficiently high to 'serve' all levels.

Circulation Space can be formed by positioning the *Spaces* surrounding the *Circulation Space* correctly. If a base sheet of coloured card is used to set out the *Space Models* the size and shape of the *Circulation Space* will be clearly seen.

Remember that this is a creative exercise and that you do not have to get everything perfect first time. Allow yourself the possibility of getting things wrong, of making a mess, of correcting your errors in your own time.

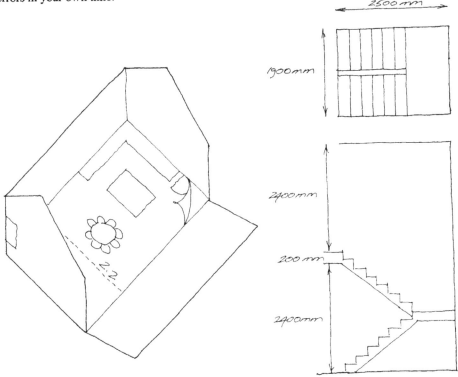

What you are going to do next is to place these *Space Models* - boxes! - in relationship to each other so as to accord with your *Layout Plan*. Over this assembly of boxes you are going to place a roof or roofs. You are also going to refine the shape of the assembly of boxes to make it simpler, more pleasing or whatever your creative impulses lead you to do to it. Then you will adjust any of the *Spaces* that have been affected by your work, make another 1:50 *model* or perhaps a bigger one. In this way the overall shape of your building will be 'smoothed' out around the *Spaces* within it. The matter of windows and doors will then be dealt with and, finally, drawings will be made to represent your final design.

Refining The 3D Shape Of Your Building

At this point it is essential to accept that what you are about is a 3-dimensional exercise - you are in fact creating a sculpture that you will live in. The drawings that you will make of this sculpture are merely informative, not creative. If this difference is not understood you will produce a design biased by the limitations of drawing technique.

To properly involve yourself in the creation of this sculpture being able to work at a 1:20 scale is most useful. At this scale you will be creating a *model* that is 20 times smaller than the finished building will be. At a scale of 1:50 your model will be 50 times smaller than the real thing - this is very small indeed and the only reason such a small model should be made at this stage of the design process is because your workspace is severely restricted in size.

The other items that need consideration at this point are - the *style* of windows and doors along with the general external *style* you wish to create. All this information will be on your *Files*. It should also be remembered that dealing with a design that has all its accommodation on a single level will be a far easier exercise than creating any form of two-tiered building.

A simple model of the evolving design

Begin the modelling exercise by pasting a copy of your *Layout Plan* onto a sheet of card then laying the *Space Boxes* in their rightful places onto this. Simple! Very quickly the 3-dimensional quality of the building will be revealed as will any inconsistencies, awkwardnesses, displeasing proportions, etc.

If you are working at 1:50 scale the attractions of 1:20 scale modelling will also be revealed - the smaller scale may simply be too small for easy working. As with many aspects of the design process you must find your own way now, choosing whichever path suits you best.

It is now critical to begin seeing your design as a 3-dimensional object that contains *Spaces* that you will inhabit. It is these *Spaces* that are now being revealed to you in miniature. Remember that 2-dimensional drawings - plans, cross sections and elevations - never show 3-dimensional space. While the seasoned reader of drawings can *imagine* the spaces illustrated by such drawings, they cannot ever actually *see* the space in the same way as is revealed by the model. Furthermore, even the most brilliant architect can never simultaneously see the congregation of spaces that even the simplest house contains. What all this means is that by following these directions you are well ahead of the game and that the modelling exercise now drives the design process. When this work is complete a set of 2-dimensional drawings will then be made to record the 3-dimensional information contained in the model.

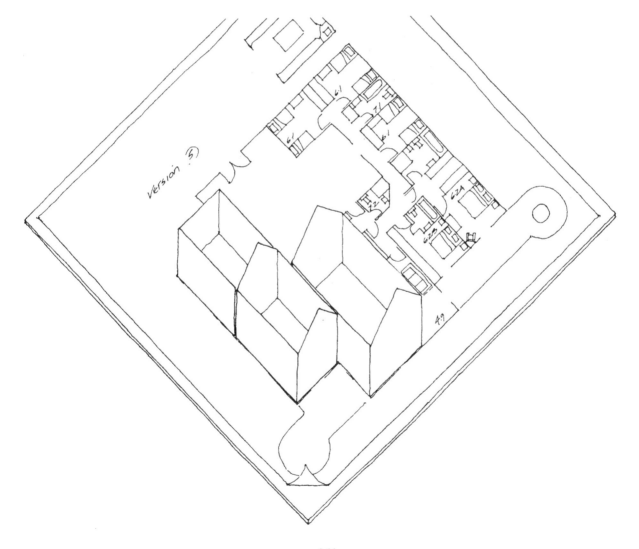

261

Readers may be chuckling at this point that I have the temerity to illustrate point about the limitations of drawings by using drawings! The accompanying illustrations are axonometric drawings that indeed do show '*space*' to some extent.They also show proportions correctly. Perspective drawings, 'walk-through' computer programmes and such methods also reveal *space* by means of drawings. Such devices however come nowhere near illustrating space in the same way as a model will, nor will they allow for the creative manupilation of the emerging 'sculpture'. These methods are best reserved for the illustration of your finished design.

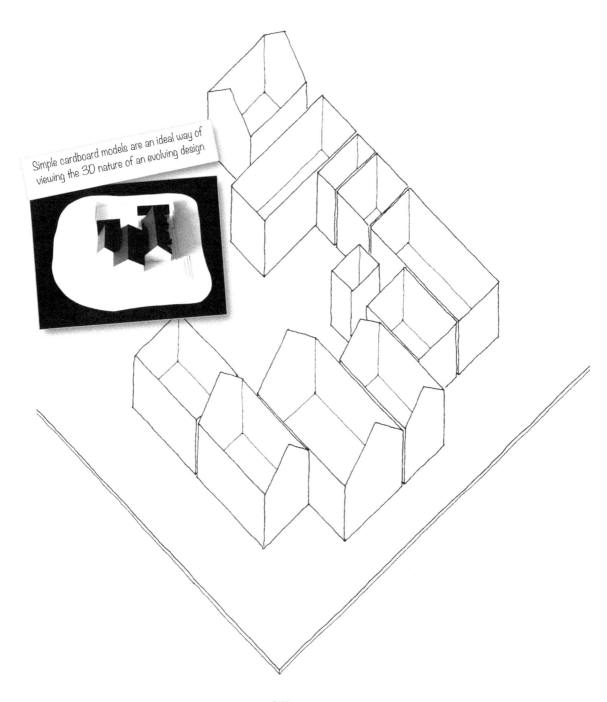

Simple cardboard models are an ideal way of viewing the 3D nature of an evolving design

When the laying out of the *Space Boxes* on the *Layout Plan* has been completed the matter of *Roofs* then has to be addressed. Reread *Part VII - Structure* (*Volume 1, Pages 153-177*). As will be gleaned from this it is the principle of *triangulation* that is most critical in making stable and workable roof structures.

Overall, it is the combination of structural and material issues that directs the roof design process. The place to start therefore is with an outline of the materials intended for use and a list of the requirements of the space design that affect the internal shape of the roof. This information should be contained in your *Brief.*

The range of roofing materials is relatively small: *slates; shingles; tiles; thatch; metal sheeting ...* In practice, local traditions and, of course, cost, will narrow this list to a choice of one or two.

Because roof design is a delicate balance of varied elements - a balance that it is critical to achieve in order to create a practical and realisable building - this phase of the design process will inevitably alter the shape and form of your evolving '*sculpture*'.

Slates, tiles and shingles have similar requirements in regards to application - they are nailed to roofing battens which are laid over roofing felt. The roofing felt acts as a second line of defence in the event that rain is blown up under the overlapping slates. If this happens the water is caught by the roofing felt and runs down to the roof's edge due to the angle of the roof and the intentional '*sagging*' of the roofing felt between the roof rafters. This roof angle is critical in making a watertight roof and will vary according to location and expected exposure. For example, in locations where snowfalls, rain and high winds are frequent a steep roof angle is recommended. Where milder conditions prevail a shallower angle will suffice.

Roof design is affected by the choice of insulation material mainly due to the need to properly ventilate the insulation. Because a roof acts as an interface between the warm interior of a building and the oftentimes extremely cold night sky, condensation can develop within the

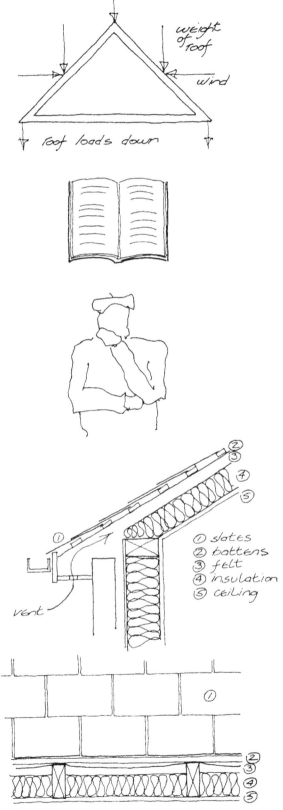

① slates
② battens
③ felt
④ insulation
⑤ ceiling

263

insulation which can render the insulating material useless. This in turn can lead to the threat of decay in the roof timbers between which the insulation is normally placed. How roof insulation is ventilated depends on the nature of the insulating material itself - whether it is synthetic or natural.

Synthetic insulation- fibreglass, rockwool, etc. - must be located within a roof construction so that a free flow of air can pass over it carrying away any moist air. With natural *'breathable'* insulation, such as cellulose fibre, any moisture build up within the insulation will evaporate outwards as long as breathable materials are used above the insulation. In practical terms these will consist of a breathable sheathing material and a breathable felt.

Because roof insulation is normally placed between the roof rafters, the breathable sheathing and felt will sit directly on top of the rafters. To create the *'sagging'* in the felt to allow any rain that makes its way under the slates to run down to the eaves, *'counterbattens'* are fixed above the breathable layers in the same line as the rafters and the normal slating battens are then fixed atop these.

Where a roofing material such as thatch is being used, a steep roof pitch will be required and no insulation at all will be necessary.

Any form of metal roofing can generally be laid to shallow roof pitches. If single skin decking is being used the ventilation of any 'synthetic' insulation needs careful detailing. Twin skin decking incorporating rigid insulation offers a more straightforward approach.

If a grass roof is to be employed, an efficient drainage layer atop some form of rubber membrane will be needed below the sod. The roof pitch can be low but to incorporate breathability into such a construction is difficult.

Apart from the technicalities of the roof construction, the need for a roof to meet design criteria in your *Brief* will be a major driving force in creating workable roofs. Such demands will probably consist of creating attic rooms, pitched ceilings, dormer windows, rooflights and so on.

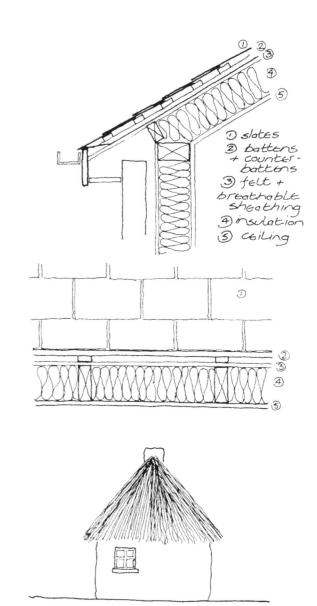

① slates
② battens + counter-battens
③ felt + breathable sheathing
④ insulation
⑤ ceiling

Generally, *Building Regulations* control issues such as clear ceiling heights in rooms - the major issue one has to deal with when designing an attic room or 'room-in-the-roof'. Refer to: *Part V - Space Mock-Ups (Volume 1, Pages 83-113)*.

To create a stable roof structure it is necessary to 'tie' the roof rafters together in some way to stop them spreading under the weight of themselves and of the roofing material that they are supporting. The simplest way to do this is to place a 'collar tie' between the lower ends of the rafters thereby creating a strong triangulated structure. Collar ties can also be located mid-way up the rafters. Premade roof trusses can also be employed though no usable attic space will result. Scissors trusses are also a very effective way of tying rafters together while at the same time creating pitched ceilings. 'Normal' roofs, using rafters and purlins can, of course, be created, though the resulting 'attics' generally do not offer any usable space.

Where metal decking is being used, the inherent structural ability of the sheeting profile allows for a minimal supporting roof structure. A combination of trusses and purlins can therefore be employed.

Any element that breaks through the waterproof 'skin' of a roof thereby creates a multiplicity of joints that in themselves need to be waterproofed. This is particularly true of dormer windows. As a result, the cost of such elements becomes excessive. Premade rooflights are easier to incorporate into a roof as they are supplied with all the necessary 'flashings' to make waterproof joints. Where rooflights are being incorporated into a roof it is a good idea to insert them at eye-level.

Where the plane of a roof changes direction a waterproof joint must be created. These are normally called 'valleys'. Valleys add to the cost of a roof but offer an excellent device where design flexibility is essential.

The physical creation of model roofs is straightforward. This is particularly true where a *space box* has been made with gables - measure the length of the gables and the length of

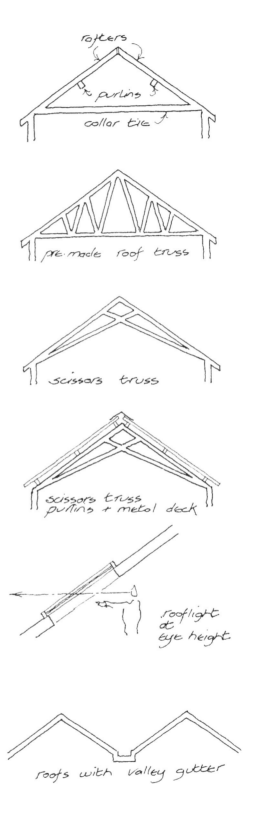

the *box* itself. Mark up a piece a piece of card
with the overall dimensions and the position of
the ridge. Lightly score along the line of the
ridge and fold. Using sellotape, fix the roof to
the model.

In reality, model roofs can be made 'by eye'
and the pitches set to satisfy visual criteria.
The actual angle can then be ascertained in
reverse by measuring the length of the pitch
and relating that mathematically to the width
of the *space box* it covers.

If this is too inexact for you, try this:
For a roof pitch of 45°, length of pitch =
X÷0.707 where 'X' is half the width of the
roof/*space box* being covered.

For a roof pitch of 30°, length of pitch =
X÷0.866 where 'X' is half the width of the
roof/*space box* being covered.

'Hipped' roofs are a little trickier to create.
Start off as if a gable roof was being made.
When the roof card has been cut out and
scored measure off the length of the hips
which will be the same dimension as the length
of the pitch. Cut out the hips, fold along the
ridge and tape the roof together. The dimensions of the missing triangular 'pieces' of the
roof can be gleaned from what has already
been made. The bottom of the triangle will be
the same width as the roof and its height will
be the same as the pitch. Refer to the diagram
to avoid confusion!

These are modelling, not mental, exercises. If
you are put off building a model because, as
you read this, you think this is all 'too much'
for you, then you are missing out on a bundle
of fun! If you stick at this, very soon you will
be hauling your friends and family in to see
your model, delighting in the cleverness of
your creation.

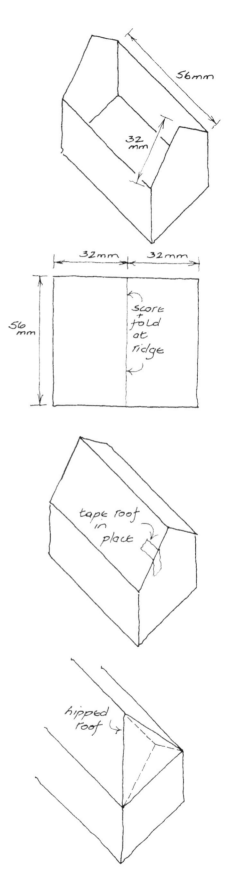

In the case of the working example, gable roofs/pitched ceilings are intended above several spaces, as can be seen in the illustration. Further, the *Planning File* indicates, in notes from the *Development Plan*, that *"new buildings should be compatible with existing forms and materials - gables; steep roof pitches, 35°+; smooth plastered walls."* These pointers give us our direction as we tackle into our 'sculpture'. The chosen 'theme', to suit the evolving design and the *Planners'* intentions, is the 'farm-yard cluster'. What this means is that the design will now strive to evoke the forms of a traditional grouping of farm buildings.

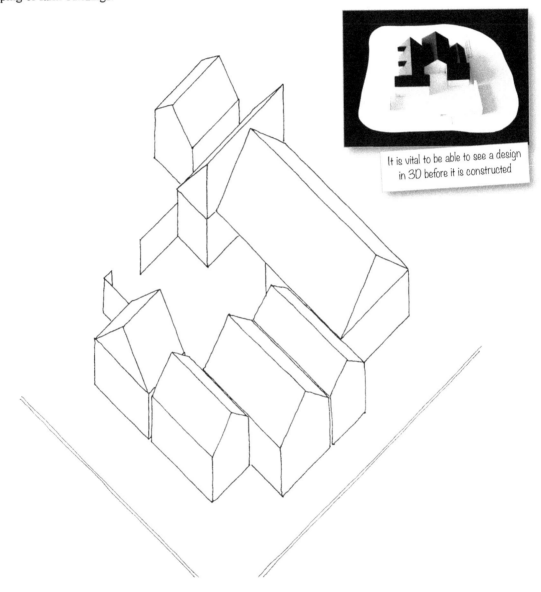

It is vital to be able to see a design in 3D before it is constructed

The pitched roofs are cut out, folded and taped into place. A tentative pitched roof is made and placed over the Study, 4.7, and the Meditation Room, 4.10. Similarly, the Bedroom 'wing' is closed in with a single roof as far as the paired bedrooms on the north side of the house - which have a monopitched roof made for them. The Courtyard wall is made and set in place. Finally, after lots of measuring and cutting, the 3-dimensional form of the building begins to clarify.

The evolving roofscape reveals several new possibilities. The attic space formed above the *Study, 4.7* and the *Meditation Room, 4.10*, when sketched out to scale, looks like it will provide sufficient space for a *Loft*. Even though the available head height does not meet the '*Regulations*' the space can be created and used nonetheless - it just cannot be considered to be part of the house proper in the '*paper-work*'.

To gain access to the *Loft* a stairs has to be installed and the plan has to be altered. Curiously, this solves the problem of the *Shower Room, 7.2,* 'sticking out'! The plan alterations are sketched in and a new *Space Box* is made, complete with new roof. The junction between the *Living Room* roof and the new roof is refined by fusing them together, forming valleys. A rooflight is cut out of the *Loft* roof to allow sunlight in and a view out.

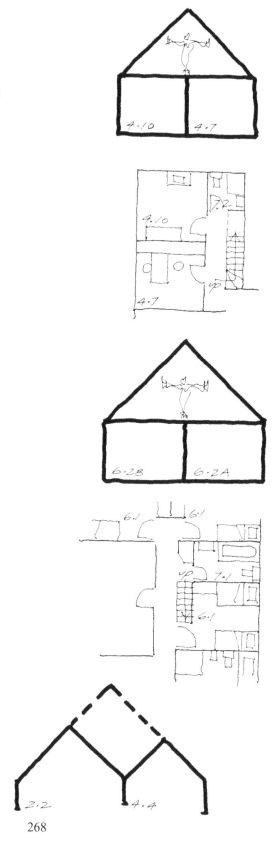

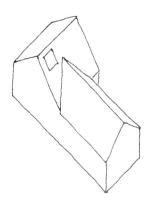

The proposed roof over the *Bedroom* 'wing' is also sketched to scale. Here again the possibility of usable *Loft* space is revealed - though, as before, this does not meet the regulatory requirments. The question of an access stairs is addressed by altering the plan.

Finally, the adjoining pitched roofs over the *Kitchen/Dining Area, 2.2,* and the *Children's Sitting Room, 4.4,* are fused to form a single roof to emphasise the central importance of these spaces.

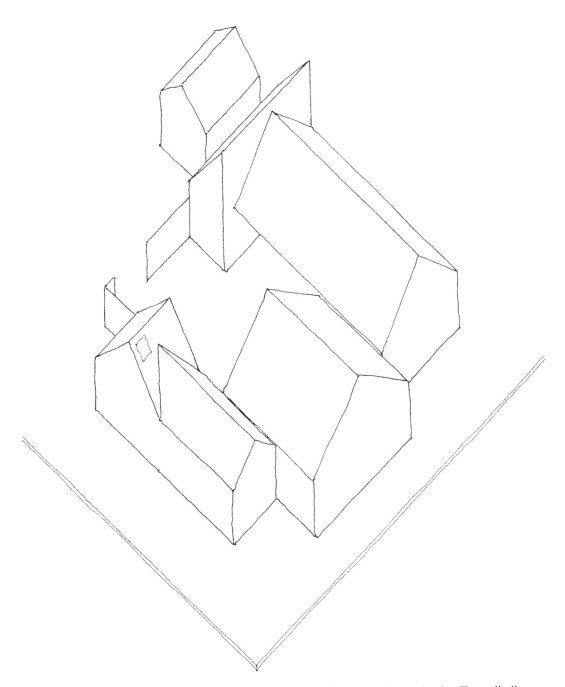

When the model reaches this level of completion it is time for drawings to be made of it. This will allow for windows and doors to be inserted and for any necessary adjustments to be carried out to individual Spaces.

Remember, these drawings will reflect the reality of the model and will serve as a means of recording the 3-dimensional information contained within it. As such the drawings are a mere 'record' of the (invisible) space contained by the floors, walls and roof of the model. The built reality of the design will have more in common with the model than it will ever have with the drawings.

269

Drawings

If any one topic strikes fear into the heart of the personal architect, it is drawing. Properly speaking this potential trauma should now have been put behind you. Should this not be the case, it is now time to confront grim reality. Should it be any comfort - professional architects hate drawing!

Drawings representing buildings fall into three categories - Plans, Cross Sections and Elevations. Of these, Cross Sections are the most mysterious and also the most useful. This is because they allow you to see within the building you are creating. Cross Sections are really 'Sideways Plans'. What this means is that where a Plan is a drawing looking down on the walls, a Cross Section is a drawing looking sideways at these walls. Where Plans are horizontal slices through a building, Cross Sections are vertical slices through a building.

Plans and Cross Sections allow one to view the inside of a building while Elevations represent the external views. These are normally four in number and are titled North, South, East & West Elevations.

When your model reaches a level of completion that you are satisfied with you must then make drawings of it in order to estimate the cost of constructing it, to examine the way the various parts of the building will go together and to show other people what your building will be like.

If one bears in mind that drawings are a very poor way of representing on paper the building you are making, you will be saved an immense amount of frustration. If you bear in mind that drawings are a necessary evil you can then value what drawings will allow you to do - that is, they will allow for an estimate of cost to be made; they will allow others to see what you intend constructing and they will allow for an orderly examination of the construction process to be carried out. All these aspects of building design are an essential precursor to the construction and planning phase of the project.

Because you have a *model* to work from, the making of drawings will be reasonably straightforward. A scale of 1:50 will be quite sufficient to use. This will allow A3 sheets to be used for the original drawings - and this size can easily be photocopied. This is essential as multiple copies of Plans, Cross Sections & Elevations will be needed for the various tasks at hand.

In addition to the basic equipment - pencils, erasers, scale ruler and so on - you will need drafting tape and

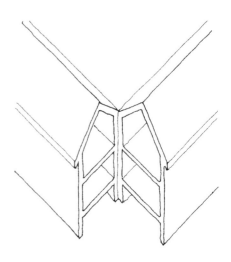

Cross Sections are the most mysterious type of drawings ... and also the most useful. What they really are is 'sideways plans'.

In terms of building design, drawings are a necessary evil. Because of what they reveal and because of the way in which they communicate, they are an indespensible tool however. Just remember - space cannot be seen, only the surfaces of walls, floors and ceilings that enclose it. Many useful tasks, such as costing, detailing and construction are carried out using drawings.

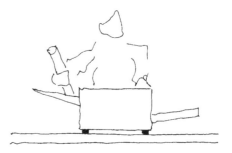

If A3 size paper is used to prepare drawings the originals can then be photocopied. It is always best to roll drawings rather than folding them.

greaseproof paper. The drafting tape - commonly referred to as masking tape - should ideally be in a dispenser while the greaseproof paper can be bought in a roll from the supermarket. You are looking for a basic greaseproof paper, not a parchment type or anything fancy. You may have to shop around a little to find a brand you like and that will 'take pencil'. What this means is that you should be able to draw onto the greaseproof paper easily using a pencil - say a HB.

Some form of drawing board would be an advantage at this point. This can be a piece of MDF 600 x 750 mm with a surface that will allow tape to be affixed and released without damage - wood veneer or melamine. The board can be propped on a table when in use and then stored quite easily.

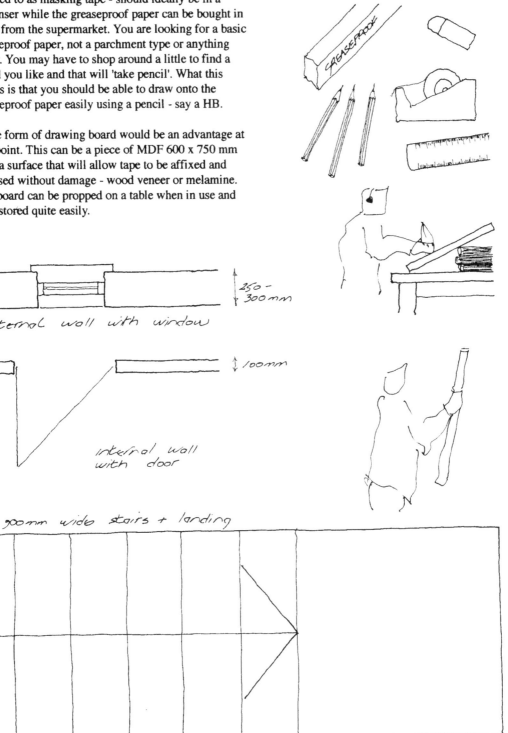

External wall with window

250 - 300 mm

100mm

internal wall with door

900mm wide stairs + landing

Drawing A Plan

The critical aspects of Plans that must be gotten right from the beginning of the drawing phase of the design exercise, are - showing correct wall thicknesses; inserting door and window openings and properly sizing stairs.

Briefly:

External walls should appear from 250-300mm thick.
Internal walls should appear as 100mm thick.
Stairs need to be a minimum of 900mm wide, including landings.

It is best to begin your Plan at one corner of the building, adding in spaces as you enlarge the drawing to include all the accommodation. Refer to *Part VI - Surveying, (Volume 1; Pages 118 -123)*, for guidance.

You may wish to use graph paper under your tracing sheet to act as a guide for the drawing of lines. But do not try to draw lines with a ruler - use freehand lines, these will give a fluency to what you are doing, a looseness that is in keeping with the stage of the project that you are at.

If problems arise with the Plan you must try to resolve these. Do this by overlaying a small piece of tracing/greaseproof on the section of the Plan you are working on. Use this small sheet - or several small sheets - to solve the problem, then draw in your 'solution' on the Plan sheet.

It does not matter that you are changing from what is represented in the model - this is all a refinement process and things will continue to change right up to the building stage of the project.

When the Plan is complete it is a good idea to title each space, to date the drawing and title the drawing also. Also, make several copies of the 'original' - and then keep this original safe. It is better to roll drawings rather than folding them.

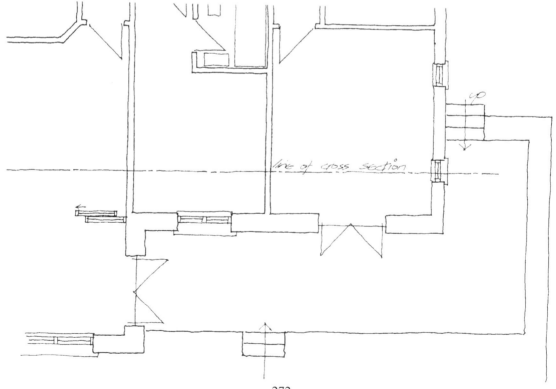

Drawing Cross Sections

The drawing of Cross Sections will follow on from the Plans. How many Sections you will need to draw will depend on how complex your building is. Basically the Sections will allow you to set floor and ceiling heights. Following on from this the junctions between floors, walls, ceilings and roofs can be examined in detail.

Normally, two Sections are drawn for a building the size of a house. The position of these can be decided by reference to the model and these can then be marked onto the Plan.

The first thing that needs to be decided is the level of the ground floor. With a suspended timber floor a minimum of 300mm must be left between the likely 'finished ground level' and Ground 'Finished Floor Level'.

A minimum floor to ceiling height of 2400mm must be left from Ground FFL to the underside of the ceiling above, though this should be considered as an absolute minimum for Living Spaces.

Where there is a habitable space above the ceiling a floor thickness of minimum 175-200mm needs to be indicated. This thickness is controlled by the distance the floor joists will need to span.

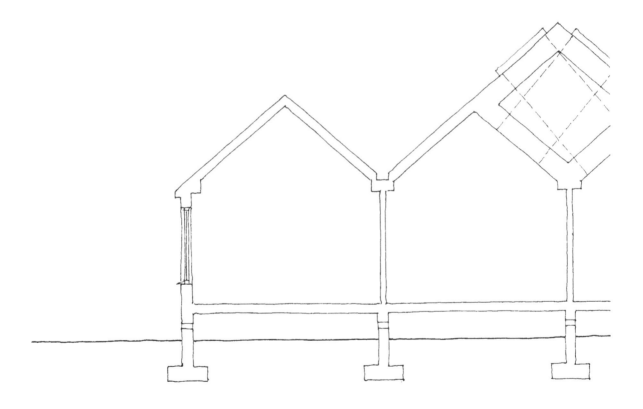

Roofs can either be open to their undersides, have flat ceilings or be a combination of both. Again the distance needed to be spanned is critical here.

Where an attic room is planned a minimum floor to ceiling height of 2400mm over at least half the room is required by the *Building Regulations*. The remaining portions of the ceiling can drop to 1500mm.

Other information appearing on Cross Sections will be wall thickness, cill and head heights of windows and heights of doors. Reference to your own eye line and of those whom the building will shelter should be considered now as well as your overall height, reach etc.

Where window seats might be considered desirable, these should be positioned and confirmed now. A final decision on ceiling heights, particularly over *Living Spaces* is also crucial at this stage.

Where a design is being developed for a particular site, some reference needs to be made to the prevailing site conditions. This is particularly true where a steep slope might need to be accommodated or incorporated into the design. Refer to *Part VI - Surveying, Page 20, (Volume 1; Page 134)*, for guidance.

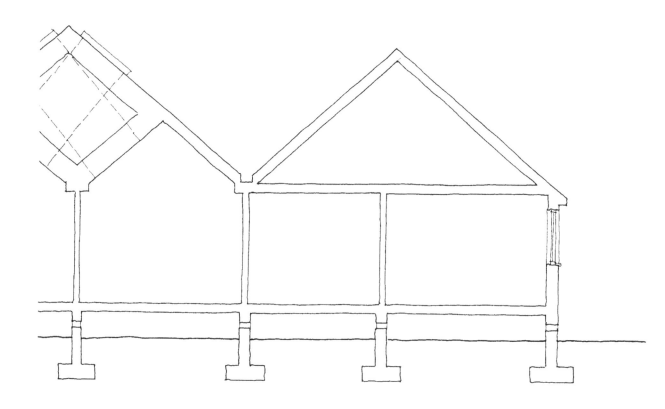

Drawing Elevations

In comparison to drawing Cross Sections, Elevations are quite straightforward. Basically four Elevations will be needed, one for each side of the building - assuming that your building has flat, regular sides of course! This may not be so, in which case you will realise how 'drawings' have conspired so much to make 'flat' buildings.

Essentially, Elevations consist of showing Door & Window heights and positions within the external walls; indicating the overall height of the building; showing the profile of the roof and giving an indication of the texture and finish of the outside walls. Elevations also allow for internal floor heights, particularly that of the Ground Floor to be viewed in relationship to Ground Level.

Elevations should be titles according to their relationship to the Four Cardinal points - that is, North, South, East & West.

In a building with a non-regular *plan form*, some parts of the Elevations will not be visible because they will be 'hidden'. Such portions of the building can be sketched out individually, or made part of Cross Sections.

west elevation

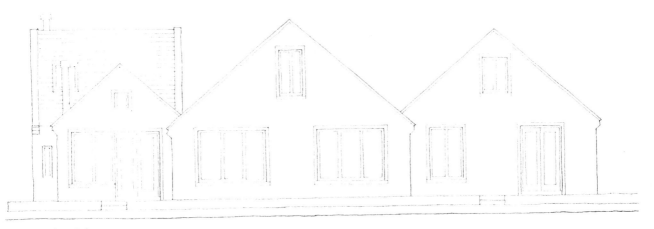

south elevation

Site Layouts

Particularly where a particular site is being utilised a Site Layout drawing is essential documentation for the next stage of the design process - that is, *Costing*.

Site Layouts should be drawn onto an outline of the actual site. This can be an enlarged OS Map containing a photocopied reduction of the ground floor Plan - both to the same scale. 1:500 is a useful scale to use for this.

Site Layouts should contain information on the *Drainage System*; Incoming *Electrical & Water Services*; Rainwater Disposal On-Site; Entrance/Exit to Roadway; Driveways/Paths; Gardens; Garden Buildings and any other items necessary to the full and proper functioning of the building and land.

This is a very easy drawing to neglect to make - with potentially disastrous consequences.

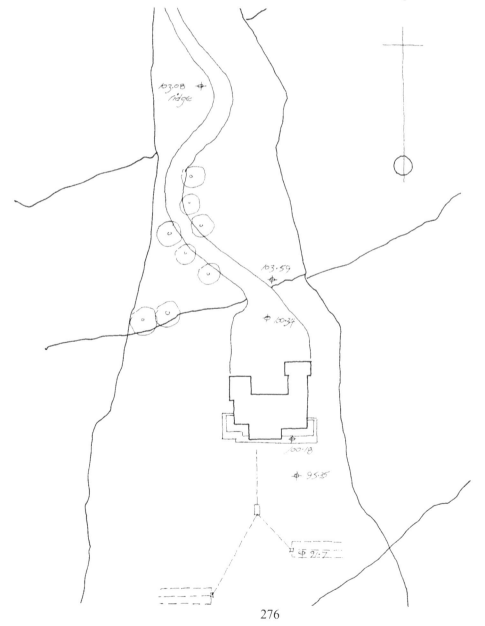

Using Plans, Cross Sections, Elevations & Site Layouts

The drawings described above comprise a set which will allow the project to enter into the *Costing/Planning/Construction* stages of the work.

Inevitably as the drawings are being made refinements will have been made to what the *model* shows. This is good and necessary. The drawings may now in fact, be used to make refinements to the *model* - or you can wait and refine the *model* later. In any event, the set of drawings are now going to be used to do a preliminary *Costing* of the work.

This is done in order to relate the project to your *Budget* and to allow any necessary alterations to be made in order to reduce costs overall.

Summary

There is never only one design solution to a building Layout exercise.

The Sun Path is the primary influencing factor on Layout Form.

The key to creating a workable Layout is to connect the individual Spaces in the design together harmoniously.

43 Sheltermaker Design Programme
Costing Your Design

It is critical that your design be accurately costed before committing it to the *Planning, Working Drawing* and *Construction* process. The reasons for this are explained in *Costing*. Read this material up as far as *'Detailed Cost Breakdown'* on page 285.

Current costs for sustainable construction in rural Ireland range from €55 to €90 per square foot, or from €600 to €1000 per square meter. The lower figures are for *Self-Build/Direct Labour*, the higher for using a *Building Contractor*. Local figures for the area you are building in should be searched out and used.

It is critical at this stage to anticipate the demands of *Mortgage Lenders* in regards to *Certification*. A suitably qualified person carrying *Indemnity Insurance* will normally have to be engaged to do this. If you are planning on using any type of unconventional materials or construction methods - such as breathable, site-constructed timber framing or hemp-lime - the *Certifying* person should be chosen for their familiarity with such materials and methods. It is a good idea to make enquiries at this stage as to who that person might be and, having tracked them down, to get their input into the project before things are finalised.

Sustainable construction is a specialist area. If you are looking for a *Building Contractor* to build a sustainable house it is best to find one with that speciality! Again, this work should begin now and any input from the *Contractor* should be invited before things are finalised.

If you are planning on building 'under the radar', in other words without being bothering with paperwork, the costing exercises will be even more important. If you over-capitalise, and, for some reason, find yourself having to sell at some point in the future, the property, because it has no papers, might have to be sold to a cash buyer because no lending institution might loan against it.

If you are working on an existing house that costing exercise will be a challenge! This will be particularly true of the labour costs! Altering existing building structures is a slow and time consuming job that is hard to quantify. Many professional builders will not be willing to cost such a job but will want to work on the basis of 'time and materials' expended. This can be a bit of a 'never never land' for the customer! So, if you are costing such a job yourself err on the side of caution in your estimates - for example double all your 'time and materials' estimates!

Print the *Costing Worksheets* and proceed with the *Costing* exercises as set out in *Costing* from page 285 onwards. The *Costing Worksheets* are quite comprehensive, following the format of the *'Bill of Quantities'* described on page 287. Included in the *Worksheets* are *Window, External Door* and *Internal Door Schedules,* allowing these items to be listed and 'quantified'. The blank *Worksheet* can be used for all other Items covered by the *Bill of Quantities*. The use of these *Worksheets* will allow for a comprehensive and realistic documentation of everything relating to the creation of your design. It may take several attempts to balance all of the conflicting demands that will emerge as one strives to arrive at an affordable *Cost* for the building. If your calculations are repeatedly coming in over budget the only way to correct this is by scaling back on floor area.

The value of this 'quantification' work cannot be over-emphasised. If these exercises are not carried out rigorously the *cost* of the building will inevitably escalate because critical decisions will have to be made during the construction process itself. The pressures of this will result in compromise and bad decision-making.

'Bargain' materials should always be looked at with suspicion. salvaged materials should be carefully assessed as to their practical usefulness and consideration given to the amount of time and effort needed to have them available on-site, ready for use. The search for low-cost ecologically acceptable materials inevitably flows back to what nature, in her bounty, can provide. If clay is available on-site and can easily be extracted, then much of the building fabric can be made with that. It is when one gets to the choice of roofing material that the 'low-cost ecologically acceptable materials' puzzle will strike one with most force! This is truly a puzzle. Traditional solutions such as thatch are now limited BY a lack of suitable material - apart from the fact that insurers will likely demand such a roof covering be underlaid with a conventional fireproof roof. Even if one is flying 'under the radar' the natural roofing puzzle will remain. One solution is to opt for something like colour-coated corrugated metal sheeting which, if carefully maintained, can be successfully be recycled at the end of a building's natural life.

Such thinking points to the fact that buildings should be made so as to be demountable! Sensible as this might seem it is rarely considered when buildings are being designed and constructed. If a building is made to come apart it can either be reconstructed at an alternative location or its various parts can be utilised individually in other building projects.

Next: SDP44 - Finalising Your Sketch Design, page 311

Building low-cost is not just about the numbers - its about how we live and how we choose to spend our time

Costing

Assessing the likely cost of your building is an essential exercise if you wish to realise your design in the real world. In other words, if you want to have your building built it is vital that before construction takes place a clear notion of cost is first determined. This exercise has implications not alone for your financial circumstance but also for the design itself and for the way and by whom it might be constructed. Further, the cost implications of the design will affect any Planning Application that might be made in respect of it and will ultimately decide the nature and content of the *Working Drawings* that must be prepared in order to have the building constructed.

If a proper and detailed *Costing* is not carried out, the implications of excessive cost might be avoided in the short term but the problems associated with this avoidance will sooner or later manifest themselves and will certainly cause greater disturbance than if they were tackled before the project moves into the critical stage of construction.

Like so many aspects of building design, *Costing* will bring to the surface many topics that have to be honestly tackled. For example if you have to borrow in order to build you will have to face the restrictions that Lending Institutions impose on borrowers. If you do not wish to obtain a Mortgage but need Capital you will have to be inventive in how you obtain money. Perhaps you will use the facilities of a Credit Union and so obtain a small loan. If you cannot possibly pay a conventional building firm to make your building for you then you will either have to utilise direct labour or do the work yourself, or at least some of it. All these and other allied matters must be clearly and honestly tackled at this stage in order that your design ambitions can be realised.

If you want to have the building you design erected, it is vital that a clear notion of the cost of doing this is first determined.

The matter of financing your building project will have to be clearly and honestly tackled in order that your design ambitions can be realised.

It should be understood that from this point onwards, as far as the beginning of the *Working Drawings & Construction* phase anyway, that the project must become malleable. What this means is that a balance must be found between the Design, Cost, Planning and Construction aspects of the project. This is why it is vital to have a sound design base - a plan - to work from, otherwise your design intentions will implode under the weight of these new considerations. If Cost, Planning & Construction become the strongest factors influencing the design the final result is bound to be lifeless, soulless and entirely lacking in individuality. *Compromise* is an expression often bandied about as being a necessity if you wish to do anything original in the world. This may be so, but if compromise is based on a firm foundation - your *Brief* - then your choices will always be clear. If you are not working from a clear *Brief* you will be pulled this way and that and then compromise will indeed rule the day.

In regards to obtaining Estimates for Construction from Building Contractors and other firms likely to be involved in the construction of your home it is essential that you yourself are in possession of independent *Costing Information* in order that a clear assessment of value-for-money can be made. Firms involved in the construction industry will furnish Estimates based on such Drawings and Specifications that you submit to them. If you are not in possession of your own estimates for such work you will have no basis for comparison of tendered estimates and so will be in no position to make a proper evaluation of these prices.

It is essential that you obtain independent, unbiased Costing Information on your project in order that a clear assessment of value for money can be made.

Preliminary Costing

The first step in the *Costing* procedure is to measure out your total floor area and to multiply this total by a Construction Cost figure.

You obtain your Floor Area by measuring within the external walls. This is best done by using a tracing or greaseproof sheet laid over a copy of your Floor Plan/s. An outline of the plan/s is all that is needed - this outline can be divided into conveniently shaped areas and these can be measured individually and the results totalled.

Alternatively, an up to date *Floor Area Worksheet* can be filled in, though this will indicate the floor area of individual spaces rather than the total area of the enclosed space that is to be enclosed. Such information as is carried on the *Floor Area Worksheet* will however

Construction Cost figures will vary according to the chosen construction system and the nature of the Labour used to make the building.

prove to be useful when it comes to costing particular items such as type of floor finish, skirtings etc. relating to individual spaces in your design.

When you have arrived at an accurate figure for the Floor Area this is multiplied by the likely Construction Cost. Construction Costs will vary according to the construction system you intend using and to the methods and nature of the construction operatives themselves. For example, if you are going to use a General Contractor that normally builds houses using materials and systems similar to what it is you want to construct then you can obtain from such a firm an estimate of construction costs that can be safely used to estimate the cost of constructing your building. With such a figure at hand you multiply this by your Floor Area and thereby arrive at a likely Construction Cost. Additions for Electricity, Telephone & Water connections should be added to this as well as a figure for the Site Works relevant to the particular conditions likely to be encountered on-site.

If you intend to utilise an alternative to a General Contractor who will provide a 'Turn-key' package you will probably be thinking in terms of using a combination of Direct Labour and A Timber Frame Construction Company. On paper such a combination will surely show itself to be potentially cheaper. It is critical however to take into account that the co-ordinating services provided by a General Contractor would in this case be absent and that someone will have to do this work in the Direct Labour scenario. If this is to be yourself it is important to realise that this job will be time consuming and demanding in a way that your job - if you have one - may not allow. Alternatively, you can employ someone to carry out the co-ordinating work on your behalf in which case you should factor in the cost of this.

An alternative to using a General Contractor is to utilise a combination of Direct Labour and a Timber Frame Construction Company.

Another alternative to a General Contractor or the Direct Labour methods is to build your house yourself. This demands of this approach requires not so much the relevant skills, which in any case can be acquired or bought in, but time. It is almost impossible to build a house and to work at the same time. At the very least one would need six to eight weeks free time in order to progress the work to the point where evening and week-end work would allow the building to be completed.

Another alternative is to build the house yourself.

Consideration of this last scenario brings to the surface the dynamics of how houses are provided in the modern world - one works and pays someone else to build the house. Not only that - one commits to working for nigh on twenty years to pay for this service! This way of providing a house for oneself and ones family has evolved from the original method which was to carry out the work oneself. Such houses were simpler, faster to construct and were essentially built out of income. The surrender of the possibility of creating ones home out of income for the allure of a 'job' has now led to a vast exploitation of peoples very real housing need. Houses have become more and more complex, larger, have become the subject of complicated legislation, have become more expensive in relationship to income and have become the foundation of western economies supporting an industrial base. It is in the growth of Industry and the consequent demand for labour that the surrender of the possibility of building ones home out of what one had, can be traced. This has now burgeoned to the point where houses are the destination of so many of the products churned out by the Industrial process. Consequently houses have become bigger, more complex, more controlled and the subject of so much propaganda that the very nature of what a home is has been lost in the blurr of disinformation.

That such manipulation can be made to endure is due to the fact that houses represent survival and consequently peoples willingness to work hard, to make sacrifices and to stretch themselves to the limit can very easily be brought into play. Much of this manipulation is carried out on an unconscious level, in other words ones need of a home and ones desire to survive are never spoken of in the same breath. This is particularly easy to do as death is very much a taboo subject in all developed economies. Consequently such matters as status front for the truth which is that we are all striving to survive and that some of us are doing it better than others.

What this leads to is the realisation that modern economies are based on peoples willingness to commit themselves to long years of hard work that oftentimes is meaningless to them as individuals. It also means that the artificial growth associated with money - interest - is revealed for what it is. It is simply the chain to which most people are shackled due to their wanting themselves and their families to survive. Unless one clearly sees this scenario for what it is the borrowing of money to create ones home will blurr the potential liberating feeling attached to *being ones own architect*. In other words you will find oneself straddling some kind of invisible fence, pulled this way by economic realities, pulled the other by your desire to take control of your individual life.

What this is leading to is the acquisition of money with which to build ones home. It also has to do with the expectation that any construction company or firm

As a consequence of the modern way of living and paying for shelter, houses have become bigger, more complex, more controlled and the subject of so much propaganda, that the very nature of what a home is has been lost in a blur of disinformation.

283

might want to provide you with particularly good value for money - in other words that you might expect to pay less for the construction of your home than what everyone else is paying. The fact that you might have figures at hand for actual cost of the material content of your home and that you might expect, based on these figures, to obtain particularly good value from a General Contractor, is a scenario likely to distance any Contractor from you rather than to bring them closer. The reason for this is that the Contractor is also labouring under the Money Interest System and so is unlikely to wish to liberate you from the tyranny!

The setting up of a Direct Labour system for the construction of your home will help to mask the fact that you intend obtaining particularly good value for your money. In other words, as there is no General Contractor only you and whoever is helping you organise the work need know how much the entire works are costing. On the downer side of this equation is the necessity to comply with the Lending Institution demands for whatever Certification they might require to ensure that 'their money' is being fed through the system of Registered Contractors etc. This is the Chain to which you will be shackled - your choice is to do it consciously or unconsciously, to know to what you are chained or to pretend that there is no freedom in life at all.

All Personal Lending is based on the security of the Home and the realisation that people will strive to maintain the Home at all costs. The notion that Houses continue to accumulate value - in contrast to all other consumer products - is based on the Money Interest System. If you calculate how much your Mortgage Borrowings will cost you at the end of the day - 20 years, say - you will realise that you will be paying a considerable amount for your home. Naturally, you would expect that your home would be worth more in the future that it would be when you buy it even though this is in total contrast to everything else that we buy. A new car, for example, we accept as being worth less the very moment we drive it off the garage forecourt! We accept the inherent contradictions of House Values continually increasing because we know that we need houses to survive.

This is a roundabout way to exploring *Costing*. Unless you have enough money of your own, or money from a clean source such as the Credit Union, you will be borrowing to build your House from a Lending Institution. Consequently you will be subject to their Terms & Conditions which will exert considerable influence on many matters to do with the built reality of your home. It is as well to tackle into this now. So, when you have

It is an illusion to expect that any Building Company or Contractor might want to provide you with a home at a lesser cost than what everyone else is paying.

The setting up of a Direct Labour system for the construction of your home will help to mask the fact that you intend obtaining particularly good value for money.

All Personal Lending is based on the security of the Home and the fact that people will strive to maintain the Home at all costs.

figured out the overall cost of building your house using a General Contractor and of borrowing conventionally to fund this construction you must then consider how you will make the necessary repayments and accept that perhaps you will be able to spend very little time within the walls you have so very carefully designed!

Alternatively you can choose to build out of income, avoid all but minimal borrowings and liberate yourself from the tyranny of Money Interest. Whatever it is you choose now is the time to make a decision as the project is now going to develop accordingly. Set your figures out in a similar manner to this for the purposes of comparison:

Construction Cost per SqM
        X General Contractors Rate   =
        X Direct Labour Rate   =
        X Self Building Rate   =

Further critical information that is required at this point of the *Costing* exercise relates to Lending Rates and Conditions. These can be obtained from Banks, Building Societies & Credit Unions. A proper and full assessment of all aspects of such information and their consequences in terms of your life and ambitions are essential in order to develop a full, proper and realistic assessment of the further development of your project.

Detailed Cost Breakdown

The exercise of reaching a detailed and accurate cost for any building project is based on the assembly of Quantities of Materials, the Specification of these Materials, Products & The Methods that are to be used in their Construction. A Building Programme specifying the time necessary for the completion of the Work is also a part of this exercise. Such information then forms the basis of a Contract for the Construction work.

Quantity Surveyors are the professionals usually employed for the task of assembling Cost Information for building work. Their expertise is more normally called upon where large construction projects are being carried out. In the case of an individual dwelling the engagement of a Quantity Surveyor is not strictly speaking necessary. In fact one might experience some difficulty in engaging a professional for so relatively small a project. Nonetheless should one wish to do so it is an approach that will remove some of the detailed

Calculate how much your Mortgage will have cost you at the end of 20 years and consider how you will make these repayments during this time.

and tedious work necessary to *Costing* the project accurately. Computer programmes are also available which carry out this work on a Personal Computer.

While the primary objective of the *Costing* exercise is to arrive at a reasonably accurate Cost for the Construction of your building, the process of *Costing* itself will allow for considerable choice to be made in balancing the various cost elements within the design. For example, the isolation of the individual cost of Windows, Doors, Walls, Floors, H&V Systems, Plumbing, Drainage & Electrical Work, Roofing, Finishes and Decoration will allow for considerable fine tuning to take place before a final Construction Cost is arrived at. This is a major function of the Costing Exercise and an important facility in arriving at a balanced and reasonable overall Construction Cost. Any Quantity Surveyor or Quantity Surveying Programme that might be used should be able to offer this facility.

The basis of the Costing Exercise will be your Plans, Cross Sections, Elevations and Site Layout. Further, the information previously gathered for your *Files* in regards to *Materials & Products* will now prove to be invaluable. If you have not already done so it is critical that you do so now. This involves the gathering of information on *Materials & Products*, their cost and their availability for use. The process of gathering such information is described in the preceding *Parts* of *Volume 2*.

The process of *Costing* should be modelled on the Quantities Breakdown outlined below. This will allow for the complete and sensible coverage of all items necessary for the Construction of your building. This information is assembled into a 'Bill of Quantities' from which an overall Construction Cost is derived.

Several versions of the 'Bill' should be assembled, beginning with the first version which will allow pertinent matters to surface and be dealt with. It will also allow you decide if the project can safely proceed into the *Planning & Working Drawing* phases without the need of making major changes brought about by budgetary constraints. It is vital therefore to tackle this initial costing exercise realistically.

Calculations of the quantities of materials can initially be reasonably 'loose'. This will allow you to become familiar with the measuring process without getting bogged down in detail. Where it may not be possible to obtain a cost estimate for some items in the Bill a 'Prime Cost' figure can be entered. These 'PC Sums' are amounts entered in the Bill that will cover the likely cost of an item - say, reinforcing bars for foundations.

The process of Costing, apart from providing you with an estimate of overall Cost, will also allow for considerable choice to be made in balancing the various cost elements within the design.

The basis of the Costing exercise will be your Plan/s, Cross Sections, Elevations and Site Layout.

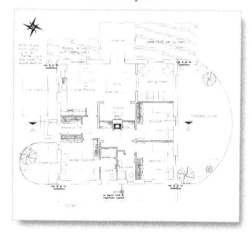

Estimates of cost should be entered onto the relevant *Quantities Worksheets*. These Costs should be broken into two elements - Basic Cost and VAT.

Apart from the necessary drawings and information on *Materials & Products*, additional materials for the carrying out of the *Costing* exercise are as follows:

Greaseproof Paper - can be bought from the supermarket in a roll. A more economical alternative would be to buy a ream of 'Butter Paper' from a wholesale supplier to food shops.

Scale Rule.

Various Felt Tip Markers

Calculator

Plain A4 paper

File Folders (20-25)

Contents of The Bill of Quantities: Preliminaries

Typically, *Preliminaries* cover items not accounted for anywhere else in the *Bill of Quantities* - this being the compilation, or *Bill*, of specific items such as the amounts of Timber, Slates, Doors, Windows etc. and the work involved in constructing these according to the proposed design.

Normally reserved for Works of greater magnitude than the construction of a house, *Preliminaries* however is a useful category under which to list such items as The Setting Out of the Works; Site Facilities; Temporary Works; The Insurance of the Work; Public Liability Insurance; Security & Safety Measures; Local Authority Charges; Plant Hire; ; Temporary Power Supply Charges; Temporary Water Supply Charges; Telephone; Removal of Rubbish; Lighting; Scaffolding; Allowances for Attendance by the Main Contractor to Sub-Contractors; Provision of Drawings and, Supervision.

While it is important to be aware of some of these 'hidden' costs. In the case of using a General Contractor these items should be covered in the tendered Cost of Construction. If you are using Direct Labour, you in the role of General Contractor would then be liable for the organisation and payment of relevant items.

If Planning Permission is sought for a design more expensive than you can afford to construct, then you will be adding unnecessary complications and problems to your life.

Setting Out the Works - This involves marking out the position of the building on-site and the location of trenches for foundations. The cost of this can be included in the General Contractors Estimate or it can be covered as an individual item. As such it would probably constitute one days work for a Surveyor or other building professional.

Site Facilities - Provision of an on-site office and possibly basic kitchen and toilet facilities. Not strictly speaking necessary though such accommodation will allow for meetings to be held, will provide safe storage as well as paying heed to the welfare of the building operatives - as well as yourself. Such consideration should be amply paid back in a commitment to do good work on your behalf. The site office could remain after completion of the work and provide valuable accommodation.

Temporary Works - This covers items that facilitate the main construction work. For example, temporary protection of an adjoining building; hoardings; fences etc. The provision of site access and roadway might also be included in this section.

Insurance of the Works & Public Liability Insurance - If there is to be a General Contractor these items will be covered by him/her. In the case of using Direct Labour these costs will be borne by you as Contractor.

Security & Safety Measures - Protection of materials and tools; protection of workers and visitors.

Local Authority Charges - These are usually specified in Planning Permissions and cover such things as restoring pavements where they need to be disturbed to allow work to be carried out. General development charges might also be levied. Charges for connection to public drains and water supplies might also be sought.

Plant Hire - This will relate to equipment necessary for the preparation and construction work to be carried out - Hymacs; Diggers; Excavators etc. Some of these charges can be incorporated into specific items such as Excavating & Filling.

Temporary Power & Temporary Water Supply Charges - These charges will relate to the supply of water and power to allow the works to be carried out.

Telephone - Installation of on-site telephone.

Removal of Rubbish - Cost of supply and removal of skips.

Lighting - Should the construction work be underway
in wintertime it might be worthwhile making provision
for temporary lighting to be installed to facititate work
carried on in the hours of darkness.

Scaffolding - This item is self explanatory. It is very
few projects that do not require the hiring of
scaffolding.

*Allowances for Attendance by the Main Contractor to
Sub-Contractors* - Where the Main Contractor sub-
contracts portions of the work or what is called a
Nominated Sub-Contractor is used - this is someone
that you yourself 'nominates' - the Main Contractor will
have to 'attend' to certain needs the Sub-Contractor
might have. For example, providing power, lights,
scaffolding etc. Such attendences are provided for by
an agreed percentage of the Sub-contract amount.

Provision of Drawings - The printing of Drawings and
other material relevant to the carrying out of the work.

Supervision - Payment to a Building Professional for
visiting the site, inspecting the work, providing advice
to the Contractor, overseeing payments etc.

Demolition & Disposal of Rubble

This section is relevant only where an existing building
has to be demolished to make way for the construction
of a new one. The removal of rubble - or where this
might be disposed of on-site - is covered in this section
also.

Alterations & Renovations

This item is of relevance only where an existing
building forms part of the new works to be carried out.
In contrast to *Demolition* this section would cover such
things as the making of openings in existing walls; the
removal of existing windows and/or doors; the filling in
of existing openings; window and door replacement;
work on existing chimneys; repairs to walls, floors etc.

Excavation & Filling

Excavation & Filling concerns itself essentially with
the making of Foundations. The type of foundations
you will be utilising will depend on the type of
structure you are going to make as well as on the soil
conditions on-site.

To take on-site conditions first. A preliminary examination of the ground conditions should be carried out, if it has not already been done. This will reveal the nature of the soil and give an indication of levels. This information can then be related to the type of foundations required for the type of structure you are proposing to build.

Broadly speaking, a clad timber framed structure needs only 'pad foundations'. These are small individual foundations that are placed under the 'legs' of the frame.

Any structure consisting of masonry - that is bricks or blocks - requires continuous foundations under such walls. These foundations need to be as level as possible.

It is obvious that in terms of foundations, masonry structures are more expensive. This holds true both for the amount of concrete required, the amount of excavation necessary as well as requiring the site to be reasonably level to start off with.

The practice of 'filling' to bring the low part of a site level with the high part can only be discouraged. The alternative, in terms of creating level foundations is to excavate the high portion of the ground to bring it level with the low part. This approach creates its own problems in that one side of your building will for all intents be below ground level. This, combined with the possible use of a concrete slab, could have dire consequences as far as damp or water penetration into the structure.

Excavation & Filling should include any work such as providing access to the site, the making of driveways to facilitate the construction, hardstands etc. Such work should appear on your *Site Layout*.

To estimate the amount of *Excavation* likely to be required you need a Ground Floor Plan of your building. Lay a greaseproof sheet over this, temporarily holding it down with pieces of masking tape. A copy of the proposed Site Layout should also be at hand.

First draw an outline of the entire area that the building will occupy making this outline a little on the 'generous' side. This area will need to be at the very least cleared of topsoil - that is, the first four to six inches of earth will have to be removed. Similarly, for driveways, hardstands etc. a tracing of this should be made. The areas involved can then be calculated and expressed in square meters. A location for the resulting spoil should be identified on the *Site Layout*. This should be conveniently located in terms of your *Landscape* proposals as this topsoil will be rich in vegetable matter and will come in useful eventually.

If the area to be occupied by your building is not level an estimate of the amount of soil to be removed will have to be estimated - taking into account the likely ground conditions that might be encountered. The same is true of driveways, though these can be built to a gradient.

After the topsoil has been removed the next step is for the excavation of foundation trenches to be carried out. Trenches are excavated to the width required for the foundations which is calculated by the thickness of the wall plus 200mm on either side. In the case of a 300mm external wall the trench would need to be a minimum of 700mm therefore. Where an internal 4in/100mm wall has to be supported on a foundation a 600mm foundation trench would be appropiate. The bottom of foundations is normally kept 600mm below finished ground level. Where pad foundations are proposed a 600mm square pad will normally suffice.

Based on this information you can outline the trench/foundation lines on a tracing sheet laid over the ground floor plan of your building. From this plan the amount of excavated material can be calculated by multiplying the trench width by the length by the depth: *Trench/Pad Width X Length X Depth.* All figures should be in meters giving result in cubic meters:
For example: For 1 Pad - .6 X .6 X.6 = .216cum
For 40m of trench - .7 X 40 X .6 = 16.8cum

Where it is proposed to use a concrete slab a calculation of the amount of filling - or hardcore - under this should be included in this section. The plan area to be occupied by the slab can be calculated from the ground floor plan. A thickness of 100-150mm (.1 - .15m) of filling can be calculated for.

The above examples assume a level site. Where deeper excavations might be required to keep the bottom of the foundation trenches 600mm below ground level the amount of material to be excavated will increase. Similarly with the hardcore - if the ground is not level and more fill is required under parts of the slab an increase in the amount of hardcore needed will result.

Estimates of the cost of hardcore - delivered - can be obtained from quarries. An amount should be included for a load of sand also. This is used to 'blind' the hardcore, that is, to provide a reasonably level, impervious surface on which to lay a dampproof membrane before the concrete slab is poured.

Concreting

In the case of continuous footings under masonry walls foundations themselves are normally 250mm thick. The volume of concrete required to fill the foundation trenches to a depth of 250mm (.25m) is estimated by multiplying the length of the trench by the width by .25m:

For 40m of 750mm (.75m) trench - 40 X .75 X .25 = 7.5cum

In the case of pad foundations a depth of 250mm will also suffice. So to estimate the amount of concrete required to fill 16, 600mm square pads to a depth of 250mm you carry out the following calculation:
16 X .6 X .6 X .25 = 1.44cum
Therefore, 1.44cum of concrete will be required. Where pads might be made deeper to being their tops above ground level to allow timber posts to be affixed to them a pad depth of 750mm would be needed. In that case the estimate of concrete volume would therefore be as follows:
16 X .6 X .6 X .75 = 4.32cum

A 25 N/mm2 concrete strength will suffice for most domestic construction.

In the case of concrete slabs the volume of concrete required is calculated by multiplying the slab area by its depth. In the case of a 150mm (.15m) slab that is 80m2, this would be:
80 X .15 = 12cum.

This section also includes 'sundry items' such as damproof membranes and reinforcing bars. These can be covered by a PC Sum.

Estimates of the delivered costs of readymix concrete can now be obtained along with information on 'minimum delivered loads', access requirements for readymix vehicles etc.

Masonry

This section of the *Bill* covers concrete blockwork, brickwork, sills, stonework and associated items such as damproof courses, wall ties and cavity wall insulation.

To estimate the quantities involved you will need plans, elevations and possibly, a cross section, of your building. You will also need to have information on door and window openings. If you have not already done so you should number external doors (D1, D2 etc.) internal doors

(ID 1, ID2 etc.) and windows (W1, W2 etc.). This information should be listed on the relevant *Schedule Sheets* for easy reference. Numbers should also be written against doors and windows on the plans, elevations and cross sections.

In the case of timber frame construction that is to be brick or block clad the first measurement of quantities is that relating to the 'rising walls' - these are the walls rising off the top of the foundations. One of these walls will rise up to become the 'outer leaf' of the structure terminating at the roof. The other wall will support the timber frame walling and will terminate at the level of the ground floor.

The amount of blockwork required to construct the rising walls is calculated by measuring from the top of the foundation to the level of the ground floor - normally around 600mm. This measurement is multiplied by the length of the entire outside walls of the building. This distance is measured off the plan:
Height of rising wall: 600mm - 0.6m
Length of outside walls: 60m
Thickness of wall: 100mm - 0.1m
Quantity of blockwork: 0.6 X 60 X 0.1 = 3.6cum
This result is multiplied by 2 because there are two rising walls:
3.6 X 2 = 7.2cum

To calculate the actual number of blocks this figure is divided by 0.01 - the volume of one block giving: 720 blocks.

Where there is to be a suspended timber floor, the number of blocks needed to construct the supporting walls underneath these is calculated in similar fashion. Account should also be taken of the vent grilles and vent bricks or openings required to provide underfloor ventilation.

To calculate the amount of bricks or blocks needed to clad a timber frame similar calculations are carried out. For example, for an exterior wall rising to a height of 6m:
Height of External Wall - 6m
Length of External Wall - 60m
Thickness of Wall: 0.1m
Area of Windows - 35sqm
Area of External Doors - 7sqm

Total Wall Area Less windows and doors:
(6 X 60) - (35+7)
   360- 42 = 318sqm

This is multiplied by the thickness of the wall:
318 X 0.1 Giving a result of 31.8cum
Divided by the volume of 1 block - 0.01 = 3180 blocks.

In the case of bricks the volume is divided by .0016, giving a result of: 19,875 bricks.

In the case of masonry cavity wall construction the same calculation is carried out - wall area minus window and door area - but the volume of blocks is doubled to account for the two walls.

Where internal walls are to be constructed in blockwork the number of blocks required for these also needs to be estimated.

Quantities of wall ties: 4 per sqm. > 318 X 4 = 1272

The amount of damproof course required will be based on the construction system - horizontal DPC will be needed in all rising walls; in masonry construction all window and external door openings will require a DPC around the entire length of the opening.

The number and quantity of window cills can be estimated from the *Window Schedule*.

The number and quantity of Lintols can be estimated from the *Window* and *External Door Schedules*.

Structural Timber

The quantity of timber required to construct your building will very much depend on your chosen construction system. In the case of a timber framed building you will, of course, require very much more timber than if you are building in masonry. Whatever the situation, plans, elevations and cross sections will be needed to give you the dimensional information required for calculations. In all cases estimates are made both for the lengths and section sizes required as well as for the overall volume of timber that will be needed.

In the case of Timber Frame construction the first estimate is for the amount of wall plate - this is the section of timber that sits on top of the rising wall. This will be a 100 X 75mm section and wall plates will be required on top of all rising walls and on top of any supporting walls under suspended timber floors.

Length of Rising Wall 60m
Length of Supporting Walls: 35m
Length of wall plate:
60+35 = 95m of 100 X 75mm section
Volume of timber: 95 X 0.1 X 0.075 = 0.7125cum

A DPC will be required under the wall plate:
Length of DPC: 95m
The wall plate will also require fixing with straps or bolts every metre or so:
Number of fixings: 95 bolts/straps.

Where a suspended floor is to be constructed - whether in timber frame or masonry construction - the volume of timber required for this is based on the chosen floor joist size and the distance apart that these are to be. The plan of the ground floor is needed for this calculation. It is best to use a sheet of tracing or greaseproof to make an outline of the floor area, breaking the area up into easily measurable zones. These can be based on the actual subdivision of the floor into rooms or spaces.

On this tracing the actual number of joists is marked in using the appropiate spacing - usually 400mm centre to centre. This exercise will give an indication of the number of joists required. The actual section size of the joists is determined by the span - the distance between the wall plates under them. The calculation for each zone is as follows:

Zone 1 - Number of joists X Span > 14 X 3.9m = 54.6m of 150 X 44mm SCB section.
The volume of timber is calculated as follows:
54.6 X 0.15 X 0.044 = 0.36cum

All the zones are thus measured and the total length and volume of timber is calculated by adding together the results for all zones.

The measurement of the floorboarding required is based on the total area of all the zones divided by the area of the boarding itself. In the case of plywood sheeting to cover a floor area of 120sqm: > Area of plywood sheet: 1.2 X 2.4 = 2.88sqm
Number of sheets required: 41.6 sheets of plywood.

Where 150mm wide T&G boarding is to be used, the area of 1m of such boarding would be:
1 X 0.15 = 0.15sqm. This figure is then divided into the floor area.
Therefore 800m of boarding would be required to surface the entire floor area.

The amount of joists and boarding required for intermediate floors is calculated in the same way using the appropiate floor plan.

The calculation for the amount of timber required to create the timber frame walling follows a similar procedure. In this case the area of windows and doors needs to be subtracted from the overall wall area. Tracings of the elevations are used for the purposes of the calculations, using the same method of marking in as was employed for the floor - a spacing of 400mm between studs which are normally 100 X 44mm in section.

The calculation for the amount of plywood required for sheathing the studding follows the same procedure as for calculating floorboarding quantities.

The calculations for the quantities of timber for the roof is again similar, though, because the roof is not flat, measuring the actual length of the rafters requires reading the plan and the cross section together. Calculations for rafters, purlins hips, valleys and ceiling joists should be carried out separately on individual tracing sheets.

Where a roof is being placed atop a masonry structure, a wall plate needs to be included in the estimate. A DPC under this should be taken account of and provision made for the number of bolts/straps needed to hold the wallplate down.

Where roof trusses are proposed for use - as opposed to creating what is called a 'cut roof' - the number of trusses can be assessed from the roof plan and the manufacturers recommended spacing.

External Cladding & Covering

Including Patent Glazing
  Roof Tiles
  Slates
  Metal Decking
  Felt
  Underlays
  Flashings
  Fascia & Soffitts

This section of the *Bill* concerns itself with the external covering to the timber structure - tiles, slates, roof glazing, flashings, fascias and soffits and so on.

These measurements are straightforward to make and will by based primerally on the elevation drawings. In the case of measuring the roof tiles, slates a roof plan and a cross section will be needed.

The area of tiling or slating required is based on a measurement of the overall roof area - remember not to rely on the plan to calculate this. Because the roof will slope it is necessary to calculate the area of the roof by using the pland and the cross section together. Remember to take account of dormers if there are to be any in your design.

When the area of roof to be covered has been arrived at this figure is divided by a measure of the 'coverage' of the chosen roofing material. For example it normally requires 13 slates to cover 1sqm of roof. In the case of metal decking the area of one sheet can be divided into the roof area to calculate the number of sheets needed:
Area of Roof: 120sqm
Area of Metal Decking Sheets: 2.16sqm
Number of Sheets required: 55.5 sheets

Number of slates required for the same roof area:
120 X 13 = 1560

Where timber framed walls might be clad with decking, tiles or slates similar calculations are carried out based on the appropiate elevation drawings.

Similarly, where timber weatherboarding is to be utilised the length of boarding required is calculated as for timber floorboarding described earlier.

The roof plan will also yield up information on the amount of ridge, hip and valleys required to complete the outer roof covering. These should be marked onto an individual tracing sheet and expressed in terms of their length:

Length of Ridge - 20m
Length of Hips - 15m
Length of Valleys - 12m

Ridges and hips will require individual covering to match your chosen roof finish. Valleys will need to be either lead lined or in the case of something like metal decking, lined with a specially manufactured valley.

Outlets for soil vents and attic roof vents should also be taken account of. Most roof coverings come with an appropiate fitting to allow such outlets to be neatly incorporated into the roof. An approximation of the number of vents is all that is required.

Where any form of roof light is to be incorporated into the roof this should be taken account of in this section. In the case of pre-made Velux type rooflights, this is fairly straightforward and the cost of the window and the 'flashing' needed to marry it into the roof covering can be fairly easily obtained. Where a built-in rooflight - patent glazing - is to be used, the amount of glass, glazing bar and flashing needs to be calculated.

Next comes the measurement of the 'underlay' which is installed beneath tiles, slates and possibly even beneath metal decking. The overall area of this will accord with the measurement of the roof area already calculated.

Felt, where it is used on a conventional roof, is laid on top of the rafters. Where slate, tile cladding or weatherboarding is to be used vertically on the face of a timber frame, battens will need to be affixed to the plywood sheathing to allow the felt to be installed. 3m of 44 X 22mm battens will be needed for each square metre of felt.

Where brick or blockwork is to be used to face a timber frame structure, building paper or a breathing membrane should be installed on the face of the sheathing ply. The area for this will accord with your earlier measure for sheathing ply.

Where roofs meet walls and where chimneys project through roofs, 'flashings' are needed to protect the joints from moisture penetration. The measurement of the amount of flashings required should be included in this section. Use your elevations - or better still, your model - to discover how much flashing will be needed. Express this in terms of the number of meters required.

Where the roof meets the wall, and possibly overhangs it, a fascia and possibly a soffit will be required. Soffits are usually used to allow ventilation into roof spaces. The length involved will be measurable from your elevations. Express this in terms of length indicating the overall size of the fascia and soffits themselves:
Length of Fascia and Soffit: 75m
Fascia Height: 150mm
Soffit width: 150mm

Waterproofing
Waterproofing
Felt Roofing
Waterproof Rendering

This section of the *Bill* concerns itself with roofing membranes that might be used on a flat roof or where a sod roof is proposed. Relevant areas can be obtained from plans and cross sections.

Where portion of a structure might be underground or require asphalting or waterproof rendering to prevent water penetration, the relevant areas should be measured within this section of the Bill also. Estimates of cost for this work should be obtained from specialist firms.

Measurements should follow these general guidelines:

Area of Flat Roofing - sqm
Area of Waterproof Membrane under sod roof - sqm
Area of Asphalting - sqm
Area of Waterproof Rendering - sqm

Linings

Sheathings
Dry Partitions
Flooring

This section of the *Bill* concerns itself with all types of internal linings, vapour barriers, the construction of stud partitions in masonry structures and with the covering of concrete slabs. Plasterboarded ceilings are also included.

In timber frame structures, linings will generally consist of plasterboard incorporating a vapour barrier. These areas can be measured from plans and cross sections or can be gleaned directly from the Floor Areas Worksheets. Ceiling areas can be measured from the plans.

Dry partitions - stud partitions - in timber framed structures will have been measured as part of the timber frame measurements so this section relates primerally to the measurement of stud partitions in masonry structures.

Generally plasterboard is 'skimmed' with a thin coat of plaster to cover over joints and to give a smooth consistent finish. Areas to be skimmed should be measured in this section.

This section of the *Bill* also covers linings other than plasterboard - for example, T&G boarding to ceilings and walls.

Again, in timber frame structures or where a suspended timber floor is being used in a masonry structure, flooring will have been accounted for. Where a concrete slab is being used however, a suitable finish for this should be measured and estimated under this section.

Typical measurements under this section of the *Bill* will be as follows:
Area of Regular Plasterboard: - sqm
Area of Foil Backed Plasterboard: - sqm
Number of 1.2 X 2.4m Sheets - Divide Area by 2.88

Timber in Dry Partitions:
With studs at 400mm centres plus head and base plates calculate length of timber required.
Volume of timber - Length X 0.075 X 0.044m = cum

Area of Plasterboard to Dry Partitions:
Length X Height X Number of Sides - sqm/number of sheets

Area of Plasterboard to Ceilings: Length X Width -
sqm/number of sheets

Area of Timber linings to Walls and Ceilings:
Area X Thickness (for T&G normally 15mm)

Finish to Concrete Floor: Length X Width to be
covered expressed in sqm.
Thickness should also be noted.

Windows, Doors & Stairs

This section of the *Bill* concerns itself with Windows,
Doors and Stairs. Information on the Windows, Internal
& External Doors should be available on the relevant
Schedules. Information on the stairs should be available
on your plan/s and cross section/s.

Generally windows and doors sizes should accord with
standard manufactures units that are readily available.
Catalogues should be available in your files detailing
what is available. Similarly estimates of cost should be
coveded in your files. An estimate of the likely cost of
these units can therefore be arrived at.

An estimate of the cost of stairs can be covered by a PC
sum or a preliminary price can be gotten from a joinery
shop based on your requirements.

Locks, latches, bolts etc. - Ironmongery - should also
be estimated within this Section. A PC Sum would be
the best way in which to do this. Similarly PC Sums
can be used to cover the costs of Windows, Doors and
Stairs if you wish.

Estimate for Windows: £ -
Estimate for Internal Doors: £ -
Estimate for External Doors: £ -
Estimate for Ironmongery: £ -
Estimate for Stairs: £ -

Surface Finishes

Items in this section of the *Bill* apply to masonry structures that are rendered or plastered externally. However a timber frame structure that is to be clad with sand/cement render on expanded metal should be measured in this section.

Brick faced structures that are to have rendered or plastered decorative surrounds to window and door openings should have such work included in this section. Also, where a decorative plinth might be proposed for the base of a structure or decorative coigns to corners are proposed.

Other items covered in this section are internal plastering and wall tiling, floor tiling and decoration.

Estimates of area for external plastering or rendering can be gleaned from the elevations making allowances for the window and door openings. Account should be taken of the window and door reveals - that section of walling within the window or door openings.

Areas for internal plastering can follow previous estimates for areas of masonry walling or plasterboard lining, whichever applies.

Areas for wall and floor tiling can be interpreted from plans etc. Estimates for this work should relate to a particular choice of tile. Internal and external decoration should be covered by a PC Sum.

Measurements should follow these general guidelines:

Area of external blockwork to be rendered:
Flat wall area - sqm
Area of Door/window reveals and heads - sqm

Rendering onto Expanded metal:
Area of expanded metal - sqm
Area of rendering   -sqm
Area of Door/window reveals and heads - sqm

Area of Decorative surround to window and door openings:
Length, Width & Thickness (20mm normally)

Area of Decorative Plinth to base of structure:
Height, Length & Thickness (20mm normally)

Area of Decorative Coigns: Height, Width & Thickness
(20mm normally)

Area of internal plastering:
Total of individual walls and ceilings - sqm

PC Sum for Decoration - £

The primary cost of much of this type of work will be
Labour. Even if you are self-building, unless you have
the appropiate skills you will be better off hiring the
experts. Estimates of cost for rendering, plastering and
tiling should therefore be obtained from a builder or
plasterer.

Fixtures

Furniture & Equipment
Built in Units
Kitchen
Sanitary Appliances

Shelving, worktops, furniture, equipment, toilets,
washandbasins and so on are estimated within this
section.

Other than perhaps the sanitary units, these items
should all be covered by PC Sums - general estimates
of cost that will ensure that the cost of supply and
installation is covered without going into too much
detail at this stage.

It is a good idea however to decide the amount of the
PC Sums by obtaining general prices for Kitchens,
Bathroom suites etc.

PC SUM for Shelving: £ -
PC SUM for Furniture & Equipment: £ -
PC SUM for Built In-Units: £ -
PC SUM for Kitchen: £ -
PC SUM for Sanitary Appliances: £ -
PC Sum for Taps and Fittings: £ -

Building Fabric Sundries

Insulation
Building Paper
Skirtings
Trim
Handrails
Architraves
Pipe Ducts
Pipe Run Box Ins
Wiring Ducts
Trenches for Incoming Services

This is really a sort of rag-bag section of the *Bill*, a gathering place for loose ends - items that if they are not taken account of can keep pushing costs up.

The area of Insulation required can be discovered from the plans, elevations etc.

The area of building paper - that is, paper applied to the external plywood face of a timber framed structure - can be estimated from the elevations or from your previous calculations for plywood.

The length of skirting boards can be discovered from your *Floor Area Worksheets* or from the plan/s.

Trim - decorative cornices, dado rails, picture rails etc - can be covered by a PC Sum. Internal window cills should be included here.

Handrails - again a PC Sum will suffice, though if you have a clear idea of the type of handrail you want on stairs it can now be estimated.

Length of architrave can be calculated from *Window* and *Internal Door Schedules* as this is where the architraves will be destined for.

The ducts and boxing in will relate to *Services Layouts* - to what extent hidden accommodation has to be made for pipes and wires. Unless your *Services Layouts* are at a detailed stage and you can tell where pipes and wires are going to run - and which ones need to be hidden - cover this item with a PC Sum.

The area of the trench needed to accommodate incoming water, electrical and telephone services can be estimated from a *Site Layout*.

Estimates in this section can be as follows:

Area of Insulation:
Totals of Individual Areas - Length X Width/Height X
Thickness expressed in cum.
Area of Building Paper: - sqm
Quantity of Skirting Board: Length X Section Size
Internal Window Cills: Length X Section Size
Picture Rail: Length X Section Size
Plaster Cornice: Length X Size
Handrails: PC Sum
Architrave: Length X Section Size
Also mention number of units to receive architraving.
Services Ducts: PC Sum
Trench for Incoming Services: PC Sum

Exterior Items

Paving
Planting
Fencing
Outside Furniture & Equipment
Roads
Driveways

Items in this section of the *Bill* concern themselves with
things outside of the building itself. The most vital of
these, in terms of moving into the completed building,
would be a Road or Driveway and, to some extent, the
Paving outside of Doors that will allow the immediate
comings and goings to be catered for in a reasonable
manner.

The *Site Layout* drawing should yield up the relevant
information necessary to estimate quantities and
prepare estimates of likely cost.

These should be set out in a manner similar to this:

Area of Paving: - sqm
PC Sum for Planting - £ -
Area of Fencing:
Length X Height - sqm (Or use a PC Sum)
PC Sum for Outside Furniture & Equipment - £
Area of Roadway:
Length X Width - sqm
Area of Driveway:
Length X Width - sqm

Drainage

RWG / pipework
Foul Drainage above Ground
Drainage Stacks
Drainage below ground
Septic Tank
Trenches for drains
Land Drainage

Disposal systems to take care of rain and waste water are considered in this section of the *Bill*. At this stage of the project a PC Sum should be sufficient to cover the likely cost of these items. Such an estimate should take account of the likely extent of the drainage system - for example if a septic tank and percolation area are required - and the prevailing ground conditions on-site. Should the site be prone to waterlogging provision should be made for Land Drains to be installed to protect the building from water penetration.

The PC Sums can be organised as follows:

PC Sum for Rainwater Disposal System
PC Sum for Soil pipes, traps, vents and fittings
PC Sum for gullies, manholes, pipes and fittings.
PC Sum for Septic Tank
PC Sum for Percolation Area
PC Sum for Constructed Wetland
PC Sum for Excavation & Trenches
PC Sum for Land Drains

Plumbing, Heating, Gas & Mechanical Services

Plumbing
Pressurised Water
Natural Gas
Central Heating
Boiler
Stove
Mechanical Services

The estimate for Water, Gas and Heating Services is covered in this section of the *Bill* as well as any other mechanical services that might be required. These estimates will be based on the proposed systems. Such estimates are best obtained from Plumbing & Heating and other specialist firms as, even if you are self-building, you are unlikely to attempt these installations yourself.

Estimates for the cost of individual items such as stoves and boilers should however be obtained independently as well as pricing such items as cylinders, water tanks etc.

PC Sum for Plumbing System: £ -
PC Sum for Heating System: £ -
PC Sum for Boiler & Flue: £ -
PC Sum for Cylinder: £ -
PC Sums for other plumbing items: £ -
PC Sum for Stoves and Flues: £ -
PC Sum for Mechanical Services (E.g. Heat Recovery Ventilation): £ -

Electrical

The estimate for the *Electrical System* should be based on the proposed *Layout*. As with *Plumbing and Heating Services* an expert should install the system and therefore should be the source of the estimate. Independent investigation however should be carried out as to the cost of fittings etc.

Remember that the Electrical Supply Company may charge for bringing power to the site.

If you are proposing to utilising a system that is independent of the National Grid obtain an estimate for the system components and for the commissioning of these.

Estimates can follow these guidelines:

PC Sum for Power Hookup: £ -
PC Sum for Installation of System: £ -
PC Sum for Fittings - switches etc.: £ -
PC Sum for Lights: £ -
PC Sum for Alternative System: £ -

Security Systems

This item, if required, can be covered by a PC Sum.

Labour

The most difficult section of the *Bill* to quantify is the Labour content of the construction work. Obviously the more straightforward the work is and the simpler the building fabric is to erect the faster the building will be to erect - and consequently the smaller Labour costs will be. Items such as the Plumbing, Heating and Electrical that have been estimated by reference to specialist firms will have had a Labour content already included in them. The remainder of the estimated costs will have been for Materials only - Structural Timber, Masonry etc. - and it is the Labour involved in utilising these materials to construct the building that must now be estimated.

At minimum, a doubling of these basic Materials costs will give some indication of what to expect if a General Contractor is to be employed to carry out the work on your behalf. If some other method of carrying out the work is to be used - Direct Labour, for example - paying yourself or some other person to organise the work should be factored in.

A period of 12 to 18 weeks should be sufficient to complete the construction of a home using a team of four or five people working a full week. This does not include the specialists such as the Plasterers and Electricians who will merely come to carry out their part of the work during the general construction period.

Based on a 15 week Construction Programme, utilising a 5 person team, a total of 375 Man Days would have to be paid for. At an average daily rate of £30 the Labour bill for this would be £11,250. If the average daily rate is more like £50 then the Labour bill would jump to £18,750.

A General Contractor estimating the cost of erecting your building will be using such methodology in arriving at a quotation for the work. Full time employees not only have to be paid for their work but the Government has also to be paid for Social Insurance, Levies etc pushing the cost of a Man Day relentlessly upwards. Also, vehicles have to be kept on the road, an office equipped and staffed and equipment paid for. These are some of the realities of being in the Construction Business and it is you, as a potential Customer, that would be helping to support these costs should you enter into a contract for the construction of your home.

On the positive side you can - in theory - sit back and have the work done for you and comfort yourself with the notion that the money you are spending is going into bricks and mortar and will therefore gain magically in value once the building is completed. If such thoughts are not comforting however you will have to be resourceful in your approach to having your house built - using direct labour and maybe even rolling your sleeves up and getting involved yourself.

Using The Cost Plan

When the initial *Cost Plan* has been completed and totalled you will have a fairly detailed as to how much each part of the building is going to cost to be completed. This figure can then be compared with your earlier Cost Estimate based on Floor Area/cost per square foot. If the detailed estimated cost far exceeds how much you want to spend, now is the time for revisions to be made to what you propose doing otherwise you will have to extend yourself beyond what you can borrow and/or pay. If Planning Permission is sought for a design more expensive than you can afford to construct you will be adding unnecessary complications to your life. Now is the time to be realistic and to make whatever changes to the design and construction proposals to ensure that the project can move forward on a realistic footing.

Several versions of the *Cost Plan* should be made, reducing costs where necessary in each successive exercise. It will be found that even reductions of £100 will add up to considerable overall savings. Where the costs of *Materials & Products* can be pared and reduced by shopping around for the best deal, the Cost of Labour is less easy to estimate, not alone reduce! This reality has the effect of emphasising the necessity of a strong and realistic *Costing* of *Materials & Products* as well as underlining the need to create a building that is straightforward to construct and finish, thereby keeping construction time to a minimum.

It should be said, in the context of the Cost of Labour, that everyone should be fairly paid for their work. What this means is that savings should not be made by shopping around for the cheapeat workers! This would certainly be a false economy. Where savings can be made in this sector however, is in the reduction of the amount of time needed to make and complete the building. This points towards simplicity and organisation, both in terms of providing the *Materials & Products* when they are needed, as well as streamlining the process of their assembly. To succeed in this, a clear and realistic *Construction Programme* is needed that details the construction process from the turning of the first sod to the final completion of the work.

In theory, a General Contractor employed to construct your building, will devise a *Construction Programme* to allow the work to run smoothly in this way. The incentive to streamline this process in order to make savings on your behalf is however likely to appear in only one form - money! The expectation that a General Contractor will work hard to pass on savings to you is therefore not realisable. General Contractors are in business to make a profit - for themselves, not for you. Where savings might be made therefore, they will likely go no further than the Contractor's Bank Account! Also, a Contractor is likely, in preparing an Estimate of Cost, to cover himself for the possibility that savings might not be made and, in fact, to even cover himself for the likelihood of cost overruns! For the person wanting a house built by using the services of a General Contractor, the possibility of making substantial savings is virtually non-existent.

What this means is that to make substantial savings in the cost of constructing your building you need to act, or employ someone to act, in the role of General Contractor. In other words, the organisational aspects of the construction project is placed in the hands of someone that is acting in your best interests and that whatever savings can be made are passed on to you.

Apart from making savings, such an approach brings one substantially closer to the reality of what creating shelter is all about and allows one to draw on the considerable amount of energy that we all have available to ensure our own survival and that of our nearest and dearest. Further, by acting as your own General Contractor, it is possible to draw on the willingness of friends and family to assist in sheltering you and to enjoy the euphoria of the almost forgotten houseraising experience.

Summary
Assessing the cost of your building is essential before a planning application is made or construction commences

44 Sheltermaker Design Programme
Finalising Your Sketch Design

The changes wrought by the *Costing* exercise will require the preparation of a set of *Sketch Design* drawings incorporating these changes. This exercise may take several attempts to complete satisfactorily. Indeed, you may find yourself retreating back to your *List of Spaces* and moving forward again to achieve the desired results. This is both normal and even desirable. Bear in mind that repeating the steps of the *Design Programme* can be carried out more rapidly and effectively with each successive attempt.

The *Sketch Design* drawings prepared of one's 'final' design proposal should mirror what will be required for *Planning* and for construction purposes. These are called *'Planning'* and *'Working'* Drawings respectively.

Working Drawings include what is called a *'Specification'*. This is a written instruction 'specifying' the *Materials & Products* to be used in the building. It also includes directions as to how these items are to be installed and to the quality of the workmanship, etc.

Because *Planning* drawings are required before *Working Drawings* they are usually prepared first, a *Planning Application* is then made and, subsequent to the granting of *Planning Permission*, the working drawings are made. This will work effectively if the preparation of the *Planning* drawings takes account of what the working drawings will contain that might affect the appearance, shape, size or height of the building. This is done by examining in detail how the various components of the building will be assembled. If the *Planning* system in your area is considerably different, adjust your approach to take account of this.

The structure of the building should be the first thing to be examined in detail, particularly the depth, height and thickness of walls, floor and roof; the roof pitch and floor to ceiling heights. This work can be carried out by drawing a cross section or cross sections at 1:20 scale. Other questions of detail will arise as these drawings are prepared, particularly where the cross section passes through a window or external door. The wall/floor and roof/wall junctions are also worth examining. Details at these locations can be 'exploded' and worked on at 1:5 or 1:10 scale.

The nature of the construction details themselves will depend on the materials being used and the type of structure being created. There are many 'standard' details available for particular types of constructions such as breathable timber frame. Effectively, these can be 'copied' and the building 'detailed' very quickly. If one is using some innovative form of construction such as hemp-lime, new details will have to be developed which involves an amount of head scratching and a lot more work. Bear in mind that it is 'fine detail' that makes a building attractive on a human scale.

The *Plumbing, Drainage, Electrical* and *H&V* systems also need consideration, preferably in consultation with the likely installers. Even though much of this is 'post-planning' work if it is not carried out now when this work finally gets underway changes to the design might be necessitated. Again, this work will anticipate the contents of the *Working Drawings*, ensuring that when these are being prepared - subsequent to a grant of *Planning Permission* - no nasty surprises await! Information on products, components, performance and so on are readily available, allowing one to 'size' the various systems if an expert is not on hand to do the work for you.

The external appearance of your building - an aspect of your proposal which the *Planners* will show particular interest in - is governed largely by the overall proportions, by the external finishs, by the size and style of windows and doors openings, by the form of the roof and by the covering on this. How the building will 'sit' in the landscape is also critical to take into account. Bear in mind that certain building forms look strange when drawn in 2-dimensions. If it is the case that your building has a strange appearance because of this, consider making a model. Photographs of this can accompany the *Planning Application*.

The detailed work outlined above will, for the most part, not appear on the *Planning* drawings except for information on the *Drainage* system. However, by examining the hidden details of the building and incorporating these into the *Sketch Design*, its appearance will be much enhanced. This will both assist in the quest for *Planning Permission* as well as facilitate the construction process which will follow.

After this detailed work has been carried out the *Sketch Design* drawings can proceed reflecting the 'refined' quality of the building. This set should include plans of all floors, cross Section/s, elevations and a site layout. An 'outline' of the *Specification* will have to be included as well. This will comprise outline information on things such as the structure, insulation, heating, drainage and external finishes. The format of this follows the *Costing Worksheet - Bill of Quantities*. Your files will contain the bulk of the information which will make up the *Specification* - your choice of windows, doors, roofing, insulation, finishes and so on.

A draughtsperson may then be required to 'draw up' your *Sketch Design* in AutoCAD. These drawings will then form the basis of the *Planning* drawings to be submitted as part of a *Planning Application*. Ideally, the same person will prepare *Working* drawings and therefore can anticipate this when the *Sketch Design* is being 'drawn up'. It is best to agree with a draughtsperson the amount of time to be devoted to revision of the computerised *Sketch Design* drawings as they grow into a set of *Planning* drawings. Changes can be kept to a minimum if detailed work has been carried out as suggested.

45 Sheltermaker Design Programme
Creating Planning Drawings

The preparation of *Planning* drawings is the first step in having your design constructed. This is where your dreams meet the real world. The trick to achieving the best result is to find a comfortable balance between your personal expectations and the guidelines laid down by the *Planning Office*. These are set out in the *County Development Plan* and possibly in a *Design Guidelines* booklet. It is worth studying such information again, noting which specific aspirations your design harmonises with. If you are designing for another jurisdiction, adjust your approach accordingly.

If you are flying under the radar your sensitivity can attune to your surroundings, endeavouring to harmonise with these on all levels, visible and invisible.

Read up to page 320 of *Planning & Working Drawings*. Bear in mind that the opportunities for pre-Planning meetings have considerably diminished. This makes it even more critical to study the *County Development Plan* [or its equivalent in your area] and any design guidelines, closely. It also means that the human aspects of the proposed design will have to highlighted in the *Planning* drawings themselves. Such individualisation will amount to you telling your story within the context of the drawings while, at the same time, articulating the required 'technical' information.

Planning Applications are subject to rigorous *Checklist* scrutiny before they are accepted for processing. It is worth getting a copy of this *Checklist* from the relevant *Planning Office* and using it to verify that you are submitting everything that they are asking for in the form that they require. This is the soulless face of the design and construction process. It is best to accept this, protecting the flame of your dreams with a veneer of normalcy. All of these considerations will influence the choice of draughtsperson.

You should also obtain several copies of the *Planning Application Form*. Fill one of these out to discover which questions require you to get *Letters of Permission* and so on. The *Form* will also list the drawings and documents which must be submitted with the *Application*. Use this as your guide.

To ensure a successful collaboration with the draughtsperson you should brief them on all aspects of the *Sketch Design* and on the 'tone' you intend to strike with your *Application*.

46 Sheltermaker Design Programme
Making The Planning Application

It is critical that all of the requirements of the *Planning* process are met in terms of the information submitted. This should follow the guidelines set out in the *Planning Application Form* itself and should accord with the *Checklist* used by the *Planning Office* to initially scrutinise *Applications*. The level of information required will depend on whether an *Application* for *Outline* or for full *Planning* is being made. For information on the distinction between these two types of *Application* refer to page 182 in the *Planning & Building Regulations* chapter. In all cases refer to your local jurisdiction to ascertain the required procedures in your area.

Generally, an *Application* for *Planning Permission* will consist of a selection of the following:

- Completed Application Form
- Cheque for Application Fee
- Letter of Consent from Site Owner with Map of Lands held in the area
  (If the site is being purchased subject to the granting of Permission)
- Letter of Consent from Trustees of Group Water Scheme
  (Where connection is being sought to an existing water main)
- Copy of Newspaper Ad
- Copy of Site Notice
- Plan indicating position of Site Notice
- Certified Trial Hole & Percolation Test results
  (Where on-site drainage system is being installed)
- 6 copies of Site Location Map
- 6 copies of Plan/s & Outline Specification
- 6 copies of Elevations & Cross Section/s
- 6 copies of Site Layout & Drainage System Details

A period of 8 weeks will elapse before a *Decision* is made on an *Application*. If *Further Information* is requested this period can be extended by up to a further 8 weeks. With a *Decision to Grant Planning Permission* work can commence, subject to the terms of the *Decision* and barring *Objections* or *Appeals*, after a period of 4 weeks. *Objections* to *Decisions* on *Applications* for *Outline* or full *Planning Permission* can be made by third parties or by the *Applicant* who might be unhappy with some of the *Conditions of the Grant of Planning Permission*. *Objections* and *Appeals* are made to *An Bord Pleanala* and the processing of these can take up to one year. No work can be carried out in the interim period. Refer to page 323 for further information on this.

47 Sheltermaker Design Programme
Preparing Working Drawings

With a Grant of Planning Permission in place work can commence on the construction of the building. This requires the preparation of a set of *Working* drawings including a *Specification*. This package of information will be based on the work carried out when *Finalising Your Sketch Design* **SDP44** on page 311, and will incorporate any changes necessitated by the terms of the *Planning Permission*. Because of the risk of such changes it is probably better to await the *Grant of Permission* before commencing the *Working Drawings*. However this can add additional time to the process. From the date of an initial *Application*, all going well and with no request for *Additional Information*, it can take four to five months to having the completed *Working Drawing* package ready. If key technical decisions have been made in regards to structure, finishes, windows, doors, services and so on and particularly if tradespeople have been involved in the design of particular systems, such a timeframe can be adhered to. If detailed design work on the content of the *Working Drawings* only commences with a *Grant* *of Permission* then considerably more time will be required.

Working Drawings are generally beyond the scope of the unskilled individual. Ideally, the draughtsperson who prepares the *Planning Application* drawings will also prepare the *Working Drawings*. If your design information is comprehensive this collaborative effort will be enjoyable as well as fruitful. If your expectation is for the draughtsperson to have all the answers you will be disappointed. A list of what is generally required in a *Working Drawing* package can be found in pages 320-325.

In many ways it is ideal to select a builder who can be involved in the preparation of the *Working Drawing* package. If you are self-building then you are the builder! Issues of finance, guarantees, certification, insurance and so on will also have to be taken into account. All of this points to the creation of simple buildings with simple systems within them. The more complex the design the more complex the construction will be.

48 Sheltermaker Design Programme
Constructing Your Design

Unlike the issue of design, there is much information freely available on self-building. This type of information should be sought out and studied at as early a stage as possible. Generally speaking the more thought-out a building design is, the easier it will be to construct. Good site organisation and practices will all assist in keeping morale high and keep things moving forward smoothly. Bad feeling should never be allowed to infest the building work as this will become 'locked in' and can never be eliminated. Sensitivity is the order of the day. This contrasts with the normal macho vibration on building sites.

You have arrived at the core of *Living Architecture*. This can be imagined as a threshold between inner & outer worlds. The mysteries enshrined in this cannot be articulated but must be experienced.

49 Sheltermaker Design Programme
Living In Your Architecture

Living in your design is an experience that will occur in future time. Because of this it is impossible to experience it in the here and now. However, if one imagines that the potential for this future 'you' is an inherent part of your 'self' as you presently exist, this wisdom will infuse the design process allowing you to live your life and your architecture to the full.

Planning & Working Drawings

When the *Cost Plan* and the design have been harmonised - in other words when you have arrived at a satisfying design that you can afford to build - the project can move into its final stages. This involves obtaining Planning Permission and producing Drawings with which to effect both the Planning Application and the construction process itself.

Preliminary Planning Assessment

Because it is vital that the design you obtain Planning Permission for is the design that you are going to build, it is important to have a preliminary meeting with the Planning Office before a formal Application is lodged. This will allow for an informal exchange with the local Planning Officer and for any areas of difference to be identified and corrected before the submission becomes formal.

This type of meeting is vital to the smooth flow of the project onwards. Ideally, the Two Month digestion period during which your Application will pass through the Planning Process will be the time for you to organise the construction end of things so that work can begin at the earliest possible date. If this is your aim it is important to know of any likely changes that the Planners will want you to make to your design before you submit the Application formally.

It is vital that the design you obtain Planning Permission for is the design that you are going to build.

Informal meetings of this sort do not in any way ensure that your Application will be treated in a particular way. It is more by way of establishing yourself in the Planners mind as being a person, as being real and as a way of communicating the more abstract dimensions of the project, the things that cannot go down on paper. If this is done then a link between you as a person and you and your design will have been established. This will allow the formal submission to have a human dimension when it comes across the Planners Desk formally.

A preliminary Planning Assessment Meeting is made through the Planning Office. The appointment for this can be made in writing or by telephone. The location of the site in question and any relevant File Number should also be given at this stage.

What you should bring to the meeting is a concise presentation that shows your design off to its best. This will probably consist of Plan/s; Elevations; Cross Section; Site Layout and Photos of a Model. Also, photographs from your *Design & Style File* illustrating the proposed outward appearance of your building particularly in terms of the walling, roofing and window treatment, would be very useful.

It should be borne in mind that the Planner will be assessing your Application in the light of the local Development Plan, the proposed outward appearance and the location. The internal layout will not be the subject of scrutiny. Items such as the disposal of waste water will be within the orbit of the local Engineer and again will not be the subject of detailed scrutiny at this stage.

The real opportunity presented you in a Preliminary Planning meeting of this sort is the establishment of a human connection between you and the Planner. This is no time to hide your light under a bushel. Modesty in terms of the amount of material presented is fine but the amount of work that has gone into the design can be openly and clearly stated. Also, your knowledge of the aims of the Development Plan can be flaunted. Finding the proper balance in all of this will be important of course - but if the Planner can be seen as an ally and not as an enemy, then much will have been achieved.

In regards to 'suggestions' that might be made to modify the design proposals - these should be noted and decided upon before the formal submission goes in.

The Area Planning Official dealing with your Planning Application, should be seen as an ally - not as an enemy.

The Planning Application

Three sets of drawings will usually need to be submitted to the Planning Authority with a Planning Application, as well as a copy of the Newspaper Ad and Site Notice, the Fee and the completed Application Form.

Drawings For Planning Permission

1. Plan/s 1:50 scale.
Ground floor plan should show the drainage system immediately outside the building. North point should be indicated. All spaces should labelled.
Position of cross section/s should be clearly marked.
Main dimensions should be indicated.

2. Section/s 1:50 or 1:20 scale.
The number of sections needed to indicate the overall shape of the building will depend on the individual design. A 1:20 scale cross section will enable a large amount of detail to be shown. A general Specification written onto this drawing should outline the type of materials that are to be used in the construction.
Main dimensions should be indicated.

3. Elevations 1:50 scale.
Elevations for all sides of the building should be produced. These should be labelled North, South, East and West. The type of finish to be applied to the outside of the building should be noted on the elevations.
Main dimensions should be indicated.

4. Site Plan 1:200 or 1:500 scale.
The Site Plan should show the connections from the drainage system of the proposed building to the public drain or the septic tank and percolation area etc. The north point should be clearly indicated on the site plan. Also gateways, driveways etc.

5. Location Map 1:1250 or 1:2500 scale.
This will be a copy of a portion of the Ordnance Survey Map indicating the site in question. Clearly note the Sheet Number from which your Location Map comes.

Drawings & Documentation for a Planning Application for Full Planning Permission:

Plan/s 1:50
Section/s 1:50
Elevations 1:50
Site Plan 1:200 or 1:500
Location Map 1:1250 or 1:2500
Completed Application Form
Copy of Site Notice
Copy of Newspaper Ad
Fee

Drawings Generally

All drawings should carry a number as well as an indication of the scale they are drawn to. Original drawings, when they are altered, should have a Revision Number added to the Drawing Number. For example Drawing Number 7, when it is altered in any way becomes Drawing Number 7A. If Revision Numbers are not used confusion can very easily arise. Revised drawings should also carry a note indicating the changes that have been made to them.

Planning is the most important stage of the design and build process. It is essential to build according to the drawings submitted and consequently these should be what you want to build. The Planning Application set of drawings, with the addition of *Services Layouts*, can also be used to obtain a construction price from a builder/s.

Preparing Planning & Working Drawings

You must decide at this stage whether to prepare the drawings necessary for Planning and Building yourself or whether to engage a qualified technical person to do the work for you. There are many advantages to having the work done for you but it is crucial to realise that you remain in control of the project and so must provide the draughtsperson with clear information from which to work.

Draughtsperson

If you are engaging a draughtsperson to draw up your design, find someone that you can get on with, that is familiar with the type of construction you are proposing to use and that draws in a way that you like and admire. Approach all dealings with the person from the point of view that you are the boss and that you know what you are doing. What you want this person to do is to produce a set of drawings for *Planning* and *Construction* purposes for an agreed price and within an agreed timescale. This will involve the careful drawing of what you yourself have drawn at 1:50 and 1:200 scale - plans, cross sections and a site plan. You will also need at least one cross section at 1:20 scale showing the detailed construction of the building as well as some as 1:5 or 1:10 details of critical junctions within this cross section. You will also need *Plumbing, H&V* and *Electrical Layouts*.

All drawings should carry a Number and an indication of their Scale.

Planning is the most important stage of the design and build process.

If you proceed with this course of action you will be duplicating what most professional architects do anyway - they pass on their 'sketch' designs to a draughtsperson or technician for rendering into *Planning & Construction Drawings*.

Explain your design carefully to the person you engage even if this means paying for their time. If someone understands your decision making process they will have a better chance of producing a set of drawings just how you want. It is inevitable that things will come under discussion as this set of drawings is being prepared - be prepared to make clear decisions and think things out thoroughly. There is always a temptation to rush at this point in the project but this will only mask over errors that will manifest themselves sooner or later.

Working Drawings

These drawings are the drawings which Contractors will use to estimate the cost of erecting your building as well as to organise the construction work itself. Working drawings can be the drawings which are submitted for Planning even though there will be more detail on them than the Planning Office needs. One advantage of submitting *Working Drawings* for Planning Permission is that invariably these will indicate exactly what is to be built. If proper consultation has been made with the Planning Office before a submission is made the risk of having to alter your *Working Drawings* will be minimised.

The list of *Working Drawings* required to obtain a properly estimated price for the erection of your building will be the same as that outlined above for Planning Permission plus the following:

6. Electrical Layout 1:50 scale.
This can be a tracing off the plan/s. All plugs, switches, outlets etc. should be indicated and notes on this drawing should indicate the type of fittings to be used.

7. Plumbing Layout 1:50 scale.
This can also be a tracing from the plan/s. All sinks, toilets, washing machines, radiators, boilers, cylinders etc. should be indicated plus the pipe runs, water tanks and so on.

8. Details 1:5
Details at eaves, wall and floor junctions; rising walls; foundations; window and external door openings can be keyed into the 1:20 cross sections prepared at the planning stage.

If you engage a draughtsperson to prepare drawings for you, you will be duplicating what most professional architects do anyway.

Working Drawings are those drawings used to estimate the final Construction Cost ... as well as being used to organise the construction work itself.

A Typical Set of Working Drawings:

Plan/s 1:50
Section/s 1:50
Elevations 1:50
Site Plan 1:200 or 1:500
Details 1:5
Electrical Layout 1:50
Plumbing Layout 1:50

9. Quantities & Specification.
This will be an up-to-date version of the work carried out earlier - the *Bill*. This will form the basis of costing the work and negotiations.

Building Programme

Apart from the need to have a clean, straightforward Planning Permission and a good set of *Working Drawings*, it is critical that a comprehensive *Building Programme* is also drawn up. In the event that you are Self-Building, this Programme is of even more critical importance.

A Building Programme sets out the sequence of the construction work, allows deadlines to be set, allows for materials to be ordered in a timely fashion, allows for Sub-Contractors to be properly scheduled and generally gives an overview of how and when the work should begin, progress and be completed.

Where a General Contractor is to be engaged to carry out the work, in theory he will work to a *Programme* of his own. This is not always the case however. Without a *Programme*, Construction Work runs on in a random fashion and vast inefficiencies creep into the process pushing costs relentlessly upwards.

Where any form of Self-Building is being tackled, a *Building Programme* will be as essential as a set of Working Drawings or being in possession of the money with which to carry out the work!

Any *Building Programme* should list the Sequence of Work; the Materials and Skills required to carry out the work; a note of any Decisions that must be made to allow the work to be done; and, a Timescale which details the progress of the project from start to finish.

A Building Programme sets out the sequence of the construction work, allows deadlines to be set and materials to be ordered, allows for Sub-Contractors to be properly scheduled and generally gives an overview of how and when the work should begin, progress and be completed.

Without a Building Programme, Construction Work runs on in a random fashion and vast inefficiencies creep into the process, pushing costs relentlessly upwards.

Selecting A Builder

It is a sensible idea to investigate the builders local to the area in which you are going to build. This can be done by enquiry in the locality. A short list can be drawn up and the various comments that have been gleaned can be entered alongside the relevant builder. Examples of work completed should be inspected - at this point merely a casual outside view is all that is required. Much can be ascertained from this exercise.

From this simple exercise one or two builders will surely emerge ahead of the others. These should then be contacted directly. The idea of this is to find out the builders capabilities, what he can offer, what he can and cannot do and most of all, how you get on with him.

The normal methods of construction used by the builder should be enquired of and the average cost of these. This will be expressed in a cost per square foot. If you want a timber framed house with a brick or block skin will the builder do this? If you wish to use a factory prepared timber frame will the builder prepare the foundations and complete the work when the frame has been erected?

When you have narrowed down your search for suitable builders for your house you then have to formally request that they submit a 'Tender' for carrying out the construction work. If you wish to obtain competitive tenders you will need to send out documentation to at least three builders. On the other hand, if there is one particular builder that you want to work with you can negotiate a price for the construction work.

Negotiating a price for building work has many advantages. Firstly, it allows you to develop a working relationship with a builder before construction commences. Secondly, it allows the builder to attend to the matter of estimation in more detail. This is in contrast to competitive tendering where the builder has at best a one-in-three chance of getting the work. On a negotiated price a builder can be reasonably assured of obtaining the work once the budget price has been met. Also, with a negotiated price the final details of the work to be done can be more easily fined tuned to come within your budget parameters.

If you decide to go it alone and build by Direct Labour you will be going through a similar procedure as is followed above except that smaller segments of the work will be under separate consideration - for example, the Excavation, Foundations & Rising Walls; Plumbing & Heating; Electrical work etc.

Whichever way you decide to proceed, you yourself will need to have a good idea of what everything is going to cost so that your negotiating position is tenable. You do this by following the procedure set out in *Part XVII - Costing* and basing this work on the final design drawings.

Quantities

The final *Bill of Quantities* will form part of the information supplied to any Building Contractor or Services Contractor, along with relevant drawings, so that such firms can supply you with an estimate for the carrying out of the work.

Any fine tuning of the price will also be based on the Bill and any necessary changes or alterations must be included in this to form the basis of the Contract/s.

Invitation To Tender

If you are inviting bids from several Contractors you must send them all the same set of documentation. It should be clearly indicated just what the Contractor is to price for. At least three prices are needed to make a reasonable assessment of value for money.

A specific period of time should be given for the Contractors to prepare a price and submit it to you. The prices you receive should also be accompanied by an indication of the time required for erection of the building.

Preparing prices can be a time consuming job for any builder. It is important to make the job as easy as possible to do - remember, the unsuccessful bidders will receive no payment for their work.

The price obtained should be a broken-down estimate, based on the Bill - not just an overall figure. In this way particular items can be isolated in terms of cost and allow for the price to be fine-tuned if necessary. A *Building Programme*, indicating Start-Up and Completion Dates should also be provided.

If you are inviting Tenders from several Building Contractors, you must send them all the same documentation.

At least three Tenders are required to make a reasonable assessment of value-for-money.

Planning Decisions

Eight weeks will elapse before any decision will be made and then you will be notified by post of the Decision. A further period of four weeks must elapse before work can commence.

During the initial eight week period of the Application the Planning Office might request Additional Information. If this is done, a new period of 'eight weeks' begins with the submission by you of the requested Additional Information.

During the eight week period of a Planning Application, a Third Party - someone with an interest (usually negative) in what you are doing - can submit their views to the Planning Office and these views will be considered by the Planning Office in reaching a Decision on your Application. All correspondence in connection with such Third Party interests will appear on the Planning File and will be available for your scrutiny.

When a Planning Decision is issued, you may, within a period of four weeks of the date of issuance of that Decision, object to the Decision or to any Condition attached to it. Such an objection must be made through the Planning Appeals Board.

In the case of a Third Party objecting to any aspect of a Planning Decision, they must, within a period of three weeks from the date of issuance of that Decision, register their objection with the Planning Appeals Board. A Fee must also be paid.

Contracts

It is a good idea to include in your set of Tender Drawings an indication of the type of Contract you intend to use. This Contract can be very simple and can be drawn up by your Solicitor.

Any Contract should respect the interest of both parties to the agreement. A method for resolving any disputes that arise should be indicated as well as an outline of how payment will be made as the work progresses. Liability for the work in progress and Insurances should also be covered.

A Defects Period can be stipulated covering a period of 6 months - 1 year. Normally an amount of money - an agreed % of the Contract Price - is held over, to be paid after the Defects Period is over.

A Building Contract should respect the interests of both parties; outline a method for resolving disputes; outline how payments will be scheduled and made; and, detail responsibility for Liability & Insurance.

Supervision

Once the work is underway some level of supervision is needed to ensure that the work is being properly carried out. This is a job that you can do yourself or you can engage someone to do it on your behalf. The draughtsperson you get to prepare your drawings might be a good person or a retired Foreman or Clerk of Works.

This is a position that requires an understanding of the world the builder inhabits otherwise misunderstandings can very quickly arise. If you are supervising the job yourself you must establish a good rapport with the builder at an early stage. Your primary concern is to see that the work is carried out as set out in the drawings. How the builder chooses to do this is up to him.

Any additional items of work that arise as the work progresses should be priced by the Contractor in writing and agreed before the work commences. Prices for Alterations should also be agreed in writing.

It will be found very easy to praise good work and this should be done at every opportunity. If the people building your home have their work admired you will receive a level of service impossible to specify in the Contract.

Visits to the site should follow an agreed pattern - you should not hang around all the time, make surprise visits or act as if you own the place. The building site should be regarded as the builders territory. Soon enough the place will be yours to do what you like in!

Summary

It is vital that the building design you get Planning Permission for is the design that you are going to build.

Planning Officers should be seen as allies - not enemies.

If you engage a draughtsperson to prepare drawings for you, you will be duplicating what most professional architects do anyway!

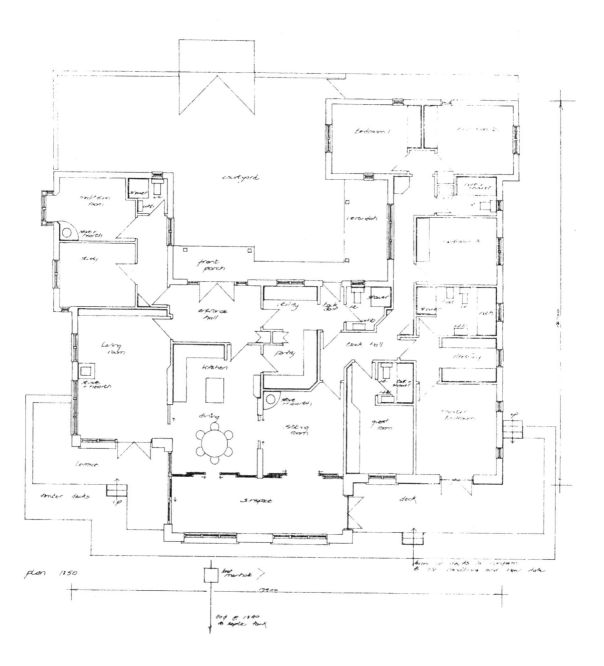

Plan

A Plan 'drawn up'. This can be compared to the 'Version 5 Plan' in Part XVI, Layout, Page 40. This type of drawing is used for the purposes of a Planning Application. It is also used to begin the process of preparing Working Drawings – those drawings used to direct the construction process.

north elevation 1:50

west · east cross section 1:50

h elevation 1:50

Elevations & Cross Section

These drawings form part of the set prepared for a Planning Application. They also allow for scrutiny of the various parts of the building they depict – junctions, heights, window openings, etc. As such they are an essential precursor to the Working Drawing stage of a project. It is essential that Planning Drawings reflect the expected final appearance of a building. This is because a Grant of Planning Permission is based on the drawings submitted and so the building must largely be constructed to reflect what these drawings show.

east elevation 1:50

west elevation 1:50

Elevations

Because they are 2-dimensional, Elevations are really a false representation of reality. Pasted onto card however elevations can be used to create a 3-dimensional model which will reflect reality much better!
Refer to Part VI, Surveying, Page 32, for guidance on building a model using Elevation drawings.

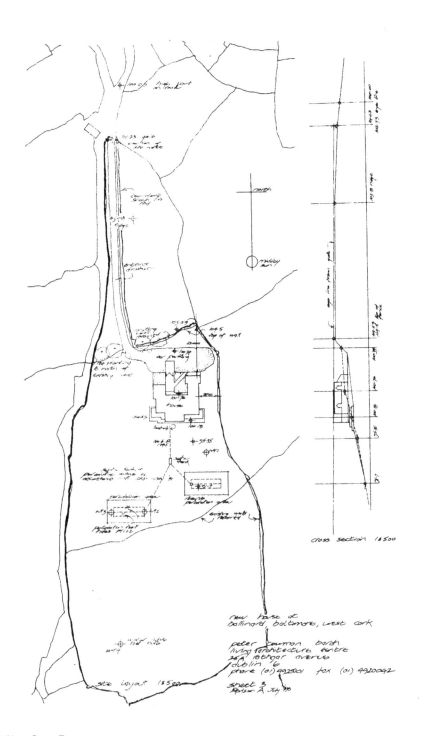

The Site Layout

This shows the building located on the site, the road entrance, driveway, position of the septic tank and percolation areas, boundaries, levels, landscaping, etc.

329

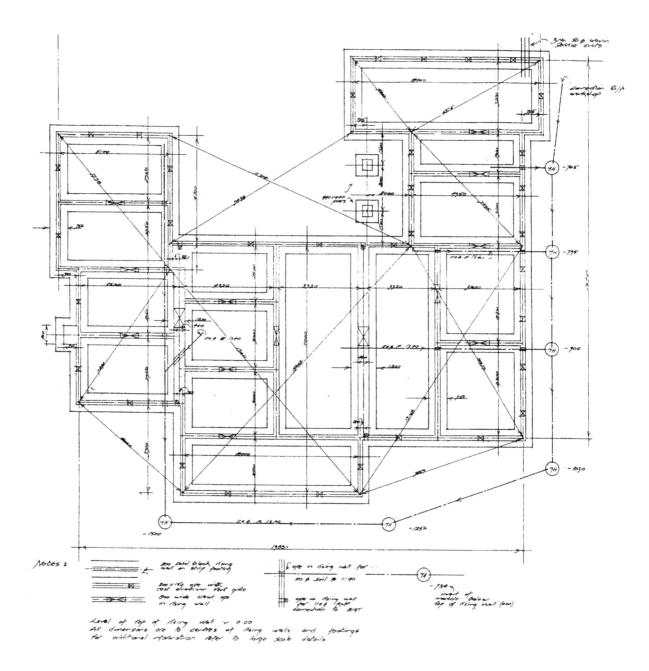

Foundation Plan

This drawing shows the position and size of the foundations as well as the location of the 'rising walls' which will sit atop the foundations. The diagonal lines indicate check dimensions to ensure that the foundations can be built 'square'. Openings for underfloor vents, drainage pipes, crawl holes, cables, ducts, etc. are also shown. A Specification also forms part of this drawing. This describes the materials to be used in the construction process.

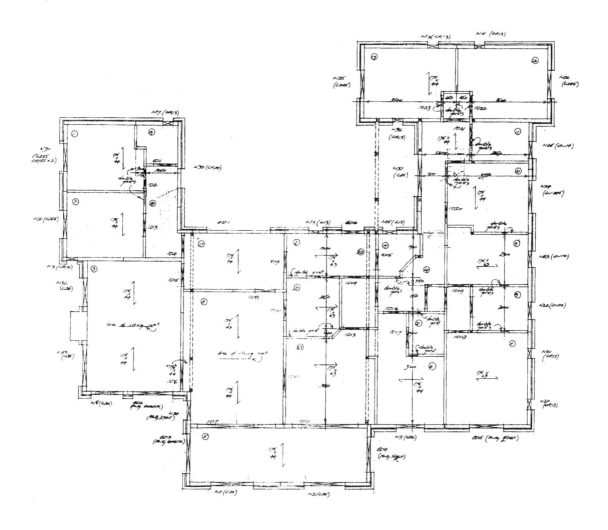

Framing Plan

This drawing indicates the direction and size of the timber joists that form the floor — these joists span between rising walls. This drawing also shows the layout of the timber frame panels which will sit atop the suspended timber floor — the walls. The openings in these wall panels for doors and windows are identified by numbers.

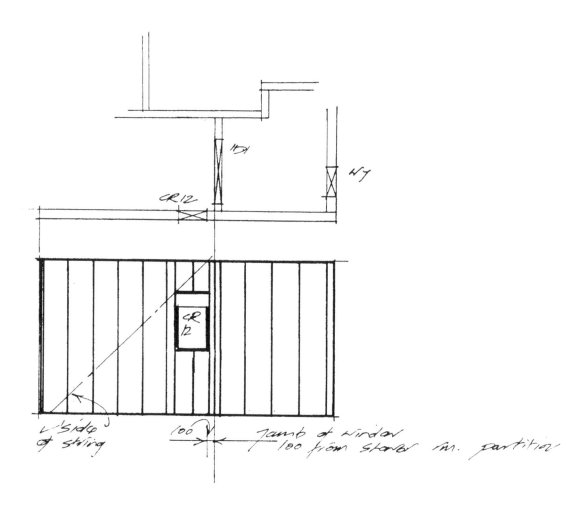

Typical Panel Drawing

Elevation and plan of a typical wall panel. The elevation shows the panel height, general stud positions and identifies a window opening. The exact information on the size of this opening will be detailed elsewhere. Drawings are produced for all panels that will form part of the house. These drawings are also used to 'quantify' the amount of materials that will be needed to construct what they illustrate.

332

Index

C

I

K

L

P

T

U

Volume 1 Contents

LIVING ARCHITECTURE CENTRE.COM

The Living Architecture Centre is an internet-based school of vernacular architecture, founded and directed by Peter Cowman who was born in Ireland. He is an architect, eco-builder, writer and teacher delivering Courses & Workshops internationally on the subject of sustainable house design and construction. He has a special interest in the creation of affordable, low-impact buildings.

The Living Architecture Centre offers a wide range of resources on all aspects of the role of eco-architecture in the achievement of a sustainably way of life – Articles, Sheltermaker Magazine, LIVE & Distance Learning Courses, Talks, Workshops, Sheltermaker Theatre presentations as well as Consultancy & Mentoring Services.

Mentoring for users of *The Sheltermaking Manual*

Students can submit *Assignments* and receive written *Feedback* and *LIVE Video Consultation* on their projects. Further details available from livingarchitecturecentre.com

EconoSpaceMaking Course

Sustainability begins in your own backyard - that is the compelling argument put forward on this dynamic combination of text, drawings, photographs and video information which is supplied on a DVD.

By learning how to create a small sustainable shelter - with no need to first obtain planning permission - you are offered the opportunity to regain territory lost to an economic system which depends on mortgage debt to satisfy its insatiable appetite and growth.

From drawing to modelmaking, from concept to built reality, EconoSpaceMaking provides you with the means to create your own living architecture and to discover, in the process, who you really are.

EconoSpaceMakers can also participate in a dedicated online Forum where they can exchange ideas and information as well as keeping up with the latest developments.

See page 286, *Vol. 1* for further details or go to livingarchitecturecentre.com

Living Architecture PRIMER

Not certain if the Living Architecture is for you? Then try the Living Architecture PRIMER. This is a disc-based compilation of published *Articles, Course Handouts, Films* and *TV* documentaries, plus *Sheltermaking Manual* and *EconoSpaceMaking Course* material, all of which will serve as an excellent introduction to the subject of *Living Architecture*. The budget-priced PRIMER includes a discount voucher redeemable against the cost of the full *EconoSpaceMaking Course* when you are ready to upgrade. To order or to obtain further details go to livingarchitecturecentre.com

PYTHON PRESS BOOKS

Books on sensitive and sustainable living, esoteric agriculture and
awareness of the spiritual dimensions of life and planet

Available at bookstores around the world or buy directly from:
Python Press PO Box 929, Castlemaine, Vic 3450, Australia

www.pythonpress.com

pythonpress@gmail.com

Sensitive Permaculture
- cultivating the way of the sacred Earth

by Alanna Moore

This 2009 book explores the living energies of the land and how to
sensitively connect with them. Positive and joyful, it draws on the
indigenous wisdom of Australasia, Ireland and elsewhere, combining the
insights of geomancy and geobiology with eco-smart permaculture
design to offer an exciting new paradigm for sustainable living. It
includes the authors experiences of negotiating with the local fairy
beings over land use in Australia and Ireland.

Readers say:

"A delight to read" Callie

"You make permaculture so easy and alive---and sweet" Joy, Taiwan

"...Hard to put down" Celia, Permaculture Association of Tasmania

Reviewers comments: *"A very practical and thoughtful guide for the eco-spiritual gardener,
bringing awareness to the invisible dimensions of our landscape"*
Rainbow News, New Zealand

"An adventure in magical and practical Earth awareness"
Nexus magazine

Divining Earth Spirit   by Alanna Moore
An Exploration of Global & Australasian Geomancy

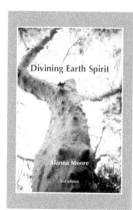

A global look at geomancy and geobiology from an Australasian
perspective, from English ley lines and fairy folk, to geopathic stress and
the paradigms of the Aboriginal Dreamtime. The environment is alive
and conscious!

*"This book is a classic for anyone wanting to get involved with Earth healing.
It contains information by the bucketload... The research that has gone into this
book is incredible and no doubt will stir you into wanting to use it yourself"*
Radionics Network Vol. 2 No.6

"Excellent reference book" Don McLeod, Silver Wheel

*"Love of the topic clearly shows, as Moore brings clarity and a sense of the
necessity of personal involvement and engagement with the Earth. The great
advantage of Moore's book is in its detailing all the salient aspects of Earth
Spirit phenomena....all covered succinctly and with precision... the perfect
introduction to the topic."*   Esoterica magazine, No. 4, 1995

Backyard Poultry - Naturally   by Alanna Moore

From housing to feeding, from selection to breeding, from pets to production and from the best lookers to the best layers, this book covers everything the backyard farmer needs to know about poultry husbandry - including preventative and curative herbal medicines and homeopathics, plus permaculture design for productive poultry pens. It has long been Australia's best-selling 'chook' book!

The Reviews:

"A wonderful resource! Alanna Moore has provided poultry enthusiasts with all the information they need to raise healthy poultry without using harmful chemicals."
Megg Miller, Grass Roots magazine.

"The poultry health section is the best I've seen."
Eve Sinton, Permaculture International Journal.

"An interesting and worthwhile book that will no doubt have a lot of appeal for the amateur or part-time farmer."
Kerry Lonergan, Landline, ABC TV.

Stone Age Farming - tapping nature's energies for your farm or garden
(2nd edition, 2012)   by Alanna Moore

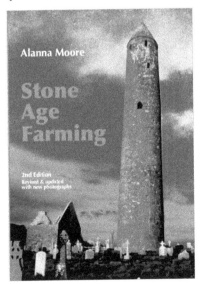

From Irish Round Towers to modern Towers of Power for enhancing plant growth. In this book ancient and modern ideas about the energies of rocks and landscapes are explored for practical use in the garden, including the application of dowsing, Earth wisdom and geomantic understandings.

What reviewers have said of the 1st edition (2001):

"Simply fabulous!"
Maurice Finkel, Health and Healing.

"Quite fantastic."
Roberta Britt, Canadian Quester Journal.

"Clear, lucid and practical" Tom Graves

"A classic"   Radionics Network.

"Will change your perception of the world"
Conscious Living magazine.

A Geomantic Guidebook to

Touchstones for Today

- designing for Earth harmony with stone arrangements and subtle energy dowsing

by Alanna Moore, 2013

Ancient and enigmatic, the standing stones, labyrinths and stone circles that still haunt various corners of the world have often been subject to systematic destruction. But yet, in some form, they have survived over several millennia. Their enduring presences beg so many questions. How did the ancients manage to erect the huge megalithic monuments, when it is a struggle to replicate them today? For what purposes were they made? They must have been highly significant, given the enormous amount of effort involved. Science and folklore can provide clues. But personal experience of sites and energies detected at sacred stones can be much more revealing and rewarding than bland facts.

Today, sensitive people find that the ancient standing stones, both natural and intentionally placed, can act as transmitters of beneficial Earth energies, providing anchor points for the power and spirit of the land. Not surprisingly, old traditions of healing, divination, wish fulfillment and fertility associated with certain sacred stones continue to find currency today. And anyone may potentially tune in to the sacred stones by taking up the ancient art of dowsing (also known as divining), or other forms of psychic attunement. It can be personally most enriching!

This Guidebook encourages people to discover for themselves the magical and transforming energies associated with both ancient megalithic sites and modern stones of power; and to be inspired to create one's own energetic stone arrangements, as Touchstones of interaction with the Sacred Earth.

144 pages, with 90 black & white illustrations

About the Author

Alanna Moore was a co-founder of the New South Wales Dowsing Society 1984. A professional dowser, she is internationally known for her writing and teaching of dowsing and geomancy. She lectures worldwide and also makes films. A permaculture farmer and teacher as well, her writings are archived at www.geomantica.com as well as at Australia's National Library.

Diary of A Sheltermaker   by Peter Cowman

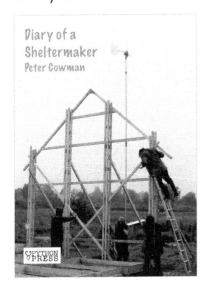

When architect Peter Cowman opts to follow his own 'living' architecture philosophy he's in for a few surprises. After 30 years of itinerant life, the lure of the acre of boggy meadow in Ireland's northwest is compelling.

Juggling work commitments alongside construction of his low-cost, low-impact, mortgage-free cabin, his adventures are both amusing as well as hair-raising.

True to his own predictions, the issues which the design and construction process raise track to the very core of his being, challenging his grasp on reality.

Rooted in the here and now, his timepieces are the sun, the moon and his commitment to unravelling the mysteries of sheltermaking.

Living off the grid and off his wits, surprises appear out of nowhere, demanding time and attention.

Nestled by the warm stove of his imagining, absorbed within the gentle beauty of the ancient land, the dreams which sustain him have an agenda of their own.

When sheltermaking activities hit a blockage, despite having willing volunteers and materials on hand, Peter has to call a halt to further progress.

In an instant his plans are turned on their head and he suddenly finds himself on the other side of the planet!

This resumption of his itinerant life leads to unexpected discoveries.

Piecing together shards of the past, the picture he has long imagined is suddenly complete!

So, the mystery unfolds and the reluctant hero finds solace in the realisation of his freedom to act out his sheltermaking dreams wherever he happens to be.

GEOMANTICA

Correspondence Course
Diploma of Dowsing for Harmony

This correspondence Course imparts techniques and applications of pendulum dowsing that will help you to create a more energetically harmonious world and to potentially have a career doing this work. Originally written in 1989, many hundreds of students from around the world have enjoyed this opportunity for distant study. It has been revised and updated over the years. The Course can be bought in ten parts or all at once.

The Course includes comprehensive notes, dowsing charts and lists, practical exercises and personal Assessments from Course originator and internationally acclaimed tutor Alanna Moore, who has over 30 years dowsing and teaching of dowsing experience. You can start now or anytime and complete it in your own time, although generally it is usually undertaken over one or two years. No obligation when to finish. (It has also just recently been made available to a wider audience, for people who don't want to achieve a Diploma.)   See www.geomantica.com/dowsing-correspondence-course

The 10 Units of in-depth study are these:

Unit One: The Basics of Dowsing - Theories that help to explain dowsing. Clear, simple techniques and useful exercises.

Unit Two: Wholistic Diagnosis – The philosophical basis of holistic health and harmony, the importance of seeking balance of the mind, body, emotions, spirit and environment. Dowsing the levels of being and divining peoples' esoteric psychology with the Seven Rays.

Unit Three: Body Systems – An integrated approach to anatomy and physiology – from the physical to the energetic in global traditions, including Chinese medical philosophy.

Unit Four: Analytic Dowsing – Dowsing for causative factors in disease, diet selection, food and water testing, allergen detection. The problem of pesticides, additives and pollutants in food and water and how to test for them. Using samples for analysis.

Unit Five: Dowsing for Solutions – Selecting remedies and therapies by pendulum and Seven Ray analysis. Working with vibrational remedies made from flowers, gems, shells etc. Dowsing for homeopathic remedies.

Unit Six: Distant Dowsing and Healing – Remote health analysis and energy balancing techniques. Using symbolic patterns plus crystals and gems for remote healing work. Chakra balancing with the pendulum and more.

Unit Seven: Earth Energies and Health – How underground streams, geological faults and the like can cause geopathic stress. How to create and maintain harmony with geomancy and feng shui. Working with the devic dimensions – the nature spirits.

Unit Eight: Building Biology – Our homes are our third skin, and should protect us to some degree. Unhealthy homes can poison or irritate us with their toxic building materials and electro-magnetic fields etc. How to check for sick building syndrome and find healthier alternatives.

Unit Nine: Map Dowsing and Environmental Remedies – Distant dowsing by map to seek out harmful zones in the home and environment. Geomantic cures such as Earth acupuncture methods using copper pipes, crystals, etc to neutralise noxious zones.

Unit Ten: Towers of Power & The Professional Dowser - How to locate and make Towers of Power for environmental energising and harmonising. Professionalism in dowsing.

Geomantica Films
by Alanna Moore
Only available from www.Geomantica.com
(See extracts of Geomantica Films on You Tube.)

* The ART of DOWSING & GEOMANCY
140 minutes of dowsing and geomancy training sessions with Alanna Moore and her students, ideal for beginners.

* DOWSERS DOWNUNDER
102 minutes of interviews and demonstrations with a diverse range of amazing dowsers filmed around Australia.

Three film series (with each film around half an hour):

* EARTH CARE, EARTH REPAIR (8 films)
Dowsing, Greening & Crystal Farming (including interview with broadscale wheat farmers about crystal farming). *Eco-Gardeners Down-Under* (featuring Bill Mollison and David Holmgren). *Grassroots Solutions to Soil Salinity* (with dowsers saving landscapes from dryland salinity). *Growing & Gauging Sustainability* (using Universal Knowledge to Brix meters). *Remineralising the Soil* (the value of paramagnetic rock dust and dowsing its qualities). *Making Power Towers* (shows the construction of a paramagnetic antenna, or Power Tower). *Agnihotra / Homa Farming* (an ancient Indian fire ritual that has marvellous effects on plant growth).

* GEOMANCY TODAY (5 films)
Megalithomania (stone circles and the like from Europe to Australasia). *Divining Earth Harmony* (5 geomancers talk about their diverse approaches.) *Discovering the Devas* (yes, they are out here and you can dowse for them!) *Helping the Devas* (interview with Swedish dowsers who work with the devic kingdoms). *The Sacred World of Water* (from mythology to a geomantic appreciation of water in the landscape).

* STATE of PILGRIMAGE (6 films)
Glastonbell Dreaming (interview with Australia's first white geomancer). *Pilgrimage to Central Australia* (exploring Aboriginal sites and culture). *A Thirst for Ireland* (indigenous geo-mythos). *Bali – geomantic journeying in paradise. South Australian Sojourn.*

Lightning Source UK Ltd.
Milton Keynes UK
UKHW030741270721
387842UK00010B/1144